HUMAN RIGHTS OF INDIGENOUS PEOPLES

HUMAN RIGHTS OF INDIGENOUS PEOPLES

(In 2 Volumes)

Volume 1
(Protecting the Rights of Indigenous Peoples)

Editor
Aman Gupta

ISHA

ISHA BOOKS

Delhi-110033

Human Rights of Indigenous Peoples
(Protection of the Rights of Indigenous Peoples)

Rs. 1800 (Set)
Rs. 900 (Each Volume)

ISBN : 81-8205-205-X (Set)
ISBN : 81-8205-275-0 (Vol. 1)

Published in 2005 in India by
Isha Books
D-43, Prithviraj Road,
Adarsh Nagar, Delhi - 110033
e-mail : ishabooks@hotmail.com

Laser Typesetting at : Global Printers, New Delhi
Printed at : Chawla Offset Press, Delhi

Contents

Preface

People who inhabited a land before it was conquered by colonial societies and who consider themselves distinct from the societies currently governing those territories are called indigenous peoples. Indigenous peoples worldwide number between 300-500 million, embody and nurture 80 per cent of the world's cultural and biological diversity, and occupy 20 per cent of the world's land surface. They live in nearly all the countries on all the continents of the world and form a spectrum of humanity, ranging from traditional hunter-gatherers and subsistence farmers to legal scholars. Like all cultures and civilisations, indigenous peoples are always adjusting and adapting to changes in the world. They recognise their common plight and work for their self-determination; based on their respect for the earth.

Despite the extensive diversity in indigenous communities throughout the world, all indigenous peoples have one thing in common — they all share a history of injustice. They have been killed, tortured and enslaved. In many cases, they have been the victims of genocide. They have been denied the right to participate in governing processes of the current state systems. Conquest and colonisation have attempted to steal their dignity and identity as indigenous peoples, as well as the fundamental right of self-determination.

Over the last several years, the international system—particularly as embodied in United Nations and other international institutions—has exhibited a renewed concerns of indigenous peoples. The Draft Declaration on the Rights of Indigenous Peoples is the most comprehensive statement of the rights of indigenous peoples to date, establishing collective rights to a greater extent than any other document in international human rights law. It establishes the rights of indigenous peoples to the protection of their cultural property and identity as well as the rights to education, employment, health, religion, language and more. It also protects the right of indigenous peoples to own land collectively. The Universal Declaration of Human Rights, also guarantees the fundamental rights of all human beings. The ILO Indigenous and Tribal Peoples Convention was the first international convention to address the specific needs for indigenous peoples' human rights. The Convention outlines the responsibilities of governments in promoting and protecting the human rights of Indigenous Peoples.

Despite international recognition and acceptance of these declarations and conventions, in practical fact indigenous peoples' human rights remain without specifically designated safeguards. To this day, indigenous peoples continue to face serious threats to their basic existence due to systematic government policies. In many countries, they rank highest on such underdevelopment indicators as the proportion of people in jail, the illiteracy rate, unemployment rate, etc. They face discrimination in schools and are exploited in the workplace. National governments continue to deny indigenous peoples the right to live in and manage their traditional lands. In some cases, governments have even enforced policies of forced assimilation in efforts to eradicate indigenous peoples, cultures, and traditions.

This book is an in-depth study of the rights of indigenous peoples. It looks at the socioeconomic status, human rights situation and burning issues of indigenous peoples around the world. It also discusses the role of international laws and modern human rights programmes to protect the indigenous peoples' aspirations to survive as distinct communities in control of their own destinies. This book will have a wide audience including anthropologists, sociologists, demographers, development studies specialists in addition to activists working in organisations dealing with the issues of indigenous peoples.

Editor

1

Status of Indigenous Peoples

Indigenous peoples are generally defined as peoples living in an area within a nation-state, prior to the formation of a nation-state, but who do not identify with the dominant nation. They are sometimes referred to as aborigines, native peoples, first peoples, first nations or as autochthonous, a Greek term that means "sprung from the earth". Greek authors of the classical period referred to the indigenous people of Greece, who had lived there since before any of the waves of Hellenic migration, as "Pelasgians." In antiquity, the Greek term for all non-Greek speaking peoples was "barbarians".

Indigenous peoples are also sometimes identified as primitives, savages, or uncivilized. These terms were common during the heyday of European colonial expansion. By the 17th century, indigenous peoples were commonly labeled "uncivilized". Proponents of civilization, like Thomas Hobbes, considered them merely savages; critics of civilization, such as Jean Jacques Rousseau, considered them to be "noble savages". Those who were close to the Hobbesian view tended to believe themselves to have a duty to civilize and modernize indigenes. Although anthropologists, especially from Europe, used to apply these terms to all tribal cultures, it has fallen into disfavor as demeaning and, according to anthropologists, inaccurate.

After World War I, however, many Europeans came to doubt the value of civilization. At the same time, the anticolonial movement, and advocates of indigenous peoples, argued that words such as "civilized" and "savage" were products and tools of colonialism, and argued that colonialism itself was savagely destructive. In the mid 20th century, Europeans began to recognize that indigenous and tribal peoples should have the right to decide for themselves what should happen to their ancient cultures and their ancestral lands.

The United Nations defines indigenous peoples as follows:

> "Indigenous communities, peoples and nations are those which, having a historical continuity with pre-invasion and pre-colonial societies that developed on their territories, consider themselves distinct from other sectors of the societies now prevailing in those territories, or parts of them."

Advocates of the concept of indigenous peoples argue that, despite the diversity of indigenous peoples, they share common problems and issues in dealing with the prevailing, or invading, society. They are generally concerned that the cultures of indigenous peoples are being lost and that indigenous peoples suffer both discrimination and pressure to assimilate into their surrounding societies.

Several criticisms of the concept of indigenous peoples are:

— In many cases, such as with some Native American tribes, some people claim that the people termed indigenous arrived in an area after the people termed non-indigenous.

— Peoples have invaded or colonised each other's lands since before recorded history and so the division into indigenous and non-indigenous is a matter of judgement. Even in recent centuries there are difficulties: for example, are the Zulu people indigenous to South Africa?

— Lumping indigenous peoples into one group ignores the vast amounts of diversity among them and at the same time imposes a uniform identity on them, which may not be historically accurate.

Some feel that those who argue that indigenous peoples should have the right of self-determination often are simply replacing the stereotype of the barbaric savage with another stereotype, that of the noble savage possessing mystic truths and at peace with nature, and that this second stereotype ignores some of the real issues of indigenous peoples such as economic development.

However, advocates of rights for indigenous peoples consider these arguments to be specious; if a tribe has lived self-sufficiently in an area for many centuries, why should "economic development" suddenly now be an issue when it never has been before? They argue that these arguments are usually put forward by industrialists who want to exploit the land for economic gain, or by governments who consider the indigenous population to be inferior and to be an obstruction to their plans for development.

An example of this occurred in 2002 when the Government of Botswana expelled all the Kalahari Bushmen from the lands they had lived off for at least twenty thousand years. Government ministers described the Bushmen as "stone age creatures" and likened their forced eviction to a cull of elephants. These events passed almost without comment in the world's media, at a time when the eviction of a number of white people from land in nearby Zimbabwe was headline news.

In response, many have pointed out that in many cases the indigenous peoples often haven't been living self-sufficiently in an area for centuries, and that economic development was not an issue before because it was not an option. They point out that when given a choice, indigenous peoples themselves often want economic development, and that this has indeed caused conflicts with environmental groups when indigenous peoples have been given title to land and then proceed to develop just like non-indigenous people.

Furthermore, it has been pointed out that indigenous peoples are not necessarily any more self-sufficient or in tune with nature, and that indigenous peoples have themselves created environmental disasters such as those experienced by Easter Island, the Maya civilization, or the disappearance of Australian and North American megafauna.

Indigenous behavior in history many times is the opposite of what many film writers and authors portray. When the Spanish conquistadors invaded the new land, the indigenous behavior is portrayed as welcoming, friendly, and humble human being, but in actuallity the majority of the submissive attitude towards the Spanish was because they feared the strength of the Spaniards. In other words the Spaniards greatly outpowered the Indians. The Spaniards actually killed some of the indigenous peoples when they first invaded the indigenous territory. In most related history films the indigenous peoples are compared to child-like social animals that were being mistreated by the Spaniards. In actually many indigenous peoples hated and envied the Spaniards.

The early church was closely related to the indigenous people and the Spaniards. Catholic missionaries often times served as mediators of the Spanish government and the indigenous people. The Spanish had many agendas such as profitting for the New World and taxing the indigenous people. There were many members in indigenous life that were a part of a ayllu.

For some people, indigenous peoples may be victims of biopiracy when they are submitted to unauthorised use of their biological resources, of their traditional knowledge on these biological resources, of unequal share of benefits between them and a patent holder. A controversial case of biopiracy was reported on human genes of a tribal community reported to be resistant to malaria and leprosy.

Origin and Status of Indigenous People of the World

Details of some improtnant indigenous communities of the world are discribed below.

Ainu

The Ainu are an ethnic group indigenous to Hokkaido, the northern part of Honshu in Northern Japan, the Kurile Islands, much of Sakhalin, and the southernmost third of the Kamchatka peninsula. There are over 150,000 Ainu today, however the exact figure is not known as many Ainu hide their origins or in many cases are not even aware of them, their parents having kept it from them so as to protect their children from racism.

History

The origins of the Ainu are uncertain. Although their traditional homeland has been inhabited since the end of the last ice age, it is impossible to track the movements of the peoples of Northeastern Asia until well after the beginning of the historical period. At first, contact with the Japanese people was friendly and both were equals in a trade relationship. However, eventually the Japanese started to dominate the relationship, and soon established large settlements on the outskirts of Ainu territory.

As the Japanese moved north and took control over their traditional lands, the Ainu often gave up without resistance, but there was occasional resistance as exemplified in wars in 1457, 1669, and 1789, all of which were lost by the Ainu. Japanese policies became increasingly aimed at reforming the Ainu in the Meiji period, outlawing their language and restricting them to farming on government-provided plots. Ainu were also used in near-slavery conditions in the Japanese fishing industry. Japan used to called the Ainu's home island "Ezo", but changed the name to "Hokkaido" during the Meiji Restoration.

The Ainu are now governed by Japanese laws and judged by Japanese tribunals, but in former times their affairs were administered by hereditary chiefs, three in each village, and for administrative purposes the country was divided into three districts, Saru, Usu and Ishikari, which were under the ultimate control of Saru, though the relations between their respective inhabitants were not close and intermarriages were avoided.

The functions of judge were not entrusted to these chiefs; an indefinite number of a community's members sat in judgement upon its criminals. Capital punishment did not exist, nor was imprisonment resorted to, beating being considered a sufficient and final penalty, except in the case of murder, when the nose and ears of the culprit were cut off or the tendons of his feet severed. Intermarriages between Japanese and Ainu are not infrequent, and at Sambutsu especially, on the eastern coast, many children of such marriages may be seen.

Today, many Ainu don't like the term Ainu and prefer to identify themselves as Utari ("comrade" in the Ainu language). In official documents both names are used.

Geography

For historical reasons, nearly all Ainu live in Japan. There is, however, a small number of Ainu living on Sakhalin, most of them descendants of Sakhalin Ainu who were evicted and later returned. There is also an Ainu minority living at the southernmost area of the Kamchatka Peninsula and on the Kurile Islands. However, the only Ainu speakers remaining live solely in Japan. There, they are concentrated primarily on the southern and eastern coasts of the island of Hokkaido.

Culture

Traditional Ainu culture is quite different from Japanese culture. Never shaving after a certain age, the men have full beards and moustaches. Men and women alike cut their hair level with the shoulders at the sides of the head, but trim it semicircularly behind. The women tattoo their mouths, arms, clitorides, and sometimes their foreheads, starting at the onset of puberty. The soot deposited on a pot hung over a fire of birch bark is used for colour. Their traditional dress is a robe spun from the bark of the elm tree. It has long sleeves, reaches nearly to the feet, is folded round the body, and is tied with a girdle of the same material. Women also wear an undergarment of Japanese cloth.

Both sexes are fond of earrings, which are said to have been made of grapevine in former times, as also are bead necklaces called tamasay, which the women prize highly. Their cuisine consists of the flesh of the bear, the fox, the wolf, the badger, the ox or the horse, as well as fish, fowl, millet, vegetables, herbs, and roots. They never eat raw fish or flesh, but always either boil or roast it. Their habitations are reed-thatched huts, the largest 20 ft. square, without partitions and having a fireplace in the centre. There is no chimney, but only a hole at the angle of the roof; there is one window on the eastern side and there are two doors. The house of the village head is used as a public meeting place when one is needed. Instead of using furniture, they sit on the floor, which is covered with two layers of mats, one of rush, the other of flag; and for beds they spread planks, hanging mats around them on poles, and employing skins for coverlets. The men use chopsticks and moustache-lifters when eating; the women have wooden spoons.

Religion

The Ainu believe in animism, or that everything in nature has a "kamui" (spirit or god) on the inside. There is a hierarchy of the kamui. The most important is grandmother hearth (fire), then kamui of the mountain (animals), then kamui of the sea (sea animals), lastly everything else. They have no priests by profession. The village chief performs whatever religious ceremonies are necessary; ceremonies are confined to making libations of wine, uttering prayers, and offering willow sticks with wooden shavings attached to them. These sticks are called Inau (singular) and nusa (plural). They are placed on an altar used to sacrifice the heads of killed animals. The Ainu people give thanks to the gods before eating and pray to the deity of fire ("Huchi") in time of sickness. They believe their spirits are immortal, and that their spirits will be rewarded hereafter by ascending to kamui mosir (Land of the Gods) or punished in hell. Some Ainus in the north are members of the Russian Orthodox Church.

Australian Aborigine

Australian Aborigines are the indigenous peoples of Australia. Their ancestors probably arrived in Australia just over 50,000 years ago, although the date remains in dispute.

History

Pre-colonisation: The Aboriginal and Torres Strait Islander people are the indigenous people of Australia. At the time of first contact with the European colonists in the late 18th century, most Aborigines were hunter-gatherers with a complex oral culture and spiritual values based upon reverence for the land and a belief in the Dreamtime. The Dreamtime is at once the ancient time of creation and the present day reality of dreaming.

The exact timing of the arrival of the Aborigines' ancestors has been a matter of dispute among archaeologists. The most common view is that their ancestors came from southeast Asia more than 50,000 years ago. This means there have been more than 1250 generations in Australia. The 50,000 BP date is based on a few sites in northern Australia dated using thermoluminescence. A large number of sites have been radiocarbon dated to around 40,000 BP, leading some researchers to doubt the accuracy of the thermoluminescence technique. Thermoluminescence dating of the Jinmium site in the Northern Territory suggested a date of 120,000 BP. Although this result received wide press coverage, it has been seriously questioned by most archaeologists.

The Aboriginal people lived through many climatic changes and adapted successfully to the different environments. There is much debate about the degree to which Aboriginal people modified their environment. One controversy revolves around the role of Aborigines in the extinction of the marsupial megafauna. Some argue that natural climate change killed the megafauna. Others claim that, because the megafauna were large and slow, they were easy prey for Aboriginal hunters. A third possibility is that Aboriginal modification of the environment, particularly through the use of fire, indirectly led to their extinction.

Despite their reputation as stone-age relics, there is evidence of substantial change in Aboriginal culture over time. Rock painting at several locations in northern Australia has been shown to consist of a sequence of different styles linked to different historical periods. Harry Lourandos has been the leading proponent of the theory that a period of hunter-gatherer intensification occurred between 5000 and 3000 BP. Intensification involved an increase in human manipulation of the environment, population growth, an increase in trade between groups, a more elaborate social structure, and other cultural changes. A shift in stone tool technology, involving the development of smaller and more intricate points and scrapers, occurred around this time.

There were a great many different Aboriginal groups, each with their own individual culture, belief structure, and language. These cultures overlapped to a greater or lesser extent, and evolved over time. Lifestyles varied a great deal, and the stereotyped image of a proud and naked hunter standing one-legged in the red sand of the central Australian desert cannot be applied across the board. In present-day Victoria, for example, there were two separate communities with an economy based on fish-farming in complex and extensive irrigated pond systems; one on the Murray River in the state's north, the other in the south-west near Hamilton, which traded with other groups from as far away as the Melbourne area.

British colonisation: In 1770, Captain James Cook took possession of the east coast of Australia and named it New South Wales in the name of Great Britain. The Aboriginal population was decimated by British colonisation which began in 1788, when news of the land's fertility spread to Europeans causing them to begin settling in the Aborigines' land. A combination of disease, loss of land and outright murder reduced the Aboriginal population by an estimated 90% during the 19th century and early 20th century. A wave of massacres and resistance followed the frontier. The last massacre was at Coniston in the Northern Territory in 1928. Poisoning of food and water has been recorded on several different occasions.

In the arid centre of the continent, where small communities were spread over a vast area, the population decline was less marked, and Aboriginal communities were able to continue in an approximation of their traditional lifestyle for considerably longer—in many cases, until the late 19th century and in a few instances well into the 20th.

Nevertheless, European settlers gradually made their way into the interior, appropriating small but vital parts of the land for their own exclusive use, and introducing sheep, rabbits and cattle, all three of which ate out previously fertile areas and degraded the ability of the land to carry the native animals that were vital to Aboriginal economies.

In general, the first European colonisers were welcomed, or at least not opposed, but there were violent conflicts from time to time frequently culminating in murder. In the Northern Territory, both isolated Europeans and visiting Japanese fishermen continued to be speared to death on a semi-regular basis until the start of the Second World War in 1941. It is known that some European settlers in the centre and north of the country shot Aboriginal people during this period. It is reasonable to presume that many more Aboriginal people died than Europeans, but such events were seldom recorded and the number of murders is a matter for speculation.

Australian independence from Britain changed little in the relationship between Whites and Aborigines. As the European pastoral industries developed, several economic changes came about. The appropriation of prime land and the spread of European livestock over vast areas made a traditional Aboriginal lifestyle less viable, but also provided a ready alternative supply of fresh meat for those prepared to risk taking advantage of it.

As large sheep and cattle stations came to dominate outback Australia, Aboriginal men, women and children became a significant source of labour, usually on a voluntary basis but sometimes under conditions that amounted to virtual slavery. For European workers, life in the outback was harsh, dangerous and ill-paid. For Aboriginal workers it was usually worse yet, wages often being restricted to food and other basic items, particularly in the early years. Typically, an Aboriginal stockman could expect to earn half as much as a European doing the same job. This system lasted until the introduction of equal pay legislation in 1965, which—paradoxically—brought about widespread unemployment and yet more hardship.

During the first half of the 20th century, native welfare boards were established in the various states. These instituted a policy of separating children from their parents based upon racial stereotyping. Pale-skinned children were forcibly removed, and Aboriginal parents often darkened up their children to keep them. This aspect of Aboriginal history is also open to considerable debate. See Stolen Generation.

The Australian Constitution originally did not permit Aborigines to be counted in the census, thereby effectively denying their right to vote. In 1967, a referendum was held to allow Indigenous Australians to be counted in the census and to allow the Federal Government to make laws for the benefit of Indigenous Australians. This referendum was successful with a huge majority favouring the constitutional amendments.

Recent history: Many aborigines now live in towns and cities around Australia, but a substantial number live in settlements in what are often remote areas of rural Australia. The health and economic difficulties facing both groups are substantial and the root causes are poverty, grog and the brutality of individuals towards one another. The solutions to these root causes have been, again, contentious in political issues.

The Australian government has begun a process it calls "Reconciliation". Some notable former Prime Ministers, such as Bob Hawke and Malcolm Fraser have made many symbolic gestures and speeches in support of respect for Aborigine culture. Many Aborigine leaders such as Isabell Coe reject such moves, demanding actual sovereignty instead.

In 1972, the Aboriginal Tent Embassy was established on the steps of Parliament House in Canberra, the Australian capital. The continuous protest has remained in place for over thirty years to demand sovereignty for the Aboriginal peoples.

In 1992, the Australian High Court handed down its decision in the Mabo Case, declaring the previous legal concept of terra nullius to be invalid. This decision legally recognised the presence of Indigenous Australians in Australia prior to British Settlement. Legislation was subsequently enacted and later amended to recognise Native Title claims over land in Australia.

In 1999 a referendum was held to change the Australian Constitution to include a preamble that, amongst other topics, recognised the occupation of Australia by Indigenous Australians prior to British Settlement. This referendum was defeated by a huge majority, though the recognition of indigenous Australians in the preamble was not a major issue in the preamble referendum discussion, and the preamble question attracted secondary attention compared to the question of becoming a republic.

Most recently, in 2004, the Federal Government of Australia has proceeded with plans to abolish The Aboriginal and Torres Strait Islander Commission—ATSIC — which had been Australia's peak Indigenous organisation. The Commonwealth cites corruption and in particular the mis-use of public funds as principal reasons along with the fact that the body had become largely irrelevant and served mostly as a symbol of "Aboriginal self-determination".

Awa

The Awa are an endangered indigenous group of people living in the eastern Amazon forests of Brazil. Originally living in settlements, they adopted a nomadic lifestyle about 1800 to escape incursions by Europeans. During the nineteenth century, they came under increasing attack by settlers in the region, who cleared most of the forests from their land. From the mid-1980s onward, some Awa moved to government-established settlements, but for the most part they were able to maintain their traditional way of life, living entirely off their forests, in nomadic groups of a few dozen people, with little or no contact with the outside world.

In 1982, the Brazilian government received a loan of nine hundred million US dollars from the World Bank and the European Union. One condition of this loan was that the lands of certain indigenous peoples would be demarcated and protected. This was particularly important for the Awa because their forests were increasingly being invaded by outsiders. There were many cases of tribespeople being killed by settlers, but perhaps more significantly, the forest on which they depend was being destroyed by logging and land clearance for farming. Without government intervention it seemed very likely that the Awa and their ancient culture would become extinct.

However, the Brazilian government was extraordinarily slow to act on its commitment. It took twenty years of sustained pressure from campaigning organisations such as Survival International and the Forest Peoples Programme before, in March 2003, the Awa's land was finally demarcated.

During this time, encroachment on their land and a series of massacres had reduced Awa numbers to about 300, of whom only about 60 were still living their traditional, isolated, hunter-gatherer way of life.

Ayero

The Ayoreo are one of around 18 different tribes living in Paraguay. The Ayoreo's home is in the Chaco, a huge region of dry scrub forest, rivers and swampland which encompasses the whole of the western half of Paraguay and extends into other countries. The Ayoreo live in the north-west of Paraguay and part of eastern Bolivia. There are different sub-groups of Ayoreo, including the Totobiegosode (whose name means 'people from the place of the wild pigs').

The Ayoreo are a nomadic, hunter-gatherer people, who once inhabited a vast area of scrub forest. Their first sustained contact with white people came in the 1940s and 1950s, when Mennonite farmers established colonies on their land. Subsequently missionaries attempted to contact and settle them. Although the Ayoreo resisted contact and largely rejected the missionaries, they did begin to come out of the forest; there is now only a small group of nomadic Totobiegosode living uncontacted in the forest. Most Ayoreo land is now owned by private landowners, who hire work-teams to clear the forest of valuable timber and then introduce cattle. Some is still owned by the Mennonites and another religious group, the US-based New Tribes Mission (NTM).

During the 1970s and 1980s, the Ayoreo experienced intensive missionary activity, as the NTM pursued a policy of aggressive attempts to convert them. They would encourage groups of missionised Ayoreo to go into the forest to capture the uncontacted, nomadic Ayoreo, their traditional enemies, and bring them back to the NTM base. This resulted in violent clashes and several deaths as the Indians were exposed to diseases to which they had no immunity at the mission camp. The Ayoreo also suffer greatly from the theft of their land – although the Paraguayan constitution guarantees Indian land ownership, the Ayoreo's land has almost all been taken over by ranchers, forcing them out of their forest and making it very difficult for them to support themselves.

Basque

The Basques are an indigenous people who inhabit parts of both Spain and France. They are found predominantly in four provinces in Spain and three in France. This area - the Basque Country—is to be found around the western edge of the Pyrenees on the coast of the Bay of Biscay.

Origin of Basques

The most important sources about the early history of the Basques are the classical writers, especially Strabo, who confirms that at about the time of the birth of Jesus, the western part of the Pyrenees were inhabited by a people known as the Vascons. This is quite identifiable as the origin of the Romance word "Basque". Further evidence for these people speaking the Basque language (Euskara) is provided by lists of personal names and place names.

The Basques have occupied a single region of Europe longer than any other identifiable ethnic group. There is also considerable evidence that the Basque language was once spoken over a much wider area than the modern day Basque country. The Dark Ages and the Reconquista extended the Basque territory beyond the limits of the Roman age.

It is believed that the Basques arrived before the Indo-Europeans and thus that they are the oldest surviving people continuously inhabiting a particular location in Europe. It is believed that they have lived in their present location for thousands of years, unmoved by any of the calamities of war, plague, or famine that destroyed all the other ancient civilizations of Europe, a relatively small group of people surviving when many others were overwhelmed by the waves of invaders that have swept Europe. A number of Basque writers seeking to explain this have speculated about racial superiority, but the endurance of the Basques can also be explained by luck: they happened to be in the right place over and over again.

The Basques either chose their easily defended home in the Pyrenees or, what is more likely, were forced into it at some time in the past. It is common for mountainous regions to remain as bastions of an all-but-vanished group of people. When the Celts of Europe were overwhelmed by the Germanic peoples from the East and North, and attacked by the Roman Empire from the south, the only areas left speaking Celtic languages were Ireland and a number of mountain bastions, which still retain Celtic speakers to the present day. These regions include Brittany in the northwest of France as well as Scotland and Wales in the British Isles. In these regions the Celtic cultures have survived fifteen hundred years after the assimilation of others into other cultures.

The Basque homeland is well suited to survival. Its low mountains are combined with dense forests and heavy vegetation to make the region almost impassable to outsiders, but still temperate enough to support a large agricultural base. Despite this growth, the soil is of much lower quality than the surrounding plains in Spain and France, leaving the area a much less tempting target for invaders. For invaders bent on plunder, the Basque areas have few reserves of precious metals, especially in comparison to the gold reserves to the west in Spain or to the wealth in Gascony just to the north of Basqueland. The Basques seem to have ended up in the best locale for uninterrupted survival on the continent. The first two known invasions the Basques survived were those of the Indo-Europeans and then the Celts. These two invasions occurred in prehistory and the secret of the Basque survival is only hinted at by limited archeological evidence.

Geography and Distribution

The current autonomous Basque area of Spain, known as "Euskadi" in Basque, "Pais Vasco" in Spanish, "Pays Basque" in French and the "Basque Country" in English, is composed of three provinces or territories: Araba/Alava, Bizkaia/ Vizcaya and Gipuzkoa/Guipúzcoa. There are 2,123,000 people living in the Basque Country: Araba, 279,000; Bizkaia, 1,160,000; and Gipuzkoa, 684,000. The most important cities are: Bilbo/Bilbao, Donostia/San Sebastian and Gasteiz/ Vitoria. Both Euskara and Spanish are official languages. Knowledge of Spanish is virtually universal; 27 per cent of the people speak the Basque language, but this number is increasing for the first time in many centuries.

There is also a substantial Basque population in the adjacent Spanish autonomous community and province of Navarre, and in nearby parts of France — see Basque Country for more information. There is at least some ethnic Basque presence in many countries of the Americas, including Argentina, Chile, Venezuela, Uruguay and a community in Idaho, eastern Nevada, and throughout California who first came over to herd sheep.

The destination of the majority of Basque emigrants was Argentina, with Basque culture contributing much to Argentine culture. There are Basque cultural centres in most large cities, as well as pelota courts and Basque language schools. Many places have been given Basque names, including the main international airport, Ezeiza. Several of Argentina's Presidents have been of Basque descent, including Irigoyen, Aramburu and Urquiza, not to mention other figures, notably Che Guevara. There are an estimated 15,000 surnames in Argentina of Basque descent.

The largest community of Basques in North America exists in the greater Boise area. Boise is home to the Basque Museum & Cultural Center. The area around the center includes a variety of stores and restaraunts featuring Basque culture in a so-called "Basque block." The current mayor of Boise, David H. Bieter is Basque.

In the Caribbean, Basque descendants exist in the hills of Esperón in the province of Habana, where many originally settled during the Spanish colonial period.

Culture

There are interesting social differences between the Basques and their neighbours. The Basque people have an unusually close attachment with their homes. A person's home is their family in Basqueland. Even if one does not still live there and has not for generations a Basque family is still known by the house in which it once lived. Common Basque surnames could translate as "top of the hill", or "by the river" all relating to the location of their ancestral home. This is interesting evidence for considering the Basques to be the only people who have always had a fixed and stable abode.

Though matriarchality has been sometimes attributed to Basque society, today it seems clear that the actually known familiar structure is patrilinear, being the top position given to the father, as in neighbour cultures. Nevertheless there are some signs that this could have not always been that way. Also it must be said that the social position of women has always been rather better than in neighbour countries.

In spite of this, until the Industrial Age, poor Basques (usually the younger sons) have emigrated to the rest of Spain or France and the Americas. Saint Francis Xavier and Conquistadores like Lope de Aguirre were Basque.

Despite ETA and the crisis of heavy industries, the Basques have been doing remarkably well in recent years, emerging from persecution during the Franco regime with a strong and vibrant language and culture. For the first time in centuries, the Basque language is expanding geographically led by large increases in the major urban centres of Pamplona, Bilbao, and Bayonne, where only a few decades ago the Basque language had all but disappeared. The opening of the new Guggenheim Museum in Bilbao is widely seen as a symbol of a linguistic and cultural revival.

Religion

Most Basques are practicing Roman Catholics. The region has been a source of missionaries like Francis Xavier and Michel Garicoïts. Also, Ignatius Loyola, founder of the Society of Jesus, was a Basque. A sprout of Protestantism in the continental Basque Country produced the first translation of the new Testament into Basque by Joannes Leyçarraga. After the king of Navarre converted to Catholicism to be king of France, Protestantism almost disappeared. Bayonne held a Jewish community mainly from Sephardic refugees from Spain.

Bororo

The Bororo are a Macro-Jê-speaking people in the Mato Grosso region of Brazil; they also extended into Bolivia and the Brazilian state of Goias. The Western Bororo, now extinct, lived around the Jauru and Cabaçal rivers, while the Eastern Bororo (Orarimogodoge) live in the region of the São Lourenço, Garças, and Vermelho rivers.

Bushmen

The Bushmen or San peoples of South Africa and neighbouring Botswana and Namibia, who live in the Kalahari, are part of the Khoisan group and are related to the Khoikhoi. However, they have no collective name for themselves in any of their languages. They have a sign language that they use while hunting. With the pygmies of Central Africa, they have been considered root of female DNA lineage - the legendary

Mitochondrial Eve.The term San was historically applied to them by their ethnic relatives and historic rivals the Khoikhoi; as the term means outsider and was derogatory, many of this group prefer to be called Bushmen, despite the fact that the term is considered politically incorrect by most Westerners.

In modern South Africa, the Bushmen have largely been absorbed into the so-called Coloured or Cape Coloured population of the Western Cape. Since 2002, the Bushmen of Botswana are seeking legal action to prevent the Botswana government from removing them from the Central Kalahari Game Reserve, their ancestral homeland. The Bushmen are arguing that the Government of Botswana is attempting to destroy their culture through forced relocation and persecution based on their identity.

Celt

In ancient times, the Celts were a number of interrelated peoples in central Europe sharing a branch of Indo-European languages indicative of a common origin. Today, "Celtic" is often used to describe the people and their respective cultures and languages of several ethnic groups in the British Isles, the French region of Brittany and the Spanish region of Galicia. They also share many of the same traits in their cultures and languages as the original Celts. Nowadays "Celt" is usually pronounced as kelt.

Orgin and Geographical Distribution

The Celtic language family is a branch of the larger Indo-European family, which leads some scholars to a hypothesis that the original speakers of the Celtic proto-language may have arisen in the central Asian steppes. However, the Celts enter history and archaeology located in central Europe, whence they spread over a range from Ireland in the west to Anatolia in the east, and from Denmark and Scotland in the north to the Iberian peninsula and northern Italy in the south.

It is not known whether the Picts of Scotland were Celts or the remnant of an earlier population of the British Isles who had been pushed to the margin by Celtic invasions. However, in historical times Scotland was colonized by the Celtic Scotti from Ireland. Additional forays into Greece and central Italy during the historical period did not result in settlement, though the same movement that brought Celtic invaders to Greece pushed on through to Anatolia, where they settled as the Galatians.

As there is no archaeological evidence for large scale invasions in some of the other areas, one current school of thought holds that Celtic language and culture spread to those areas by contact rather than invasion. However, the Celtic invasions of Italy, Greece, and western Anatolia are well documented in Greek and Latin history.

Some scholars think that the Urnfield culture represents an origin for the Celts as a distinct cultural branch of the Indo-European family. This culture was preeminent in central Europe during the late Bronze Age, from c. 1200 BC until 700 BC. The period of saw a dramatic increase in population in the region, probably due to innovations in technology and agricultural practices. The spread of iron-working led to the development of the Hallstatt culture directly from the Urnfield.

The subject of the replacement of the Hallstatt culture by the La Tène culture, the final stage of the Iron Age, and its gradual transformation into the explicitly Celtic culture of early historical times, is complex. However the technologies, decorative practices and metal-working styles of the La Tène were to be very influential on the Celts. The La Tène style was highly derivative from the Greek, Etruscan and Scythian decorative styles with whom the La Tène settlers frequently traded. The La Tène culture was distributed around the upper reaches of the Danube, Switzerland, Austria, southern and central Germany, eastern France, Bohemia and Moravia, and parts of Hungary.

It was not the Celts, but rather earlier inhabitants of Europe who built Stonehenge and the other megalithic monuments in the areas settled by the Celts. But though the Celts did not construct the monuments, the religious significance of these places may well have endured among the conquered people and the Celts eventually adopted the practice of worshipping there as well.

The conventional historical view holds that the Celtic influence in the British Isles was the result of successive invasions from the European continent by diverse Celtic-speaking peoples over the course of several centuries.

The nature of their interactions with the indigenous populations of the isles is unknown. However, by the Roman period most of the inhabitants of the Isles were speaking Goidelic or Brythonic languages with close counterparts to Gaulish languages spoken on the European mainland. The degree to which the spread of Celtic languages was due to peaceful cultural interaction, or to military conquest, is a debated point among historians. The relative paucity of surviving information about the inhabitants of the British Isles prior to Celtic influence suggests conquest.

An alternate theory, proposed during the 1970s by Colin Burgess in his book The Age of Stonehenge theorized that Celtic culture in Great Britain 'emerged' rather than resulted from invasion and that the Celts were not invading aliens, but the descendants of the people of Stonehenge. Support for this idea comes from the study by Cristian Capelli, David Goldstein and others at University College, London which shows that genes typical of Ireland and Scotland are common in England and Wales and these genes are similar to the genes of the Basque people, who speak a non-Indo-European language. This similarity, they argue, shows that the non-Indo-European native inhabitants of Britain were not wiped out by invasions of either Indo-Europeans bringing farming or Celts in 600 BC. They suggest that 'Celtic' culture and the Celtic language were imported to Britain by cultural contact not mass invasion. The genetic similarity is less marked in women in Britain who have a genetic makeup closer to that of Northern Europe —possibly because women tended to move to their husbands' homes.

At the dawn of history in Europe, the Celts who had settled in present-day France were known as Gauls, and were described by Julius Caesar in his Gallic Wars. Other Celtic tribes invaded Italy, establishing there a city they called Mediolanum (modern Milan) and sacking Rome itself in 390 BC. Not until 192 BC did the Roman armies conquer the last remaining independent Celtic kingdoms in Italy.

Under Caesar the Romans conquered Celtic Gaul, and from Claudius onward the Roman empire absorbed parts of the Celtic British Isles. Roman local government of these regions closely mirrored pre-Roman 'tribal' boundaries, and archaeological finds suggest native involvement in local government. Latin was the official language of these regions after the conquests.

Later these regions adopted Christianity along with the rest of the Roman empire. The unconquered Ireland adopted Christianity as well, and was a major source of missionary work in central Europe.

Degar

The Degar (referred to by French colonists as Montagnard) are the indigenous people of the central highlands of Vietnam. The term Montagnard means "mountain people" in French and is a carry over from the French colonial period in Vietnam.

Before the Vietnam War, the population of the Central Highlands, estimated at between 3 and 3.5 million, was almost exclusively Degar. Today, the population is approximately 4 million, of whom about 1 million are Montagnard. The 30 or so Degar tribes in the Central Highlands comprise more than six different ethnic groups drawn primarily from the Malayo-Polynesian and Mon Khmer language families. The main tribes, in order of population, are the Jarai, Rhade, Bahnar, Koho, Hmong, and Stieng.

Originally inhabitants of the coastal areas of the region, they were driven to the previously uninhabited mountainous areas by invading Vietnamese and Cambodians beginning prior to the 9th century AD. Physically, the Degar are darker skinned than the Vietnamese and do not have epicanthic folds around their eyes.

Although French Catholic missionaries converted some Degar in the nineteenth century, American missionaries made more of an impact in the 1930s, and many Degar are now Protestant. Of the approximately 1 million Degar, close to half are Protestant, while around 200,000 are Catholic. This has made the Degar suspect to Vietnam's Communist Party, particularly during the Vietnam War, since it was thought that they would be more inclined to help the American forces.

In the mid 1950s, the once-isolated Degar began experiencing more contact with outsiders after the Vietnamese government launched efforts to gain better control of the Central Highlands and, following the 1954 Geneva Accord, new ethnic minorities from North Vietnam moved into the area. As a result of these changes, Degar communities felt a need to strengthen some of their own social structures and to develop a more formal shared identity.

In 1950, the French government established the Central Highlands as the Pays Montagnard du Sud (PMS) under the authority of Vietnamese Emperor Bao Dai, whom the French had installed as nominal chief of state in 1949 as an alternative to Ho Chi Minh's Democratic Republic of Vietnam. When the French withdrew from Vietnam and recognized a Vietnamese government, Degar political independence was decimated. However it is not just the Degar's aspirations for greater autonomy that have led the Vietnamese government to crack down on the Degar.

The Degar have a long history of tensions with the Vietnamese majority that is comparable to the tensions between American Indians and the population of European descent in the United States. While the Vietnamese are themselves heterogeneous, they generally share a common language and culture and have developed and maintained the dominant social institutions of Vietnam. The Degar do not share that heritage nor do they have access to the country's dominant institutions. There have been conflicts between the two groups over many issues, including land ownership, language and cultural preservation, access to education and resources, and political representation.

In 1958, the Degar launched a movement known as BAJARAKA (the name is made up of the first letters of prominent tribes, compare to the later Nicaraguan Misurasata) to unite the tribes against the Vietnamese. There was a related, well-organized political and military force within the Degar communities known by the French acronym, FULRO, or Forces United for the Liberation of Races Oppressed. FULRO's objectives were autonomy for the Degar tribes.

The 1960s saw contact between the Degar and another group of outsiders, the U.S. military, as American involvement in the Vietnam War escalated and the Central Highlands emerged as a strategically important area, in large part because it included the Ho Chi Minh trail, the North Vietnamese supply line for Viet Cong forces in the south. The U.S. military, particularly the US Army's Special Forces, developed base camps in the area and recruited the Degar, roughly 40,000 of whom fought alongside American soldiers and became a major part of the U.S. military effort in the Highlands. The Degar's legendary bravery and loyalty earned them the respect and friendship of the U.S. Special Forces as well as sympathy for the Degar struggle for independence.

Thousands of Degar fled to Cambodia after the liberation/fall of Saigon, fearing that the new government would launch reprisals against them because they had aided the US Army. However, in Cambodia, they soon suffered much more brutal treatment under the Khmer Rouge. Back in

Vietnam, the government did carry out retributions, by imprisoning or executing nearly all prominent Degar tribal leaders. In addition, the Vietnamese government has steadily displaced thousands of villagers from Vietnam's central highlands, in order to use the fertile land for coffee plantations.

The Degar population has decreased by nearly two-thirds in only 32 years, due to very high death rates and low birth rates. This has prompted several human rights organizations to argue that the Degar are subject to an ongoing and continual genocide by the current Vietnamese government.

Enxet

The Enxet are an indigenous people of about 17,000 living in the Gran Chaco region of western Paraguay. Originally hunter-gatherers, many are now forced to supplement their livelihood as laborers on the cattle ranches that have encroached upon their dwindling natural forest habitat. Nevertheless, the Enxet are still engaged in an ongoing conflict with the government and ranchers, who want to destroy what remains of the forest to open the land for massive settlement. Today, only a handful of Enxet are still able to maintain their traditional way of life, while the majority live in small settlements sponsored by various missionary organizations.

Frisians

The Roman historian Tacitus, in his Germania, mentioned the Frisians among people he grouped together as the Ingvaeones. Their territory followed the coast of the North Sea from the mouth of the Rhine river up to that of the Ems, their eastern border according to Ptolemy's Geographica. Pliny the Elder states in Belgica that they were conquered by the Roman general Drusus in 12 BC, and thereafter the Frisians largely sank into historical obscurity, until coming into contact with the expanding Merovingian and Carolingian empires. In the 5th Century, during this period of historical silence, many of them no doubt joined the migration of the Anglo-Saxons who went through Frisian territory to invade Britain, while those who stayed on the continent expanded into the newly-emptied lands previously occupied by the Anglo-Saxons. By the end of the sixth century the Frisians occupied the coast all the way to the mouth of the Weser and spread farther still in the seventh century, southward down to Dorestad and even Bruges. This farthest extent of Frisian territory is known as Frisia Magna.

Modern Frisians

The modern remnants of Frisia Magna are small and scattered. Most of it became dominated by its expanding neighbors: the Saxons and the Frank). Western and Middle Frisia are solidly within the modern state of the Netherlands, which now includes the "heartland" of the Frisians from the North Sea coast from Alkmaar in the modern province of Noord-Holland, along the coasts of the modern provinces of Friesland and Groningen, and up to the mouth of the Ems. Culturally, it has shrunk down to the province of Friesland alone.

The Frisian language is now spoken only there and in parts of only the Wadden Sea islands of Terschelling and Schiermonnikoog. Eastern and Northern Frisia have been absorbed into the northern states of Germany, with only the marshes of Saterland, well inland from the coast, still retaining any cultural identity. There are also descendants of Frisians living on the coast of the Jutland peninsula and nearby islands. It is unclear when they arrived there, or even whether they lived first on the islands and then spread to the mainland, or vice-versa. What remains of their language is under heavy pressure from Low German, High German, and Danish, and is generally expected to become extinct.

Native Hawaiians

Native Hawaiians are the indigenous Polynesian peoples of the Hawaiian Islands who trace their ancestry back to antiquity before the arrival of British explorer Captain James Cook in

1778. According to the U.S. Census Bureau report for 2000, there are 476,000 people who identified themselves as being native Hawaiian, part native Hawaiian and mixed native Hawaiian. Most native Hawaiians are residents of the United States in California, the State of Hawaii, Nevada and Washington. Two-thirds live in the State of Hawaii while the other one-third is split among mainland states. Almost half of the mainland share of the population is in California.

Identifying and classifying native Hawaiian subgroups has become a delicate issue among native Hawaiians. Different government agencies have different methods of classifying native Hawaiians. However, it is widely accepted that such classifications are necessary to facilitate laws, trusts and wills governing native Hawaiian programs.

According to the Hawaii Revised Statutes, section 10-2, Hawaiians are defined as: any descendant of the aboriginal peoples inhabiting the Hawaiian Islands which exercised sovereignty and subsisted in the Hawaiian Islands in 1778, and which peoples thereafter have continued to reside in Hawaii. Within this definition, Hawaiians are sub-classified into two major groups: native Hawaiians consist of the population who claim over 50% ancestry dating back to antiquity. Also, there are part Hawaiians who claim less than 50% of ancestry dating back to antiquity.

Culture and Arts

Native Hawaiians and community allies have established several cultural preservation societies and organizations over the course of the twentieth century. The largest of those institutions is the Hawai'i State Museum of Natural and Cultural History, established in 1988 and is administered by the Bernice Pauahi Bishop Museum. It houses the largest collection of native Hawaiian artifacts, documents and other information available for educational use. Most are held for preservation alone. The repository has established links with all the major colleges and universities throughout the world to facilitate research.

Native Hawaiian culture saw a revival in recent years as an outgrowth of decisions made at the 1978 Hawai'i State Constitutional Convention, held exactly 200 years after the arrival of Captain Cook. At the convention, the Hawai'i state government committed itself to a progressive study and preservation of native Hawaiian culture, history and language.

A comprehensive Hawaiian culture curriculum was introduced into the State of Hawaii's public elementary schools teaching: ancient Hawaiian art, lifestyle, geography, hula and Hawaiian language vocabulary. Intermediate and high schools were mandated to impose two sets of Hawaiian history curricula on every candidate for graduation. Statutes and charter amendments were passed acknowledging a policy of preference for Hawaiian place and street names.

Innu

The Innu are the indigenous inhabitants of an area they refer to as Nitassinan, which comprises most of the Quebec-Labrador peninsula in Eastern Canada. Their population in 2003 was between 15,000 and 20,000. They are known to have lived on these lands as hunter-gatherers for several thousand years, living in tents made of animal skins. Their most important resource is the caribou, and the animal is culturally very significant to them. Their language, Innu-aimun, is spoken throughout Nitassinan, with certain dialect differences.

The Innu people are sometimes sub-divided into two communities, the Montagnais ["mountain people" in French] who live along the shore of the Gulf of Saint Lawrence, and the less numerous Naskapi ["inland people" in Innu-aimun] who live farther North. However, the Innu themselves dislike these terms, and according to most sources the distinction is anyway largely an artificial one invented by the French colonists. Neither group has any common heritage with the Inuit, a completely separate people whose lands lie much further North.

The Innu have never officially surrendered their territory to Canada. As a consequence of this they are not registered under the Indian Act and the government does not afford them the same protection, tax-breaks and benefits as other First Nations. From the 1950s on, the Canadian government and the Catholic church attempted to "civilise" the Innu, inducing them to settle in fixed encampments and to abandon their nomadic lifestyle. Before long, life in these artificially constructed settlements became marred by extremely high levels of alcoholism, petrol-sniffing amongst children, domestic violence, and suicide. Between 1975 and 1995 the Innu settlements averaged 178 suicides per 100,000 persons per year. This is more than twelve times the Canadian average.

Inuit

Inuit is a general term for a group of culturally similar indigenous peoples of the Canadian Arctic who descended from the Thule. The Inuit Circumpolar Conference defines its constitutency to include Canada's Inuit and Inuvialuit, Greenland's Kalaallit people, Alaska's Inupiaq and Yupik people, and Russia's Yupik. However, the Yupik are not Inuit in the sense of being descended from the Thule and prefer to be called Yupik or Eskimo.Canadian Inuit live primarily in Nunavut, Nunavik and in Nunatsiavut. The Inuvialuit live primarily in the Mackenzie River delta, on Banks Island and part of Victoria Island in the Northwest Territories. There have been Inuit settlements in Yukon, especially at Herschel Island, but there are none at present. Alaskan Inupiaq live on the North Slope of Alaska, while the Yupik live in western Alaska and a part of Chukotka Autonomous Area in Russia

The Inuit are traditionally hunters who fish and hunt whale, walrus, and seal by kayak or by boat or by waiting at airholes the seals make in the ice. They use igloos as hunting or emergency shelters. They make use of animal skins in their clothing. Dog sleds, known as qamutiit, are used for travel pulled by Inuit Sled Dogs in a fan hitch, though snowmobiles have largely replaced this mode of travel.

The Inuit living in North America were formerly classified together with other Native Americans, but they are now considered to be an entirely separate ethnic group who arrived in North America a few millennia after the latter did, probably around 500 as the Thule, replacing the so called paleoeskimos. Accordingly, in Canada the Inuit are not considered First Nations, although they are included in the term "Native Peoples," "First Peoples," or "Aboriginal Peoples" along with Indians and Métis.

The European arrival caused a great deal of damage to the Inuit way of life, causing mass death and other suffering. Circa 1970, Inuit leaders came forward and pushed for respect for the Inuit and their territories. One of the resulting land-claims agreements created the Canadian territory of Nunavut, the largest land-claims agreement in Canadian history. In recent years, circumpolar cultural and political groups have come together to promote the Inuit people and to fight against ecological problems, such as the greenhouse effect and resulting global warming, which heavily affects the Inuit population due to the melting and thinning of the arctic ice and die-offs of arctic mammals. Nunavut premier Paul Okalik took the lead in this regard in a First Ministers' meeting discussing the Kyoto Accord.

Culture

One of the most famous Inuit artists is Pitseolak Ashoona. Susan Aglukark is a popular Canadian singer. In 2002 the feature film Atanarjuat: the Fast Runner directed by Zacharias Kunuk was released world wide to great critical and popular acclaim. Jordin Tootoo became the first Inuk to play in the National Hockey League in the 2003-04 season, playing for the Nashville Predators.

Jarawa

The Jarawa are a largely uncontacted people, living on the Andaman Islands in the Indian ocean. Both British and Indian settlers have moved onto their islands over the last 150 years, but the Jarawa have chosen to maintain an almost complete isolation. They are very different in appearance to their Indian neighbours, and DNA tests suggest that their closest relatives are African.

Because of the Jarawa's voluntary isolation, and the fact that no one outside the tribe really speaks their language, very little is known about them. We do know that the they live a hunter-gatherer lifestyle, hunting pig and monitor lizard, fishing with bows and arrows, and gathering seeds, berries and honey. They are nomadic, living in bands of 40-50 people. They resisted all contact with the outside world until 1998, when some Jarawa started coming out of their forest to visit nearby towns and settlements. From what can now be understood of their language, it seems that pressure from poachers on the coast had driven them inland. Although a few Jarawa, particularly women and children, still come out onto the road or into settlements to visit they continue to live a self-sufficient life in the forest.

The main threats to the Jarawa are encroachment on their land – sparked by the building of a road through their forest in 1970 – and the risk of being settled forcibly – as planned by the authorities in 1991 and urged by a local lawyer in a court case brought in 1999. The road has increasingly brought settlers, poachers and loggers into Jarawa land, who steal the tribe's game and expose them to disease. Forced resettlement was fatal for other tribes in the Andaman Islands, and has always been so for newly contacted tribal peoples worldwide: it introduces diseases; destroys the sense of identity and society; robs tribes of their self-sufficiency; and leaves them vulnerable to alcoholism and despair.

Maasai

The Maasai or Masai are an indigenous African tribe of semi-nomadic people located primarily in Kenya and northern Tanzania. The Maasai are probably one of the most familiar tribes of East Africa. Despite the growth of civilisation, the Maasai have largely managed to stay out of the mainstream and maintain their traditional ways, although this becomes more challenging each year.

The Maasai are part of the Nilotic family of African tribal groups, and probably migrated from the Nile valley in Sudan to central and south-western Kenya and northern Tanzania sometime after 1500 AD, bringing their domesticated cattle with them. Although other African tribes organised themselves into civilisations and kingdoms, the Maasai never surrendered their semi-nomadic lifestyle. The ability to graze their cattle over large territories has diminished considerably in recent years, due to increased urbanisation and the declaration of the Maasai Mara and Serengeti game reserves, which was all formerly Maasai grazing land.

Despite their reputation as fierce warriors, Maasai culture revolves around their cattle. One of their spiritual beliefs is that their rain god Ngai gave all cattle to the Maasai people, and therefore anyone else who possesses cattle must have stolen them from the Maasai. This has led to some fatal altercations with other tribes of the regions over the centuries when the Maasai attempt to reclaim their "property". The huts of the Maasai are built from dried cattle dung, and certain sacred rituals involve the drinking of cow blood.

There are numerous traditions and ceremonies performed by Maasai men. Perhaps best known is the warrior "jumping" dance, where young Maasai morani (warrior-youth) leap into the air from a standing position, in order to demonstrate their strength and agility. Until recent times, in order to earn the right to have a wife, a Maasai moran was required to have killed a lion. Officially this practice has stopped, although there is evidence that it continues in the more remote regions of

Kenya. Also in earlier times a group of young boys were required to build a new village and live in it for a lengthy period (often years) as part of the passage to manhood. This practice is dying out due to lack of land.

Unlike many tribal cultures, Maasai women have a strong voice in their culture. Maasai women are easily identified by their shaved heads, bright clothing and beads, and the removal of one of the bottom teeth. Circumcision is performed on both sexes, with the elder men circumcising the teenage boys, and the elder women circumcising the teenage girls. Attempts by the Kenyan government to stamp out this practice have failed, primarily due to the fact that it is the Maasai women who defend the practice, not the men.

The Maasai share their language, Maa, with the Samburu tribe (indicating a common origin at some stage), but most Maasai also speak Swahili, the lingua franca of East Africa.

Makuxi

The Makuxi are a hunting and farming people living in a hilly region known as the 'Guyana shield', on the border between Brazil and Guyana. The Makuxi believe that they and the neighbouring Ingarikó tribe are descended from the children of the sun, who left for their descendants the gift of fire but also disease and the hardships of nature.

Makuxi land is a spectacularly beautiful region of mountains, tropical forest and savanna, where they raise cattle. During the long dry summer months, they hunt, fish in any rivers that are not dried up, and visit neighbouring villages. This is also when they build and repair their houses, which they make from wood, clay and palm leaves. The winter, from May to September, is a period of very heavy rain, making many of their summer activities impossible. Makuxi communities vary greatly in size, and are based on ties of marriage and family – when Makuxi marry, the couple live in the bride's family's village. Extended families hunt together, but each household grows its own crops for personal use.

The Makuxi have endured vicious violence and the theft of their land since colonisation in the 18th century. Today, they suffer particularly from invading ranchers and gold miners who not only destroy their land, and expose them to disease, but also treat them with extreme brutality – some ranchers, for example, employ hitmen to intimidate and murder the Makuxi. The Brazilian government has so far failed to comply with its own constitution by officially recognising and protecting Makuxi land, and many powerful politicians side with the ranchers and miners. The Indians are now facing a new threat from the Brazilian army, which is seeking to militarise their area, building barracks and moving in troops. This will expose the Makuxi to more disease.

Maori

Te Puni, Maori ChiefMaori is the name of the indigenous people of New Zealand, and their language. It is also the name of the people and language of the Cook Islands, referred to as Cook Islands Maori.

The word maori means "normal" or "ordinary" in the Maori language and is widely applied ("wai maori" is fresh water as distinct from seawater). "Maori" has similarities in some other Polynesian languages such as Hawaiian in which the cognate word maoli means native, indigenous, real or actual. The use of the term Maoris as the plural of Maori is now generally used only outside New Zealand.

Maori are believed to have migrated to New Zealand from eastern Polynesia in the latter part of the 1st millennium AD. Archaeological evidence suggests that there were probably several waves of migration over the period between 800 and 1300. Maori oral history describes their arrival from the mythical Hawaiki by large ocean-going canoes (waka). Migration accounts vary among Maori tribes or iwi, whose members can identify with the different waka in their genealogies or whakapapa.

Despite significant social and economic advances during the 20th century, Maori still suffer significant disadvantage including negatively performing in most health and education statistics, labour participation as well as over-representation in criminal and corrections statistics.

Mapuche

The Mapuche are the pre-Hispanic inhabitants of Central and Southern Chile and Argentina. They are also known by the Spanish name Araucanos. Mapuche means people (che) of the land (mapu). They had an economy based on agriculture; their social organisation consisted of extended families.

Mapuche encompasses different ethnic groups which shared a common social and religious structure with language and economics as a basis. Their influence extended between the river Aconcagua and the Argentinian pampa: the Picunches lived in the central valleys of Chile , the Mapuches inhabited the Valleys between the Itata and Toltén Rivers, the Huilliches, the Lafkenches, and the Pehuenches. Also, the northern Aonikenk ethnic group of the pampa regions made contact with some Mapuche groups, adopting their language and some culture; they are the Tehuelches.

Mapuches successfully resisted attempts by the Inca empire to subjugate them, in spite of lacking a nationwide organization. The Mapuche fought against the Spaniards, and, using the Bio Bio River as a natural frontier, they resisted colonization; this war is known as the War of Arauco, and is immortalized in the epic poem La Araucana. When Chile split from the Spanish crown, some Mapuche chiefs sided with the colonists. After Chile's independence from Spain, Mapuches coexisted and traded with their neighbors .

The Chilean Army put an end to the War of Arauco in the 1860s, and, using a combination of force and diplomacy, Chile's government and some Mapuche leaders signed a treaty to incorporate the Araucanian territories into Chile.

Mapuche descendants now live across southern Chile and Argentina; some maintain their traditions and continue living from agriculture, but a growing majority have migrated to cities in search for better economic opportunities. In recent years, there has been an attempt by the Chilean government to reddress some of the inequities of the past, by, for example, validating the Mapudungun language and culture by including them in the curriculum of elementary schools around Temuco.

Moriori

Moriori are the indigenous people of the Chatham Islands, east of the New Zealand archipelago.

Moriori are a Polynesian people. Although it was once speculated that they settled the Chatham Islands directly from the equatorial Polynesian islands, scholars now agree that they were Maori who migrated from the southern South Island of New Zealand. Evidence supporting this theory is found in the similarity of the Moriori language to the Maori dialect spoken by the Ngai Tahu tribe of the South Island, comparisons of Moriori and Maori genealogies ("whakapapa"), and prevailing wind patterns in the southern Pacific. The Chatham Islands thus became the last corner of the Pacific to be settled during the period of Polynesian discovery and colonization.

The Chatham Islands environment is more cold and harsh than the one the original settlers had left behind, and barely capable of supporting a population. The Chathams being unsuitable for the cultivation of most crops, Moriori adopted a hunter-gatherer lifestyle.Moriori embraced a pacifist culture which rigidly avoided warfare, substituting it with ritual fighting and conciliation.

Native American

Native Americans (also Indians, Aboriginal Peoples, American Indians, First Nations, Alaskan Natives, Amerindians, or

Indigenous Peoples of America) are the indigenous inhabitants of The Americas prior to the European colonization, and their modern descendants. This term comprises a large number of distinct tribes, states, and ethnic groups, many of them still enduring as political communities.

History

Based on anthropological and genetic evidence, scientists generally agree that most Native Americans descend from people who migrated from Siberia across the Bering Strait, at least 12,000 years ago.

European colonization of the Americas: The European colonization of the Americas forever changed the lives and cultures of the Native Americans. In the 15th to 19th centuries, their populations were ravaged, by the privations of displacement, by disease, and in many cases by warfare with European groups and enslavement by them. The first Native American group encountered by Columbus, the 250,000 Arawaks of Haiti, were violently enslaved. Only 500 survived by the year 1550, and the group was extinct before 1650.

In the 15th century Spaniards and other Europeans brought horses to the Americas. Some of these animals escaped and began to breed and increase their numbers in the wild. Ironically, the horse had originally evolved in the Americas, but the last American horses died out at the end of the last ice age. The re-introduction of the horse had a profound impact on Native American culture in the Great Plains of North America. This new mode of travel made it possible for some tribes to greatly expand their territories, exchange goods with neighboring tribes, and more easily capture game.

Native Americans in the United States: From the outset, European colonists had, at best, lived in an uneasy truce with the Native Americans. While the groups sometimes cooperated, the Natives were inexorably displaced from the most favorable land, and frequently resisted this process with violence. Although in recent years it has become popular to assert that Native Americans learned scalping from Europeans, historical evidence suggests that scalping by Native Americans had been practiced long before contact with Europeans.

Indian Wars and forced relocations: In the 19th century, the Westward expansion of the United States incrementally expelled large numbers of Native Americans from vast areas of their territory, either by forcing them into marginal lands farther and farther west, or by outright massacres. Under President Andrew Jackson, Congress passed the Indian Removal Act of 1830, which forced the Five Civilized Tribes from the east onto western reservations, primarily to take their land for settlement. The forced migration was marked by great hardship and many deaths. Its route is known as the Trail of Tears.

Conflicts generally known at the time as "Indian Wars" broke out between U.S. forces and many different tribes. Authorities entered numerous treaties during this period, but later abrogated many for various reasons. Well-known military engagements include the atypical Native American victory at the Battle of Little Bighorn in 1876, and the massacre of Native Americans at Wounded Knee in 1890. On January 31, 1876 the United States government ordered all remaining Native Americans to move into reservations or reserves. This set about the downturn of Prairie Culture that had developed around the use of the horse for hunting, travel and trading.

American policy toward Native Americans has been an evolving process. In the late nineteenth century reformers in efforts to civilize Indians adapted the practice of educating native children in Indian Boarding Schools. These schools, which were primarily run by Christians, proved traumatic to Indian children, who were forbidden to speak their native languages, taught Christianity instead of their native religions and in numerous other ways forced to abandon their Indian identity and adopt European-American culture. There are also many documented cases of sexual, physical and mental abuses occurring at these schools.

Current status: Military defeat, cultural pressure, confinement on reservations, forced cultural assimilation, outlawing of native languages and culture, forced sterilizations, termination policies of the 1950s, and 1960s, and slavery have had deleterious effects on Native Americans' mental and ultimately physical health. Contemporary health problems include poverty, alcoholism, heart disease, diabetes and New World Syndrome.

As recently as the 1960s, Indians were being jailed for teaching their traditional beliefs. As recently as the 1970s, the Bureau of Indian Affairs was still actively pursuing a policy of "assimilation", the goal of which was to eliminate the reservations and steer Indians into mainstream U.S. culture. Even their lands are perhaps no longer safe; as of 2004, there are still claims of theft of Indian land for the coal and uranium it contains.

Culture and arts

Native American music is almost entirely monophonic, but there are notable exceptions. Traditional Native American music often includes drumming but little other instrumentation, although flutes are played by individuals. The tuning of these flutes is not precise and depends on the length of the wood used and the hand span of the intended player, but the finger holes are most often around a whole step apart and, at least in Northern California, a flute was not used if it turned out to have an interval close to a half step.

Performers with Native American parentage have occasionally appeared in American popular music, most notably Shania Twain, Robbie Robertson, Rita Coolidge, Wayne Newton, and Redbone (band). Some, such as John Trudell have used music to comment on life in Native America, and others, such as R. Carlos Nakai integrate traditional sounds with modern sounds in instrumental recordings. A variety of small and meditum-sized recording companies offer an abundance of recent music by Native

American performers young and old, ranging from Pow-wow drum music to hard-driving rock-and-roll.

The most widely practiced public musical form among Native Americans in the United States is that of the pow-wow. At Pow-wows, such as the annual Gathering of Nations in Albuquerque, New Mexico, members of drum groups sit in a circle around a large drum. Drum groups play in unison while they sing in a native language and dancers in colorful regalia dance clockwise around the drum groups in the center. Familiar pow-wow songs include honor songs, intertribal songs, crow-hops, sneak-up songs, grass-dances, two-steps, welcome songs, going-home songs, and war songs. Most indigenous communities in the United States also maintain traditional songs and ceremonies, some of which are shared and practiced exclusively within the community.

Native American art comprises a major category in the world art collection. Native American contributions include pottery, paintings, jewelry, weavings, sculptures, basketry, and carvings.Artists have at times misrepresented themselves as having native parentage, most notably Johnny Cash, who traced his heritage to Scottish ancestors and admitted he fabricated a story that he was one-quarter Cherokee. The integrity of certain Native American artworks is now protected by an act of Congress that prohibits representation of art as Native American when it is not the product of an enrolled Native American artist.

Negrito

The Negritos include the Atis, and at least 5 other tribes of the Philippines, the Semang of the Malay peninsula, and 12 Andamanese tribes of the Andaman Islands. The Malay term for them is orang asli, or original people. They are likely the indigenous people of south-east Asia, including New Guinea. Pygmy-sized, they are numerically and physically among the smallest as well as among the least-known of all living human races.

Semang, Field Museum of Natural History, ChicagoThe word is Spanish for "little Negro" and was given by early explorers who thought that the Negritos were from Africa. Nevertheless it has been used for the past more than 300 years to denote the generally short-statured, peppercorn-haired, dark-skinned people found in small surviving pockets all over tropical Asia and perhaps beyond.

The theory of the connection to Africa collapsed the moment the first unbiased scientific observers met living Andamanese Negritos face to face. Apart from dark skin and curly hair, they have little in common with any African population, including the African pygmies. There are, however, a few fascinating connections to the Khoisan of South Africa. It is therefore quite sure that the Negritos are not African in origin. Clear archaeological evidence found so far of Negrito settlements in the Andamans does not go back more than 2,200 years but absence of evidence is not evidence of absence. Besides, there is now little doubt that the Negrito race represents an ancient, if not the most ancient, component in the prehistoric peopling of Asia by anatomically modern humans. As such they could go back 70,000 years. The Negritos of the Philippines could make fire, whereas the Andamanese could not, as of 1911. The Semang are recorded to have made clothing of pounded tree bark, and to have lived in both caves and leaf-covered shelters. They are distinct from the Formosan-Indo-Malay peoples who arrived in boats or balangay. The current mainstream Filipino at times commemorate the Negrito and the Spanish by dressing up as these peoples, during local celebrations.

For the Negritos themselves the term has no meaning since they know themselves only by their local tribal names and are not (yet) aware that they may belong to a people called "Negrito". The term "Negrito", a term of long historical standing, is regarded by some as a misnomer. "Black Asians" has been proposed but this would include the Negritos along with the Melanesians, Veddoid and some other Asian people, giving undue importance to the minor genetic trait of skin colour and ignoring more profound genetic and other differences between these groups.

Others think that until the Negritos themselves are aware of their situation and in a position to decide the matter for themselves, the term should not be changed. In this view, non-Negritos should not arrogate to themselves the right to rename a people without their knowledge and consent. It is proposed that "Negrito" is a perfectly acceptable term as long as it is used without derogatory intent.

Northern Indigenous Peoples of Russia

The northern indigenous peoples of Russia incude Finno-Ugric, Turkic, Eskimo-Aleut, and other groups. Many of these groups are now extinct or almost so, or assimilated.Many of these peoples live in Siberia, and their names here are transliterations from Cyrillic, rather than self-names.

Nuba

Nuba is a collective term used for the peoples who inhabit the Nuba Mountains, in Kordofan province, Sudan, Africa. Although the term is used to describe them as if they were a single tribe, in fact the Nuba are quite diverse, and are made up of different ethnic and linguistic groups.Estimates of the number of Nuba vary widely; the Sudanese government estimated that they numbered 1.1 million in 1993.

Ogiek

The Ogiek are one of the few remaining hunter-gatherer peoples of East Africa. Their home since time immemorial has been the Mau mountain forest, overlooking Kenya's rift valley.

The Ogiek are hunter-gatherers – some in the deep forest live purely by hunting and gathering, while the majority grow vegetables and keep livestock also. They have traditionally hunted such animals as antelope and wild pigs, which is now generally illegal. They gather not only wild plants, but also honey from beehives which they make from hollow logs and place in the high branches of the forest trees. Trees at different heights on the mountain slopes flower at different seasons, meaning that the Ogiek can collect honey all year round. Its taste varies according to when and where it is gathered. This honey plays a central part in Ogiek society; it is used for food and for brewing beer, and also to trade with neighbouring peoples outside the forest.

Ever since colonial times there have been attempts to evict the Ogiek from their ancestral forest, usually on the pretext that they are degrading it. But when the Ogiek are removed, their forest is not protected but rather exploited by logging and tea plantations – some owned by government officials. In some parts of the Mau forest, groups of Ogiek are now resisting eviction, while in others they face influxes of settlers onto their land. The most serious threat currently facing them all comes from the government's plan to open up around one tenth of Kenya's forests – most of it in the Mau forest – to outsiders. This will open the way for more settlers, loggers and tea plantations.

Penan

The Penan live in Sarawak, the Malaysian part of the island of Borneo, the largest of the Malaysian states. Much of it is covered by dense rainforest and has abundant resources of natural gas and oil. The Penan are just one of the tribal peoples of Sarawak, but they are the only nomadic tribe. Sarawak is dominated by non-tribal Malays.

The Penan are nomadic hunter-gatherers. Although many have now been settled, about 500 Penan lead a completely nomadic life in the forest. Even the settled Penan still rely heavily on the forest. The Penan have a gentle and egalitarian society without any hierarchy. Sharing is taken for granted in Penan society: there is no Penan word for 'thank you', and a hunter must not eat a single bite more than he gives to others, however small his prey. The forest is essential to the Penan, providing them with everything they need to survive. In particular, they rely heavily on sago, which they use for building houses, making baskets and to eat – the Penan love to eat it fried in pig fat and mixed with blood.

Since the 1970s, all the tribal peoples of Sarawak have had their land taken to make way for logging, dam construction and oil palm plantations – driving them into towns where they are reduced to abject poverty. The Penan have been told by the government that they have no rights to land at all until they 'settle down' or start farming. The logging industry has a particularly devastating impact. The Malaysian government claims that Sarawak is being logged sustainably – but in fact its forests are being destroyed at one of the fastest rates in the world. As the forests are logged, the rivers are silted up, pollution is killing the fish and the game is being scared deeper into the few remaining forests. Since 1987, the Penan have been fighting back by blockading the logging roads – and suffering acute food shortages as a result. Many Penan have been arrested for holding these peaceful blockades but finally they are starting to see some results. Some of the companies are now agreeing not to log Penan forest, but the Penan still have to stay constantly vigilant as many companies do not keep their promises.

Pygmy Peoples

There are many different 'Pygmy' peoples – for example, the Bambuti, the Batwa, the Bayaka and the Bagyeli ('Ba -' means 'people') – who live scattered over a huge area in central and western Africa, in the Democratic Republic of Congo (DRC), Congo (Brazzaville), Cameroon, Gabon, Central African Republic, Rwanda, Burundi and Uganda. In many places they are recognised as being the first inhabitants of the region. The different Pygmy groups speak different languages, mostly related to those of neighbouring non-Pygmy peoples. However there are a few words which are shared between even widely separated Pygmy tribes, suggesting they may have shared a language in the past. One of these shared words is the name of the forest spirit, Jengi.

The 'Pygmy' peoples are forest dwellers, and know the forest, its plants and its animals intimately. They live by hunting animals such as antelopes, pigs and monkeys, fishing, and gathering honey, wild yams, berries and other plants. For them, the forest is a kindly personal god, who provides for their needs. All Pygmy groups have close ties to neighbouring farming villagers, and work for them or exchange forest produce for crops and other goods. At its best this is a fair exchange, but it can involve exploitation of the Pygmies, especially where they have lost control of the forest and its resources.

'Pygmy' peoples see their rainforest homes threatened by logging, and are driven out by settlers. In some places they have been evicted and their land has been designated as national parks. They are routinely deprived of their rights by governments, which do not see these forest-dwellers as equal citizens. In Cameroon, the life of the Bagyeli is being disrupted by a World Bank-sponsored oil pipeline which is to be built through their land. The Batwa of eastern DRC, Rwanda, Burundi and Uganda have seen nearly all their forest destroyed, and barely survive as labourers and beggars.

Sami Peoples

The Sami People are an indigenous people of northern Sweden, Norway, Finland and Russia, covering a total area in the Nordic countries corresponding to the size of Sweden. The Sami are one of the largest groups of indigenous peoples in Europe. Their languages are the Sami languages, which are classified as Finno-Ugric. They call their ancestral lands Sapmi. Traditional occupations are hunting, fishing, reindeer herding and farming, but today only a minority of the Sami making a living from these things alone. The population is estimated to about 85,000, although it is difficult to establish exactly how many there are. Roughly half live in Norway, although Sweden also has a significant group. Finland and Russia only have smaller groups located in the far north, including the Russian Kola peninsula. The Sami in Russia were forced by the Soviet authorities into one collective called Lovozero / Lojàvri, in the central part of the Kola peninsula.

Traditionally, the Sami had a variety of livelihoods; fishing on the coast and in the inland, trapping for fur animals, sheep herding etc. The best known livelihood is reindeer herding, but only a small percentage of the Sami have been mainly reindeer herders over the last centuries. Today, many Sami lead modern lives in the cities inside and outside the traditional Sami area, with regular jobs.

History

Up to around 1500 the Sami were mainly fishermen and trappers, usually in a combination, leading a nomadic lifestyle decided by the migrations of the reindeer. Around 1500, due to excessive hunting, again provoked by the fact that the Sami had to pay taxes to Norway, Sweden and Russia, the number of reindeer started to decrease. Most Sami then settles along the fjords, on the coast and along the inland waterways to pursue a combination of cattle raising, trapping and fishing. A small minority of the Sami then started to tame the reindeer, creating the well-known reindeer nomads, that although often portrayed by outsiders as the archetypical Sami lifestyle, only represent around 10% of the Sami people.

The Sami crossed the borders freely until 1826, when the Norwegian/Finnish/Russian border was closed. Sami were still free to cross the border between Sweden and Norway according to inherited rights down to 1940, when the border closed due to Germany's occupation of Norway.

For long periods of time, the Sami lifestyle reigned supreme in the north because of its unique adaptation to the Arctic environment, enabling Sami culture to resist cultural influences from the South. However, in the 19th c. Norwegian authorities put the Sami culture under pressure, in order to make the Norwegian language and culture universal. On the Swedish and Finnish side, conditions were a lot more lax. The strongest pressure took place from around 1900 to 1940, when Norway invested a lot of money and efforts to wipe out Sami culture. After World War II, the pressure was relaxed somehow, and from the 1980's onward, Sami rights are on the agenda.

Religion

The term Sami religion is usually referring to the pre-Christian religion, practiced till about 18th century. Christianity started already in the 11th century but the Lutheran Bible was first translated in much later time. In the 16th century, priests had tried to convert them, sometimes by cruel means such as burning rune drums (and peoples) on the stake, but it was not until the bible was translated that major parts converted.

Sami religion shared many common elements to the Norse mythology and the latter's spiritual parts are often considered to be derived from an aboriginal life style. By mainly a French initiative, from J.P Gaimard, Lars Levi Laestadius started to do research in the Sami mythology. His work resulted in four bands or fragments, since it in his own word only contained only a few percents of what had existed. The fragments were termed Theory of Gods, Theory of Sacrifice, Theory of Prophecy, or short reports about rumorous Sami magic and Sami sagas. Generally, he filtered out the Norse influence and derive common elements between the South, North and Eastern Sami groups. The mythology have also common elements with other Circumpolar religions -- such as those in Siberia and North America.

Semang

The Semang are the Pygmy-sized Negritos of the Malay peninsula. They are probably the indigenous peoples of this area, and have been recorded to have lived here since before the 200s. They are a fairly pure branch of the woolly-haired Negrito race, which includes the natives of the Andaman Islands, the Aetas of the Philippines and the dwarfs of Central Africa.

The men average about 4 ft. 9 or 10 in., while the women are 3.5 in. shorter. Their color is a very dark brown or black. The shape of the head is round, or intermediate between round and long. The forehead is low and rounded, and projects over the root of the nose, which is short, depressed and pyramid-shaped. The eyes are wide open and round, showing no obliquity, the iris being of a very rich, deep brown. Lips vary from moderate to full, the mouth is rather large, the chin feebly developed, and the jaws are often slightly projecting.

The hair is very dark-brown black, never blue-black as among Chinese and Malays. It grows in short, spiral tufts, curling closely all over the head. The arm-stretch is almost always greater than their height. The feet are usually short and splayed, with a remarkable inward curve of the great toe, and are very prehensile.

The Semangs live in caves or leaf-shelters formed between branches. A waistcloth for the men, made of tree bark hammered out with a wooden mallet from the bark of the terap, a species of wild bread-fruit tree, and a short petticoat of the same for the women, is the only dress worn; many go naked. Tattooing, or rather scarring, is practised, by drawing the finely serrated edge of a sugarcane leaf across the skin and rubbing in charcoal powder.They have bamboo musical instruments, a kind of Jews' harp and a nose flute. On festive occasions there is song and dance, both sexes decorating themselves with leaves. The Semangs bury their dead simply, food and drink being placed in the grave.

Taiwanese Aborigine

Taiwanese aborigines or aboriginal peoples are the indigenous peoples of Taiwan. They are a group of Austronesian people, who are descended from the inhabitants of Taiwan who lived on the island before Han immigration in the 1600s. Today, most tribes that the Republic of China (ROC) recognizes are concentrated in the highland mountains of Taiwan and speak a linguistic grouping of archaic Formosan languages, which like the related Malayo-Polynesian languages, belong to the Austronesian language family. The total population of these tribes is around 400,000 as of 2004.

Tsimshian

The Tsimshian, translated as "People Inside the Skeena River," are Native Americans who live around Terrace, Prince Rupert, and Kitimat, on the north coast of British Columbia and the southernmost corner of Alaska on Annette Island. Currently there are about 10,000 Tsimshians, of which about 1,300 live in Alaska.

Canadian Tsimshian live along the Skeena and Nass rivers, as well as the many inlets and islands on the coast. The Tsimshian obtained food through fishing (halibut and salmon) and hunting (seals, sea lions and sea otters).

The Tsimshian speak their own language, referred to by the same name as the tribe itself. There are four main dialects of Tsimshian:

— Northern Tsimshian, spoken along the lower Skeena River and north to Alaska

— Southern Tsimshian, spoken south of the Skeena River

— Gitksan, spoken along the upper Skeena River

— Nisga'a, spoken along the Nass River

The Tlingit claim that their art of weaving Chilkat blankets is derived from Tsimshian sources, although this has not been historically corroborated. The Tlingit also trace a number of other arts to Tsimshian sources. Intermarriage, name exchange, trade, and slaving were very common between the Tlingit, the Tsimshian, and the Haida.

Wends

The Wends are partly a term by some held equivalent to Vandals through a latinized form of Wendland, and partly a German abbreviation (also often used in English) for some Slavic people from north-central Europe. The term has not historically enjoyed consistent usage, but is most employed specifically for one or two Slavic groups and as an over-arching term. The Franks referred to most Slavs living between the Odra and Laba as either Wends or Sorbs, while in Slavic literature these people are called Polabian Slavs.As a result, it is still difficult today to present a coherent picture of the Wends as a people. For the Slavic interpretation, the term Wends was presumably used in the history in the following meanings:

1. In general - a German name for West Slavic people formerly inhabiting teritories of present day Pomerania and Eastern Germany. The term Wends was used in connection to all Slavs inhabiting west of Poland and north of Bohemia - Polabians, Pomeranians and Sorbs.

2. German and English name for Sorbs, a Slavic people who moved into Central Europe during the great migration, most likely in response to pressure by the westward movement of warlike peoples such as the Huns and Avars. Some of their descendants, also called Wends or Lusatian Sorbs, still live in Lusatia today, where the Sorbian language is maintained in schools. Many Wends were driven out of Prussia during the revolutions of 1848. The Prussian government insisted that Wends living in the area give up their language in schools and other public arenas. Moreover, the Wends who wished to continue living in the Empire were compelled to practice Lutheranism. A large part of the Wendish population of Prussia emigrated to countries that welcomed immigrants as a source of cheap labor, including the United States and Australia. In the United States, the majority of Wends landed in Texas, where they became some of the earliest

members of the Missouri Synod of the Lutheran church. A notable settlement of Wends in Texas is the town of Serbin, in Lee County, where a church, St. Paul's Lutheran Church, stands as a typical example of Wendish architecture. In St. Paul's, the pulpit is located in the balcony of the church.

3. German name for Kashubians.
4. Some Finnish historians claim that the words Wends or Vandals used in Scandinavian sources occasianally meant all peoples in Eastern coast of Baltic from Pomerania to Finland, including some Finnic peoples. The existance of these supposed Finnic Wends is far from clear. In 13th century there was indeed a people called Wends or Vends living as far as in Northern Latvia around the city of Wenden and it is not known if they were indeed Slavs as their name suggests. Some researchers think they were related to Finnic speaking Votians.

Yanomami

The Yanomami are an indigenous people of Brazil and Venezuela. They were studied by Napoléon Chagnon, who called them "the Fierce People" in his first edition of The Yanomamo, but later changed his title after spending more time with them and coming to a better understanding of their culture. Chagnon also described, among many other things, their use of a hallucinogen called ebene.

The name generally refers to a people who live in an area that spans parts of the northwest Amazon Rainforest and southern Orinoco, share the culture, and who speak languages from the Yanomami group of languages. Traditionally, a Yanomami village is a relatively temporary wood and thatch house called a shabono. The shabono is circular in shape and surrounds a central open space. Each family has their own area within the shabono. The Yanomami are known as hunters, fishers, and horticulturists, cultivating as their main crops plantains and cassava in "gardens," areas of the forest cleared for cultivation.

As with many other native Americans of tropical South America, the Yanomami traditionally wore essentially no clothing. The sole exception to this was a string-like belt worn by the men, into which the foreskin of the penis would be clamped. As with many other tribes, body hair was considered repugnant and would usually be plucked out.

In the Yanomami language, if a vowel is phonemically nasalized, all vowels after it in the word are also nasalized. So if the ogonek is written under the first vowel, the whole word is nasalized. All the vowels in "Yanomami" are nasal, but it is unclear whether they are phonemically nasal or nasal just because of the nasal consonants. There are many different variations and dialects of the language, such that people from different villages cannot always understand each other. The Yanomami language is believed by linguists to be unrelated to all other South American indigenous languages, and indeed the origins of the language are unknown.

There is tremendous debate among anthropologists over why the Yanomamo are so fierce, and over whether the Yanomamo are indeed so fierce at all. Indeed, the word 'fierce' comes from a possibly inaccurate translation of a Yanomami word 'waiteri', the meaning of which can connote a multiplicity of things such as strength or generousness. Chagnon later changed the title of his ethnography to omit "the fierce people" after coming to the conclusion that this was an inaccurate and unfair label. Gold was recently found in Yanomami territory and the inevitable influx of miners that arrived soon after have brought with them disease, alcoholism, and violence. Yanomami culture is in a real threat of disappearing from Earth entirely unless more measures are taken to protect it.

Yora

The Yora are one of the isolated tribes living in the Amazonian rainforest in south-east Peru, close to the border with Brazil.

Their land is in a remote part of the rainforest which is the source of several tributaries of the Amazon river. The Yora are one of several tribal groups which speak related languages.

The Yora and other tribes in their area first fled into the headwaters where they now live around 100 years ago. Their retreat into the deep forest was an attempt to escape massacres, slavery and disease as companies moved in to exploit the Amazon's rubber trees during the so-called 'rubber boom'. The Yora today live in voluntary isolation, largely uncontacted by outsiders. They are nomadic, living in small family groups which move around frequently. During the dry season families tend to live by the rivers, as fishing is relatively easy and turtle eggs can be collected from the sandy beaches. In the wet season they retreat further into the forest to hunt and collect fruits, berries and nuts.

The Yora's refuge was invaded in the 1980s by Shell, who were looking for oil. The oil exploration paths subsequently acted as an easy entrance for colonists, who brought with them colds, flu and other diseases which the isolated Indians had never encountered. In the ensuing epidemic, between 50 and 100 Yora died in the forest. In 1996, the oil company Mobil also explored in this region, but international protests eventually led the company to pull out, and the government to declare much of the area an Indian reserve. However, a crucial area was left out of the reserve, and now logging companies are operating nearby, and vigorously lobbying the government to allow them to log inside it. If the loggers go in, many of the isolated Indians will flee from the noise and destruction, some will no doubt be frightened into responding to intruders with violent confrontations – and many will die as diseases spread into the area.

Wichi

The Wichi have lived for millennia on their land in northern Argentina, in what are now the provinces of Salta, Formosa and Chaco in a larger region known as the Chaco. Along with other Indian tribes, they live between the Bermejo and Pilcomayo rivers near the border between Argentina, Paraguay and Bolivia.

The Wichi traditionally supported themselves by hunting, fishing, and growing food in small gardens. Their land was once fertile grassland and forest which supported them and provided them with all their needs. But the introduction of cattle onto their land has turned it into a dry sandy desert, leaving them vulnerable to periods of real hunger and starvation, and much more dependent on occasional employment by outsiders for their survival.

The Wichi's land has steadily been invaded over the last 100 years. Since then, loggers have felled their forest, and settlers have introduced cattle. These cattle not only turn the land already stolen from the Wichi into desert, but also break into the tiny plots of land which the Wichi have managed to hold on to, destroying their crops. The Wichi have been left almost landless and without their livelihood. The local Salta authorities have, since 1966, repeatedly promised to recognise Indian territory in their province – but have failed to fulfil one single promise. On the contrary, they have worked with the landowners to continue to deny the Wichi their land, handing it to settlers, and authorising its deforestation. The local government wants to build a trunk road connecting the bridge into Paraguay to the state highway system, opening up the area to further commercialisation.

2

Economic Exclusion and Discrimination

Although indigenous peoples will usually constitute a numerical minority and be a non-dominant group, indigenous peoples' cultures and lifestyles often make them distinct from other minority groups; consequently, they may or may not choose to identify also as minorities in the national context. Indigenous peoples' claims to ancestral land rights and other natural resource rights, to manage economic and social affairs using traditional customs, law and practice, and their historical continuity with the land inhabited by their communities, generally distinguishes indigenous peoples from other minority groups.

Indigenous peoples have also had some success in asserting their right to self-determination as peoples, resulting in, for example, recognition of certain forms of autonomy and communal land ownership. The issues surrounding discrimination against indigenous peoples in terms of their exclusion from social and economic institutions are similar to those related to minority groups.

Is the economic exclusion of minority groups and indigenous peoples a result of discrimination? The answer is almost certainly yes, in that discrimination can at least be regarded as a factor in economic exclusion. Exclusion may well arise as a result of implicit or explicit discrimination against minority groups and/or indigenous peoples, for example through excluding minorities from citizenship through ethnically biased qualifying criteria; not establishing or adequately implementing and monitoring anti-discrimination legislation and measures; under-funding public services in regions inhabited primarily by minorities or indigenous peoples; or the use of a majority official language in legal, economic, social or political transactions, without provision for minority language access.

But causality may be difficult to establish, especially because of the difficulty in proving intent to discriminate. Moreover, the diversity of experiences and social, cultural, economic and political characteristics of minority groups across the world means that a multitude of factors may be influencing their exclusion. However, given the strength of evidence from some countries, we can infer a link to discrimination by showing that exclusion and poverty are greater among minority groups and indigenous peoples. Furthermore, the fact that inequalities between majorities and minorities persist or become worse over time is indicative of a failure, first, to recognize the problem and, second, to take action to reduce inequality and exclusion. Both may be seen as discriminatory.

Ideally, in order to make a case that minority groups and/or indigenous peoples are excluded or poorer than other groups, qualitative and quantitative indicators for the minority group and/or indigenous people need to be compared with those for the remaining or total population. A number of problems immediately arise. First, data is not available systematically for every minority group or indigenous people, or even a large proportion of them. Household surveys that are truly nationally representative and reasonably recent do not exist for all countries. Even the dollar-poverty figures used in measuring progress towards the Millennium Development Goals do not cover the entire population.

Approximately 88 per cent of the developing world's population is covered by the household surveys used to construct the dollar-poverty estimates, a figure that rises to 97. 9 per cent in South Asia as a whole and falls to as low as 52. 5 per cent for the Middle East and North Africa. If the population not covered by the surveys is similar to that which is, then there is no problem. But this is not generally the case. Remote rural areas are often not covered by surveys, but this is often where minority groups and especially indigenous peoples are to be found.

The accuracy or representativeness of data for certain groups (e.g. minorities) is questionable if these groups are less likely to respond to questions, either because of poor communication or misunderstanding, or because of apprehension and mistrust. Second, where data is collected on minority groups and/or indigenous peoples, it is collected only for those groups that are recognized by the survey planners (usually the national statistics institute) as being minority groups or indigenous peoples, and often using clusterings of race, ethnicity, language, etc. that preclude meaningful analysis. So, for example, the Brazilian surveys ask respondents their 'colour', with the choice of categories being branco (white), preto (black), amarelo (yellow), pardo (mixed or mulatto) and indigena (indigenous). This classification has led some to argue that the Brazilian population is statistically 'whitened'.

For example, research has shown that, when faced with the above classification, a large proportion of respondents declare themselves to be 'white'. When the same respondents were asked to classify their own colour, far fewer said 'white' but many more said moreno, which 'can be used to describe very dark black people or very light mestizos'.

Minorities and indigenous peoples are sometimes grouped into a small number of categories that do not allow indicators to be produced on specific ethnic groups. For example, in Vietnam, the population is made up of predominantly (around 85 per cent) Kinh (ethnic-Vietnamese), with around 10 per cent being from one of Vietnam's 54 ethnic groups and around 2 per cent ethnic Chinese. But the household survey data used to estimate poverty and living standards groups the 54 ethnic minorities into just eight categories. Although small sub-sample sizes would make sophisticated analysis unreliable, the classification does not even allow simple descriptive statistics to be estimated.

Hence not only do officially collected statistics use terms that distort the demographic profile of the population, they also make it much more difficult to understand the complexity and diversity of the experience of exclusion, poverty and inequality within and between minority groups. This makes a strong case for ensuring the participation of representatives of different ethnic, religious or linguistic groups in preparing and delivering census surveys.

One way to overcome the lack of detail on specific groups is to adopt a case study approach, and there are many that provide rich data about specific minority groups or indigenous peoples. The drawback with these is that they often lack comparability with data for the whole population, in terms of the coverage of issues and topics and, crucially - given the vulnerability of poor people to economic, seasonal and climatic shocks - the timing of the studies.

Properly planned, studies that combine qualitative and quantitative approaches provide a rich resource. Third, an important limitation is that data does not always capture the diversity of experience among minority groups and indigenous peoples. One important source of diversity of experience is gender. Evidence from several countries illustrates intersecting discrimination on the basis of gender and membership of a minority group faced by minority women, which often renders them among the most marginalized of all groups. Too often, however, data is analysed by ethnicity or gender, which does not allow for deeper analysis of ethnicity and gender differences.

Finding systematic empirical evidence on poverty and social exclusion among minority groups is therefore difficult, and hampers attempts to establish causality. Current data is inadequate so far as minority groups and indigenous peoples are concerned. This is in itself a form of exclusion, denying minority groups and indigenous peoples information about themselves and their position relative to that of others. Lack of data may result from lack of integration of discrimination issues in development policy. For example, the 'nonracialism' belief in Brazil that refused to acknowledge the existence of distinct races and racial discrimination was reflected in the removal of questions relating to race and colour from the 1970 Census and the failure of the national household surveys to collect data on race until the late 1980s, almost a hundred years after slavery was officially abolished.

While governments may have legitimate concerns about collecting disaggregated data through censuses, these concerns can be overcome if the participation of minority groups in the drafting of census questionnaires and data collection is ensured. A good standard on this point was set by the World Conference Against Racism (WCAR) Programme of Action in Article 92, where states are urged to collect, analyse and disseminate disaggregated data on discrimination, and to do so with the participation and consent of the targets of discrimination. Once discrimination issues are fully undertaken in development research, data will start being collected.

Experiences of Social and Economic Exclusion

The concept of economic exclusion can be understood best within the overall framework of social exclusion. The concept of social exclusion has captured the phenomenon of certain individuals and/or groups being excluded from participation in social relations, an important dimension of poverty and deprivation. The idea originated from the debate on social policy changes in European countries, particularly employment and social security policies, during the 1970s. The concept was further re-endorsed by the Stockholm European Council in March 2001, which declared the fight against social exclusion to be of utmost importance for the European Union (EU).

The term 'social exclusion' is usually applied to encompass both economic and political exclusion, so for example many studies will define the socially excluded to include those who may be economically excluded (for example unemployed, with little or no access to assets such as land, housing and credit) and/or politically excluded (for example, not able to participate in local, regional or national political processes).

One problem with the concept of social exclusion is that it is broad and, according to some, lacks theoretical underpinnings. Indeed, Sen writes of the explosion in the use of the term 'socially excluded' to cover almost every type of deprivation imaginable, and argues that it would be better employed as a relational concept, linked to capability failure. He writes that social exclusion includes exclusion from:

> '... a livelihood; secure, permanent employment; earnings; property, credit, or land; housing; minimum or prevailing consumption levels; education, skills and cultural capital; the welfare state; citizenship and legal equality; democratic participation; public goods; the nation or the dominant race; family and sociability; humanity, respect, fulfilment and understanding'.

Using this plethora of exclusions it is hard to imagine anyone ever being included. Certainly such a large proportion of the population in most countries would be defined as socially excluded using these criteria that the concept would be rendered meaningless. Social exclusion can only be a meaningful concept if it used to describe and understand the underlying processes that result in a particular 'negative' outcome. One of the most common ways that researchers analyse the economic dimensions of exclusion is by examining unemployment. If unemployment arises from practices in the labour market that tend to work against certain groups of people, then the language of social exclusion becomes useful. But Sen argues that 'in general the causes of unemployment need not be seen to be resulting ... from any exclusionary process'. These points are valid and, as in the analysis of poverty, drive researchers and policy makers to seek to understand the causes of social exclusion in terms of relational failure.

Recently, Atkinson and colleagues have developed a set of indicators of social exclusion. Atkinson et al. argue that social exclusion (which they use to encompass social, economic and political exclusion) occurs along several dimensions and is associated with five main areas of human lives: material deprivation, lack of education, lack of a productive role, poor health and poor housing. A recent OECD study that looks at social exclusion along four similar dimensions: self-sufficiency (proxied by indicators such as employment and unemployment); equity (proxied by indicators such as poverty and income inequality): health (proxied by indicators such as life expectancy and morbidity); and social cohesion (proxied by indicators that measure its absence such as industrial unrest, criminality, drug usage, suicides and number of people in prison).

The exact choice of indicator may vary from region to region, or between developed and developing countries. These dimensions of exclusion are naturally related as, for instance, material deprivation can be seen simultaneously as a cause and a consequence of lack of education whereas lack of education, in turn, may inhibit the access of individuals to adequate employment and thus lead to lack of an economically productive role in society.

Material deprivation and unemployment can also be seen as both causes and consequences of poor health and lack of access to suitable housing. Similarly, Sen has argued that poor health and/or disability are fundamental reasons why, in some circumstances, households will not be able to transform entitlements into actual welfare gains.

The indicators of social exclusion developed by Atkinson et al. and by the OECD were constructed in order to analyse the extent of social exclusion in European countries. Although the dimensions of social exclusion and the objectives of policies that address social exclusion and discrimination may differ between developed and developing countries (given, for instance, the higher rates of poverty observed in developing countries), the analytical framework proposed by these studies is useful for the analysis of social exclusion in developing countries since it highlights important issues associated with social exclusion that will be shared by both sets of countries.

Therefore, the notion of social exclusion is being quickly adopted by the literature on the analysis of poverty and inequality and has been applied to developing countries in recent studies. The concept and indicators of social exclusion may be a useful way of addressing particular situations of social exclusion among minority groups and indigenous peoples and therefore useful in understanding the nature and/or extent of discrimination against such groups. Atkinson et al. and the OECD study recommend that the indicators of social exclusion should be disaggregated where possible by region, gender and household type, but no mention is made specifically of minority groups defined along religious, ethnic, linguistic or cultural lines.

However, both studies recommend that the indicators be country-specific in order to reflect the specific dimensions of exclusion within each society. It is therefore the responsibility of each individual country to incorporate concerns with minority groups and indigenous peoples in their own indicators of social exclusion, especially when discrimination against, and exclusion of minority groups is a feature of economic, social and political relations in that country.

Providing statistics on exclusion, broken down by ethnicity and gender for example, can highlight important differences and relative deprivation, and contribute to a better understanding of the extent and nature of the exclusionary process. However, countries where exclusion of minorities and indigenous peoples arises out of discrimination are unlikely to give priority to such activities precisely because the concerns of these groups are not heard.

Economic exclusion of minority groups and indigenous peoples is a phenomenon that occurs both in developed and developing countries. Data limitations affect the breadth of statistical evidence that can be presented here. The data available is derived from very diverse regions, where minority and indigenous status and relations may differ widely. Nevertheless, the evidence available does give some indication of common experiences across regions, and from this we can draw some general conclusions on the link between discrimination and economic exclusion.

Poverty

Approximately a fifth of the world's population is defined as being extremely poor. Although minority groups may not necessarily constitute the largest identifiable group among the poor, the incidence of poverty is often high for minority groups and indigenous peoples, and a range of other development indicators are often worse for those groups. Empirical evidence from numerous countries shows that minorities are more likely to be income-poor, and experience lower levels of educational attainment and formal job skills, poorer health and limited access to mechanisms of power. Table 1 summarizes some of the evidence on the extent of poverty among minority groups and indigenous peoples from a number of countries. Minority groups and indigenous peoples are both more likely to be poor than the rest of the population and they have much higher poverty rates than the rest of the population.

Table 1. Poverty among minority groups and indigenous peoples (selected countries)

Country (year)	GNP per capita ($US 1999)	% population below poverty line[a]	% of minorities and indigenous peoples in total population	% of minorities and indigenous peoples below poverty line
Vietnam (97/8)	370	37	Ethnic minorities:[b] 14	67
India (93/4)	450	38	Scheduled castes: 17	50
			Scheduled tribes: 8[c]	50
Peru (97)	2390	43	Indigenous: 24[d]	65
Brazil (95)	4420	38	Black: 6	54
			Mixed: 40	53
			Indigenous: <0.1%	67
South Africa (93)	8318	25		Black: 32
				Coloured: 8
				White: 0
Bulgaria (95)	4914	15	Roma	85

Sources: for GNP *per capita* see World Bank, *World Development Report, 2000–2001*
Notes: (a) poverty lines vary across countries and are not comparable; (b) excludes the Kinh majority and the Chinese majority; (c) data refers to the 1991 census; d indigenous peoples in Peru are defined as individuals living in households where the head reports her/his first language to be one of the indigenous languages.

These typical facts remain true for countries spanning the whole 'development spectrum', from very low-income developing countries, through middle income countries like Brazil, to rich countries such as the United States of America (USA).

Although the available data is limited, a survey of evidence from various regions is indicative of a global problem of poverty for minorities and indigenous peoples. Among developed countries, the USA is probably the country with the richest source of data on inequalities, exclusion and discrimination, as well as persistent and large socio-economic gaps between ethnic minorities and indigenous peoples on the one hand and the majority ethnic group on the other.

If the USA were to be divided into two countries on the basis of ethnicity, the one with a solely white population would be in first place in the Human Development Index ranking, whereas the one with a solely black population would be number 31. Furthermore, black children are much more likely to grow up in poverty than white children. Similarly, households in Great Britain where the head of the household is from an ethnic minority group are more likely to appear in the bottom 20 per cent of the income distribution than those from non-minority groups.

In Slovakia, where they form 5-10 per cent of the population, the Roma are frequently discriminated against in a variety of economic, social and political arenas. They suffer from much higher levels of poverty and unemployment, and have very limited access to social services. In Bulgaria approximately 7 per cent of the population are Roma but as many as 85 per cent of Roma are poor, compared to a national poverty rate of 15 per cent. In Serbia and Montenegro, poverty among the Roma is around 65 per cent, almost three times the national figure. The UN Development Programme (UNDP) recently published a regional human development report on the Roma, which revealed that across the region of five Central and Eastern European countries (Bulgaria, Czech Republic,

Hungary, Romania and Slovakia) Roma experience similarly high levels of poverty.

In Latin America, ethnicity - usually defined as having a first language other than Spanish (or Portuguese in Brazil) - has received special attention from development agencies, particularly the World Bank and the Inter-American Development Bank, and good data is available for a number of countries. Ethnicity is an important correlate of poverty, especially in rural areas.

Indigenous peoples and Afro-descendants are often the poorest of the poor in many Latin American countries. Indigenous peoples in the Amazon, Central America and the Andes, and the Indians of the chaco in Argentina and Paraguay are particularly poor, as identified by a number of poverty assessments. In Guatemala, 45 per cent of the poor belong to indigenous households (defined as where the first language of the head of household is not Spanish), and 93 per cent of indigenous people are below the nationally defined poverty line.

In Bolivia, 88 per cent of rural indigenous households are poor. In Mexico, indigenous peoples account for only around 15 per cent of the total population, but approximately 30 per cent of the poor population, and 80 per cent of indigenous peoples are poor. In Peru, the indigenous peoples of the Amazon have the highest levels of poverty in the country: 59. 48 per cent of the indigenous forest peoples are poor and 41 per cent live in absolute poverty.

Statistics on Afrodescendants are much more difficult to identify, since many countries in the region do not disaggregate census information according to ethnic group. Seventy-six per cent of Afro- Colombians live in extreme poverty, and poverty is higher in regions where there are large proportions of indigenous peoples. Africa has some of the highest poverty levels in the developing world but an extreme lack of data on inequalities between ethnic and other minority groups.

Given the emphasis in the economics literature on the relationship between ethnic tensions and economic growth, and the spate of recent ethnic conflicts, this is extremely surprising and represents a real gap in development knowledge. The chief exception is South Africa, due to the legacy of apartheid that explicitly made reference to differences between white people and other groups and, in a perverse way, facilitated the collection of disaggregated data and indicators. According to the 1993 Human Development Report, in South Africa, the richest 5 per cent of the population (mostly white) owns 88 per cent of all private property, half of the population (mostly black) lives below the poverty line and one-third of the black population over 15 years old (about 3 million people) is illiterate.

In the year that saw elections bring an end to years of apartheid, poverty rates among the black population far outweighed those of any other group: 32 per cent of black individuals were below the poverty line, compared to 8 per cent among the coloured population and none among the white population, and black household incomes per capita were only one-sixth of those of white households.

Evidence from other African countries is patchy but suggestive: the bottom 20 per cent of the Kenyan population encompasses socially excluded ethnic groups and other lower social classes. In Namibia, the San indigenous communities have the lowest income and record a Human Development Index rate that is nearly twice as low as the rate recorded for the next highest group. In Asia and the Pacific poverty is also associated with ethnic minorities and indigenous peoples. In China, approximately 8 per cent of the population are from ethnic minorities but make up approximately 40 per cent of the poor.

Minority groups in China generally live in areas with poor soil (even for subsistence crops), which has made them particularly vulnerable to recent trade shocks. In India, scheduled castes and tribes are much more likely to be poor, with much worse social indicators. Jayaraj and Subramanian find in their study on caste and class discrimination that scheduled castes and scheduled tribes have average consumption levels only around 15 per cent higher than the subsistence poverty line, compared with that of the rest of the population, which is 51 per cent higher than the poverty line. Ethnic minorities in Vietnam tend to have the highest levels of poverty in relation to the Vietnamese (Kinh) majority. In 1997-8, while 37. 4 per cent of the whole Vietnam population was below the poverty line, 67 per cent of all ethnic minority households were poor.

Ethnic minority households also had the highest probabilities of remaining poor and of falling into poverty, and the lowest probabilities of escaping poverty between 1992/3 and 1997/8. The evidence above suggests that poverty is indeed higher among minority groups and indigenous peoples. Most of the evidence presented here is based on a poverty line and monetary indicators of poverty.

However, poverty is a multi-dimensional concept that should encompass not only income shortages but also access to entitlements and political participation. A review of many participatory poverty assessments concluded that poor people report their condition largely in terms of material deprivation, for example, low incomes, lack of or unstable employment, shortage of food, inadequate housing, combined with inadequate access to health services and clean water.

But they also give weight to non-material social and psychological factors such as insecurity, social and political conflict, lack of autonomy and exclusion from decision-making institutions. This non-material elements may in fact be of utmost importance when discussing poverty among minority groups and indigenous peoples, for whom issues of participation, autonomy, identity and dignity may be as or more relevant than achieving a certain level of consumption, expenditure or income. Hence, standard methods of measuring poverty that focus on the monetary approach may overlook other dimensions of poverty. This may lead poverty levels to be measured wrongly, that is, under- or overestimated. Exactly whether in any particular country poverty among minorities and indigenous peoples is under- or overestimated will depend on where these groups live, on their livelihoods and on the nature and extent of discrimination against them.

Income poverty on its own is not sufficient evidence of discrimination and social exclusion on other fronts. This is important to consider if we want to understand the extent and nature of marginalization of minority groups and indigenous people. Examining other. non-monetary indicators of poverty, suggests that minority groups and indigenous peoples remain among the poorest.

Education

Low educational attainments are an important aspect of social exclusion and a significant contributing factor to economic exclusion. Globally, minorities and indigenous peoples struggle to achieve equal levels of education with majority groups. In the USA, only around 53 per cent of Hispanics and 74 per cent of black people completed four or more years of high school, compared to 82 per cent of white people, and gaps are larger for college education.

In Mexico, 63 per cent of the indigenous population is illiterate compared to 42 per cent of the non-indigenous population. In Colombia, the primary school enrolment rate for indigenous children is just 11. 3 per cent and 44 per cent of adults in the indigenous population are illiterate. Van de Walle and Gunewardena have looked at the situation of ethnic minority groups in Vietnam in detail and found that education attainments are lower on average for minorities than for the majority.

Minority women sometimes fare even worse, because of the intersecting of gender and minority status: in Romania, there is evidence for this, where 19 per cent of Roma men are illiterate but 35 per cent of Roma women are illiterate. In India only 19 per cent of rural women from scheduled castes in 1991 were literate, compared with 46 per cent of scheduled caste men and 64 per cent of the country as a whole. These low educational attainments may be due to several factors.

The remote location of many minority and indigenous groups may mean that access to school facilities or teachers for their regions may be very limited. In Kenya, where minority groups are often regionally concentrated, large disparities exist in access to schools and in attainment between regions, with the North Eastern Province having much lower access to schools than other regions.

In Peru, the national average illiteracy rate is 13 per cent, but among the indigenous population it reaches 33 per cent, and in the case of indigenous women it is 44 per cent. Literacy, as well as school attendance and attainment rates, are much lower than national averages in regions where indigenous peoples are concentrated.

The limited educational resources available to remote minority or indigenous communities may or may not be due to direct discrimination by government authorities in delivering services, but the evidence suggests that more effort is needed to promote education within regions where minorities and indigenous peoples are concentrated. Where evidence of discrimination is stronger is in the curriculum and delivery of teaching to minorities and indigenous peoples.

Textbooks commonly omit any reference to minority or indigenous histories and cultures, or may even denigrate the value of these cultures and their communities. Parents also are sometimes dissatisfied with school curricula that do not attempt to educate their children in line with their own community values and livelihoods.

The impact of access to first-language education affects many minority or indigenous groups and states commonly fail to make access to first-language education available at least at the primary school level to facilitate an easy transition to schooling for children from these groups. Students may also experience discrimination from students or teachers. All of these factors combine to lessen the chances of minority or indigenous children of reaching higher education.

The fact that minority or indigenous children are already more likely to come from poor households further impedes their access to higher education. In Brazil, for example, Afro-descendants have just two-thirds the level of education of the white population and a quarter of them have no schooling at all, compared to around a sixth of the white population. The system of education is so skewed in favour of the better off that only those able to afford private tuition at school can hope to gain access to the publicly funded universities.

Health and health care Exclusion of minority groups and indigenous peoples often begins at birth as shown by indicators of children's health. Infant mortality rates (IMR) for white people in the USA are much lower and have fallen proportionately more than for black people and other ethnic groups: the US Bureau of the Census estimates that the white IMR almost halved from 10. 9 to 6. 6 per 1, 000 live births between 1980 and 1994, while the black IMR fell by a third from 22. 2 to 15. 8 per 1, 000 live births.

The infant mortality rate in Canada for indigenous children is twice as high as for the population as a whole. In Peru, 27 per cent of all children under age five suffer chronic malnutrition. In the Amazon region of Peru, however, this figure reaches 70 per cent, and in places such as Atalaya with an Ashaninka population, 91 per cent. Health deprivation can be seen in other statistics for adults. Life expectancy in the USA among black males is estimated to be ten years less than that for white males, and the gap appears to be widening. Life expectancy for Inuit males in Canada is 58 years compared to 75 years for all Canadian males. In South Africa, black people have a life expectancy nine years below that of the white population, and infant mortality rates three to five times higher than that of the white population, depending on the survey to which one refers. In Asia, similar health disparities exist.

In Nepal, although segregation on the basis of caste has been made illegal, low-caste people are still marginalized. For instance, 'untouchables' in Nepal have a life expectancy of 46 years, 15 years less than for Brahmins. These inequalities in life expectancy for minority and indigenous groups could be attributed to several factors. In South Africa, for example, diseases, like HIV/AIDS and TB, are much more prevalent among the black population, reflecting in part poorer housing conditions, nutrition and education. In Vietnam, Van de Walle and Gunewardena find that ethnic minorities are more likely to live in communes with no clinic or other health services.

The discrimination factor can contribute directly to inadequate access to health care for minorities, for example because health clinics in their regions are not funded by the government on an equal basis with other regions; or because their ancestral community land rights have been violated forcing their displacement to poorer living conditions. There may also be indirect factors related to other aspects of exclusion, such as poverty, which impact on the ability of minorities to have adequate nutrition or to pay for medical services.

Employment

Minorities and indigenous peoples are often found working in low-wage employment, or without employment; this is perhaps the most prevalent characteristic of their economic exclusion across regions. In Bulgaria unemployment rates among the Roma are as much as 90 per cent; in the Czech Republic, Roma unemployment is 70-80 per cent while unemployment among the whole population is around 3 per cent. In South Africa, white people and Indians are much more likely to hold senior management or professional jobs. Forty per cent of black people and 'coloureds' in 1995 were employed in 'elementary occupations' compared to just 1. 6

per cent of white people, and unemployment rates among black people were almost 40 per cent, compared to just over 5 per cent for white people.

The impact of discrimination on this aspect of economic exclusion is perhaps more easily confirmed through employment statistics and qualitative evidence than it is in other aspects of economic exclusion, such as health and education above. Nascimien to and Nascimiento on Brazil show that earnings of white men are almost two-and-a half times higher than those of black men and four times higher than those of black women, illustrating the extent of discrimination in education and employment along both race and gender divisions. Job and pay discrimination is common. For example, there is evidence that job vacancies in Brazil are advertised expressing the colour preference of the employer in the belief that different racial groups embody different work ethics and attributes. In a detailed study of the town of Arni in northern Tamil Nadu, Basile and Harriss-White found that scheduled castes and scheduled tribes constitute around 80 per cent of the causal labour force and take on the poorly paid jobs.

Furthermore, 10-15 per cent of all firms in Arni only employ labour of their own caste, and some employers refuse to hire scheduled caste and scheduled tribe workers. These findings are illustrative of a situation still present in most Indian states. This is not to conclude that all employment or underemployment of minorities and indigenous peoples is due to discrimination. For example, in Canada, where 35 per cent of Inuit men are unemployed, compared with 10 per cent of other Canadian men, the inequalities may be attributed largely to the absence of job opportunities in the remote region in which the Inuit live, where there are few industries.

In addition, the informal work of Inuit men and women, linked to their traditional livelihoods of hunting and fishing, may not be accurately recorded or understood in official employment statistics. This same experience may be applied to other minorities and indigenous communities living in remote areas and/or relying on traditional livelihoods for their existence.

Housing, Infrastructure and Other Assets

Minority groups are more likely to be excluded from holding assets such as housing. In the USA, housing conditions are generally poorer among the black and Hispanic population: they are less likely to own their own properties and more likely to rent compared to the white population; they have higher reported incidences of poor conditions such as rats, holes, cracks, exposed wiring, and they have smaller and fewer rooms than white-owned and white-rented properties. The basic infrastructure to service housing for minorities and indigenous peoples is also often lacking. In Mexico, housing quality and access to services such as piped water, electricity and communications are much worse for indigenous peoples.

In Ecuador, a key group vulnerable to poverty is indigenous peoples, who have higher rates of illiteracy, child malnutrition and infant mortality, and tend to be located in areas with lower service provision. In Brazil, black people have less access to treated (safe) drinking water, sewage disposal, garbage collection, fridges, televisions and are more likely to live in rural accommodation.

While all the white urban population in South Africa, and most of the white rural population, can expect to have indoor water, only around half of the black urban population, and a mere 10 per cent of the black rural population, have indoor water. Only 31 per cent of Dalit (formerly 'untouchable') households are equipped with electricity, compared to 61 per cent of non-Dalit households.

Only 10 per cent of Dalit households have access to sanitation. Furthermore, the state deliberately excludes Dalits from basic amenities. In many villages, it installs electricity, sanitation and safe drinking water in the upper-caste section, neglecting to do the same in the areas inhabited by the Dalits.

Although it is difficult to prove intent, the lack of services to minority and indigenous communities in other countries may stem from similarly discriminatory policies by local or national governments. The economic exclusion of minorities and indigenous peoples is also often related to their rights to traditional lands and territories, the resources of those lands and the traditional livelihoods that they furnish.

Indigenous peoples in particular have struggled to secure recognition of their land rights, through titling, in order to prevent involuntary displacement or resettlement. In Malaysia, only two of the indigenous Orang Asli out of 10, 000 have legally recognizable titles to their land. In Namibia, only around one-fifth of the San have de jure rights to land. Other minority groups have similar problems in challenging government plans to resettle them, usually in the name of large-scale development projects. Minorities and indigenous peoples often find their communities further impoverished as a consequence of displacement, having lost not only their housing but often also their means of livelihood connected with their habitat.

In Sri Lanka, indigenous groups are disappearing due to government resettlement programmes that have disturbed traditional livelihoods. Even the quality of land that minorities and indigenous peoples have been displaced to may be of lesser quality, thus inhibiting their potential to use it for their livelihoods. In Vietnam, minority households have poorer access to irrigated and good quality land. The minority groups are concentrated in upland and mountainous areas, where access to public services is difficult and adequate basic infrastructures are not in place. So while governments may claim to be displacing minorities in the name of wider economic development, the neglect of proper resettlement strategies and compensation leaves these groups in a much worse economic position than before.

Moreover, the denial of land rights to these groups makes access to credit for small and medium enterprises much more difficult. Poor access to credit is also common in developed countries. In the USA, for example, black people and Hispanics are rejected for home loans 60 per cent more often than equally qualified white people, and pay higher mortgage interest rates; and house prices in predominantly black residential areas rise much slower than in predominantly white areas. Social cohesion While the concept of social cohesion may make most sense in relation to the framework of social exclusion, it also has important implications for combating economic exclusion of minority and indigenous groups.

Social cohesion, proxied as it is by indicators such as industrial unrest, criminality, drug usage, suicides, number of people in prison, and political participation, has a significant impact on minorities and indigenous peoples who are more likely to find their communities on the periphery of society. The cause(s) of this marginalization will vary according to the group, but would often include discrimination as a factor. Regardless, the outcome for minorities and indigenous peoples is that they are more likely to experience weaker political participation in all countries. In developed countries, some minority or indigenous groups will have higher rates of suicide, imprisonment and involvement in crime.

In the USA, for example, despite efforts to close gaps between black and white people on education, health and employment, crime statistics suggest that black people are still more likely to be arrested, more likely to be convicted, and then more likely to be imprisoned than white people. In states where the death penalty is still used, black people 'have been disproportionately subject to death by state execution because of a racist law enforcement system'. Social cohesion in relation to minorities and indigenous peoples may be undermined by endemic discrimination and social structures that exclude them, such as those found in India and other countries with so-called 'untouchable' classes. In India, scheduled castes and tribes are much more likely to be poor, with much worse social indicators.

Poverty and socio-economic inequalities in India are largely explained by the caste system, which although legally abolished still defines 'the structural basis of Indian civil society'. Despite the process of industrialization and modernization of the Indian economy, and changes in the attitude of government and society towards the integration of the lower castes in the structures of employment and organization of the civil society, 'caste still persists as a fundamental principle of social organization even if under different guises'. Although the apartheid system in South Africa has been dismantled, the legacy of years of discrimination persists in unequal living standards and opportunities.

Although much is changing in South Africa, the gaps between white and black people in particular persist, and some of the current debate is about seeking to balance redressing of past inequalities and issues of merit. In other developed countries, evidence of discrimination and exclusion can be found. According to the 2000 UNDP Human Development Report, police have recorded hundreds of violent hate crimes and discrimination against immigrants and ethnic minorities in Germany, Sweden and elsewhere in Europe.

In 1998, more than 7, 700 hate crimes were reported in the USA: 56 per cent of those crimes were against people of a different race, 18 per cent against people of a different religion and 16 per cent against people of a different sexual orientation. In recent years, minority and indigenous communities have been involved in or affected by conflicts. Many have been displaced or left their homes as refugees.

The establishment of social cohesion and trust between communities that is necessary both for peace and for stable economic development has been undermined. Recognition of identities is also an important aspect of social cohesion. Creating homogeneous societies through assimilation is not the best way of ensuring stability because distinct ethnic, religious and cultural identities are too important to individuals' psychological and social welfare to eliminate. Many states nevertheless pursue a passive or active form of assimilation through subtle policies that deny citizenship to certain ethnic groups, or that fail to acknowledge their true identities as distinct.

Peru recognizes both Spanish and ethnic languages as official, but the latter only in the zones where they predominate. The Constitution also recognizes the special jurisdiction of indigenous communities in the Amazon region but, while the Peruvian state recognizes Amazon peoples as distinct ethnic groups, it does not recognize the Quechua and Aymara communities as indigenous peoples.

Defending Discriminations

Discrimination is often difficult to prove, particularly when it is not expressed in specific legislation or when there is a lack in commitment among dominant groups to recognize the problem. One of the most visible forms of discrimination against minority groups and indigenous peoples is reflected in the fact that minority groups and indigenous peoples constitute a disproportionately large and persistent percentage of the poor, both in developing and industrialized countries. Another visible form of discrimination relates to the exclusion of minorities and indigenous peoples from key social, political and economic institutions.

Although it may be difficult to establish that poverty and exclusion are caused by discrimination, the fact that poverty and other forms of exclusion are more persistent among minority groups and/or indigenous peoples is indicative that discrimination may be a contributing factor. Furthermore, poverty and exclusion are not independent and often we will not be able to distinguish between the two phenomena. In the context of minority groups and indigenous populations, the incidence of poverty and exclusion can be seen as different manifestations of the same phenomenon: the marginalization of minority groups and indigenous peoples from the process and benefits of social, economic and political development.

Poverty incidence and exclusion are higher among minority groups and indigenous peoples than the rest of the population of given countries. Much of social, economic and political exclusion, and deprivation, may be rooted in past or present discrimination. However, minority groups and indigenous peoples do not necessarily constitute in all cases the majority of the poor or the majority of the excluded groups.

A large amount of evidence has shown other types of discrimination against women, persons with disabilities and older persons, etc. and their marginalization in development policies. Moreover, discrimination might not always be directed specifically at minority groups. Why then should the development community be concerned with discrimination against minority groups? This concern can be defended from a number of perspectives, ranging from the body of legislation in international human rights law to the analysis of a variety of social, economic and political outcomes.

Right to Non-discrimination

Perhaps one of the most concrete defences can be made from an international law perspective. The right to non-discrimination is a principle of customary international law, which means that all states are obligated to respect this right for all people in their territory. This is strengthened further in the two main international treaties on human rights, the International Covenant on Civil and Political Rights (ICCPR), and the International Covenant on Economic, Social and Cultural Rights (ICESCR) which stipulate respect for non-discrimination in the realization of human rights. This right is elaborated in the UN Convention on the Elimination of All Forms of Racial Discrimination (ICERD), now ratified by 166 States. This treaty allows states to take 'special measures' in the economic, social, cultural or other spheres to ensure that all people can enjoy their rights equally without discrimination.

Notably, all of the treaty monitoring bodies require that states provide disaggregated data in their regular reports to the UN on the implementation of the treaties. Very few actually provide such information. Although there is no universal treaty on minority rights, the UN has adopted the Declaration on the Rights of Persons Belonging to National or Ethnic, Religious and Linguistic Minorities (UNDM), which proclaims that states must protect the existence of national, ethnic, cultural, religious and linguistic minority identities and encourage conditions for the promotion of those identities. The Declaration also requires that states take measures to ensure that minorities may participate in economic progress and development in their country. Together, these international human rights provisions provide a framework of states' responsibilities towards minority groups that cannot be ignored.

Reducing Poverty

The ethical principles established by legislation aimed at protecting minority groups and/or indigenous peoples from social, economic and political forms of discrimination have been taken into account in recent work on poverty and inequality. The 1993 Human Development Report stressed the importance of participation of traditionally excluded groups in development and in the establishment of fully democratic regimes.

The 2000/2001 Human Development Report argued for a human rights approach to development and emphasized the importance of freedom from discrimination, want, fear and injustice; and freedom for the realization of one's human potential, freedom of participation, expression and association, and access to decent work as fundamental bases for the alleviation of poverty and inequality and the promotion of socially and politically sustainable economic growth.

Despite these efforts, commitment to human rights is still rare in development initiatives. Combating discrimination against minority groups and indigenous peoples, however, is slowly being recognized as a central element in the fight against world poverty. The International Development Targets set out at the UN Social Summit in Copenhagen included the halving of poverty in developing and transitional countries by 2015, as well as the improvement of a range of health, education and environment targets.

Recent assessments of these targets have shown that, during the 1990s, poverty in Eastern Europe and Central Asia has risen and is predicted to rise even further by 2015, and that decreases in poverty elsewhere have been minimal. Those increases in poverty have been localized among certain population groups, of which minority groups and indigenous peoples form a large fraction, and have persisted over time.

The overlap between persistent poverty and minority groups and indigenous peoples makes a strong case for including minority groups and indigenous peoples as central targets of development policies. This is not to say that reducing poverty among groups in a numerical minority is going to have a large impact on total poverty reduction. However, recognizing that the persistence of poverty among minority groups and indigenous peoples is to a large extent a consequence of exclusion, marginalization and discrimination may have important implications in terms of the elimination of one important barrier to the reduction of world poverty.

Although minority groups might not be the largest identifiable group among the poor in all developing countries it is usually the case that poverty incidence and a range of other development indicators are worse for minority groups and indigenous peoples, and, furthermore, it is often the case that poverty reduction is slowest among these groups. The 2000/2001 World Development Report examines three key elements in the fight against poverty: the promotion of opportunities, the empowerment of disadvantaged groups and the enhancement of security. These elements cannot be addressed without expressed concern for the rights of minority groups and indigenous populations.

The promotion of opportunities can be achieved by promoting economic growth and adequate market reforms that reflect the institutional and structural characteristics of the economy in question. Creating opportunities, however, also depends to a large extent on the implementation of policies that address socio-economic inequalities across gender, ethnic and social divides. Lower socio-economic inequality will, in turn, facilitate the access of vulnerable groups to new opportunities and diminish the extent of the shocks these households are bound to suffer during economic reforms.

The empowerment of disadvantaged groups expresses a more direct concern with the problems brought about by the marginalization of these groups. It implies greater political accountability, the creation of efficient legal and public services and the removal of structural barriers that exclude some population groups from the decision-making process. The final element is the enhancement of security and, consequently, the reduction of vulnerability to all types of shocks. The poor generally are often more vulnerable to shocks and less able to cope with their consequences. For example, lack of access to credit means that not only can poor households not build up sustainable livelihoods, but also they cannot cover basic needs when there is adverse weather or an economic shock.

Evidence presented above from various countries shows that minority groups and indigenous peoples have worse access to credit, are more likely to suffer from ill-health, be unemployed or be affected by ethnic conflict. This third element implies promoting the diversification of activities of vulnerable households, establishing adequate social insurance and social assistance programmes, creating the conditions for stable socio-political environments and strengthening the assets of poor and marginalized people, including minority groups and indigenous peoples, whose levels of poverty and exclusion from social, economic and political institutions are particularly high.

Participation in Decision-Making

Efforts to reduce poverty globally need to address the particular problems of minority groups and indigenous peoples. This implies the establishment of policies that guarantee the participation of minority groups and indigenous peoples in the process of decision-making in every country. But minorities and indigenous peoples may be wary of policies and institutions that are overly integrative or assimilationist, given concerns about loss of their identity, and of their own cultural and social values, languages, practices and institutions.

Therefore a level of meaningful participation is necessary in order to ensure the protection of the rights of minorities. This participation 'signifies the ability ... to bring relevant facts to decision-makers, argue their position before decisionmakers, veto legislative or administrative proposals, and establish and manage their own institutions in specific areas'.

The participation of minorities in the national decision-making process will not only help to address the problems of persistent poverty and exclusion among these groups, but will also yield important gains for those minority groups and indigenous populations that are excluded from fundamental social, economic and political institutions. These gains will not be entirely material but will also affect the dignity, self-worth and feeling of integration and participation of minorities and indigenous peoples in social, political and economic decisions that have important consequences for their lives.

Often minority and indigenous groups become estranged from national decision-making processes because they perceive no role for them in that process, or because they believe themselves to be incapable of influencing political, social or economic policy outcomes. These facts imply important private costs for those individuals, households and groups that suffer from discriminatory actions in terms of the loss of their cultural identity and loss of their basic human rights, freedoms and interests.

A particularly important issue in decision-making is land ownership. Land is not just an economic resource but also plays an important role in the culture and traditions of many minorities and indigenous peoples, particularly those whose land use is based on collective or communal forms of ownership. There is a large body of evidence of attempts against the land rights of indigenous populations. In Vietnam, the large increase in the international price of coffee led to the non-authorized occupation of indigenous land in the Central Highlands for the production of coffee. Minority groups and indigenous peoples are much more likely to be displaced by so-called development projects such as dams and infrastructure projects. They have at best only partially recognized land rights and little political leverage.

For example, in India, siting of dams has disproportionately affected the Adivasis, and thousands have been displaced from their homes, with little attempt to help them resettle and re-establish their livelihoods, or create new ones. In Brazil, appropriation of indigenous lands by commercial agriculture has contributed to high suicide rates among indigenous peoples, particularly among young people, who perceive their cultural identity as being eroded and devalued. Where land rights are more fully recognized, minorities and indigenous peoples can have greater authority and autonomy in decision-making as it affects their territories and livelihoods. This in turn can help mitigate the effects of land loss and displacement on their communities.

Business Case for Inclusion

It can be argued that eliminating discrimination against minority groups is also highly desirable from an economic perspective - this is the so-called 'business case' for inclusion.

The persistence of poverty and inequalities due to discrimination, social exclusion and difficult access to services and institutions may undermine efforts to decrease poverty and create poverty traps. These have important economic effects that undermine the country's potential for the establishment of sustainable development paths, including the decrease in the demand potential of internal markets, the reduction of the human capital potential of societies where discrimination against minorities is significant, and the creation of political instability.

Poverty and deprivation among minority groups imply that private consumption is low, and this may be particularly acute in countries where minority groups are numerically significant proportions of the population. Forms of discrimination against minority groups and their exclusion from social, political and economic institutions may also create important constraints on the accumulation of social and physical capital by those groups. These factors create barriers that may prevent the enlargement of internal markets. This, in turn, may decrease effective demand and thus economic growth. This is particularly relevant in developing countries where the size of internal markets is considered an important constraint on development and economic growth.

Furthermore, high levels of poverty and socio-economic inequalities among specific population groups reduce the productive capacity of those groups. Discrimination 'deprives society of unity and the cooperation of all their people in pursuit of the common good [and . . .] wastes talent, productivity and lives'. Improving the economic conditions of minority groups would thus 'amount not to a consumption transfer but to a productive investment'.

Thus, the whole economy would benefit from an improvement of its human capital resources. O'Connell and Birdsall describe education as being the people's asset, and for many it is the only asset they have with which to generate an income. In the longer run, 'the transformation of poverty groups into more productive members of society is likely to raise the incomes of all'.

Human capital plays a central role in theories of economic growth and development, and much empirical work across and within developed and developing countries shows a robust, strong and positive effect of educational attainment on growth rates. Birdsall et al. found that increasing a country's primary and secondary enrolment rates from 75 per cent to 90 per cent and from 22 per cent to 34 per cent would raise annual per capita growth rates by 1. 5 percentage points, which by 1990 would have been translated into a relative increase in GDP per capita of 40 per cent compared to countries that had not increased enrolment rates.

The relationship between education and economic growth is a feature of growth theory that stresses the positive effect of education on innovation and adoption of new technology. The accumulation of human capital brought about by the improvement of education and health care, and the elimination of extreme forms of destitution among excluded groups could improve the productive capacity of these groups.

The productive activities of minorities and indigenous peoples are integral to their cultures and lifestyles, and therefore cannot easily be transformed without serious consequences for their identities. This must be considered seriously in any analysis of the human capital potential of minority or indigenous groups and should not be ignored in favour of particular economic outcomes.

Addressing discrimination requires a huge effort on the part of governments, international organizations and the media. But the incentives to do so are high. Studies that have sought to estimate the gains of ending long-term exclusion and discrimination against minority groups and indigenous peoples suggest huge potential economic gains, as well as private gains to previously excluded groups and broader social benefits. Gaps in investment in education and health and the resulting gaps in wages, and high and concentrated poverty among minorities and indigenous peoples, lead to losses in output, GDP and wealth (although it must also be recognized that the low-wage labour of minorities and indigenous peoples, and appropriation of their lands for development purposes, has also perversely contributed to gains in output, GDP and wealth for some sectors of the population).

Discrimination in education is perpetuated in the labour market through pay and gender discrimination, and restrictions on occupational choice. In many countries these inequalities are persistent and have led to social divisions. Not only is this violation of human rights morally indefensible and highly detrimental to the well-being of those discriminated against, there are also important social costs: reducing discrimination can benefit everyone not just those formerly discriminated against or excluded. There are two main ways of estimating the economic cost to society of discrimination through this education route, developed by Brimmer for the USA.

One method is to simply calculate the gains in total output and income that would arise from the full use of the existing education, skills and experience of the excluded discriminated group, that is, the excluded group is assumed to have the same levels of earnings and productivity as their nonexcluded counterparts, usually estimated by age, gender and education. This essentially gives an estimate of the gains for removing discrimination in the labour market. Given that individuals from minority groups and indigenous peoples earn less than their majority or elite counterparts with the same levels of education, these gains would be significant.

The second method goes one step further by calculating the gains that would arise if we removed discrimination in education, that is, made use of the potential skills, education and experience of the group that is discriminated against. There is sufficient evidence that minority groups and indigenous peoples have much lower levels of education than the rest of the population and that these inequalities are essentially reproduced in the labour markets. Adding the two estimates together simulates the effects of removing discrimination in education as well as in employment. Each method requires detailed data on education, age, work experience, wages and employment for both the minority group and the rest of the population.

Zoninsein has estimated the gains in earnings and GDP for four Latin American countries, Bolivia, Brazil, Guatemala and Peru, plus South Africa and the USA. Peru has much smaller estimated gains because the household survey contained less information on indigenous peoples - highlighting the importance of data coverage. Table 2 summarizes these findings.

Although these estimates are only simulations of the gains from removing discrimination, and the method is subject to debate, they are indicative of possible economic benefits. They suggest that even partial removal of discrimination in some spheres would be hugely beneficial in improving economic performance, and ultimately poverty reduction.

The removal of discrimination against minority groups and indigenous peoples will not only have large social benefits but will also yield, large private benefits for those individuals, households and groups that suffer the effects of discrimination and consequent poverty and exclusion from key social, political and economic institutions.

Stability and Security

Finally, income inequality and persistent poverty among particular groups of the population can also increase feelings of unfairness. This promotes social discontent and may lead to social unrest which can have negative effects on economic growth. In fact, the recent attention paid to minority rights by the international development community originated from the emergence of various types of inter-ethnic conflict.

Table 2. Gains in earnings and GDP from removing discrimination

	Labour market discrimination		Education discrimination		Both	
	Earnings	GDP	Earnings	GDP	Earnings	GDP
Bolivia (1997)	57.8%	17.12%	66.1%	19.56%	123.9%	36.68%
Brazil (1997)	36.7%	4.85%	60.3%	7.98%	97.0%	12.83%
Guatemala (1998)	32.2%	4.59%	63.5%	9.04%	95.8%	13.63%
Peru (1997)	35.9%	1.76%	50.0%	2.45%	85.9%	4.21%
Brazil (1990)	–	–	–	–	24.94%	9.04%
South Africa (1993)	–	–	–	–	183.7%	96.6%
USA (1992)	2.7%		2.04%		4.74%	2.8%

There is a growing literature on the economic and social causes of conflict, including civil wars, and discrimination, inequalities between social groups, and inequality between minorities and nonminorities play an important role. And conflict, whether caused or merely fuelled by discrimination against minorities or indigenous peoples, has devastating consequences on prospects for total not just minority poverty reduction.

Elbadawi finds that civil wars can be influenced by the extent of ethnic fractionalization in segmented societies. Easterly and Levine find similar results for Africa. Dollar et al. and Collier and Hoeffler, using a cross-section of more than 100 countries, find identical results for their ethnic fragmentation variables. Justino investigated the case of Kerala, India, and found that the persistence of caste inequalities could be a strong determinant of labour instability there. A large fraction of the more or less violent forms of conflict that have taken place in both developed and developing countries in recent decades have been in part influenced by the discontent of some parts of the population with rising poverty and unemployment, and deteriorating living conditions.

Discrimination and extreme rural poverty experienced by indigenous peoples across the globe, from Indonesia to Central America have been associated with rural social and political conflict. There is also the increasingly common phenomenon of so-called 'development conflict'. Where economic development priorities clash with the needs and rights of minority or indigenous groups, the result can be local or widespread conflict. For example, some indigenous groups have engaged in armed resistance to oppose forced appropriation of their lands without their full prior informed consent to such action.

Even if the use of the land and its resources is claimed to be necessary for the economic development of the country as a whole, the denial of minorities' and indigenous peoples' human rights cannot be justified as a trade-off. Moreover, such actions can force minority and indigenous communities into further marginalization and poverty, and commonly destroys their cultures and livelihoods.

A commitment to sustainable and peaceful development requires a commitment to development paths that respect minority and indigenous rights, and works with them to find appropriate solutions to local and national development challenges.

Given the evidence discussed above, we can argue that policy programmes that reduce discrimination among minority groups and increase their socio-economic participation can create an element of socio-political stability, essential for the success of any economic growth and development strategy.

However, despite the high development costs of discrimination, and the links between discrimination against minority groups and the emergence of civil wars and other types of socio-political conflicts, the inclusion of minority rights in development policies should not be solely justified in terms of cost-efficiency or conflict-prevention measures.

Although discrimination may entail large costs for economic growth and development, the elimination of discrimination will not guarantee large economic growth rates. In fact, it may lead to lower economic growth if it implies the transfer of large amounts of resources towards minority groups, and greater control for minorities and indigenous peoples over their traditional lands and natural resources.

The inclusion of minority rights in development policies is, however, an important element in the creation of sustainable and integrated development strategies. The incidence of high levels of poverty among many minority groups and indigenous peoples, and their exclusion from important social and economic institutions, should be the object of attention of the international development community.

In addition, the clear prohibition of discrimination in international human rights law places strong obligations on the part of states to take positive steps to eliminate discrimination and its effects - including through development cooperation activities. A key part of the solution is ensuring that minorities and indigenous peoples can participate meaningfully in decision-making on development policies that might affect them.

3

Discrimination against Indigenous Women and Children

There are about 300 million indigenous men, women and children worldwide. They are extremely diverse – more than 5,000 different groups of indigenous peoples live in more than 70 countries. They make up one third of the world's 900 million extremely poor rural people. In many countries, indigenous peoples are the most severely disadvantaged. They are often forced to live on the least productive terrain, denied rights to land, forests and other natural resources that they have managed sustainably for millennia, and marginalized by modern society.

Yet, their value systems, spirituality, capabilities and cultures have huge untapped potential for sustainable development. They play a crucial role in the stewardship of natural resources and biodiversity and provide environmental services at local, regional and international levels. Indigenous peoples have rich, varied and locally rooted knowledge systems and their immense cultural diversity is extremely valuable in a world threatened by the homogenizing trend of globalization.

Today, there is a growing consensus that accountability is crucial to poverty reduction, human development and human security. The human rights approach to poverty reduction emphasizes the obligations of governments and all partners in the development process and requires that they be held to account for their conduct in relation to international human rights. This has led to greater emphasis on the obligations of governments and UN agencies towards indigenous peoples.

Dicrimination against Indigenous Women

Within indigenous communities, indigenous women are playing a crucial role in securing the livelihoods of their families, while preserving the cultural worldviews and values of their indigenous group. In most countries, indigenous women are facing a triple exclusion: for being poor, indigenous and a woman.

Indigenous women, often the most powerless people in society, bear the brunt of both criminal and political violence. They suffer multiple layers of discrimination, including gender and racial violence in all its forms. This is a cultural genocide in a modern-day context.

The indigenous women are in a particularly desperate situation since so much of the country is in turmoil. They have been oppressed and marginalized by central and state governments for a long time. They are victims a number of atrocities included rape, torture and murder. In India violence agianst indegenous women often occurs in the remote hill country so it is hard to get the news out to the wider world. In addition, the governments does not want to recognize that it is the perpetrator of the violence. Indigenous women have been disappearing but it has never been reported because there is no mechanism to get information out. The same thing is happening all over wolrd — disappearances, land confiscation, trafficking in women, and agriculture and other traditional livelihood systems are destroyed.

In low-intensity armed conflicts in Bangladesh, India, Indonesia, Laos, Myanmar, Nepal, the Philippines and Vietnam, indigenous women are targets in these conflicts because of their gender and ethnic origins. In Nepal, the army fighting Maoist guerrillas raped indigenous women as the guerrillas moved into indigenous territories. It is the assertion of the civilized society that barbaric methods of law enforcement will be dealt with by upholding the majesty of the rule of law.

Sherpas in Nepal are being forced into combat in the so-called movement for liberation led by non-indigenous people. Indigenous women and young are being targeted for misuse by the Maoists and therefore government forces hold them in suspicion. Because of the surrounding armed forces, the rates of violence against women have been increasing in this ongoing armed conflict.

Indigenous women are not only victims of war-related violence. In Canada, some 500 indigenous women have disappeared over 20 years. There are two layers of justice, one for non-aboriginal people and one for aboriginal people. When aboriginal women go missing, police take little notice.

Rights of Indigenous Women

International instruments adopted through the United Nations system, including the Universal Declaration of Human Rights, the Convention for the Prevention of Genocide, the Convention for the Elimination of Racial Discrimination and the International Covenants for Economic, Social, Cultural, Civil and Political Rights, have created the basis for a body of human rights law. Civil society and the Indigenous movement have been important actors in this process, working to ensure that advances in individual human rights law are accompanied by progress in the area of collective human rights. The Indigenous movement in particular has worked to advance collective rights in both international and national arenas.

Despite this current Indigenous participation in the UN, it was not until 1971 that the UN Economic and Social Council first authorized "a general and complete study of the problems of discrimination against Indigenous populations" suggesting national and international measures "necessary to eliminate such discrimination, in collaboration with other organs and entities of the UN and with competent international organizations."

The resulting report, the "Study of Discrimination Against Indigenous Populations," or the Martinez Cobo Report, was presented in 1984. It clearly documented that the large majority of Indigenous Peoples were subject to discrimination, oppression and exploitation. It noted that in many countries, Indigenous Peoples did not have the same employment opportunities, access to public services, health services, religious and cultural freedoms or access to justice as other groups. The report also showed that Indigenous Peoples did not have access to meaningful participation in political life. It found that many Indigenous Peoples had either resigned themselves to their situation or turned to assimilation as the only way to improve their living conditions.

Along with the disparities between Indigenous Peoples and other ethnic communities revealed in studies like the Martinez Cobo Report, basic indicators on literacy, health, education, and salary document a gap between men and women within Indigenous communities. Indigenous women recognize that the wellbeing of their peoples depends on "equality between men and women in decision-making in the public and private life". Their advocacy in the international arena is tied to the Indigenous struggle to be fully recognized as Peoples with unique philosophies, worldviews, and knowledge. One of these is a belief in a dualist relationship between men and women. Indigenous women recognize that the cultural wealth of Indigenous Peoples has its origin in the transmission of values and community education. Women, as the community's midwives, advisors, spiritual guides and leaders are principally responsible for the preservation of knowledge, traditional values, wisdom and abilities.

The publication of the Martinez Cobo Report was followed in the UN by the creation of a Working Group on Indigenous Populations. Since the 1980s this group has served as an important space for hundreds of organizations and Indigenous leaders from all over the world to convene annually and present grievances. Although not a binding mechanism, the Working Group helped open new spaces for Indigenous Peoples within the UN system.

It is clear that eradicating disparities between Indigenous Peoples and non-Indigenous sectors will require much more than just broadening access to services. It requires the recognition of self-determination as a collective, fundamental human right of all peoples, like Indigenous Peoples, who share a language or a culture different from the majority. There is much progress to be made in this area. International legislation is limited because it uses the term "people," rather than Peoples to refer to Indigenous Peoples.10 While Indigenous pressure has succeeded in forcing some states to use the term Peoples, these states have established clauses restricting the rights attached to this term.

Today there are only a limited number of judicial instruments that recognize collective rights. The United Nations and the OAS are currently debating Draft declarations on the rights of Indigenous Peoples. Though these resolutions would not be binding, their adoption would be an important step for Indigenous Peoples and the construction of a body of collective human rights law.

To date, Indigenous Peoples achievements in the UN system include ILO Convention 169, along with Declaration and Recommendations on the Environment (Rio de Janiero), Human Rights (Vienna), Gender (Beijing), Health (OMS/OPS), Education (UNESCO), Informed Participation (World Bank, Convention on Bio Diversity), creation of an Iberoamerican Indigenous Fund, and the Permanent Forum on Indigenous Peoples, which has already established a plan of action.

A number of States have ratified ILO Convention 169, while others have established their own policies to improve relations with Indigenous Peoples. The ILO has always recognized Indigenous Peoples as distinct from traditionally-understood rural communities. In 1957, after a long study, it adopted the Convention on Indigenous Populations and Tribal Populations, known as Convention 107.

Convention 107 was significant because "for the first time, an international institution established binding, obligatory standards with respect to a range of Indigenous problems (not only labor conditions)". The convention recognized collective land rights, the right to native-language education and the validity of common law. But it had a paternalistic and protectionist perspective and its ultimate objective was the assimilation of Indigenous Peoples in the name of a homogenous national state. "As a consequence of the growing criticisms of this perspective, the ILO decided to push for a revision of the Convention. This led the General Conference to adopt Convention 169 on the Indigenous and Tribal Populations in 1989. Convention 169 is now ratified by various member states and, to date, it constitutes the only international judicial instrument on the human rights of Indigenous Peoples."

Convention 169 establishes fundamental aspects of human rights and Indigenous law, including traditional land rights, common law and the right to health and life. It states that Indigenous Peoples must be consulted in good faith prior to the establishment of any policies that concern them and stresses that governments must consider Indigenous Peoples' values and insights in relation to environmental conservation. It also recognizes Indigenous Peoples' right to be protected from exploitative labor agreements. The convention stipulates that governments, in collaboration with interested Peoples, must submit "a coordinated and systematic plan for protecting the rights of Peoples and guaranteeing respect for their integrity"(Article 2, Convention 169).

ILO Convention 169 is the first international judicial instrument that uses the term "Indigenous Peoples," although it restricts the meaning of the term Peoples in order to conform to other international conventions.

Important aspects of Convention 169 include:

— Article 3, which states: "Indigenous and tribal peoples must fully enjoy the fundamental human rights without obstacles or discrimination."

— Article 4, which declares that, "the values and social, cultural, religious and spiritual practices of said peoples" must be recognized.

— Article 8, which establishes that "before applying the national legislation to interested peoples, governments must appropriately take into consideration their customs and common laws."

— Article 10, which establishes that "when penal sanctions are imposed by general legislation to members of said peoples, they must take into account their economic, social and cultural characteristics." It also establishes that states should give preference to sanctions other than incarceration.

— Article 12, which states that "The interested peoples must have protection against violations of their rights and be able to initiate legal procedures, either on their own or through representative organizations in order to assure respect for their rights."

These successes in international legislation are achievements of a dynamic Indigenous movement which is articulating its goals in the international arena and throughout the Americas, as well as through the World Council of Indigenous Peoples, the Continental Campaign of 500 Years of Indigenous, Black and Popular Resistance, the Indigenous Summit and, more recently, the First Summit of Indigenous Women.

Indigenous women are an especially valuable part of this movement. By promoting multi-ethnic democracy and a more integrated and balanced respect for human rights, Indigenous women are forcing a re-conceptualization of the nature of the state.

The Convention for the Elimination of Discrimination Against Women, the Optional Protocol of Belem do Para and the recommendation from Beijing and its successors have been important opportunities for Indigenous women to give voice to their issues and ideas. Through these processes, Indigenous women have formed their own spaces—including the international network of Indigenous Women and the international Forum of Indigenous Women—in which to articulate their positions and proposals and, above all, to assert their own identities.

At the First Summit of Indigenous Women, held in December 2002, Indigenous women reaffirmed the urgent need to increase their own participation in the international arena, noting that existing international conventions had been "formulated from positions of power and the perspective of the dominant discourse." The Summit enabled Indigenous women to develop and reach consensus on a Plan of Action, which includes a chapter on human rights, and provided a valuable space for exchanging ideas and strengthening international participation.

At the Summit, Indigenous women also reaffirmed their fundamental demand for states to adopt the UN Draft Declaration of Rights of Indigenous Peoples. This Declaration emphasizes fundamental issues including collective rights, Indigenous self-determination and the right to economic, social and cultural development. Though the Declaration would not be binding, its approval would, for the first time, establish the bases of intercultural co-existence in our societies.

Indigenous Peoples see the UN and OAS Draft Declarations on the Rights of Indigenous Peoples as means to establish states' political will to effectively confront exclusion and institutionalized racism against Indigenous Peoples and create new relationships between states and Indigenous communities. The UN Draft Declaration in particular is the result of a participatory process begun in the 80s, which has successfully established broad agreement through dialogue between states and Indigenous organizations. The UN Working Group on Indigenous Populations was integral through this process.

The United Nations Draft Declaration aims to establish the basic conditions necessary for Indigenous Peoples to exercise their human rights to health, education, development, land and collective intellectual property, while recognizing their diversity as subjects of collective rights. It recognizes Indigenous Peoples' right to collectively-owned lands, collective intellectual property, self-determination, autonomy and political participation in all levels of government as well as their right to have a say "in any laws and administrative measures that directly affect them."

The Draft Declaration recognizes the collective identity of Indigenous Peoples. It acknowledges that Indigenous Peoples view themselves as parts of a distinct and collective whole and that, as a result, they have the right to self-determination separate from the State or any international organizations. The Declaration also proclaims that States must accept Indigenous Peoples' distinct identity and co-exist with Indigenous communities within a framework of peace and development. It requires that States meet the needs of Indigenous Peoples, including allowing international relations with these collectives. The Draft Declaration, therefore, establishes the basis for States' to recognize Indigenous autonomy and self-determination.

Indigenous organizations have been involved in creating the OAS Draft Declaration of the rights of Indigenous Peoples as well. When the draft began in 1989, the OAS did not establish means to facilitate Indigenous participation. But in 1999, through a General Assembly resolution, the Assembly opened itself to Indigenous Peoples' participation. A Working Group was formed and there is now an annual meeting between governments and Indigenous Peoples in order to advance the discussion of the draft.

But the most relevant recent development in Indigenous rights in the Inter-American system is the Interamerican Court of Human Rights (IACHR) judgment in the Awastingni case. In this case, an Indigenous community (the Sumu/Mayangna of Nicaragua) demanded that the State concede control over its ancestral territory. The Court ruled in favor of the Indigenous community, recognizing its right to the territory even in the absence of a title of community property and ordered the Nicaraguan government to develop a procedure to define and delineate Indigenous territories.

The Awastingni case established a basis for increasing recognition of Indigenous Peoples' territorial rights and right to self-determination. For Indigenous Peoples, having autonomy and self-determination means having the power to govern their own communities and to establish and maintain their own institutions and projects, while also having access to effective means of political participation at the national and international level.

The Awastingni case illustrates the importance of Indigenous Peoples' participation in both theoretical and practical advances in human rights at the international level. Legal changes are generating shifts in the balance of power and establishing means through which Indigenous Peoples can exercise their rights as autonomous peoples with full capacity to decide on economic, social and cultural polices and to recover and reclaim their development and recognize their individual and collective rights.

The recent decades of Indigenous women's international participation– from walking the halls of the UN to winning the Nobel Peace Prize in 1992 – have served as a beginning for a long and complex process of reconciliation and negotiation. Indigenous women have laid a foundation that will nurture the spirits of justice and fairness. They have won agreements between Indigenous Peoples and non-Indigenous communities, and built bridges of trust to facilitate change. But Indigenous women confront many challenges in continuing their human rights work at the international level. Creating new alliances with Indigenous and non-Indigenous women and consolidating old alliances is a fundamental task. International organizations like MADRE have valuable experiences to share in this respect. The job ahead is to continue the work which has been started: fostering recognition and respect for the Indigenous wisdom, knowledge, and science of which women are the ultimate bearers and advancing Indigenous women's alliances, capacity and individual and collective leadership.

Opportunities for Development

The United Nations International Decade of the World's Indigenous People (1995-2004) and the Fourth World Conference on Women (held 4-15 September 1995 in Beijing, China) are providing indigenous women with unique opportunities to increase public awareness of their situation. Indigenous women's special concerns include survival of their communities and of their cultural identity and recognition of the central role of women in the efforts to advance the interests of indigenous people everywhere. They hope that the International Decade and the World Conference will result in UN Member States adopting constitutional reforms incorporating the rights of indigenous people and that more countries will ratify ILO Convention No. 169, which calls for the protection of the rights of indigenous and tribal peoples. Indigenous women want to see concrete results at the end of the Decade, including improvements in health, education and housing, cleaner and more adequate water supplies and the adoption of policies regarding land demarcation.

Indigenous women successfully lobbied to have their concerns included in the Beijing Declaration and Platform for Action adopted at the Fourth World Conference on Women. In those documents, Governments and other actors of society are asked to take particular measures to promote and strengthen national policies and programmes in favour of indigenous women in the following areas:

— *human rights*: by promoting the human rights of indigenous women and translating human rights instruments into indigenous languages;

— *health*: by reducing the negative effects of environmental degradation on the health and life of indigenous women;

— *education*: by promoting a multicultural approach to education, taking into consideration the needs, aspirations and cultures of indigenous women.

— *economic development:* by supporting the economic activities of indigenous women, taking into account their traditional knowledge, and encouraging their access to capital;

The need for the full participation of indigenous women in decision-making on issues that affect them was also emphasized.

More and more indigenous women are taking the lead in supporting their communities and have been in the forefront in advancing the cause of their people. Nobel Peace Prize winner Rigoberta Menchu Tum, a Mayan Indian, was internationally honoured for promoting the human rights of indigenous people. She lived in exile in Mexico from her native Guatemala, a country ravaged by a long and destructive civil war, for more than 10 years and used her own personal experience of torture and injustice to fight for the rights of Indians everywhere. In 1992, she was awarded the Nobel Peace Prize for her activities in promoting peace.

Participation of indigenous women in national political structures, though insufficient, is increasing. Some indigenous women now participate in national politics at the highest levels. In Australia, Lois O'Donoghue, an Aborigine, started to fight for the rights of her people in the 1950s, when she was refused admission to a nursing school because of her race. She fought for five years and finally won the right to register in a teaching hospital. She has been involved in the aboriginal movement at the grass-roots and national levels ever since. Today, she is the Chairperson of the Aboriginal and Torres Strait Islander Commission, an organization responsible for advancing the cause of aboriginals in Australia. She sees women as the backbone of all indigenous organizations and central to the development of their communities.

Many more women are not internationally known but are making a difference in their societies. In Colombia, Eulalia Yagari, at the age of 14 and against her father's will, was the first woman in her community to participate in a public awareness meeting on land recovery, a process successfully used by some indigenous groups to regain possession of their ancestral lands. In Eulalia's village, 900 people were living on 60 hectares of land. Because of her work, her community was eventually granted more land as a result of the land recovery campaign.Eulalia also played an important role within her tribe in trying to revive their cultural traditions. She consulted with the elder women of her tribe, who taught her old songs and stories. She later taught the music to children in the village's child-care centre, a cultural programme that gave the children a new sense of pride and self-esteem. Today, Eulalia is a member of the Provincial Assembly of Antioquía, in the north-west of Colombia, and is still devoting herself to social issues to alleviate the distress of her people.

In 1986, in the Northeast of Brazil, Eliane Potiguara created GRUMIN (Grupo Mulher - Educaçao), an organization which mobilizes indigenous women, holds conferences and seminars and organizes vocational training to raise indigenous women's awareness and to help them take control of their own lives. Ms. Potiguara who experienced problems as an indigenous woman herself, lived for a time in Rio de Janeiro and saw the way indigenous people were discriminated against in the cities. This gave her the impetus to return to her village to help her people, the Potiguara, who were suffering from social disintegration. GRUMIN has started a variety of projects, including opening a pharmacy of herbal medicines and creating community gardens, where families that have lost their land can grow food. Today, GRUMIN has grown into a nationwide organization, with an extensive network of offices.

In Arequipa, in southern Peru, Celina del Carpio, who works at the National University of San Augustin, is very active in her community and tries her best to improve the life of indigenous women. Convinced that women can move forward in society only through their own empowerment, she holds meetings to inform women about their rights. As a result of their activism, women have organized soup kitchens to feed the hungry and the poor and have also launched a programme entitled "the glass of milk", to provide milk to indigenous children who are malnourished.

Indigenous women face tremendous challenges. Like most women in the world, they have been victims of discrimination for centuries. But as indigenous women, they have been doubly discriminated against: for being indigenous people and for being women.

Discrimination against indigenous people has included forcible removal from their traditional lands; exclusion from mainstream political, economic and social spheres; and genocide.

As indigenous women, in certain communities, they have often been kept in a situation of dependency. They have been marginalized, refused access to land or subjected to other forms of discrimination.

In certain regions, the status of indigenous women was greatly reduced at the time of colonization, with the imposition of new political, economic, social and cultural systems. As stated at the Forum on Indigenous Women of Ecuador, which was held 7-11 September 1994, "Colonialism comes down to the loss of our lands, to the introduction of a language with no sense of poetry, of an irrational political and administrative structure irrespective of the laws of nature, and of the forceful imposition of a Judeo-Christian religion in which woman is synonymous with sin."

Once indigenous women played an important role in their communities: they were, along with men, part of the decision-making processes affecting the future of the whole group. They were consulted and their words listened to. They were respected.

In many cases, the introduction of foreign values destroyed this equilibrium. It had a negative impact on the relationship between men and women, as well as on women's role within their communities. Women were relegated to a position of secondary importance and the traditional complementarity of roles was broken.In their daily lives, within their families and communities, indigenous women deal with hardships stemming from lack of basic services and from inappropriate or no education, among other problems. These factors greatly impair their ability to participate fully in society.

Education and Training

The authoritarian approach of most educational systems imposed on indigenous people did not take into consideration the importance of the traditional and cultural values of these populations. Rather, the educational systems emphasized integration of indigenous groups into the national mould. Most indigenous children failed to adapt to these systems and, as a result, indigenous communities have very high illiteracy rates and poor educational qualifications. In Bolivia, for instance, schooling levels of indigenous people are three years less than for non-indigenous, and the difference is greater for indigenous women.

Innovative measures have been recently introduced to remedy this situation. At schools in Guatemala and Bolivia, for example, indigenous children are taught in their own languages as well as in Spanish, helping to preserve their cultural identity. In certain areas, an education system based on linguistic and cultural diversity has been developed for each ethnic community.

Poor education means that most indigenous women can expect low wages, if they can find jobs at all. According to a report released by the Australian Bureau of Statistics in 1991, aboriginal women usually obtain qualifications in the traditional female fields of health, education and office skills. Those without qualifications mainly work in the informal sector as domestic or farm labourers.

Thus, indigenous women find it very difficult to escape the cycle of extreme poverty, exploitation and low-paid employment. According to the International Labour Organization, incomes earned by Aboriginals in Australia are half the national average and Aboriginal unemployment is five times higher than the national unemployment rate.

Investing in women — giving priority to women's education and training — ultimately benefits all the members of the community. And for indigenous women, appropriate education is especially important, since they are often the primary guardians and transmitters of their rich, diversified culture. In Bolivia, the United Nations Voluntary Fund for the International Year of the World's Indigenous People financially supported a project by the Organización de Mujeres Aymaras del Kollasuyo (OMAK) to teach Andean indigenous women the concept of democracy and human rights. The project emphasized the importance of the process of voting as a significant step towards enabling indigenous women to empower themselves and have their concerns included on the national political agenda. The training was carried out through a series of seminars and radio programmes.

Economic and Social Aspects

The empowerment of indigenous women is the key to better standards of living. Women themselves want to be given the means and the tools to increase their independence. The concept of empowerment has been clearly described in the words of an Aboriginal woman from Australia: "If you came only to help me, then you can go back home. But if you consider my struggle as part of your own survival, then perhaps we can work together."

There has been a dramatic shift in the general concept of technical assistance, which used to impose without consultation a certain kind of development on the populations concerned, thus creating long-term dependency. This top-down approach proved to be very ineffective. Now, emphasis is being put on self-reliance and independence.

The importance of women's participation in the development process of their countries has been recognized and stressed in various United Nations fora. Some United Nations agencies have engaged in bilateral programmes with indigenous communities to enable them to regain some economic autonomy. Indigenous women prove to be very receptive to income-generating activities.

With many men from indigenous communities migrating to urban areas in search of employment, women have to take on greater responsibilities.In spite of their strong involvement and participation in the economic aspects of their communities, indigenous women are still confronted with harsh social problems. Poverty and the lack of job opportunities that affect these communities give rise to alcoholism, drug abuse, domestic violence and prostitution.

Another area of concern for indigenous women is limited access to medical care. At the Forum on Indigenous Women of Ecuador, women drew attention to the alarming deterioration of health conditions within their communities. Even though many villages are provided with basic health services, these services are still inadequate and do not cover the needs of the population.

In 1990, for instance, out of 1,000 indigenous births in Ecuador, 517 children died of respiratory and intestinal infections or malnutrition, easily curable diseases. Certain

Governments maintain that the reason for the absence of adequate medical facilities is the remoteness of tribal communities and the reluctance of certain indigenous groups to use the available health centres, rather than neglect.

In Venezuela, the Anu people of the Laguna de Sinamaica face serious health problems owing to industrial development, which has caused environmental problems: water is highly polluted, and fish, the main source of food, are increasingly scarce. Consequently, indigenous populations in the area suffer from malnutrition and various diseases. Local organizations have launched projects involving women and designed to improve health conditions and to teach women about immunizing children, nutrition and hygiene, as well as women's health issues.

The land-tenure situation is also a major issue for indigenous people. In northern Arizona, in the United States, indigenous families have been resisting relocation from their reservations, in the face of private developers taking over their commmunities' land and sacred sites. To support their action, a group of elder women have organized themselves and started a weaving project. Through the sales of hand-woven rugs, women supply resisting families with income for survival.

The determination of indigenous women to take charge of their destinies is unequivocally expressed in the growing number of indigenous women who are taking on leadership roles in their communities and participating in national and international fora. At the international level, the Decade of the World's Indigenous People provides an excellent opportunity for indigenous women to develop new relationships with the United Nations system and with other indigenous groups, thus laying the ground for greater cooperation and communication. Strengthening these partnerships will greatly enhance local and national efforts to solve the problems faced by indigenous women around the world.

Discrimination against Indegenous Children in India

India has one of the largest populations of indigenous peoples in the world. According to the Government of India classification of Scheduled Tribes the population is close to 70 million. However, this does not include many indigenous peoples who resist being named "tribal" or are excluded from this category by legislative fiat. All told the actual population of those considering themselves indigenous to their ancestral territories may be as much as 10 to 15 per cent over this figure.

Out of the 5653 distinct communities in India, 635 are considered to be 'tribes' or 'Adivasis'. In comparison, one finds that the estimated number of [Scheduled Tribes] varies from 250 to 593." Again this does not include those who consider themselves distinct "nations" rather than "tribes" or "adivasi". This section will focus largely on the indigenous children of the North Eastern region of India, in the overall context of the Indian Union.

Discrimination against the indigenous population in South Asia has many roots: conquest and displacement in ancient history, exclusion from the mainstream class and caste structures, into which they do not fit, isolation geographically from the more settled and feudal social and cultural environments of the ancient and medieval "Indian" kingdoms.

Colonization played a contributing role in the enhancement of this discrimination in British India. Despite imperialism, considerable regard for the classical South Asian social and cultural mainstreams developed in academia and subsequently in the political acknowledgement of these. Indigenous peoples on the other hand, were largely perceived as "primitive" worthy of anthropological rather than any other consideration, to be at best benevolently either brought into the fold of civilization or preserved in their splendid barbarity!

The successor government of the Indian Union has continued in such modes, tempered however with the insatiable thirst of a new born and impoverished country struggling to find a prominent place in the economic and political hegemonies that rule the world today. With this substantial population of indigenous peoples it is both surprising that these are some of the most discriminated group entities in the supposedly democratic Indian polity and obvious why they should be kept so.

It is only with the acceptance of this unpalatable truth: that it is in the immediate interest of the development thrust of Indian state to maintain indigenous peoples in their disenfranchised condition, that it is possible to make sense of the systemic action and inaction that characterizes discrimination against indigenous children in India.

Indigenous Children and the Convention Rights of the Child

What is the position of the Convention of the Rights of the Child concerning the specific needs of indigenous children? At first glance there are only two Articles that explicitly address the question of indigeneity. However, the numerous references to family, community participation and culture appropriateness of interventions and services , the prohibitions against discrimination on any grounds make it clear that the drafters of the Convention intended the broadest interpretation of its language, in favour of the child, in every circumstance.

Moreover the language of the Preambular section and the overall language of the Convention is evidently enabling rather than limiting, "[taking] due account of the importance of the traditions and cultural values of each people for the protection and harmonious development of the child"

What is or must be expected as "due account" in the case of indigenous children in order that the Convention may be applied in a non-discriminatory, inclusive, participatory and effective manner, in general and in the Indian context? It may be of value here to look at specific cases of the systemic impact of nonrecognition or discrimination in order to answer such a question.

Basis of Discrimination

The first question that comes to mind in the search for information is who and where are these millions of children? Their identity and location. The geographical locations are spread across India Indigenous peoples' territories exist in every state of the country, in larger or smaller areas .

A major concentration is the North East region of India; one of the largest territories in the country still dominated by indigenous peoples in their traditional territories . They are coastal or plains peoples, riverine or mountain dwellers, with a range of cultures to match the terrain. However large and increasing populations of indigenous peoples also live in nontraditional environments, rural or urban, even in those areas where the Census of India does not reveal their presence.

The primary line of discrimination being drawn, it is not surprising that discrimination permeates every level of policy, and, concomitantly, of planning and social services. Indigenous peoples' identities are not recognised nor, therefore, are their rights or needs visible as legitimate aspirations in this gargantuan democracy.

Status of Indigenous Children in the North East India

The situation of the peoples of the North East region of India, home to over 200 indigenous peoples, is strongly illustrative of this situation. In terms of food security and food availability, data is not available in most of the areas except for the State of Assam, which is identified as having a moderate problem .

However considering that indigenous and tribal child populations in even the more prosperous states of India are suffering malnutrition and starvation incidence far higher than the national average it is not surprising that the Union Health Minister in January 2001 commented on the increasing neonatal morbidity and mortality in the region .

The word used by the Minister himself needs to be stressed - "increasing". This is an apparent anomaly. The usual contexts of strong male child preferences, extreme discrimination in caring for girl children, lack of education, especially of women or low status of women are not largely present in the majority of societies in the region . Why then, when India is claiming to have improved its performance on these basic indicators, are these regions demonstrating a noticeable downward trend?

It is well recognised, all over the world today, that the survival and development of indigenous peoples is closely tied to their traditional lands . These lands provide not only food and medicinal products, shelter materials and other tangibles without which mere physical survival and well-being are threatened, but also are the basis of community, identity, history and culture.

What is the record of the Government of India in protecting indigenous peoples' rights to lands in this region?

Anachronistic colonial law based on the premise of terra nullius governs indigenous peoples' lands like all other lands in the territory of the Union of India. A range of laws therefore limits indigenous peoples' rights to their ancestral territories and policies including forest and conservation laws, land acquisition laws and development polices demanding land resources .

Massive influxes, encouraged by the State, of mainstream ethnoses, into indigenous lands , the on-going situation of armed conflicts, rapid and imposed urban development, the growth of extractive industry and plantations all make exorbitant demands on these lands, many of which support unique, sensitive and fragile ecosystems which have been maintained and possibly enhanced, for thousands of years by the indigenous peoples, while supporting their survival and unique development of cultures.

There is not only a lack of but a reluctance to comprehend the critical importance of traditional land resources held by indigenous law and practice to the survival and well being of indigenous peoples and consequently to indigenous children.

There is, therefore, neither serious political commitment nor effort to assure that indigenous children are not deprived of these rights. With the growing marginalization of those called the Poor, whether they are indeed poor or more accurately rendered poor by deprivation of their wealth and non-recognition of their rights to it, indigenous children are probably the one of the most vulnerable sections of Indian society today.

The Government of India's First Periodic Report to the Committee on the Rights of the Child clubs together minorities, backward classes and Scheduled Tribes and Castes, under a chapter on "Special Protection measures" listing the constitutional and policy provisions allocated for these and the statistical evidence to demonstrate India's commitment .

However a very superficial look at the ground realities would disabuse any observer, regarding the actual extent of discrimination. Indigenous children remain at the bottom of all the statistics on survival, development.

Development and Displacement

The irony is that indigenous peoples' lands are the focus of much development activity especially in the last few decades. The exploitation of mineral resources, other natural resources such as timber or plantations of agro-industry, hydro-power generation are largely if not all implemented or planned on indigenous territories.

Why, therefore, do indigenous peoples and their indigenous children, not benefit from these initiatives? The answer is a two-fold discrimination. On the one hand, when such initiatives take place, no provisions are made for inclusion of indigenous peoples into the development paradigm posited by the projects.

On the other hand indigenous peoples (including their children) are very often perceived as an obstruction that must, one way or another, be removed at the lowest cost to the project. This almost always implies displacement without rehabilitative measures (which are extremely high cost). The statistics on displacement in India (some 40 million people at the lowest estimate) are in the majority indigenous.

Armed Conflict

The refusal of India to recognize that it hosts a number of extended armed conflicts results in endemic discrimination against children in such areas. Specifically, in the North East region of India and in some Eastern States, indigenous children are the sufferers of multiple discrimination. While in the North Eastern States, conflict between India's Security Forces and the numerous armed opposition groups is consistently reflected as "Terrorism," thereby allowing the Government to impose what amounts to extended martial law in the region.

In some areas several generations of children have grown up in this abnormal environment of suspension of their civil rights , including the right to life. While children of members of security forces receive considerable support, the vast majority who are inevitably indigenous, are discriminated against in rehabilitation or support programming.

Not only this, children are frequently targeted for aggressive or reprisal action by Security forces. The jurisdiction of the Juvenile Justice Act, itself a Special Legislation , is in conflict with national Security Legislation which awards martial law powers and impunity in the national courts to the Security forces . This in fact removes the vast majority of children taken into custody or sought to be taken into custody from the purview of the JJAct in these regions .

Corrective Measures in the Child Rights Framework

A clear understanding needs therefore to be developed regarding the linkage between children's issues and indigenous children's issues by all sectors of society and civil society in particular. While anti-discrimination positions and laws regarding children in general are a good baseline on which to start, this cannot be the standard set for indigenous children. Standards set for indigenous children must take into account their own realities: Primarily that they are indigenous. Their survival, protection, development and participation depend on their identification as indigenous in the first place. The refusal to name or identify them as such is the foundation of discrimination against them.

Request that Governments including of India, the International Community and the United Nations with its family of agencies, urgently consider following recommendations:

a. Governments must effect appropriate changes to ensure that the collective rights of children is addressed by the Convention on the Rights of the Child, including the rights of children, as addressed in the United Nations Draft Declaration on the Rights of Indigenous Children. (UNDDIP).

b. Committee on the Rights of the Child to urge upon governments to endorse the United Nations Draft Declaration on the Rights of Indigenous peoples.

c. Committee on the Rights of the Child to urge upon governments to formulate and implement policies and programme for promoting the rights of indigenous peoples.

d. Governments must ensure that the policies and programme on Employment, Healthcare, Education, Housing, and Public Representation does not discriminate against indigenous peoples.

e. Countries must promote and protect the right to life, physical and mental integrity of indigenous peoples, especially those in armed conflict.

f. Governments must ensure prompt and just punishment on all those found responsible for violations of human rights committed against children, including violations of the rights of juvenile detainees.

g. Governments must adhere to the principles and the provisions of the International Covenant on Civil and Political Rights, International Covenant on Economic, Social and Cultural Rights, International Covenant on the Elimination of Discrimination of all Forms of Discrimination with special consideration for indigenous children.

h. Expedite ratification and implementation of the Convention Against Torture and Other Forms of Cruel, Inhuman or Degrading Treatment or Punishment.

i. Ensure that countries respect the need for taking prior informed consent, participation of indigenous peoples in formulation, implementation and benefit sharing in all development projects

j. Mandatory training and education on the Convention on the Rights of the Child and collective rights of children, and the rights of Indigenous peoples among all levels of administrative institutions, civil authorities and armed forces in all countries and areas where indigenous peoples live.

4

Challenges to the Intellectual and Cultural Property Rights

Indigenous.people view the world they live in as an integrated whole. Their beliefs, knowledge, arts and other forms of cultural expression have been handed down through the generations. Their many stories, songs, dances, paintings and other forms of expression are therefore important aspects of indigenous cultural knowledge, power and identity. The Study on the Protection of the Cultural and Intellectual Property [Heritage] of Indigenous Peoples, by UN Special Rapporteur, Erica Irene Daes, of the Economic and Social Council's (ECOSOC) Sub-Commission on the Prevention of Discrimination and Protection of Minorities, confirms this approach.

According to Daes, a song or story is not a commodity or a form of property 'but one of the manifestations of an ancient and continuing relationship between people and their territory'. So she considers it is more appropriate and simpler to refer to the collective cultural heritage of each indigenous people rather than to make distinctions between indigenous peoples' 'cultural property' and 'intellectual property'. Any attempt 'to try to subdivide the heritage of indigenous peoples into separate legal categories such as "cultural", "artistic" or "intellectual" or into separate elements such as songs, stories, science or sacred sites', would be inappropriate. 'All elements of heritage should be managed and protected as a single, interrelated and integrated whole.'

> '... heritage includes all expressions of the relationship between the people, their land and the other living beings and spirits which share the land, and is the basis for maintaining social, economic and diplomatic relationships - through sharing - with other peoples. All of the aspects of heritage are interrelated and cannot be separated from the traditional Territory of the people concerned. What tangible and intangible items constitute the heritage of a particular indigenous people must be decided by the people themselves.'

The cultural and intellectual heritage of indigenous peoples comprises the traditional practices, knowledge and ways of life unique to a particular people. The guardians of an indigenous peoples' cultural and intellectual property are determined by the customs, laws and practices of the community, and can be individuals, a clan or the people as a whole. The heritage of indigenous people includes:

— language, art, music, dance, song and ceremony;
— agricultural, medicinal, technical and ecological knowledge and practices;
— spirituality, sacred sites and ancestral human remains;
— documentation of the above.

Included in indigenous peoples' heritage is intellectual property, which includes the information, practices, beliefs and philosophy that are unique to each indigenous culture. When traditional knowledge is removed from an indigenous community, the community loses control over the way in which that knowledge is used. In many cases, this system of knowledge evolved over centuries and is uniquely bound up with the indigenous people's customs, traditions, land and resources. Indigenous peoples have the right to protect their intellectual property, including the right to protect that property against its inappropriate use or exploitation.

As science and technology advance while natural resources dwindle, there is increased interest in appropriating indigenous knowledge for scientific and commercial purposes. Some research and pharmaceutical companies are patenting, or claiming ownership of traditional medicinal plants, even though indigenous peoples have used such plants for generations. In many cases, these companies do not recognize indigenous peoples' traditional ownership of such knowledge and deprive indigenous peoples of their fair share in the economic, medical or social benefits that accrue from the use of their traditional knowledge or practices.

Worldwide, despite international recognition of the right of indigenous peoples to preserve and protect their traditional practices, knowledge and ways of life, the cultural heritage of many indigenous peoples is under threat, and many indigenous peoples are prevented from enjoying their human rights and fundamental freedoms. In some countries, traditional and sacred sites are exploited or destroyed by the tourist industry. Many of these sites of spiritual and cultural significance are also ecological reserves that have been developed, conserved and managed by indigenous peoples through their traditional knowledge and practices. In other cases, indigenous art and sacred materials are used without the knowledge or permission of the indigenous artist or community. Many cultural artifacts and ancestral human remains that were taken from sites without the permission of indigenous peoples, are held in museums and collecting institutions around the world.

Struggles of Indigenous People

The struggle of indigenous peoples to protect intellectual and cultural rights ranges in form from resisting subjugation, territorial take-over, resources exploitation, the destruction of traditions, and infringement on customs and lifestyles, to fighting inhumane treatment, abuse and deprivation of human rights. The colonization of many countries resulted in oppression of indigenous peoples that continues to this day. In South-East Asia much of the struggle is over land and resources, as mining, timber and oil corporations encroach upon indigenous peoples' lands in search for profit. Indigenous peoples are becoming victims of forced resettlement, toxic pollution, diseases, militarization, starvation, social and cultural destruction, and the ruin of traditional ways of life.

According to some commentators, levels of global consumption are contributing to the threat to indigenous lands and the environment. Oil and mining companies have turned to indigenous lands to keep up with demand and indigenous peoples are subject to a 'discourse of dominance' by corporations and governments, which leaves them out of decisions affecting their lands. This process has been exacerbated by a shift in project financing away from shareholders and states and towards multilateral development agencies and regional banks.

An important part of the struggle has been the recognition and elucidation of the connections between environmental destruction and human rights abuses. Asian indigenous peoples' close connection to the land makes them particularly vulnerable to ecological damage. Extractive activities threaten patterns of subsistence, living conditions and cultural practices. In some cases governments deny indigenous peoples' civil and political rights in order to prevent them from resisting the incursions. Some states face challenges in reconciling international human rights commitments to indigenous peoples with the requirements of foreign direct investment.

Struggles of Asian Indigenous Groups

Since the early 1950s, Asian indigenous groups have sought and exploited pressure points to bolster their fight for their rights with varying degrees of success. They pursue multilateral strategies that include litigation, mass mobilizations, shareholder resolutions and public education. They have refined their rhetoric, linking environmental concerns to traditional human rights issues. Perhaps the most important innovation has been the increased flow of information through transnational networks and electronic media.

Asian indigenous peoples are now often able to wage their local struggles on a global front by working closely with international allies. A transnational movement of environmentalists, human rights workers, lawyers and indigenous organizations is emerging to defend indigenous rights. The greater international recognition now granted to indigenous rights issues has allowed indigenous organizations to gain legitimacy in their own countries.

Against the odds, indigenous peoples have had some successes. 'Divide and rule' tactics intended to break down their opposition have failed. Often, there are clear connections between resource extraction, human rights abuses and militarization. In some countries, governments have attempted to stifle the growing resistance of their indigenous populations. From the Philippines, Indonesia and Malaysia to Papua New Guinea, there is a burgeoning indigenous movement against both governments and resource depleting companies. This movement has brought together concerns about human rights and the environment. It is rural-based, grassroots-initiated and multiracial.

The movement also has concerns about globalization and unfair trade. Multinational corporations have sought to undermine opposition to their activities through mass media campaigns, challenges to tribal sovereignty and to local authorities. With their financial resources and political connections, oil, timber and mining companies can sometimes buy off impoverished communities. Yet the indigenous opposition remains vibrant and effective.

Support to initiatives by indigenous peoples

International support has focused on a number of indigenous peoples' initiatives, as discussed below.

Bangladesh. The struggle of the Jummas, the original inhabitants of the Chittagong Hill Tracts (CHT) is primarily to do with rights to land and resources. Many Jummas are losing their lands; they have been forcibly evicted by government military forces. Even when a government decree ordered that land should be returned, only a few were able to reclaim their lands. The Jummas are also being displaced because of the discovery and development of a gas-field in June 2002. The gas reserve development has affected traditional food sources like home-gardens and age-old community forests, and has caused environmental degradation.

On another front, more than 100, 000 Jummas have been uprooted over nearly four decades because of the construction of the Kaptai reservoir. Jummas are Buddhists and they also suffer from religious intolerance and discrimination by the majority Muslim population. NGOs like the Bangladesh Rural Advancement Committee (BARC), Bengalis' Union Council and the Tracts NGO Forum are leading the struggle for the full recognition of the Jummas' intellectual and cultural property rights as well as the preservation of their ethnic, religious and cultural identity. But there is little chance of success unless the government becomes genuinely concerned.

Nepal. The indigenous people of Nepal are campaigning for the amendment of the present Constitution to give indigenous peoples the right to self-government, so that they can control their own social, cultural and political development. They also demand equal language rights, inclusion of ethnic identity in the population census and the bill on nationalities, an end to the traffic in women and an end to bonded labour of the indigenous people, the Thamus.

India. Indigenous peoples in India are waging a struggle against the widespread plunder of germplasm (i.e. plant cells) and indigenous knowledge. Already, many plant resources have been lost, without recognition or recompense. Equally, they are campaigning against mega-dams which have displaced millions of people worldwide and have drowned large tracts of land once occupied by indigenous communities. Not only has their land been lost, but also natural resources, cultural treasures, traditions, lifestyles and customs. Under the government's new industrial policy, indigenous peoples' lands are being transferred to non-indigenous persons and to foreigners with corporate investments in India. The Adivasis, in particular, are trying to restore their rights over forests and to resist mining adventures that have already spoiled much of the land that still remains to indigenous peoples.

Sri Lanka. The Wanniyala-Aetto (forest beings), the Sri Lankan indigenous people, are being uprooted from their forest dwellings, shot at, detained, placed in reservations and sold as slaves or prostitutes. The International Movement Against All Forms of Discrimination and Racism (IMADR), an NGO, campaigns on their behalf. But the government has done little to intervene. The Wanniyala-Aetto women, in particular, bear the brunt of this inhuman treatment.

Tibet. The Tibetans are denied their fundamental right to self-determination and suffer from human rights abuses, underdevelopment, marginalization and repression. The Chinese authorities do not consult with the Tibetans over development processes, and the Tibetans are discriminated against in terms of employment. Their culture is also in danger: many of their schools have been closed, their monasteries destroyed and customary lifestyles repressed. Tibetans in the diaspora continue to put pressure on the Chinese government, but, so far, to no effect.

Taiwan. In 2001, indigenous activists won a victory when the government granted autonomy to indigenous peoples. This has meant that indigenous peoples are now included in parliamentary elections, and they can elect their local chiefs and councillors. The Pangcah people (one of 12 indigenous tribes) were also allowed to elect a chieftain.

Philippines. Many NGOs are working for indigenous peoples' intellectual and cultural property rights in the Philippines and, seemingly, their efforts have paid off, with the passing of Indigenous Peoples' Rights Act (IPRA) in 1997. But the body set up to implement IPRA, the National Commission on Indigenous Peoples (NCIP), suffered from political infighting and has yet to be reorganized.

Land ownership remains an issue because of holdups in processing the Certificates of Ancestral Domain Titles (CADTs) by the NCIP. CADTs give formal recognition of indigenous peoples' ancestral rights to land. As of June 2002, only one CADT had been completed, of the 100 promised by President Gloria Macapagal Arroyo. The government has also reneged on earlier promises, allowing the construction of two mega-dams, San Roque and Casecnan, despite the protests of indigenous people, and the laying of oil pipelines in Palawan, which is causing tension among indigenous people.

Indonesia. The most significant result of indigenous peoples' struggle for recognition of their rights is the government's granting of decentralized power. It gave 'adat'-based (traditional-based) villages powers beyond the standard notions of indigenous rights in international legal discourse. One power transferred is that 'the adat village has the authority to regulate and manage the interests of the local community based on its origins, local customs and traditions that are recognized within the system of national government'. It is important to note that there is explicit reference to indigenous cultural and political traditions.

The decentralization law 'recognizes and honours the adat communities as well as their traditional rights as far as these remain a living reality and are in line with the development of the society, as well as the principles of the Republic of Indonesia as a unitary state, and as they are regulated by laws'. However, some smaller adat communities are oppressed by larger groups and the state is finding it difficult to address this. Examples of these oppressed minorities are the shifting cultivators and hunter gatherer tribes like the Kubu, Orang Rimba, Talak Mamak, Sakai and the Punan.

Malaysia. Encroachment into ancestral lands and intimidation are two of the many problems facing Malaysian indigenous peoples. There is no pause in the exploitation of their resources and appropriation of indigenous territories. However, two small victories have been won by the indigenous peoples. Four Iban people won their cases against a pulp and paper company that trespassed into their lands. In another victory, a Malaysian court ordered that the Orang Asli have the right to use and derive profit from their customary and ancestral land. Apart from these victories, however, the struggle to give indigenous peoples the right to their traditional territories has been waged for some time without much success, as the government shows little interest in addressing the problem.

Thailand. In 1997, the Chao-Chaos, a mixed grouping of indigenous tribes in northern Thailand numbering almost a million, were granted a peoples' Constitution which allowed them to participate in the democratic process in the country. They are led by the Assembly of Indigenous and Tribal peoples of Thailand (AITT). Together with the Northern Farmers Network, AITT is pressing for the adoption of a community Forest Bill, which will give indigenous peoples recognition of their right to their traditional resources and management practices.

Cambodia. The year 2001 saw positive developments in Cambodia with regard to indigenous peoples' struggle for land rights and the protection of their forests and natural resources. Local activists and NGOs headed the campaign for a new law that gave provision for land tenure for indigenous people. Those who now have ownership and control of their lands are enjoying their rights to their resources, such as in the tapping of resin and development of inland fisheries. The government created the Department of Ethnic Minorities Development in

January 2002, and heeded the complaints of the Khmers against a military general who almost defrauded the local peoples of their lands and forest resources.

Vietnam. Vietnam has a government that is oppressive towards its indigenous population and does not allow advocacy activities. In October 2001, the government's Ministry of Agriculture and Rural Development and the Department for Sedentary Farming announced a campaign to 'wipe out traditional nomadic life and swidden farming' of its indigenous population. The government is attempting to eradicate traditional shifting agriculture, which is the lifeline of most highland indigenous peoples including the Banar, Ehde, Jarai, Koho and Mnong tribes, thousands of whom were imprisoned after calling for independence in February 2001.

The lifestyles, customs and traditions of these people are affected as the military conduct restrictive campaigns. Many of these indigenous people have fled to Cambodia. The government has allowed the construction of three mega-dams, which threaten the livelihood of indigenous people living along the banks of the Mekong and Da rivers, and some 100, 000 people have already been forcibly evicted. Today, social activists working with and for Vietnamese indigenous tribes plan and work covertly, in danger of being imprisoned or put to death as 'traitors' to the new republic.

Laos. Laos has a similar policy to that of Vietnam, which aims to eradicate all traditional forms of agriculture by its indigenous peoples. As a result, hundreds of thousands of Hmong are being removed from their ancestral lands and relocated to areas which are not suitable for their lifestyle and cultural practices. There is little resistance from the Hmong, even as they continue to live under extreme pressure. The government has removed the indigenous populations using military force and allowed gold and copper mining concessions on ancestral lands. There is also a plan to build a mega-dam on the Nakai Plateau, where some 350, 000 indigenous people live.

Burma/Myanmar. It is perhaps only in Burma/Myanmar, out of all the states in Asia, that the indigenous peoples form a majority. But under its military rule, political detentions, harassment, militarization, military offensives, forced labour in labour camps and an educational crisis are widespread. Women face rape, 'marriage' to military men and are trafficked by the military as slaves, labourers and prostitutes. With the popular democratic leader Daw Aung San Suu Kyi still banned from making a political comeback, the future remains uncertain. As many as 2 million internally displaced persons and refugees have been generated during decades of conflict.

The Mataatua Declaration

One initiative by indigenous peoples' representatives and advocates was the First International Conference on the Cultural and Intellectual Property Rights of Indigenous Peoples held in Aotearoa/New Zealand on 12-18 June 1993. It declared that 'Indigenous peoples of the world have the right to self-determination and in exercising that right must be recognized as the exclusive owners of their cultural and intellectual property.' The conference was held at a time when, as its way of recognizing the role of indigenous peoples in biodiversity protection and conservation, the UN had declared 1993 the International Year for the World's Indigenous Peoples. Over 150 delegates from 14 countries attended the historic conference, including indigenous representatives from Aotearoa/New Zealand, Australia, the Cook Islands, Fiji, Japan, Panama, Peru, the Philippines, Surinam and the USA.

The representatives met over six days to discuss a range of issues - the value of indigenous knowledge, biodiversity and biotechnology, customary environmental arts, music, language and other physical and spiritual cultural forms. The conference resulted in what is now referred to as the Mataatua Declaration on Cultural and Intellectual Property Rights of Indigenous Peoples. The Mataatua Declaration reaffirms a call put forward in Rio de Janiero, Brazil, a year earlier. In its Preamble, the Declaration reaffirms the efforts of the UN Member States to adopt Agenda 21, particularly Chapter 26, Section 4b. The section states: 'Adopt or strengthen appropriate policies and/ or legal instruments that will protect indigenous intellectual and cultural property and the right to preserve customary and administrative systems and practices'.

The Mataatua Declaration also listed various recommendations. Among them was the recommendation that states, and national and international agencies, must recognize that indigenous peoples are the exclusive owners of their cultural and intellectual property rights. On biodiversity, the Declaration affirms that states, and national and international agencies, must recognize the 'traditional guardianship' of indigenous flora and fauna. The Declaration also provides that indigenous peoples should manage the commercialization of any traditional plants and medicines. The Declaration includes a set of recommendations for indigenous peoples themselves; for states and national and international agencies; and for the UN.

Charter of the Indigenous-Tribal Peoples of the Tropical Forests

Indigenous peoples' organizations were also responsible for another similar initiative. This is the Charter of the Indigenous-Tribal Peoples of the Tropical Forests, a federation of organizations of indigenous peoples in tropical forest countries in Africa, Asia and the Americas. Particularly emphasizing indigenous peoples' forest communities, the Charter seeks to reverse the 'hundreds of years of continual encroachment and colonization of our territories and the undermining of our lives, livelihoods and cultures' because of destructive industries such as logging and mining.

Formulated on 15 February 1992 in Penang, Malaysia, the Charter also makes bold pronouncements on indigenous peoples' ownership of the tropical forests of the world. Article 2 states: 'We declare that we are the original peoples, the rightful owners and the cultures that defend the tropical forests of the world.' In declaring ownership over the tropical forests of the world, indigenous and tribal peoples have asserted their right to control, use and manage their own ancestral territories, which include tropical forests and all their wildlife and biodiversity resources.

The Charter also challenges the precept that forests and their resources are simply economic commodities with price tags. 'Our territories and forests are to us more than an economic resource', states Article 3. 'For us, they are life itself and have an integral and spiritual value for our communities. They are fundamental to our social, cultural, spiritual, economic and political survival as distinct peoples.' Under a section on 'Respect for Our Rights, 'the Charter contains provisions which call for other peoples to respect indigenous and tribal peoples' 'human, political, social, economic and cultural rights ... and right to self-determination'. Incorporated in this section is a call to approve and apply the Draft Declaration on the Rights of Indigenous Peoples, which 'must affirm and guarantee our right to self-determination'. The same section stresses the need for 'an effective international mechanism and tribunal to protect us against the violation of our rights ...'The call of the federation for other peoples to respect indigenous and tribal peoples' right to self-determination also includes indigenous peoples' right to have full control over their biodiversity resources and intellectual and cultural knowledge. But the Charter has separate sections on Biodiversity and Conservation and on Intellectual Property. Article 40 specifically provides:

> 'Programs related to biodiversity must respect the collective rights of our peoples to cultural and intellectual property, genetic resources, gene banks, biotechnology and knowledge of biological diversity; this should include our participation in the management of any such project in our territories, as well as control of any benefits that derive from them.'

Another important provision is Article 44: ' Since we highly value our traditional technologies and believe that our biotechnologies can make important contributions to humanity, including developed countries, we demand guaranteed rights to our intellectual property, and control over the development and manipulation of this knowledge.' In summary, the Charter, like the Mataatua Declaration, has strong provisions on indigenous and tribal peoples' sole control over their ancestral territories and over their natural and biodiversity resources. The Charter is also strong in calling for international recognition of indigenous and tribal peoples' right to their cultural and intellectual property and knowledge.

UN Efforts to Protect Indigenous Peoples' ICPR

As indigenous peoples in Asia strengthen their effort to win recognition of their rights, a number of international instruments have been initiated by the UN to support the rights of indigenous peoples to protect and enjoy their cultural heritage. One was the Draft Principles and Guidelines for the Protection of the Heritage of Indigenous People, which recommends standards for governments to ensure that the heritage of indigenous peoples survives for future generations and continues to enrich the common heritage of humanity. The UN Educational, Scientific and Cultural Organization (UNESCO) also co-established the Model Treaty on the Protection of Expressions of Folklore against Illicit Exploitation.

The Treaty recognizes indigenous peoples as the traditional owners of artistic heritage, including folklore, music and dance, created within indigenous territories and passed down through the generations. Yet these international enactments have failed to provide a working system and applicable standards that could ensure the implementation and enforcement of the instruments. In particular, the nature of indigenous peoples' intellectual property, which is often inseparable from spiritual, cultural, social and economic aspects of indigenous life, and the notion of collective ownership of such property, are not adequately addressed in existing international intellectual property law.

This is not to say that there have been no international efforts to address the problem of indigenous peoples' resources. The most widespread and fundamental threat to indigenous peoples' resources is the failure (often by states) to respect and protect the right of indigenous peoples to control their own territories under their customary forms of ownership. Recognizing this, the UN has sponsored several initiatives to resolve the problem.

The Stockholm Conference

The 1972 UN Conference on Human Environment in Stockholm was the first major international discussion on environmental issues. The conference started the process of investigating the contradictions between the priorities of economic growth and environmental protection. The governments of some Northern countries, which have used up their own resources and appropriated the resources of the South through colonization, have begun to push for environmental protection. In contrast, governments of Southern countries have sought to exploit whatever is left of their natural resources to bring about more economic growth. Since the Stockholm Conference, the debate on how to balance environmental concerns and economic development has continued. Also, the issue of biodiversity has gained legal and political prominence.

World Commission on Environment and Development

Taking off from the Stockholm Conference, the UN General Assembly created the World Commission on Environment and

Development (WCED), which issued its report, Our Common Future, popularly known as the Brundtland Report, in 1987. The report introduced the concept of 'sustainable development', which attempts to make economic growth and environmental protection complementary and mutually dependent. The Brundtland Report also emphasized the role of indigenous peoples in preserving biodiversity.

> 'The isolation of many such people [i. e. indigenous peoples] has meant the preservation of a traditional way of life in close harmony with the natural environment. Their very survival has depended on their ecological awareness and adaptation. ...These communities are the repositories of vast accumulations of traditional knowledge and experience that links humanity with its ancient origins.'

> 'Their disappearance is a loss for the larger society, which could learn a great deal from their traditional skills in sustainably managing very complex ecological systems. It is a terrible irony that as formal development reaches more deeply into rainforest, deserts, and other isolated environments, it tends to destroy the only cultures that have proved able to thrive in these environments.'

The Brundtland Report recommended:

> 'The starting point for a just and humane society for such groups [i. e. indigenous peoples] is the recognition and protection of their traditional rights to land and the other resources that sustain their way of life - rights they may define in terms that do not fit into the standard legal systems. These groups' own institutions to regulate rights and obligations are crucial for maintaining the harmony with nature and environmental awareness characteristic of the traditional way of life. Hence the recognition of traditional rights must go hand in hand with measures to protect the local institutions that enforce responsibility in resource use. The recognition must also give local communities a decisive voice in the decisions about resource use in their area.'

The Rio Earth Summit

The concept of 'sustainable development', introduced in the Brundtland Report, became the theme of the June 1992 UN Conference on Environment and Development (UNCED) in Rio de Janiero, Brazil, also known as the Rio Earth Summit. The Earth Summit was a watershed, and led to the production of vital documents, including Agenda 21 and the Convention on Biological Diversity (CBD).

Despite their limitations, Agenda 21 and the CBD can help advance the struggle of indigenous peoples in protecting their intellectual and cultural property rights. Agenda 21, particularly Chapter 26, recognizes and seeks to strengthen the role of indigenous peoples and local communities in 'sustainable development'. Chapter 26, Section 3 provides that in 'full partnership' with indigenous peoples and their communities, governments and, where appropriate, intergovernmental organizations should aim to set in motion 'a process to empower indigenous peoples'.

Convention on Biological Diversity

Critics say the Convention on Biological Diversity (1992) was produced at the 'behest of interests mostly from the North (governments, corporations and NGOs)'. As one critic noted, the CBD actually evolved from the initiatives of Northern groups such as the IUCN (World Conservation Union), which led to the exploration of the possibility of negotiating an international treaty on bio-diversity. The IUCN prepared various drafts on in situ conservation within and outside protected areas.

It is not surprising that the initial driving force for Northern groups such as the IUCN was the issue of conservation, because Northern governments were concerned and continue to be concerned about how to access the South's biodiversity. Before the 1972 Stockholm Conference, genetic resources were regarded as open-access resources, meaning anybody had the right to use these resources for free. Genetic resources are the heritable characteristics of a plant or animal of real or potential benefit to people. They include modern cultivars (i. e. cultivated varieties) and breeds; traditional cultivars and breeds; special genetic stocks (breeding lines, mutants, etc.); wild relatives of domesticated species; and genetic variants of wild resource species.

The situation that the CBD seeks to address is not only the alarming loss of biodiversity, but also its uneven distribution in the world. The developed North is biodiversity-poor but, in many cases thanks to indigenous peoples, the South has retained some of its biodiversity resources. Southern countries have found it necessary to assert their sovereign rights over their natural and biodiversity resources. Principle 2 of the Rio Declaration, and the CBD, reiterated the sovereign right of states over their natural and biodiversity resources. Article 3 of CBD states:

> 'States have, in accordance with the Charter of the United Nations and the principles of international law, the sovereign right to exploit their own resources pursuant to their environmental policies, and the responsibility to ensure that activities within their jurisdiction or control do not cause damage to the environment of other states or of areas beyond the limits of national jurisdiction.'

The national sovereignty principle answers key concerns of Southern governments. But critics like the Barcelonabased Genetic Resources Action International (GRAIN) say it does not necessarily work in favour of indigenous peoples, who are acknowledged to have helped sustain and nurture the world's biodiversity resources. Governments of both North and South still do not recognize the rights of indigenous peoples to their territories and resources, much less their right to self-determination. Indigenous peoples' leaders and advocates also complain that the CBD does not explicitly recognize that indigenous peoples have such rights.

Vandana Shiva, a noted Indian environmentalist and physicist, commented early on that the USA agenda was to have the CBD pave the way for free access to the South's biodiversity while at the same time ensuring that intellectual property rights to the USA's own technologies, particularly biotechnology, are protected. Critics have pointed out that the CBD is strong on patents but weak in protecting the rights of indigenous peoples and local communities to their biodiversity and knowledge. According to those who have been monitoring the CBD's formulation, the CBD is basically a framework convention which lays down the goals and policies for achieving the objectives stated in Article 1:

'The objectives of this Convention, to be pursued in accordance with its relevant provisions, are the conservation of biological diversity, the sustainable use of its components and the fair and equitable sharing of the benefits arising out of the utilization of genetic resources, including appropriate access to genetic resources and by appropriate transfer of relevant technologies, taking into account all rights over these resources and to technologies, and by appropriate funding.'

The CBD's Article 8j outlines what benefits should redound to indigenous peoples:

— respect and protection for the knowledge, innovations and practices of indigenous peoples and local communities;

— promotion of the wider application of these with the participation and prior informed consent of the knowledge holders; and

— equitable sharing of benefits.

It should be noted, however, that the Article does not mention any rights at all. It merely calls for respect and protection of indigenous knowledge. In various arenas, such as the Conference of Parties, indigenous peoples' representatives and advocates have tried to lobby for the inclusion of indigenous rights in the CBD, but without success. Indigenous peoples can put the provisions of Article 8j to good use, however, particularly the three main components cited earlier.

The CBD affirms the sovereignty of nations over their biological resources. It also accepts the concept of intellectual property over living things and encourages bilateral arrangements between those who want access to resources and knowledge (for example, corporations) and governments. The Convention does not define protection at the level of the community, thus setting the stage for intercommunity conflicts or conflicts between a government and its communities. Overall, the Convention lacks teeth: it has no mechanisms to control outsiders' access to indigenous bio-resources (for example, a binding code of conduct) and no mechanisms to determine the equitable sharing of benefits.

Draft Declaration on the Rights of Indigenous Peoples

Now almost a decade old, the Draft Declaration on the Rights of Indigenous Peoples has remained just that - a draft. The Draft was produced by a special UN body -the UN Working Group on Indigenous Populations (WGIP), which was created under the Sub-Commission on the Prevention of Discrimination and Protection of Minorities of the UN Commission on Human Rights (UNCHR). The Draft is far from perfect, according to those who helped shape it, for example Vicky Tauli-Corpuz, who said the Draft has many limitations because it still operates within the 'statist framework' of the UN. But she also said that the Draft seeks to address indigenous peoples' collective rights, such as their right to self-determination, right to survival, right to cultural, religious, spiritual and linguistic identity, and the right to control of ancestral territories and resources.

Despite its imperfections and limitations, the Draft contains provisions that lobbyists for indigenous peoples can use in pushing for strong policy recommendations. The following are some Articles relevant to the relationship of indigenous peoples to their territories and resources, genetic resources, and intellectual and cultural heritage or indigenous knowledge:

— Article 24: 'Indigenous peoples have the right to their traditional medicines and health practices, including the right to the protection of vital medicinal plants, animals and minerals.'

— Article 25: 'Indigenous peoples have the right to maintain and strengthen their distinctive spiritual and material relationship with the lands, territories, waters, and coastal seas and other resources, which they have traditionally owned or otherwise occupied or used, and to uphold their responsibilities to future generations in this regard.'

— Article 26: 'Indigenous peoples have the right to own, develop, control and use the lands and territories, including the total environment of the lands, air, waters, coastal seas, sea ice, flora and fauna, and other resources, which they have traditionally owned or otherwise occupied or used. This includes the right to the full recognition of their laws, traditions and customs, land-tenure systems, and institutions for the development and management of resources, and the right to effective measures by States to prevent any interference with, alienation of, and encroachment upon these rights.'

— Article 29: 'Indigenous peoples are entitled to the recognition of the full ownership, control and protection of their cultural and intellectual property. They have the right to special measures to control, develop, and protect their sciences, technologies and cultural manifestations, including human and other genetic resources, seeds, medicines, knowledge of the properties of fauna and flora, oral traditions, literatures, designs, and visual and performing arts.'

As a whole, the Draft has clearly established that the rights of indigenous peoples to their indigenous knowledge, innovations and practices, which are referred to as intellectual and cultural heritage, cannot be separated from indigenous territories and resources. These rights are interlinked with the distinct relationships indigenous peoples have built up around their land and resources. Although it needs to be improved, the Draft contains minimum standards that promote the rights and welfare of indigenous peoples, including their intellectual and cultural property rights. But many governments do not support the Draft. The Draft was approved by the Sub-Commission on the Prevention of Discrimination and Protection of Minorities and was brought before the UNCHR.

But the UNCHR did not adopt the Draft. Instead, it established the Open-ended Inter-sessional Working Group to elaborate on the Draft Declaration. This body has met eight times since 1995, but the governments of Australia, Canada, New Zealand and the USA strongly oppose many of the principles and articles of the Draft. These governments were at one in rejecting, for example, the Draft's provision recognizing indigenous peoples' right to self-determination, arguing that international instruments generally speak of individual and not collective rights.

Those indigenous peoples who have been closely monitoring the Draft are united and firm in their stand that the UN should adopt the Draft in its original form. The Draft has in fact become a key reference point in discussions of indigenous peoples' rights. Indigenous peoples' representatives always cited the Draft when they lobbied at the Rio Earth Summit and over the CBD. Some governments have referred to the Draft Declaration when drafting their national laws on indigenous peoples' rights.

One of the drawbacks of the Draft Declaration is that it is non-binding, even if it is adopted by the UN General Assembly. This means that the Declaration will not create any obligations for any country under international law. In other words, the adoption of a declaration on the rights of indigenous peoples will not render a nation legally accountable to the international community for its actions towards its indigenous people. The Declaration will be an aspirational document, which imposes no obligations of implementation. It is likely, however, that the Declaration will contribute to a growing body of customary international law in the area of indigenous peoples' rights. Customary international law is associated with the concept of state practice.

ILO Convention 169

The International Labour Organization is the only international body which has produced an international legally binding instrument on indigenous peoples - ILO Convention 169. ILO Convention 169 ratified an earlier international instrument adopted by the ILO in 1957 -the Indigenous and Tribal Populations Convention 107, which was the first attempt to codify indigenous peoples' rights in international law. Adopted in Geneva in June 1989, ILO Convention 169 hails the 'distinctive contributions of indigenous and tribal peoples to the cultural diversity and social and ecological harmony of humankind and to international cooperation and understanding'. It also addresses land and resource rights concerns.

— Article 13 states: '... (G)overnments shall respect the special importance for the cultures and spiritual values of the peoples concerned of their relationship with the lands or territories, or both as applicable, which they occupy or otherwise use, and in particular the collective aspects of this relationship. The use of the term "lands" in Articles 15 and 16 shall include the concept of territories, which covers the total environment of the areas which the peoples concerned occupy or otherwise use.'

— Article 14 also provides: 'The rights of ownership and possession of the peoples concerned over the lands, which they traditionally occupy, shall be recognized. In addition, measures shall be taken in appropriate cases to safeguard the right of the peoples concerned to use lands not exclusively occupied by them, but to which they traditionally had access for their subsistence and traditional activities.'

— Article 15 states: 'The rights of the peoples concerned to the natural resources pertaining to their lands shall be specially safeguarded. These rights include the right of these peoples to participate in the use, management and conservation of these resources.'

Like the Draft Declaration on the Rights of Indigenous Peoples, ILO Convention 169 not only acknowledges, but recognizes the rights of indigenous and tribal peoples to their territories, lands and resources, which include biodiversity and wildlife resources. The Convention can serve as reference and framework for future agreements, which bear directly on indigenous peoples and their natural and biodiversity resources and intellectual and cultural property rights. Indigenous peoples who lobbied at the Rio Earth Summit and the CBD negotiations also did not fail to invoke ILO Convention 169. One problem is that, as of August 2002, only 17 countries had ratified ILO Convention 169.

The only Asia-Pacific country that has ratified the Convention is Fiji. The other countries that have ratified the Convention are Argentina, Bolivia, Brazil, Colombia, Costa Rica, Denmark, Dominica, Ecuador, Guatemala, Honduras, Mexico, The Netherlands, Norway, Paraguay, Peru and Venezuela. It is unfortunate that, over a decade after ILO Convention 169 came into force, controversy continues. The Convention has been criticized for not fully embodying the indigenous point of view. Indeed, some imply that the wording of the document is a direct affront to the rights of indigenous peoples.

Directly after the adoption of Convention 169 by the ILO, the Indigenous Peoples Preparatory Meeting in Geneva produced a resolution rejecting it and asking governments not to ratify it. Yet, despite its shortcomings, most indigenous leaders and organizations see the Convention as an important step towards an improvement of their human rights situation and are eager for governments to ratify it.

Governments' Efforts to Protect ICPR

Enactment of Laws

Creating, modifying and implementing national laws on traditional knowledge and genetic resources is the most visible action taken by governments. This law-making is spurred on by pressure to meet international agreements. The general trend in Asia is towards the commercialization of genetic resources and the expansion of IPRs over traditional knowledge. This trend is most visible in the adoption of Union for the Protection of New Varieties of Plants (UPOV)-style legislation that does little to recognize and reward farmers' innovation in plant-breeding.

UPOV is an intergovernmental organization with headquarters in Geneva, Switzerland. It was established by the International Convention for the Protection of New Varieties of Plants to oversee the protection of new varieties of plants under an intellectual property right. Attempts have been made to slow down this trend until impact assessments of the proposed changes are fully explored, but with little success. Nevertheless, many developing countries are also attempting to promote legal changes to protect biodiversity and related traditional knowledge.

In some countries, governments have seemingly made efforts to empower local communities, such as in the Philippines with the Indigenous Peoples' Rights Act (IPRA); in Thailand, where the indigenous peoples were granted a Peoples' Assembly and the introduction of the Thai Traditional Medicine Law that seeks to protect traditional knowledge related to medicinal plants; in Bangladesh, where a Department of Indigenous Peoples Development was created along with the drafting of a Biodiversity and Community Knowledge Act; and in India and Indonesia where an amendment to the Indian Constitution and the decentralization law allow village bodies (panchayats) and adat villages to take decisions on local biological resources.

But new laws can also bring in more administrative structures and accompanying bureaucracy, and often depend on political will. KAMPI (Kasamahan ng mga Magbubukid sa Pilipinas), an alliance of indigenous peoples' organizations in the Philippines, explained how the Local Government Units still fail to recognize and respect the traditional systems of self-governance in the Philippines. At the local level, multiple bodies and groups, often with overlapping jurisdictions, may increase the problem of local resource management and create unnecessary conflicts with informal systems of control and management.

Databases

Electronic databases and digital libraries are gaining popularity in several government-initiated projects for documenting traditional knowledge. There is strongly divided opinion on the efficacy of such databases to prevent biopiracy. Some say that centralization makes information inaccessible to rural communities and alienates them. Others defend documentation in the light of dying oral knowledge and the erosion of the social processes by which the knowledge of a community or tribe is transmitted to the next generation. There is consensus, however, that any collection of traditional knowledge data must have the prior informed consent (PIC) of the communities.

In situations where such knowledge is not already in the public domain, governments would need to ensure that the disclosure of traditional knowledge is voluntary. Also, much traditional knowledge that is currently in the public domain may not be there with the consent of the concerned communities. Putting such knowledge into databases supposedly to prevent patents being taken out would only be building on an earlier wrong. There are other practical issues that need to be resolved such as the basis of user fees, valuation of the information collected, possible claims of intellectual property over the databases themselves and the recovery of operational costs of these databases.

Researches

The number of research centres and research projects in the region has increased and includes domestic ventures, foreign collaborations and corporate sponsorship. Research in traditional knowledge raises questions about the relationship between academic institutions and industry. In some cases, research is apparently carried out for the benefit of local and traditional communities. For example, in India, the All-India Coordinated Research Project on Ethnobotany has identified tribal and other community uses for several thousand species of plants, including medicinal plants. It remains to be seen whether the communities actually do benefit from this project.

In Laos, a unique system of governmental promotion and protection of the population's traditional medicinal practices has evolved under the auspices of the Ministry of Health. A Traditional Medicine Research Centre has been set up, which is a potential tool for protecting traditional medicinal knowledge of the tribes in the country. However, research does not always benefit the original knowledge-holders. In Malaysia, a plant in the Sarawak rainforest is now being tested to determine whether it presents a cure for prostate cancer. The Malaysian government has not released the plant's name for security reasons, but they are reportedly working with an Australian company to bring it to the market.

In China, in what was billed as a milestone for traditional Chinese medicine, two foreign firms joined in 2000 with one of mainland China's oldest houses of medicine to research and develop Chinese pharmaceuticals for overseas markets. Pharmagenesis from the USA and Orchid from France signed a contract with Lerentang from Tienjin to invest US$9 million in joint research on the active ingredients in traditional Chinese medicines. Indigenous peoples are concerned that such projects provide income only for the pharmaceutical and medical companies and the states involved.

Research projects funded by international organizations do not necessarily challenge this phenomenon. 'Our objection is against the collection of traditional knowledge without proper benefits to locals', argued Hemantha Withanage of the Environmental Foundation Ltd, Sri Lanka, talking about a 'Conservation and Sustainable Use of Medicinal Plants' project jointly funded by the World Bank and Global Environmental Facility. Another case from Sri Lanka is that of US Cornell University's contract with the University of Sri Jayawardenapura for the export of 905 plant varieties until 2005, which provides no compensation for the peoples who helped identify the plants and explain their uses.

In one research project, a custody battle arose between Thailand and a UK university over local fungi strains with potential medicinal uses. At issue was a collection of more than 200 strains of marine fungi, taken from mangrove and coastal areas in southern Thailand, that were stored in laboratories in the UK's Portsmouth University. A Portsmouth University professor took the marine fungi specimens in 1993, as part of a research project sponsored by a pharmaceutical company. They were finally returned years later. Nepal has its share of problems of resource exploitation alongside research projects. A university professor from Illinois, USA, collected the Dhobini plant (Mussadena sp.) from the Gurung community of Chhamdila, Nepal without any arrangement for benefit-sharing in case of commercialization.

In response, some governments are tightening procedures and guidelines for research projects. For example, in India, biomedical research guidelines require that:

> 'a Folklore medicine/Ethnomedicine is ready for commercialization after it has been scientifically found to be effective, then the legitimate rights/share of the Tribe or Community from whom the knowledge was gathered should be taken care of appropriately while applying for the Intellectual Property Rights and Patents for the product'.

Also, the Indian Ministry of Environment and Forests issued a circular in 1998 to all universities and research institutes which prevented the transfer of genetic material outside the country without prior informed consent and a proper material transfer agreement.

Intellectual Property Rights Regimes

Intellectual property rights (IPRs), as the term suggests, are rights to ideas and information which are used in new inventions or processes. These rights enable the holder to exclude imitators from marketing such inventions or processes for a specified time; in exchange, the holder is required to disclose the formula or idea behind the product/process. The effect of IPRs is therefore monopoly over commercial exploitation of an idea/information, for a limited period. As IPRs are actually mechanisms to protect individual and industrial 'inventions', they are usually in effect for a specified period. These legal rights can be attached to information if the information can be applied to making a product that is distinctive and useful.

Legal rights prevent others from copying, selling or importing a product without authorization. In essence, there are six forms of intellectual property: patents, plant-breeders' rights, copyright, trademarks, industrial designs and trade secrets. Currently, there are a number of IPR regimes in operation in Europe, the USA and elsewhere. The newer laws tend to cover a broad spectrum of life forms and grant astonishing degrees of ownership to the patentholder. Corporations are well aware of how cost-efficient it is to tap the knowledge of communities that live with and depend on biodiversity for their survival. Pharmaceutical transnational corporations (TNCs) have taken plant samples from tropical forests (identified and genetically manipulated by indigenous peoples) to use as raw materials in developing new drugs.

In Asia, agricultural companies took disease-resistant seeds (identified and genetically manipulated by indigenous peoples). After some modifications, this genetic material was patented, mainly in the USA, and the resulting seeds or products were marketed. Moving a single gene from one spot to another within a cell, whether or not it causes an actual variation in the next generation, creates a sufficiently 'new' plant variety to qualify as a patentable invention. Corporations have realized enormous benefits from their free access to genetic materials, especially in the case of crop plants from developing countries. This gave birth to rights over plant varieties, or breeders' rights, which gave the right-holder limited regulatory powers over the marketing of 'their' varieties.

Until recently, most countries allowed farmers and other breeders to be exempted from the provisions of such rights, as long as they did not indulge in branded commercial transactions of the varieties. In many Asian countries, patents with full monopolistic restrictions are now applicable to plant varieties, micro-organisms and genetically modified animals. In 1980, the US Supreme Court ruled that microbiologist Ananda Chakrabarty's patent claim for a genetically engineered bacterial strain was permissible. This legitimized the view that anything made by humans and not found in nature was patentable. Genetically altered animals, such as the infamous 'onco-mouse' of Harvard University (bred for cancer research), were also patented.

Finally, several patent claims have been made, and some granted, on human genetic material, including on material that has hardly been altered from its natural state. Until very recently, these trends were restricted to some countries, which could not impose them on others. However, with the signing of the Trade-Related Aspects of Intellectual Property Rights agreement (TRIPS), this has changed. TRIPS requires that all signatory countries (that is, more than 115 states, of which 70 are from the South) accept patenting of micro-organisms and microbiological processes, and some 'effective' form of IPR on plant varieties, either patents or some sui generis (new) version.

TRIPS allows countries to exclude animals and plants per se from patentability. The history of IPRs shows that the monopolistic hold of governments, corporations and some individuals over biological resources and related knowledge is continuously increasing. A substantial amount of this monopolization is built on and through the appropriation of the resources conserved and knowledge generated by indigenous peoples.

Impact of IPRs on Asian Farmers

The demand of corporations to apply IPR regimes to biodiversity is based on the false premise that only their investments need to be rewarded. The toil of Southern farmers in domesticating, breeding and conserving biodiversity over centuries is conveniently forgotten. The existing IPR agreements fail to recognize the rights of indigenous and local communities to their own knowledge and innovations. Countries in the South have strongly argued that multinationals from the industrialized world exploit their biological wealth and then sell the patented products back to them at excessive prices.

The growth of the biotechnology industries, combined with the loss of biological diversity worldwide, has focused the attention of governments, corporations and others on access to and control of genetic resources - mainly because of the tremendous potential for generating commercial profits. The traditional lifestyles, knowledge and biogenetic resources of indigenous peoples have become commodities, to be bought, sold and traded. As a rule, farmers save some of their crop to use as seed in the following year. Under US IPR regimes, farmers would have to pay royalties on the seeds from patented seeds, and even where farmers were the source of the original stocks, they would not be allowed, under GATT rules, to market or use them. The IPR to a folk variety would include the rights to control the use of the folk variety, and the rights to the information coded in the DNA as a result of selection by farmers and their farming systems.

Commercial plant breeding is in the hands of a few TNCs that now control all the significant gene banks. TNCs are developing plants that respond to their own agrochemicals. TNCs are also working on genetic modifications aimed at converting non-hybrid fertile plants, such as wheat, into sterile hybrids. If a gene from another plant could induce sterility, seeds would have to be purchased each year. If IPR systems continue to evolve in this direction, farmers will have to pay royalties for patented seeds; will become dependent on one supplier for seed, fertilizers, herbicides and pesticides; and, in the case of hybrid, sterile plants, will have to buy new seeds each year.

A question facing Asian farmers is whether IPRs, which were developed to protect industrial inventions, are appropriate for human or other biological genetic materials. And how can such mechanisms protect a nonphysical entity such as oral indigenous knowledge (that is, farmers' know-how as to the use and conservation of plants, shamans' preparation of herbal remedies, or women's conservation practices of seeds which are passed orally from generation to generation)?

Asian farmers must decide what type of mechanisms to adopt to protect themselves: IPR systems or other types of mechanisms. The costs and administrative implications of adopting some of the new IPR systems are great: US$250, 000 per patent. At the very least, farmers must retain the absolute right to save seed, to experiment with exotic germplasm (that is, the genetic material which forms the physical basis of heredity and which is transmitted from one generation to the next by means of the germ cells) and to exchange seeds.

TRIPS

While the success of indigenous peoples' leaders and advocates in lobbying for the provisions integrated into documents such as the Draft Declaration on the Rights of Indigenous Peoples and ILO Convention 169 should be celebrated, much remains to be achieved. Various factors continue to prevent the Draft Declaration from becoming a fully fledged universal agreement. As of August 2002, only 17 countries have ratified ILO Convention 169, and many Asian countries - such as Indonesia, Malaysia and the Philippines - which account for a significant portion of the world's remaining biodiversity resources, have yet to ratify the vital document. Lobbyists admit that even if the Draft Declaration is finally adopted, it will remain a 'soft law' like the UN Declaration on Human Rights, which is not legally binding.

In contrast, the World Trade Organization (WTO) is very powerful. The WTO is an inter-governmental entity that was set up to formulate a set of rules to govern global trade and capital flows through the process of member consensus, and to supervise member countries to ensure that the rules are followed. Many countries are now feeling the far-reaching effects of its well-instituted policies and enforcement mechanisms. Its intellectual property rights regimes have been set up very efficiently.

The WTO's TRIPS presents a tough challenge for indigenous peoples. The policies and rules of TRIPS now govern and influence the economic policies of member countries. The CBD and Agenda 21 also require countries to produce national policies, but the UN has no compliance system and no strong agency to follow up vital agreements. In contrast, the WTO can sanction countries that do not abide by its rules, and it has shown it can flex its muscles, for example over issues such as child labour and forced labour.

While UN conventions and policies such as CBD and Agenda 21 talk about 'sustainable development', the WTO policies favour the 'free market' or 'globalized free trade' paradigm. The result, as noted by proponents of sustainable development, is 'a clash of paradigms' with the globalized free trade paradigm emerging as dominant. The WTO has harmonized its IPR regimes with existing regimes, ie those of Northern governments. Some international lobbyists are concerned that indigenous peoples, who have contributed their age-old knowledge to develop and protect biodiversity in their communities, could be accused of biopiracy if the rights to this knowledge are held by TNCs through IPR regimes. As the WTO's operating mechanisms have been set in place, bio-prospectors have continued to extract biodiversity resources, including the genes of indigenous peoples. Bio-prospectors continue to target the world's biodiversity-rich regions: Asia-Pacific and Latin America.

Exploitation of Indigenous Knowledge and Property Rights

Asian indigenous peoples' struggle to protect their intellectual and cultural property rights intensified in the 1990s, when transnational corporate interests began exploiting for profit indigenous peoples' cultural knowledge, genes and biodiversity resources. As a result, biopiracy became a concern for indigenous peoples. 'Biopiracy' is used to describe the manipulation of intellectual property rights by those intent on gaining exclusive control over genetic resources without giving adequate recognition or remuneration to the original possessors of these resources.

In Asia, biopiracy is practised by multinationals and governments, under various pretexts, on biological and genetic resources found mostly in indigenous peoples' communities.

It is not only genetic or biological materials that are taken, but also the priceless and age-old collective indigenous knowledge of how to use them, embodied in healing and farming practices indigenous peoples have used for generations, and which have been proved to be scientifically sound and effective.

After genetic and biological materials, and the knowledge of how to use them, have been collected, genetically manipulated 'life forms' are patented, and thus privatized and commercialized. Biopiracy began in the 1980s, a by-product of the biotechnology industry which cannot flourish without access to biological resources. Asia's rich resources provided the much-needed raw materials.

Today, developed countries have selected and domesticated all major food crops on which humankind survives. More and more scientists now acknowledge and credit indigenous peoples' wisdom and knowledge for much of the biodiversity found in indigenous upland environments. Thus the biotechnology industry has engaged in what is called 'bio-prospecting'. The race to find antidotes for diseases such as cancer, AIDS, Parkinson's disease and others has prompted multinationals to search indigenous peoples' mountains and forests for possible remedies. Alarmed by this phenomenon, indigenous peoples' leaders and advocates came together to work out how to combat exploitation of their resources.

Biotrade

Governments and companies alike are key players in the business of biotrade. 'Biotrade' refers to the movement of biological resources between countries, companies, academic institutions and individuals for potential profit. More and more governments in the region, willingly or unwillingly, are allowing overseas and domestic private enterprises to operate in the sector. Cash-poor governments like Laos, Burma/ Myanmar and the Philippines, for instance, often strike biotrade deals that might not further the interests of their traditional knowledge holders. Oxford Natural Products (ONP) from the UK has signed an agreement with PT Indofarma, one of the largest pharmaceutical companies of Indonesia, which will bring Jammu medicines onto the international market. Jammu are the traditional local botanical medicines widely prescribed for those who live in Indonesia.

This thriving trade in traditional medicine is one of the few that does well in the recession-ridden Indonesian economy. ONP has also signed an agreement with one of the leading natural medicine institutes of Vietnam. The two-part agreement embraces both development and future commercial rights, giving the company exclusive access to an important portfolio of Vietnam's medicinal plants. ONP is also involved in Bhutan, where the company used the knowledge of the Dungrshos, Bhutanese traditional-medicine doctors, and the Menpas, their assistants, to identify Bhutanese herbal plants and how they are prepared.

The Human Genome Diversity Project

Another serious concern worldwide, particularly among indigenous peoples since the 1990s, is the ambitious US$20 billion Human Genome Project of the National Institute of Health (NIH) and the Department of Energy in the United States. Scientists working on the project belong to what is called the Human Genome Organization (HUGO); they seek to map the genetic basis of diversity among humans.

As part of the project, HUGO set up a committee in 1991 to develop the Human Genome Diversity Project (HGDP). The HGDP aims to 'collect, analyse and preserve genetic samples from a host of vanishing human populations'. These 'vanishing human populations' are indigenous peoples, including the Aetas of the Philippines, the Guaymi of Panama and the Hagahai people of the highlands of Papua New Guinea, among others. They were selected because their genes contain certain characteristics absent in mainstream populations, like resistance to some diseases, and tolerance to cold, heat and pain. The HGDP seeks to project an idealistic aim. Proponents say they will map the hereditary bases for differences in human susceptibility to disease, which may help find treatments for diseases such as AIDS. But indigenous peoples are concerned about the motives of biotechnology corporations involved in the project.

The HGDP's aim of 'preserving' genetic samples from 'vanishing' human populations also sounds idealistic. But some indigenous peoples' leaders object to this aim, pointing out that colonizing countries of the North subjected indigenous peoples to genocide and ethnocide for 500 years, and that this continues in many parts of the world, so collecting their DNA is just rubbing salt on an open wound. Indigenous peoples have also found the HGDP's methods of collecting gene samples questionable. One example is the attempt of the drug firm Hoffman-La Roche to collect gene samples from the Aeta peoples of the Philippines under the guise of medical missions.

In 1993, Hoffman-La Roche approached the Hawaii-based Aloha Medical Mission, which often visits the Aetas, to contact the Aeta people when they were facing medical problems following the eruption of Mt Pinatubo, a volcano in Luzon island, in 1991. Sick and hungry after the dislocation caused by the volcanic eruption, the Aeta people welcomed such medical missions. As in bio-prospecting for plant genetic materials, the HGDP also uses universities as intermediaries.

In the Philippines, for example, there have been reports that professors from the University of the Philippines have been given contracts to collect genetic material from indigenous peoples. A submission to the Working Group on Indigenous Populations by the Office of the High Commissioner for Human Rights noted in the conclusion that: 'Some concerns of indigenous peoples . . . cannot be adequately addressed without a complete ban on projects such as the HGDP, and of the patenting of human geonome.' But the HGDP continues.

Securityn of Land

For many indigenous and upland peoples in Asia, living securely in their ancestral lands or territories means taking full control over their biodiversity resources and their cultural heritage or their intellectual and cultural property rights. The Hmong people of Mae Sa Mai, an upland community north of Chiang Mai in Thailand, have communal knowledge about particular herbs and plants that can cure rheumatism, women's painful menstruation, coughs and colds, and asthma. They grow medicinal plants in a communal herbal garden, which they consider their community pharmacy.

The Hmong people have handed down traditional knowledge on the medical importance of certain plants through the generations. As part of their spiritual practices, they have designated part of their land a 'sacred forest', where they worship gods and spirits who, they believe, are keeping watch over their community. The sacred forest, a 30-minute climb from the community proper, is also a vital headwater and watershed of springs and brooks that supply the community's potable water and irrigation needs. But they are worried because they are living within a territory that the government considers as a national park. Their aim is that the land where they have lived for 70 years, will be awarded to them.

In the Philippines, the effectiveness of the Indigenous Peoples' Rights Act (IPRA) has yet to be fully tested. Signed into law in October 1997, the law recognizes the rights of indigenous peoples to own, protect, use and manage their ancestral lands and domains according to their customary laws and traditions. Before the IPRA came into effect, the DENR issued special administrative orders, which paved the way for the issuing of Certificates of Ancestral Domain Claims or CADCs to indigenous communities. These CADCs are temporary though, until they become Certificates of Ancestral Domain Titles (CADTs).

In July 2002, Bakun town in Benguet Province in northern Philippines was awarded its CADT, the first in the country and the only one issued so far. Through this CADT, the Kankanaey-Bago peoples of Bakun can have full control over their biodiversity and wildlife resources. One prerequisite for processing of the CADT was an inventory of their wildlife and biodiversity resources. But, aware of the biopiracy phenomenon, the Kankanaey-Bago people do not intend to submit all the list of plants within their community. However some government laws and policies are in conflict with the IPRA, for example, the Mining Act of 1995. The Mining Act liberalized the mining industry, giving incentives to big mining investors who apply for large concessions, mostly in the ancestral lands of indigenous peoples. Large-scale mining is a threat to biodiversity and water systems, as well as people, who are displaced in some cases.

Indigenous Peoples' Struggles Against Biopiracy

The extraction of biodiversity resources and the genes of indigenous peoples to supply raw materials for the biotechnology industry of the North has alarmed many indigenous peoples. Northern corporations, for example, have applied for patents on the neem plant and turmeric in India, the kava in the Pacific, the ayahuasca and quinoa in Latin America, and the bitter gourd in the Philippines and Thailand. When processed or genetically engineered, these raw materials can be transformed into marketable commercial commodities. The use of resources found mostly in indigenous peoples' lands is increasing. Recently, a German agrochemical and pharmaceutical giant, Hoechst Co. , was able to apply for and win several US patents on preparations derived from the medical plant of the mint family Coleus forskohlii, which grows in India, Nepal and Thailand, for commercial production.

The plant has long been used and protected by indigenous peoples of these three countries. Since 1998, another company, Glaxo Welcome has successfully completed ethnobotanical research in Asian countries, including the Philippines, India and Indonesia, on the mint plant. The Singapore Centre for Natural Products Research (CNPR), a Glaxo Welcome-funded bio-prospecting institution, is alleged to have an agreement with India's Tropical Botanical and Garden Research Institute, which allows the results of the work carried out by CNPR and Welcome, along with the samples and any information relating thereto, to be considered 'the confidential property of CNPR or Glaxo Wellcome'. Such arrangements can seriously threaten indigenous peoples' access to and control of their collective property and their collective knowledge of the traditional uses of exotic and endemic plants, which they have been using as food and medicine for centuries.

On the global level, international NGOs such as RAFI, GRAIN, the Third World Network and others have been joining with other groups to raise awareness of the biopiracy problem. These NGO networks, along with other interest groups and some parliaments, keep watch over patent applications in various patent and trademark offices worldwide. In September 1995, more than 200 organizations from 35 countries filed a petition at the US Patent and Trademark Office. The petition seeks to revoke a patent given to W. R. Grace Company to use a pesticidal extract from neem, an endemic tree in India. The petitioners charged the company of usurping an age-old biological process.

Indigenous peoples have found an ally in the international church community. As early as 1989, the World Council of Churches came out with a statement calling for 'a ban on experiments involving the genetic engineering of the human germline' (i.e. cell block). Indigenous peoples themselves have spoken out against the Human Genome Diversity Project (HGDP), condemning it as 'sacrilegious' and unethical. Indigenous peoples' lobbyists in 1994 also asked the UN Commission on Sustainable Development to ban the

HGDP. In February 1995, Asian indigenous peoples presented a statement at the European Parliament calling for a halt to the project.

At the Fourth World Conference on Women in Beijing, the Asian Indigenous Women's Network exhorted other women to include in the Beijing Declaration a condemnation of the HGDP, and to call for it to be banned. Also in 1995, indigenous peoples from the Asia-Pacific won the backing of 17 organizations in the Americas, which signed up to the Declaration of Indigenous Peoples of the Western Hemisphere Regarding the Human Genome Diversity Project. The Declaration called on international organizations to protect all life forms from genetic manipulation and destruction, and criticized the efforts of Western science 'to negate the complexity of any life form by isolating and reducing it to its minute parts ... and [thereby] alter its relationship to the natural order'.

Indigenous peoples' representatives have organized 'parallel activities' to coincide with major WTO activities such as the WTO Third Ministerial Meeting in Seattle. After a caucus, the indigenous peoples' leaders produced the 'Indigenous Peoples' Seattle Declaration', which protested, among other things, about the patenting of life. Some indigenous peoples' representatives have also participated in negotiating for the adoption of a Biosafety Protocol in the Convention on Biological Diversity. Adopted in January 2000, the Biosafety Protocol regulates the 'transboundary transfer' of genetically modified organisms.

Action against biodiversity exploitation

India. It is in India that some of the most significant struggles to protect biodiversity are taking place. For more than 2, 000 years, Indian indigenous communities have used the sap of the Commiphora mukul tree to lower blood cholesterol level and treat other forms of illness. Now, the patent on the use of tree's sap is owned by the New Jersey-based Sabinsa

Corporation The extract from the tree is said to be an 'antioxidant and has cancer chemopreventive roles for cancer. ... The invention relates to a composition and method for products extracted from Commiphora species for use in the prevention and treatment of abnormal cell growth and proliferation in inflammation, neoplasia and cardiovascular disease.'

Indian indigenous peoples and sympathetic NGOs are asking the government for compensation for the knowledge shared on the growing, care and management, use and processing of the tree and its extract, which the local people perfected over so many years. Indigenous peoples in India have contributed much to the identification, conservation and use of medicinal plants and continue to do so, although now they are wary of this. One active indigenous peoples' organization, the Foundation for the Revitalization of Local Health Traditions (FRLHT) is drawing up the Peoples' Biodiversity Register. This local NGO is supporting sustainable local health traditions in Karnataka, Kerala and Tamil Nadu. FRLHT believes that, with regard to intellectual property rights on medicinal plants, it is a misconception that traditional knowledge can be patented when it has been documented and published.

As the general rule in patenting is that 'anything published cannot be patented as it is a prior art and already accessible in published form', FRLHT is asking local people to put oral knowledge and local health traditions into published form and into databases. The Centre for Ecological Sciences (ECOS) at the Indian Institute of Science, is helping the Tharu people set up a museum of Tharu culture and traditions, including agricultural tools and implements, traditional varieties of paddy, maize, wheat and certain herbs. These are documented and stand as proof of the Tharu's indigenous heritage. Another Indian NGO which is helping farming communities to protect their indigenous know-how and biodiversity, is the Centre for Indian Knowledge Systems

(CIKS). CIKS's model in imparting and popularizing indigenous farming techniques is the Vrkshayurveda - the ancient classical texts of Indian plant science. The system is being implemented in 35 villages with a network of 1, 200 farmers.

In the Kanchepuram district of Tamil Nadu, for instance, farmers make use of ancient pest control practices called the Ural Marundu. This involves filling pots with leaves from a variety of plants with known pesticidal properties, adding cow's urine and a little water. The pots are covered, buried and left to brew for at least two weeks. The resulting liquid is diluted with water and used as a broad-spectrum pesticide for crops.

The plants used in the decoction are known only to Tamil Nadu farmers and CIKS staff. In April 1997 villagers in Pattuvam village, in Kannur District in northern Kerala (a southern state of India), issued a declaration placing controls on identified genetic resources available and used in the village for ages. The declaration was made after the village youth prepared a detailed register of every species and all the crop cultivars in the village. The register included 26 traditional rice varieties, 93 bird species, 30 fish varieties (freshwater and saline), a number of crabs, molluscs and tortoises, 32 species of mangroves, 14 wild mammals, and other tree and plant species. The survey listed a total of 366 species of plants in Pattuvam village alone.

The group of active villagers also set up a Forum for the Protection of Peoples' Biodiversity. The Forum, together with the village's grassroots statutory authority (panchayat), would thus have to be consulted by any person or company seeking access to the register and the genetic material listed. Pattuvam villagers have concluded that there were items of considerable economic value which justified a declaration of ownership. Lawyers have yet to look into the legal implications of what the villagers have done in relation to GATT and WTO arrangements. But Vandana Shiva, a leading Indian social activist, opined: 'The declaration gives recognition to community rights to the intellectual and biological commons and provides a new interpretation to the sui generis option of TRIPS.' Indian people also hold festivals to renew their connection with nature's resources that they have long used.

The Indian Academy of Development Science periodically organizes a 'Vedu Sammelan' - a gathering of traditional healers. Under India's National Biodiversity Strategy Action Plan (NBSAP), biodiversity festivals have been held in various parts of the country, and have become platforms for seed and information exchange, celebration of cultural aspects of biodiversity and revival of traditional knowledge systems. In another local peoples' initiative, villagers of Jardhargaon, a Himalayan foothills village in Uttar Pradesh, northern India, have taken charge of the heavily degraded slopes above their village. They started the Beej Bachao Andolan (Save the Seeds Movement), and, by making many journeys to more remote villages, they have been able to collect many varieties lost elsewhere in the region. Several farmers are now at various stages of switching over to biologically diverse, sustainable agricultural practices.

Nepal. ECOS is also active in Nepal. Nepalese indigenous knowledge is being protected by the Tharu indigenous people who live in the southern plains. ECOS is helping Tharu farmers revive their indigenous farming methods by complementing them with recently developed environmentally friendly practices. One such project is in Dibya Nagar, where Tharu elders teach ECOS staff about age-old farming practices while learning about bio-pesticides from college-trained ECOS staff. Tharu elders are motivated to share their know-how on biodiversity conservation, especially on seed conservation, with the younger generation.

More often than not, it is the young women, trained by elder women, who become adept in assimilating this knowledge. For instance, the herbs used for healing and cooking are known mainly by the older women and the young women they trust with their knowledge. These women contribute a great deal to the sustainability of important food and medicinal plants. Also in Nepal, village fairs, community exchanges and biodiversity festivals are some of the innovative ways used to keep alive and celebrate biodiversity and its link with the local culture. At one such biodiversity fair, the villagers realized that almost 100 traditional rice varieties were still in use, though they had long disappeared from the market.

Malaysia. Recognizing the importance of traditional knowledge, leaders at Sahabat Alam, Malaysia are helping the villages of Long Sayan and Uma Bawang Keluan to create botanical conservation sites. These sites will be a repository for many different species of rattan, bamboo, fruit trees and medicinal plants. With funding from the Borneo Project (a project aimed at improving the life and welfare of the indigenous peoples of Borneo), these pilot programmes are helping villagers manage, preserve and restore rare plant stocks for future generations.

Indonesia. The traditional practices and belief systems of the Atoni, who inhabit West Timor, are banned, and the identity of biodiversity species that are important in farming and for the treatment of diseases are being lost as the older people die. But a few Atoni tribesmen are reviving old practices and traditional lifestyles related to the Atoni cosmovision 'underground', with the help of the Timor Integrated Rural Development Programme (TIRD-P), a consortium of four NGOs working to promote sustainable agriculture and to prevent biopiracy in West Timor.

Thailand. The UK Foundation for Ethnobiology attempted out bio-prospecting activities among the indigenous Karen communities in northern Thailand. Foundation representatives initially sought access to information about medicinal plants. Through the Riche Monde Initiative for Ethnobiology in Thailand, the Foundation sought to make an inventory of the traditional medical and biological knowledge of the Karen people. Thai NGOs discovered that the Foundation for

Ethnobiology had not sought the approval of Thailand's National Science Council for its activities. Contrary to its claims, the Foundation had not consulted groups and communities who were opposed to the project. The Foundation was able to start the inventory project under the guise of gaining access to Karen 'environmental insights'. A landmark achievement in the prevention of biopiracy in Thailand was when the Thai government, in 1997, as a result of lobbying by indigenous peoples, drafted a bill to recognize and protect the knowledge of traditional healers and Thailand's medicinal resources from private appropriation by pharmaceutical companies.

Sri Lanka. As elsewhere in the world, indigenous healers in Sri Lanka have, for centuries, prepared medicines from wild plants and flowers gathered from the country's tropical forests to treat a variety of illnesses. The ancient formulations of the ayurveda system of medicine were tightly guarded and were passed from one generation to the next in families that could trace back their ancestry for generations. Feisal Samath cites the ability of an indigenous doctor in the north-central town of Polonnaruwa to treat patients with heart problems who would otherwise require bypass surgery, which costs at least US$4, 500 in hospitals in the country. Global drug firms seek to exploit this ancient Lankan wisdom, extracting chemicals from local plants and patenting them abroad.

Export of medicinal plants or their extracts is banned in Sri Lanka. But Samath reports that biopiracy is flourishing in the country. Samath lists some of the local biological resources that have been patented abroad. One is the locally grown Kothalahimbutu plant, which helps control diabetes. Ayurveda physicians in Sri Lanka advise diabetic patients to drink water left overnight in mugs or jugs carved out of Kothalahimbutu, whose production has become a cottage industry in the country. Citing local newspaper accounts, Samath reports that a Japanese drug company patented a product based on this plant through the American Chemical Society in 1997.

The plant Weniwalgeta - used as a remedy for fever, coughs and colds - has also been registered by Japanese, European and American manufacturers. The media has played a role in exposing biopiracy in Sri Lanka. Two biopiracy cases in September 1997 were widely publicized and led to a sudden interest in the issue among environmentalists and scientists in the country. A university botanist was intercepted by customs at Colombo Airport trying to smuggle out some plant extract. In the same month, customs officials discovered a container of Kothalahimbutu - 1, 512 cups weighing some 4 tonnes - being shipped to Japan through a Sri Lanken-owned firm.

Bangladesh. In Bangladesh, an activity facilitated by UBINIG (the Bangla acronym for 'Policy Research for Development Alternatives') is the Nayakrishi Andolan -the New Agricultural Movement, a peasant initiative for biodiversity-based farming. It aims to 'incorporate traditional and indigenous knowledge of farming based on the principles of preservation, conservation and enhancement of biodiversity and genetic resources'. The traditional uses of medicinal plants are kept alive by women, and village seed banks can be seen throughout the region.

Philippines. In the Philippines, the first item collected in an act of bioprospecting was a soil isolated in a cemetery in Iloilo province in 1949 by a Filipino scientist, Abelardo Aguilar, then working for the American company Eli Lilly. The soil turned out to produce an antibiotic, a drug now known as erythromycin. Aguilar never received any recompense from his company, even after the Philippines government intervened on his behalf. The Philippines Department of Environment and Natural Resources (DENR) does not know what happened to specimens of a mountain yew called Taxus sumatrana, which two American researchers took from Mount Pulag in 1993. The 8,000-foot peak in Luzon island is a national park, and thus a 'protected area'.

An Asian Development Bank (ADB) report, Challenges for Asia's Trade and Environment, said that the country's trade policies and regulations are harming the environment, causing loss of biodiversity, infringing property rights and increasing deforestation. Trade liberalization and the facilitation of technology transfer is happening at a high environmental cost. The loss of biodiversity and property rights, especially those of ethnic and tribal peoples, is causing a widespread tendency to mismanage resources because no proper price is being paid for their exploitation.

Biopiracy has increased in the Philippines and the preservation of the ecosystems has become more controversial. The threat to Philippine biodiversity has become more serious as the government has agreed to a US$60 million biodiversity research project on drugs and medical products with the US National Institute of Health. Companies that do not have agreements with the Philippine government are continuing to carry out covert research.

In 1995, indigenous peoples' leaders in southern Philippines confiscated sacks of plant specimens collected by researchers from the Philippine National Museum. The researchers insisted their collection was legitimate and important for the National Museum's Philippine Plant Inventory Project. But the indigenous people asserted that the researchers broke both legal and traditional protocols as they failed to get the 'prior informed consent of the people', in accordance with Executive Order 247 which seeks to regulate research and bioprospecting in local communities. The indigenous tribal leaders imposed a fine on the researchers of eight water buffaloes, 27 chickens, 8 metres of cloth, and one-peso coins amounting to P150.00 (almost US$3). The researchers protested, but the indigenous people prevailed.

In the Cordillera Region of the Philippines, several villages are now engaged in community seed-banking, which is being promoted by the Igorot Tribal Assistance Group (ITAG), an environmental NGO, and the Project Initiating Employment through Training in Environmental Enterprises (PINE TREE), an environmental movement aimed at reducing poverty and facilitating environmental education. PINE TREE is supported by the New York-based Echoing Green Foundation. The seed-banking activities are intended to allow the indigenous people to document important food and medicinal crops and valuable trees, and continuously plant and conserve these.

The biopiracy phenomenon has produced a variety of responses from indigenous peoples themselves, civil society, the churches and some governments. Indigenous peoples' organizations at the national level have been monitoring biopiracy and bio-prospecting, and have been lobbying for laws to regulate these activities.

5

Indigenous Peoples' Right to Development

The right to development was accepted as a human right with the adoption by the United Nations General Assembly of the Declaration on the Right to Development (DRD) in 1986. Article 1 states:

> 'The right to development is an inalienable human right by virtue of which every human person and all peoples are entitled to participate in, contribute to, and enjoy economic, social, cultural and political development, in which all human rights and fundamental freedoms can be fully realized.'

The individual and all peoples are thus named as the right-holders of a right to development. With the DRD, a circle that had effectively been broken at the international level after the adoption of the Universal Declaration of Human Rights (UDHR) was completed.

The UDHR conceived of all the human rights as interrelated and interdependent. The unity of those rights was broken with the spread of the Cold War, the divide clearly demonstrated by the formulations of two different covenants, one dealing with civil and political rights and the other with economic, social and cultural rights. Other human rights were eventually codified in subsequent instruments recognizing and elaborating rights relating to children, women, the environment, minorities and indigenous peoples.

With the adoption of the right to development, the unity of all human rights was restored in that the right to development was presented as a composite of all human rights and fundamental freedoms. The DRD recognizes all rights and freedoms as 'indivisible and interdependent' and explicitly refers to the failure to observe civil and political as well as economic, social and cultural rights as an obstacle to development.

Development has been defined in the Preamble of the DRD as

> 'a comprehensive economic, social, cultural and political process, which aims at the constant improvement of the well-being of the entire population and of all individuals on the basis of their active, free and meaningful participation in development and in the fair distribution of benefits resulting therefrom'.

The Preamble also has the General Assembly '[r]ecognizing that the human person is the central subject of the development process ...'. The right to development can thus be understood as entailing the right to a particular process of development. A process that aims at improving human well-being has been described as having as its objective the expansion of the capabilities or freedoms of individuals to realize what they value.

The right to this particular process of development is significant in that it refers to the realization of all the rights and freedoms recognized as human rights - civil and political, economic, social and cultural as well as the specific rights articulated to promote and protect the rights of minorities and indigenous peoples, children, women and other entities identified as warranting particular attention under international law. The right to development then seeks to treat them as interrelated and interdependent, reflecting their relationship as an integrated whole and not as simply an aggregate or sum of existing rights.

A second significant element of the right to a process of development is that both the outcomes of development, as well as the ways in which the outcomes are realized, form part of the human right to development. As such, while duty-bearers have obligations to produce results, they can also be understood as having obligations of conduct. Obligations of result relate to the outcomes of the process of development while the obligations of conduct refer to the policies and programmes of development. The duty-bearers of the right to development, as the DRD makes clear, are states acting at the national level and acting individually or collectively at the international level. The conceptualization of a human right to development has thus come a long way from the concept of development.

In the 1950s and 1960s economic growth, measured as growth of Gross Domestic Product (GDP), was the principal objective of development. In the decades that followed, the human development approach added value to the conventional economic growth approach by replacing GDP growth with human development indicators such as the provision of food, health, education, nutrition, gender parities and employment, as measurements of development.

More recently, the human rights approach added value to the human development approach by converting the indicators regarding the provision of food, health, education, etc. into recognized rights to food, health, education, etc. as objectives of development. This rights-based approach thus also describes development not in terms of human needs but in terms of responding to the rights of individuals and groups.

Moreover, recognition of rights as indicators refers not just to the provision or availability of the services but also to the way in which the services are provided, and thus issues related to access, cultural acceptability and non-discrimination become equally important in the determination of whether or not development objectives are being met. The term 'human development' has come to embody the ideas of development that reach beyond the growth of material products, markets and physical infrastructure, to include the development of the human person as an out-come of development. It does not, however, address the way in which these outcomes are brought about. The integration of human rights standards and principles, both in the process and outcome of development programmes and policies, is reflected in the 'human rights-based approach to development'.

In this rights-based approach, human rights standards and principles, as derived from international human rights instruments, are meant to underscore all phases of the development process. The language of human rights.- one of rights, obligations and accountability based on binding international law - is meant to provide both the programming tools and the essential references.

The right to development, while sensitive to human development and inclusive of the rights-based approach, takes the development formula one step further by treating all rights as an integrated whole and the right to development as a comprehensive process for their achievement. A development process which takes account of the objectives that must be met to realize the right to development would include, for example, consideration of whether all rights are protected and promoted with due respect for their indivisibility and interdependence, whether all states acting at the national and international levels are contributing to the fulfilment of the right, and whether the procedures and outcomes are consistent with the rights-based approach to development.

The right to development, then, requires that states ensure that development benefits individuals, including, therefore, persons belonging to minority and indigenous communities. Minority and indigenous rights are constitutive elements of the right to development like any other recognized human right, to be respected in the process and realized in the outcomes of, development. The human rights of minorities and indigenous peoples are not simply rights comprising the right to development, but are an integral part of each civil, political, economic, social and cultural right comprising the right to development; as such, they are to be adhered to in the realization of each right, as well as in the method of realizing each right, and in any processes for realizing the right to development.

The right to development is a collective right, and can also be a group right. However, it is individuals who are meant ultimately to benefit from the exercise of that right even if they cannot individually assert the right. The implementation of the rights, whether individual or group, must ensure the centrality of the individual person as beneficiary, as stated in Article 2(l) of the DRD.

There is a danger that rights held by a group or by society as a (collective) whole will then have to be exercised by the state on their behalf but this can be addressed where mechanisms exist to establish the correspondence between the states asserting the right and the individual or group enjoying the right. These mechanisms would include a system for attributing accountability at all levels of the development process and access to remedies both for individuals who constitute the group, and for groups.

The right to development articulated and endorsed as a human right, as in the case of all human rights, implies corresponding accountability. It is indeed this binary relation which distinguishes human rights from the general valuing of freedom that exists without a correlated obligation to help bring about that freedom. This particular process, defended by the Independent Expert, is one that enables the realization of all human rights and fundamental freedoms together. It is also one which is carried out in a manner consistent with human rights and which builds on the traditional process of the expansion of wealth and allocation of resources, incorporating concerns of equity and justice along with human rights standards. This approach would seem critical to integrating the rights of minorities and indigenous peoples, who are often the unequal recipients of resource distribution, even during periods of high growth in both developed and developing countries.

Furthermore, international pressure for economic growth commonly results in the commercial exploitation of indigenous peoples' lands and territories, leading to, for example, their displacement and impoverishment, and, at times, to conflict. While there is substantial agreement on the wrongs of development, consensus on the definition of what constitutes the right to development has not been reached. For example, the rights-based approach, although enjoying considerable support, has not been universally endorsed. Similarly, framing the right to development as a right to a process of development has its supporters but also its detractors. While most, if not all, states agree that the right to development has both national and international dimensions, unsurprisingly there is widespread disagreement on whether or not there exists an obligation to cooperate internationally in the realization of the right to development, with Southern states supporting the existence of this obligation, and Northern states rejecting it.

Other areas of disagreement include: whether the right to development is an individual or collective right, with some states also arguing that it is a 'right' of states; what the appropriate balance between the national and international elements is, and what the content of the right at each level is; what practical methods of implementation are viable, as well as the most suitable permanent follow-up mechanism.

The United Nations open-ended Working Group on the Right to Development is the principal international forum for debate on the right to development qua a right. In this forum, Northern states tend to place considerable emphasis on elements of the national dimension, particularly as they pertain to the South, while the Southern states tend to focus on specific elements in relation to the international dimension.

Thus the direction of discussion set by the South is usually towards issues such as inequalities in the international financial system, greater participation of developing countries in global decision-making on economic policy, and promoting a fairer international trade regime. The Northern states tend to draw more on national implications of international cooperation, focusing on the need for suitable domestic conditions in the South, including, for example, good governance, democracy, human rights and responsible economic management.

While the focus by the North is on the implementation of certain aspects of the right to development by the South, Northern states do not sufficiently consider the incorporation of the right to development for people in their own countries. Furthermore, when the Working Group addresses both the international and national dimensions of the right to development, there is much greater scope for a people-centred debate.

Overall, much of the discussion that occurs within the meetings of the Working Group relates to interpretations of international cooperation that stems from the right to development; this means that development cooperation policy gets the most attention while the examination of obligations towards the beneficiaries of development is not considered in depth.

As set out in the DRD, the right to development entailing a right to a process of development, leading to an outcome of the fulfilment of all the human rights, involves obligations at two levels - national and international. While the state has the primary obligation to implement the right to development at the national level, in an interdependent world, economic growth in any one country is dependent on the states and other actors of the international economy that influence trade, finance and flows of capital and technology.

International cooperation therefore becomes crucial for any state to be able to formulate and execute those policies and deliver those rights to the people in the country. Whereas the obligation of international cooperation is applicable to a range of human rights, and increasingly relevant in an interdependent world, for the right to development the obligation for such international cooperation becomes almost as important as the obligation imposed on states acting at the national level. The right to development, then, is not a right of states to be developed; it is a right that entails a process of development for all people, respecting all human rights, which necessarily means a development process where effective participation allows for people to determine the terms and nature of development.

In the current international system, still largely characterized by interstate relations, governments may often be in the most suitable position to demand an equitable international system that will contribute to their ability to fulfil the right to development. However, this is in their capacity as duty-bearers. Rights and obligations and thus accountability, in relation to the right to development understood as a human right, go beyond inter-state accountability to address the accountability of the state, or the international community of states, to the people who are meant to benefit from development. The right-holders are the collective populations of a state and in the case of minorities and indigenous peoples, the right-holders are also groups with specified rights within the collective. And the ultimate beneficiaries of the right to development are individuals.

Collective Rights, Group Rights and Peoples' Rights

Discrimination and inequality, on grounds such as race, colour, language and religion, affect both minorities and indigenous peoples, yet are unequivocally prohibited in the DRD and under conventional and customary international law. Further, for minorities as for indigenous peoples, their existence is linked to the preservation of their cultural identities as a group. The rights of minorities and those of indigenous peoples may often differ, but they all aim to address these recognized fundamental needs. Though the individual is the ultimate beneficiary of the promotion and protection of human rights, it is only through certain group rights that individual rights are given meaning; that is, the enjoyment of individual human rights may require that particular human rights devolve directly upon groups.

Classified as such - individual-and group - these rights do not exist in binary opposition but complement and supplement each other. With regard to the right to development that is exercised by the collective of people within a state, the position of non-dominance occupied by minority and indigenous groups requires that their rights be addressed by policies and programmes that go beyond their rights as individual members of the collective and seek to ensure that their additional rights as groups within the collective are guaranteed. This is somewhat more straightforward in the case of indigenous peoples who, as peoples, are recognized as having certain group rights under international law. Minorities, however, are considered under international law as having collective rights which are distinguished from group rights.

From an examination of some of the literature on the rights of minorities, group rights and the rights of peoples, there appears to be conceptual and terminological inconsistency in the application of the terms. Moreover, the fact that the terms collective and group rights are often, although not always, used interchangeably in the literature adds to the confusion.

The perennial debate over the definition of individual, collective and group rights as it relates to minorities and indigenous peoples appears ill conceived, because it seems to correlate peoples (or those who are not 'peoples', e.g. minorities) with the application of either one or the other category of rights: individual (collective), or group. Moreover, even where a group is recognized as a people, as is the case with indigenous peoples, their rights as peoples are often qualified in international legal instruments. It would seem that the desire to avoid giving minority groups the capacity to vindicate their rights before a competent international body, by providing the group with international legal personality, and to limit any potential claim to secession, has underpinned the rationale for distinguishing individual/collective rights from group rights in international law. This is typified by the language of Article 27 of the International Covenant on Civil and Political Rights (ICCPR), which refers to 'persons belonging to minorities' and not simply to minorities.

Differentiating Collective Rights from Group Rights

Putting aside for a moment the notion of peoples' rights, a point to which we will return, we suggest that there is clarity to be gained by viewing collective rights and group rights, as they relate to minorities as well as indigenous peoples, as determined not by the identity of the holder, traditionally defined in international law (as persons belonging to minorities and indigenous peoples), but by the aim of the right itself.

Dinstein argues that collective rights, exemplified by Article 27 of the ICCPR, if defined just as individual rights of persons belonging to minorities as exercised in community with other members of their group, would provide little more than, for example, the right to freedom of thought, conscience and religion provided in Article 18 of the ICCPR, unless the definition goes beyond the ambit of Article 18, to provide what that Article does not: 'the granting of a collective human right qua a group right'.

The prohibition of genocide provides a cogent example of determining what constitutes a group right on the basis of what the right aims to achieve. The freedom from genocide exists to protect an entire group. It would not exist without the existence of a group that it is meant to protect. That the right is a group right, does not alter the fact that the right serves to protect individuals but it also serves to protect the group. As egregious as the killing of members of a particular group is, and although the individual's right to life would be protected by the effective application of the prohibition of genocide, the application of the term genocide to such a crime is relevant only when the aim is to wipe out the group.

In the case of the Convention on the Crime and Punishment of Genocide, and the International Convention on the Suppression and Punishment of the Crime of Apartheid, there are explicit references to, inter alia, racial groups. Similarly, the right to internal self-determination is a right to ensure the autonomy or sovereignty of a group. In the same way, sovereignty over natural resources is a group right. While groups themselves are collective entities, group rights may be said to reflect the rights of 'units and not simply as aggregations of individuals' and so, although 'the individual is the object of protection, the fundamental element is the group'. This, it seems, would apply equally to the preservation of a minority language as to the sovereignty over natural resources, suggesting therefore that the insistence on the distinction between collective and group rights, and minority and indigenous rights, which is perpetuated by the language of, inter alia, ICCPR Article 27, is factitious.

'Collective' rights as defined in international law are rights that are exercised by individuals collectively. In the case of minorities (including, where relevant, indigenous peoples) this includes, for example, the right to enjoy their own culture, to practise their own religion, or to use their own language. The right is cast as a collective one, since a minority language, for example, cannot be used and hence maintained by an individual alone.

However, according to the theory outlined above (which looks to the aim of the right itself to determine whether it is a collective or group right, and not at whether the right-holder is recognized as having collective rights or group rights), although the protection afforded by that right is aimed at the individual, a fundamental element is the group.

Collective rights that are not specific to minorities or indigenous peoples, such as the right to form a trade union or to freedom of association, or the right to strike, or the right to development (planning policies), may serve to clarify the distinction between collective individual rights and collective group rights as we have articulated it The fundamental element in the examples just mentioned is not the group, but rather the protection of the rights of individuals exercised collectively.

While the right to strike can be enjoyed only by a collective of people (a 'group'), and only the 'group' allows for the realization by the individual of the right, it is best classified as a (collective) individual right and not a (collective) group right, because the right to strike or the right to form a trade union exists only to protect the rights of the individuals. These collective rights cannot be called group rights, as we have defined it.

Even though in both cases a 'group' exercises the right, and the individual benefits, the people have formed a group in order to assert their right, and the group itself has no objective raison detre, no objective function, no quality of its own. In other words, when the maintenance or perpetuation of the group is a factor unto itself, in addition to the group being a vehicle for the realization of the rights of individual members of the group, the rights in place to protect or promote it should be recognized as group rights and thus, the people who form it should be acknowledged as constituting a group.

In the case of the rights of indigenous peoples, for example, the group exists first and when the rights are elaborated to protect the group, because the preservation of their identity, for example, is a value in itself, they are group rights. Where minorities form a cohesive group and thus where certain minority rights are meant to protect and preserve the identity of a minority group as an object in itself, the minority rights should also be regarded as group rights. This is not to say that all minorities can be identified as cohesive self-contained groups - and indeed, individuals belonging to minority or indigenous communities may claim rights aimed not at enhancing the group itself, but rather at enabling them to enjoy rights and freedoms which as individual minorities among the majority(ies) they may be denied. This way of looking at collective and group rights does not contradict the principle that it is the individuals who are the beneficiaries of the rights. In both cases the collective or the group exercises the right.

In the case of collective rights where right-holders are individuals, they are the direct beneficiaries. For group rights, the groups hold the rights and directly benefit from their exercise, in terms of well-specified criteria of enhancement of the worth or interests of the group. But the individuals who constitute the group would be the ultimate beneficiaries, at least potentially so, even if not immediately. The group and its objectives have to be conditioned so that there is an unequivocal indication when the group benefits or is better off, irrespective of whether or not all the individuals constituting the group are better off. Human rights jurisprudence accommodates this possible conflict between the right of the individual and that of the group in the application of principles of proportionality, and of reasonableness and objectivity.

In addition to collective rights and group rights there are individual rights applicable to everyone which do not require collective exercise in order to be protected or realised, such as the right to a fair trial or the right to privacy. However, some individual rights may also have a collective dimension. Obiora notes, for example, that while many economic, social and cultural rights, such as the right to education or the right to health, or to safe and healthy working conditions, can only be implemented in a collective manner, the rights are not held by the group. Although they may be best promoted by group-based policies or programmes, they are not, per se, group rights (or collective rights).

Devaluing Group Rights

While the rights of indigenous peoples need not only be framed as group rights but can also be both individual and collective rights, the rights of peoples are recognized in international law as comprising group rights. While there is no agreed definition of 'peoples' in international laws' it has been suggested that the term 'group' is broader in scope than peoples, but includes peoples. Indigenous peoples would constitute both a people and a group, and while groups include peoples, not every group can claim the rights of a people. Minorities are conceived of as individuals in a group but not as groups or as peoples under international law.

In practice the trend has been to promote respect for the human rights of the members of the relevant minority group without promoting their status as peoples. Even though group rights and peoples' rights are not the same, they seem to be applied interchangeably, resulting in a denial of group rights to national or ethnic, religious and linguistic groups not granted legal recognition as peoples.

The codification of minority and indigenous rights is aimed at guaranteeing, inter alia, the rights of those groups as well as the rights of the members of those groups. Part of the confusion that currently exists in terms of the application of international law stems from the legal fiction that regards minorities as having individual rights exercised collectively and indigenous peoples as having both those rights that are exercised collectively as well as group rights.

Procedurally, this fiction is maintained in the form of individual petition under the Optional Protocol to the ICCPR. The distinction between individual/ collective rights and group rights may address the concerns of certain states which aim to minimize grounds upon which secessionist claims might be based, but it fails to recognize the group element of minority rights, as well as the group element of indigenous peoples' rights where the reference is not to 'peoples' as it is for the-right to self-determination and sovereignty over natural resources. Alston has remarked that '[t]he language [the Human Rights Committee regarding Article 27] has chosen to use acknowledges in only a very oblique way the inevitable interplay between the individual and the group in any consideration of minority rights.

Similarly, Thornberry has noted that 'the law on indigenous peoples reflects developments in thinking about minorities and collective [e.g. group] rights generally. The two issues cannot be finally separated, despite the tendency of the international community to develop separate bodies of law. Mbaye put it simply when he wrote: 'In one case, man is considered essentially as an individual, whereas in the other he is with others, united by historical, geographical and social ties, and the rights concerned are accorded to the whole group. Legal fiction has been defined as 'the resort to pretense in the process of legal argumentation'. It has been remarked that a legal fiction is a proposition, purporting to be a principle or rule material to the determination of cases, 'which rests in whole or in part on the factual premises known to be inaccurate at the time of the fiction's invocation'.

Of equal concern to that of the inherent inaccuracy of a legal fiction is the issue of intent. While law has always made use of legal fictions, it is highly questionable as to whether they can be generally defined 'as assumptions of a beneficial or at least harmless character which are intended to promote a just outcome', as has been suggested elsewhere. Whether certain minority groups constitute 'peoples' is a question of ongoing debate, and resolution need not be attempted here.

Certain minorities may or may not constitute peoples in an anthropological or popular sense, but this does not alter the fact that they may constitute a group with common historical and ethnic attributes. Whether minorities constitute 'peoples' in a legal sense matters only if they are required to claim their rights within a constructed legal fiction which attributes certain rights, such as self-determination, to peoples but not to individuals as collectives, and further which does not recognize those collectives as groups.

While the desire to be recognized as a people may be important for a range of reasons, it is relevant in a legal sense only in so far as the legal fiction is applied. The existing legal construct that prevents minorities from being recognized as 'peoples' should not, at a minimun, prevent them being recognized as having group rights. This brings us to the crux of a question posed by Alston: is the maintenance of the legal fiction that frames minority rights only as individual rights, and not as group rights, actually harmful to their protection? And further, does the recognition of indigenous peoples as groups actually allow them to claim their rights as peoples or indeed as groups?

On the basis of the definition of group rights that we have provided, in the context of the right to development, the first question may be answered in the affirmative: casting minority rights exclusively as individual rights may be harmful to attempts to ensure their protection within the development process. And by applying our definition, indigenous peoples would be able to assert their group rights as indigenous peoples in the process of realizing the right to development, and actively claim their right as recognized groups qua peoples.

Compatibility of Group Rights with Individual Human Right

The concern is often raised that group protection might imply imposing the will of a group entity against the individual freedoms of its members and hence the debate is set in terms of a dichotomy: a choice between individual and group rights. Packer proposes that the dichotomy does not in fact exist, in that 'human beings possess both individual and social dimensions', a point of particular relevance with regard to minorities and indigenous peoples where the social dimension can also be understood in terms of group preservation. In practice, the implementation of group rights is restrained by the principles that apply to all rights under international human rights law. In the case of 'collective' rights of indigenous peoples, the UN Human Rights Committee has indicated that the right of an individual to participate in aspects of community life may be restricted if the relevant legislation reflects the legitimate aim of minority group survival and well-being, and if the restriction is not disproportionate to that aim.

Further, any restriction on the right of an individual member of a minority must be shown to have a reasonable and objective justification and be necessary for the continued viability of the minority group as whole. Group rights are not an entity created to assert 'the right of the group against its own members', but rather as a voluntarily formed group 'who agree to pool their individual rights for a specific purpose'.

The free and informed consent of the members of the group is critical, along with the effective exercise of the group rights through suitable arrangements such as legitimate representation, as is the option to opt out of the group. The exercise of group rights is considered in light of the principles that all rights are subject to limitations or modified by duties. The reasoning behind recognition of group rights is to give practical meaning to the human rights that are meant to be protected, as Obiora explains:

> 'The problem is not whether collective [group] rights are deducible from or compatible with individual human rights. In strict logic, collective [group] rights may conflict as much with other categories of human rights as they do with each other. The point is to recognize any claim made for collective [group] rights as valid only in so far as it extends, rather than deprecates other human rights.'

Group Right within the Right to Development

The right to a process of development is a right of all people in a country which is exercised collectively; within that collective there are individuals and groups of individuals, as in the case of minorities and indigenous peoples who require that their additional rights are respected within the process of development and in the outcomes of that process. The right to development is, then, an individual right exercised collectively by all the people in a given country, when the right-holders are individuals, and the collective is recognized in order to realize the right through a collective development policy. The right to development is also a group right for groups of minorities and indigenous peoples - that is, groups which exist within the broader collective.

The right to development can be understood, therefore, as both an individual right exercised collectively by the whole of a population in a given state, and a group right with regard to certain rights that pertain to minorities and indigenous peoples. When some individuals belong to a category or group defined as minority or indigenous, then the method of fulfilling those obligations will necessarily be different, requiring simultaneous adherence to policies and programmes designed for the individual as well as the group. This is necessary in order to ensure the fulfilment of the rights of minorities and indigenous peoples in the development process.

When minorities and indigenous peoples are considered as groups, the policies for their development should be designed as sub-plans of a national programme for development, with special provisions for meeting the requirement of those groups in terms of, for example, the preservation of areas they inhabit and with regard to traditional ways of life as related to work, which the usual national policies for development of all individuals may not take into account.

The rights of peoples, including indigenous peoples, to self-determination and the right to full sovereignty over natural resources, is recognized in the DRD, A and it is suggested herein that other rights aimed at the preservation of minorities and indigenous peoples should be recognized as group rights in order to, inter alia, facilitate the realization of the right to development for these groups. Recognizing group rights within the right to development therefore also allows for corresponding indicators, such as those relating to expropriation of resources, to detect forms of discrimination, determine who is excluded from the development process, and reveal the violation of group rights; conventional analysis, based on the human development approach that uses aggregated welfare indicators would not bring these issues to light.

National policies and programmes, as well as international cooperation by states acting singly or collectively, are required to consider the interdependence of all rights in order to respect the right to development. Policies must be consistent with human rights standards, which would include the rights of minorities and indigenous peoples, directed also at their identities as groups and the preservation of what makes the group distinct.

Any sub-plan aimed at ensuring that development benefits individuals as members of minority or indigenous groups would have an improved chance of realization when also aimed at the group within the particular process of development that is rights-based, including in terms of redistributive policies and economic growth.

The DRD already recognizes and diffuses the inter-relationship between individual rights, collective rights and group rights by referring to the individual as both participant and beneficiary; by emphasizing that the right to development is a comprehensive process aimed at the well-being of the entire population; and by referring to the right to development as an inalienable human right of every human person and all peoples.

While a group consists of the individual people who compose it, an approach to policy formation that recognizes the distinctiveness of the group within the collective may serve to best ensure the protection and promotion of their rights within national development, and indeed the fulfilment of their right to development.

Rights of Minorities and Indigenous People

Minorities and the need to protect and promote their rights were recognized under the League of Nations even though the rights of minorities were not incorporated into the Covenant of the League of Nations itself. In the period between the First and Second World Wars, protecting the rights of minorities was acknowledged as being of international concern and treaties related to newly created states or states that were newly expanded by war had to include provisions for the protection of religious, racial and linguistic minorities which were then placed under the guarantee of the League of Nations.

Following the Second World War the League of Nations was succeeded by the United Nations in 1945 and while any reference to minorities was omitted from the UN Charter and the Universal Declaration of Human Rights (UDHR), this decision can be seen to reflect the sense in the immediate post-war period that recognition of universal individual human rights on a non-discriminatory basis would provide the best means of underpinning the 'new world order'. Moreover, it was felt that a system of general recognition of basic human rights for all would serve to avoid political difficulties which might accompany a regime for the protection of minorities.

Although the focus on human rights for all rather than any regime that could be viewed as potentially divisive reflected the sensitivities at the time, countries of immigration were most vocal in arguing for provisions related to the prevention of discrimination without specific reference to the protection of minorities.

As a result of these factors, only a general prohibition of distinction on the grounds of race, sex, language, or religion is found in the Charter, a provision further elaborated in Article 2 of the UDHR. Despite the lack of attention paid to minority issues at the San Francisco Conference and in the UDHR, it seems that some sections of the UN recognized the

benefit of the qualitatively different form of protection that minority rights could provide.

This can be seen in the establishment as early as 1947 of the Sub-Commission on the Prevention of Discrimination and Protection of Minorities, which was mandated to 'examine what provisions should be adopted in the definition of the principles which are to be applied in the field of the protection of minorities'. Subsequently, the inclusion of a provision specifically on the promotion and protection of the rights of persons belonging to minorities was included in the International Covenant on Civil and Political Rights, which was adopted by the General Assembly in 1966 and entered into force in 1976.

Rights of Minorities in Light of the Right to Development

Article 27 of the ICCPR provides an important global and specific standard applicable to the rights of minorities. It holds:

> 'In those States in which ethnic, religious or linguistic minorities exist, persons belonging to such minorities shall not be denied the right, in community with the other members of their group, to enjoy their own culture, to profess and practise their own religion, or to use their own language.'

Article 27 explicitly refers to three aspects of the rights of minorities, namely: culture, religion and language. The logic behind Article 27 is such that in addition to protection against discrimination, members of minority groups require particular rights to enable them to preserve and develop their ethnic, religious or linguistic characteristics. In international law, minority rights are cast in terms of individual rights exercised collectively. Article 27 of the ICCPR makes this clear by stating that 'persons belonging to such minorities will not be denied the right, in community with other members of their group'. It has been remarked that

> '[t]he rights in Article 27 are a hybrid between individual rights and collective rights because of the "community" requirement: the right of a member of a minority is not exercised alone; enjoyment of culture, practice of religion, and use of language presupposes a community of individuals endowed with similar rights. Minority rights have therefore been described as benefiting individuals but requiring collective exercise.

These rights, as the Human Rights Committee (HRC) reminds us, are 'distinct from and additional to, all other rights to which, as individuals in common with everyone else, they are entitled to enjoy under the Covenant '. While Article 27 addresses the need to preserve the distinct characteristics of minorities, it falls short of explicitly referring to minorities as forming a group. In the realization of the right to development, it is recognition of the rights of minorities as having rights as a group that will provide the strongest safeguard of the very rights that the minorities legal regime seeks to protect.

It is important to note that no conclusive definition exists as to what constitutes a minority group, and recognition as a minority is to be based on self-identification and objective criteria. As has been stated by the HRC, 'The existence of an ethnic, religious or linguistic minority in a given State party does not depend upon a decision by that State party but requires to be established by objective criteria. Objective criteria can be understood as depending on the characteristics of individuals belonging to the group, such as their religion or language, and on the characteristics of the group itself, such as its size and position of non-dominance within the state.

Self-identification, on the other hand, speaks to the will or decision of those individuals to collectively see themselves as different from other inhabitants of the state, who hold or evidence a sense of belonging to the group and who wish for those differences to be maintained in order for the group in its distinctiveness to continue. It is this position of non-dominance of the group as a whole that risks limiting the protection of the rights of persons belonging to minorities in any development process. On 1 December 1992 the UN

General Assembly adopted a resolution approving a Declaration on the Rights of Persons Belonging to National or Ethnic, Religious and Linguistic Minorities (UNDM).

As the Declaration's fourth preambular paragraph makes clear, the UNDM is 'inspired by the provisions of Article 27'. The significance of having the UNDM 'inspired by', as opposed to 'based on', Article 27 of the ICCPR reflects a deliberate decision during drafting to emphasize that, while the interpretation of Article 27 may take the UNDM into account, the Declaration is not restricted by limitations of that Article.

The UNDM in fact goes beyond Article 27 of the ICCPR, addressing the rights of minorities to protect themselves and employing explicit language as to the positive action required of states. The rights of minorities have been elaborated in the Minorities Declaration, the content of which may serve to inform the scope of Article 27.

The Preamble defines the object and the purpose of the instrument and provides the framework through which the operative paragraphs should be interpreted. The preambular paragraphs of the UNDM that are of particular interest to the rights of minorities in the realization of the right to development include the desire of the General Assembly to promote the realization of the principles contained in the UN Charter, the UDHR, the two Covenants and other relevant instruments that have been adopted at the universal or regional level. Preambular paragraph 4 of the UNDM, as was previously mentioned, is '[I]nspired by the provisions of Article 27 of the International Covenant on Civil and Political Rights'. This is a significant point as the UNDM departs from Article 27 by placing considerable emphasis on participation rights, a point central to the right to development and to which we will return.

Notably, however, the HRC has repeatedly taken the view that the right to participate is to be read into Article 27.

The emphasis in preambular paragraph 6 that links the 'constant promotion and realization of the rights of ... minorities' to the 'development of society as a whole' and most specifically to the 'strengthening of friendship and cooperation among peoples and States' sums up the essential role of minority rights as a constitutive element of the right to development. It also places minority rights within the context of Article 55 of the UN Charter from which the language was derived, leading one commentator to deduce that, as such, '[m]inority rights are therefore placed in an analogous position to the principles of self-determination and human rights'.

Article 55 provides the foundation upon which the obligations of international cooperation in the DRD stem, evidenced by its reference to, inter alia, the statement that 'the United Nations shall promote ... higher standards of living, full employment, and conditions of economic and social progress and development ... solutions of international economic, social, health, and related problems ... and universal respect for and observance of human rights', a point to which we shall return later.

Article 1(1) of the Minorities Declaration, which affirms that 'States shall protect the existence and the national or ethnic, cultural, religious and linguistic identity of minorities within their respective territories, and shall encourage conditions for the promotion of that identity', moves beyond Article 27 by explicitly enshrining, in mandatory language by use of the word 'shall', the right of minorities to their existence, protected by states, and the right to the promotion by the state of their identity. While the UNDM provides no definition of existence, the scope of the right can begin to be defined in light of existing standards, such as the right to be protected from genocide, the rights to basic subsistence, and the cultural dimensions of the right to existence, such as protection from ethnocide or forced assimilation.

Further, the right to existence may be linked to the notion of individuals being able to live in community with others.

While several applications of the right may have relevance for the right to development, the right to existence as a right to subsistence and the maintenance of cultural existence are closely associated with the process of development. Although there is no specific reference to minority rights in the DRD, it speaks of the realization of all human rights.

To deprive a group of the economic resources necessary to sustain its existence, both physical and in terms of its cultural traditions in securing the right to food, such as the use of traditional farming techniques or crop selection, systems of community exchange, or nomadic lifestyle, constitutes a failure to respect minority rights. It is significant that Article 1 of the UNDM on the obligation of states to protect the right to existence (and identity) was deliberately placed as the first article (having been moved from the position of Article 2 in the draft text), reflecting the importance of its content and its logic in relation to the rest of the Declaration.

Article 1(2), again cast in mandatory language and without qualifiers that are found in other provisions, obliges states to 'adopt appropriate legislative and other measures to achieve those ends'. Article 2(1) states:

> 'Persons belonging to national or ethnic, religious and linguistic minorities (hereinafter referred to as persons belonging to minorities) have the right to enjoy their own culture, to profess and practise their own religion, and to use their own language, in private and in public, freely and without interference or any form of discrimination.'

Article 2(1) outlines the rights of persons belonging to minorities, providing an elaboration of and improvement on Article 27 of the ICCPR in several areas. Significantly, while Article 27 is cast in negative terms ('persons belonging to such minorities shall not be denied the right ...'), the UNDM replaces this with the positive ('[p]ersons belonging to ... minorities have the right to ...'), emphasizing a requirement of action on the part of states, and an aim of expanding the capabilities of minorities. While the language of UNDM Article 2(1) makes the positive obligation of states clear, ICCPR Article 27, despite its negative wording, has been interpreted by the HRC as imposing positive obligations on states:

'Although article 27 is expressed in negative terms, that article, nevertheless, does recognize the existence of a "right" and requires that it shall not be denied. Consequently, a State party is under an obligation to ensure that the existence and the exercise of this right are protected against their denial or violation. Positive measures of protection are, therefore, required not only against acts of the State party itself, whether through legislative, judicial or administrative authorities, but also against the acts of other persons within the State party.'

Additional language found in Article 2(1) of the UNDM that is not explicitly referred to in ICCPR Article 27 includes reference to the fact that minority rights may be exercised 'in private and in public, freely and without interference or any form of discrimination'. The Minorities Declaration pays considerable attention to the right of minorities to participate. The right to participate is a well-established principle of international law and a tenet central to the process of realizing the right to development. Article 2(2) of the UNDM states that persons belonging to minorities 'have the right to participate effectively' in inter alia 'economic and public life'. Article 2(3) reflects the right of persons belonging to minorities to participate effectively in decisions that 'concern[ing] the minority to which they belong or the regions in which they live'.

Article 4(5) reflects recognition of the need for states to consider taking measures 'so that persons belonging to minorities may participate fully in the economic progress and development in their county. Article 5(1) implies the participation requirement by recognizing that 'national policies and programmes shall be planned and implemented with due regard for the legitimate interests of persons belonging to minorities'. Participation can be understood as requiring the involvement of minority 'communities and associations and their representatives at the earliest stages in the development and implementation of policies and programmes affecting them and to ensure sufficient transparency about such policies', as the UN Committee on the Elimination of Racial Discrimination (CERD) has clearly stated in its 2000 General Recommendation on Discrimination Against Roma, and subsequently in its General Recommendation of 2002 on Descent-Based Discrimination.

Articles 4(5) and 5(1) of the UNDM, when read together, indicate that the 'legitimate interests' of minorities include 'economic progress and development in their country. In the interpretation of ICCPR Article 27, the HRC recognizes that the enjoyment of the rights may require positive legal measures in order 'to ensure the effective participation of members of minority communities in decisions which affect them'.

Article 25 of the ICCPR, which recognizes and protects the right of individuals to participate in processes which constitute the conduct of public affairs, of course applies equally to persons belonging to minorities. As the HRC has made clear, the term 'public affairs' is defined broadly and includes 'the exercise of legislative, executive and administrative powers [and] Hovers all aspects of public administration, and the formulation and implementation of policy at the international, national, regional and local levels'.

The provisions relating to minority participation in the UNDM and ICCPR complement the participation provisions of the DRD. The first article of the DRD refers to '[t]he right to development as an inalienable human right by virtue of which every human person and all peoples are entitled to participate in, contribute to, and enjoy ... development'. Reference to the 'active, free and meaningful participation in development' of the entire population is found in preambular paragraph 2 and in Article 2(3) of the DRD, as is reference to the 'human being [as] the main participant and beneficiary of development'. The importance of 'popular participation in all spheres as an important factor in development and in the full realization of all human rights', is found in Article 8(2) of the DRD.

Hence, development requires the full and effective participation of persons belonging to minorities and the protection of their rights in the design and implementation of development policies and programmes, both nationally and as derived through international cooperation. Just as the DRD requires a process based on the participation of all people in order to realize the right to development, the provisions of the UNDM and ICCPR reflect the particular implications of participation in promoting the rights of minorities. The application of the principle of non-discrimination is also crucial for fulfilling the right to development, as discrimination remains a key barrier to the development of minorities. The right to non-discrimination is a conventional and customary human rights norm found in, inter alia, UNDM Article 4(1), and in the Preamble and in Article 6 of the DRD.

The non-discrimination provisions in the International Convention on the Elimination of All Forms of Racial Discrimination (ICERD) and in the International Covenant on Economic, Social and Cultural Rights (ICESCR) have been applied by their respective Committees to address discrimination against minority groups in areas usually linked very closely to development. CERD's Concluding Observations of states reports, for example, have highlighted the Committee's concerns as to the impact of discrimination in the enjoyment of economic, social and cultural rights for certain minority groups within their territories under Article 5 of ICERD.

Similarly, the Committee on Economic, Social and Cultural Rights (CESCR), in its review of states' periodic reports routinely requests that States parties supply information as to the application of the provision on non-discrimination through the presentation of, inter alia, disaggregated data. CESCR has also emphasized in its statement on 'Poverty and ICESCR', that discrimination is a major factor in the perpetuation of poverty amongst many groups, and that such discrimination has 'profound implications for anti-poverty strategies'.

Article 4 of the Minorities Declaration can be seen as laying the foundation for specific requirements necessary to protect minority rights in the realization of the right to development. In addition to a non-discrimination provision in Article 4(1), it provides in Article 4(2): 'That States shall take measures to create favourable conditions to enable ... minorities to express their characteristics and to develop their culture, language, religion, traditions and customs ...'.

Article 4(3) refers to the opportunity for mother-tongue tuition; Article 4(4) refers to the need for states to consider measures in the field of education that encourage knowledge of their history and traditions etc. and, as previously mentioned, Article 4(5) specifically calls upon states to consider measures that may be required to enable minorities to participate in the economic process and development of their country. Where the language in Article 4 is qualified by the reference to taking measures 'where appropriate', analogous language in the ICESCR nonetheless requires that 'steps should be deliberate, concrete and targeted as clearly as possible towards meeting the obligations recognized'.

The resources available to states to ensure the protection and promotion of minority rights, including their participation, as laid out in Article 4(5) of the UNDM, national policies and programmes planned and implemented with due regard for their interests as per Article 5(1), cooperation and assistance at the international level as per Article 5(2), and the cooperation of states in the promotion of the rights set forth in the UNDM should all be understood to also include resources available from the international community. Applied in the context of the right to a particular process of development, the allocation of resources must be consistent with human rights standards, and economic growth must be undertaken with respect for equity and justice.

The UNDM recognizes in Articles 5(2), 6 and 7, the significance of international cooperation among states in the promotion and protection of the rights of minorities. Article 9 specifically refers to the role of 'specialized agencies and other organizations of the UN ... in the full realization for the rights and principles set forth in this Declaration, within their respective fields of competence'; this is a provision with direct relevance to, for example, the World Bank and the International Monetary Fund.

International cooperation is also a key component of the right to development, a theme to which we return in subsequent sections. The right to development has been defined in light of Article 1 of the DRD and subsequent articles in the Declaration as the right to a process of development that leads to the realization of all the human rights and fundamental freedoms and that expands the capabilities and well-being of all. These freedoms are identified with human development in both its instrumental and substantive forms.

The rights-based approach to development aims to ensure that the process and the outcomes of the process are implemented in a manner consistent with human rights standards. The essential elements of this approach is that it should respect human rights principles - be equitable, both in decision-making and sharing the benefits, non-discriminatory, participatory, accountable and transparent - as well as aim at the realization of human rights standards as derived from international human rights instruments.

While inclusive of the rights-based approach to development, the right to development goes one step further by creating all rights as an integrated whole and the right to development as a comprehensive process for their achievement. Minority rights as human rights and as constituent elements of the right to development must be understood as a part of this particular process, and as such, imposing on all duty-bearers of the right to development, not only obligations of result, but also obligations of conduct.

Right of Indigenous Peoples in Light of the Development

While indigenous peoples most often constitute a minority in the states in which they live, they are groups that have distinct identities and corresponding rights under international law from those of ethnic, linguistic and religions minorities. Indigenous peoples emphasize that they share a distinct history, culture, language and institutional structures with their own specific laws, values, traditions and unique economic, religious and spiritual relationship with their lands.

There is a clear trend in support of distinguishing the question of indigenous rights from that of minorities, evidenced by the separate treatment of the situations facing minorities and indigenous groups within the UN system and by the decision in 1995 to elaborate a declaration on the rights of indigenous peoples signifying that the Minorities Declaration does not comprehensively address the rights of indigenous peoples.

Rights chat protect minorities can apply to members of indigenous groups, exemplified by the numerous cases for the protection of indigenous rights brought under Article 27 of the ICCPR. This does not, however, preclude indigenous peoples from claiming other rights aimed specifically at their identity as indigenous peoples. The specific rights attributed to indigenous peoples, then, are in addition to all individual human rights and minority rights, if they qualify as a minority. As is the case with the term minority, there is no universally accepted definition as to who is indigenous. However, self-identification is central to the determination, as are objective criteria along with historical territorial continuity that predates colonization or invasion by other peoples.

The rights of indigenous peoples within the right to development can be closely linked to several broad international legal standards and principles: participation rights, the right to self-determination, and recognition and implementation of related group rights, such as those pertaining to land and natural resources.

As for minorities, fulfilment of the right to development includes their active, free and meaningful participation in the formulation, implementation, monitoring and evaluation of any policies and programmes that will affect them. It also refers to the ability to share in the benefits of development and requires respect for the principle of non-discrimination throughout. Another closely related standard is that of the right of peoples to self-determination, an inviolable principle of international law.

The right to self-determination is explicitly recognized in the DRD as integral to the realization of the right to development, and includes, as the DRD reaffirms, 'the exercise of [the inalienable right of peoples] to full sovereignty over their wealth and natural resources'. The provisions on self-determination in the DRD are aimed at strengthening the rights of peoples to determine for themselves the forms of development that are appropriate to their cultural values and, as such, self-determination in development includes the right to participate as a group in the design and implementation of a sustainable system of development and the policies that drive it. Another key element pertaining to the promotion and protection of the rights of indigenous peoples in the right to development is the recognition of their rights as a group, including as peoples.

Recognition of the right of the group is essential for group rights to be protected within the realization of the right to development, which is a collective right of an entire population exercised against the state and the international community of states, and which requires particular methods within its process of realization chat address the rights of specific groups. As for minorities, indigenous peoples are entitled to have their right to a process of development fulfilled by having obligations of conduct met through a set of policies that are necessary in order for those results to be achieved. These policies will be aimed at particular groups (devised with their full participation) within the broader national collective. With regard to international standards, the International Labour Organization (ILO) was the intergovernmental body to take the lead on addressing indigenous rights and in 1957 adopted the Indigenous and Tribal Populations Convention 107.

Eventually recognized as assimilationist, it was revised by the 1989 ILO Convention Concerning Indigenous and Tribal Peoples in Independent Countries, No. 169. Convention 107 was ratified by 27 states and while it is closed to further ratification it remains in force for States parties that have not subsequently ratified Convention 169, such as Bangladesh and India, although these States parties are still subject to more contemporary interpretations of the rights contained in it. Convention 169 came into force on 5 September 1991 and has been ratified by 17 countries.

Although it is considered by some indigenous peoples as outdated in light of more recent developments and trends involving indigenous rights, and has a low level of adherents to date, its impact on the process and programmes in the realm of development is nonetheless seen as significant. According to the Guide to the Convention,

> 'In spite of the relatively slow rate of ratifications, this Convention has had significant influence on domestic policies and programmes, as well as the policy guide-lines of several funding agencies. This shows that, to induce changes in the perception of the problems and the ways to solve them, ratification, though desirable and in the long term necessary, is not indispensable in the short and medium term.'

Moreover, despite certain shortcomings, Convention 169 is significant in that it is currently the only binding international instrument, still open for ratification, dedicated to the rights of indigenous peoples. The term 'indigenous populations' was widely used until the adoption of Convention 169 which, in the process of revising Convention 107, replaced the term with 'indigenous peoples'. This was the result of strenuous lobbying by, among others, the representatives of indigenous organizations who felt that the term 'indigenous populations' failed to reflect their fundamental identity as peoples and their distinct attributes, beliefs, traditions and historical relationship to land.

The reticence of states to embrace the term 'peoples' reflects their perpetual concern that the unqualified use of the term might imply a right to (external) self-determination such as through secession. It is not therefore uncommon to see references to indigenous peoples followed by a clause stating that the use of the term 'peoples' shall not be construed as having any implications as regards the rights which may attach to the term under international law. This general acceptance by states that indigenous groups have a distinct identity and corresponding rights, combined with the unwillingness of certain states to apply the term free from explicit references that offer legal safeguards to their territorial integrity, was still apparent in the language endorsed in the Durban Declaration of the World Conference Against Racism in 2001.

Significantly, however, the UN World Summit on Sustainable Development held in 2002 adopted its final documents with an unqualified use of the term, which is largely felt to reflect a vital step in appropriately defining the rights of indigenous peoples. The rights of indigenous people relevant to the development process as articulated in ILO Convention 169, include their right to participate in the process. Specific reference can be found in the Preamble, which recognizes 'the aspirations of these peoples to exercise control over their ... ways of life and economic development'. Article 2(2)(b) refers to the responsibility of governments 'for developing, with the participation of the peoples concerned, co-ordinated and systematic action to protect the rights of these peoples and to guarantee respect for their integrity ... [and] shall include measures ... promoting the full realisation of the social, economic, and cultural rights of these peoples'.

Article 6 insists chat governments, when applying the provisions of the Convention, shall '(a) consult the peoples concerned, through appropriate procedures ... (b) establish means by which these peoples can freely participate ... at all levels of decision-making [in all bodies] responsible for policies and programmes which concern them'. Article 6(2) makes clear that '[t]he consultations carried out in the application of this Convention shall be undertaken in good faith and in a form appropriate to the circumstances with the objective of achieving agreement or consent to the proposed measures'. Article 7 refers specifically to the rights of indigenous peoples in the process of, development, stating in Article 7(1) that indigenous peoples shall 'have the right to decide choir own priorities for development ... and to exercise control, to the extent possible, over their own economic, social and cultural development.

In addition, they shall participate in the formulation, implementation and evaluation of plans and programmes for national and regional development which may affect them directly' Regarding the conditions of life and work and levels of health and education, Article 7(2) states that 'their participation and co-operation, shall be a matter of priority in plans for overall economic development of the areas they inhabit'.

The Guide on Convention 169 suggests that while Article 7 does not provide for a right of veto by indigenous peoples over development plans, there must be:

> 'actual consultation in which [indigenous and tribal] .. . peoples have a right to express their point of view and a right to influence the decision. This means chat governments have to supply the enabling environment and conditions to permit indigenous and tribal peoples to make a meaningful contribution.'

In relation to land which indigenous peoples have traditionally occupied, Article 14 provides that 'measures shall be taken in appropriate cases to safeguard the right of [indigenous] peoples to use lands not exclusively occupied by them, but to which they have traditional access for their subsistence and traditional activities'. With regard to natural resources, Article 15 recognizes the rights of indigenous peoples to have such land specially safeguarded, including through the right 'to participate in the use, management and conservation of these resources', and by ensuring that if the state retains ownership of the resources,

> 'governments shall establish or maintain procedures through which they shall consult [indigenous] peoples, with a view to ascertaining whether and to what degree their interests would be prejudiced, before undertaking or permitting any programmes for the exploration or exploitation of such resources pertaining to their lands. The peoples concerned shall wherever possible participate in the benefits of such activities, and shall receive ... compensation ...'.

Article 16 addresses compensation if 'as an exceptional measure' indigenous peoples have been removed from the lands which they occupy. The criteria to be applied in the determination of compensation, including in the case of relocation, should be 'their free and informed consent' and entail 'wherever possible, the right to return to their traditional lands, as soon as the grounds for relocation cease to exist'. Although many indigenous groups are not satisfied with the promotion and protection afforded them under Convention 169 (and are contemptuous of Convention 107), it does provide a minimum standard.

Furthermore, it can be considered as far-reaching in its recognition of the group rights of indigenous peoples, it commits states to positive action, and has codified standards that have been instrumental in increasing the awareness of indigenous rights. '55 Beyond Convention 169, there is a large body of universal and inter-American law that also deals with indigenous rights; some of which goes further than Convention 169 and serves to strengthen the scope of their rights, thereby giving further practical meaning to the particular process and content of the right to development. In addition to the monitoring mechanisms of the ILO, human rights monitoring bodies, including the Committee on the Elimination of Racial Discrimination, the Human Rights Committee, and the Inter-American Commission on Human Rights (IACHR), have paid particular attention to the rights of indigenous peoples.

These bodies have contributed to the progressive development of international human rights law through the interpretation of human rights instruments of general applicability to the specific rights of indigenous peoples. The African Commission on Human and Peoples' Rights has also recently turned its attention to the rights of indigenous peoples by establishing a Working Group on indigenous peoples in Africa. This forum could provide a meaningful contribution to the importance of indigenous peoples' rights and the right to development, given that the African Charter on Human and Peoples' Rights clearly recognizes the rights of peoples and provides for a binding right to development.

While the Convention on the Elimination of All Forms of Racial Discrimination does not specifically mention indigenous peoples, they are clearly entitled to the protection of the Convention. This is reflected in CERD's extensive consideration of the obligations of States parties with regard to indigenous issues in the review of states' reports, and in its adoption in 1997 of a General Recommendation on the Rights of Indigenous Peoples.

The General Recommendation addresses several key rights integral to the fulfilment of the right to development. The areas it covers include the provision by States parties of conditions 'allow[ing] for sustainable economic and social development compatible with their cultural characteristics'; ensuring 'equal rights in respect of effective participation in public life and that no decisions directly relating to their rights and interests are taken without their informed consent'; recognizing and protecting 'the rights of indigenous peoples to own, develop, control and use their communal lands and territories and resources traditionally owned or otherwise inhabited or used without their free and informed consent'.

With regard to restitution, the General Recommendation also refers to 'the right to just, fair and prompt compensation [which] should as far as possible take the form of lands and territories'. The General Recommendation uses both the terms 'indigenous peoples' and 'indigenous communities', and elsewhere is individual in its construct, referring to 'members of indigenous peoples'. One commentator has recognized the normative potential of ICERD to cope with 'new forms of racism'. 115 While racial discrimination against indigenous peoples is not new, CERD's interpretation of the Convention reflects the latter's normative potential to cope with new forms of oppression, and hence new ways in which discrimination impacts on the lives of those who are discriminated against.

The Committee has remarked on threats to indigenous lands posed by, for example, displacement in the case of the Philippines, mining activities in Panama, and privatization of Saami lands in Sweden. In the Concluding Observations on Australia's report, the Committee emphasized the need to 'ensure effective participation by indigenous communities in decisions affecting their land rights' and the 'importance of ensuring "informed consent" of indigenous peoples'. Indeed, the General Recommendation refers to the discrimination against indigenous peoples and the deprivation of their rights not only at the hands of colonists, but by 'commercial companies and State enterprises'.

The right to participate and rights related to the land, territories and resources of indigenous peoples is increasingly recognized as a right to free, informed and prior consent, as recent work of CERD reflects. While Convention 169 refers to 'free and informed consent' in respect of relocation as a result of the removal of indigenous peoples from the lands which they occupy, the same language is not used in the provisions addressing the rights of indigenous peoples to participate, including in rights integrally linked to the development process. This lacuna is addressed in Article 30 of the UN Draft Declaration on the Rights of Indigenous Peoples, which explicitly states:

> 'Indigenous peoples have the right to determine and develop priorities and strategies for the development or use of their lands, territories and other resources, including the right to require that States obtain their free and informed consent prior to the approval of any project affecting their lands, territories and other resources ...'.

In meetings such as those of the UN Working Group on Indigenous Populations, denial of access and control over their own resources is noted as one of the most important causes of the poverty faced by indigenous peoples. International standards recognize the rights of indigenous peoples over their lands, territories and natural resources, as evidenced in Article 14 and Article 15 of Convention 169, Chapter 26 of Agenda 21 and the recent normative developments emerging from the Draft Declaration on the Rights of Indigenous Peoples. The relevance of these rights to the fulfilment of the right to development is made clear in Principle 3 of the Rio Declaration on Environment and Development, and in both the Preamble and Article 23 of the Draft Declaration.

The Preamble reflects the concern that: 'Indigenous peoples have been deprived of their human rights and fundamental freedoms, resulting, inter alia, in their colonization and dispossession of their lands, territories and resources, thus preventing them from exercising, in particular, their right to development in accordance with their own needs and interests', and Article 23 states that: 'Indigenous peoples have the right to determine and develop priorities and strategies for exercising their right to development ... '. The Human Rights Committee which monitors state compliance with the ICCPR, both in its views on individual communications under Article 27 and in its Concluding Observations on states reports, recognizes that 'development' measures may pose a threat to the traditional way of life and culture of indigenous peoples in violation of their rights under the Covenant.

In the case of the Lubicon Lake Band v. Canada, the Committee decision affirms that projects aimed at the economic development of a country are to be assessed with consideration to their obligations under Article 27 which protects, inter alia, the cultural rights of persons belonging to minorities. In the Lansman case of 1992, the HRC remarked that the scope of the state's freedom to encourage development or allow economic activity by enterprises 'is not to be assessed by reference to a margin of appreciation, but by reference to the obligations it has undertaken in article 27'. In its Concluding Observations on the report submitted by Mexico, the Committee remarked on the importance of the sovereignty of indigenous peoples over natural resources when it noted:

> 'The State party should take all necessary measures to safeguard for the indigenous communities respect for the rights and freedoms to which they are entitled individually and as a group; to eradicate the abuses to which they are subjected; and to respect their customs and culture and their traditional patterns of living, enabling them to enjoy the usufruct of their lands and natural resources and that appropriate measures should also be taken to increase their participation in the country's institutions and the exercise of the right to self-determination.'

As the DRD makes clear, participation is central to the right to development, a right also emphasized by the HRC with regard to the participation of members of indigenous communities in decisions that affect them. In the Lansman case of 1995, the Committee recalled the terms of paragraph 7 of its General Comment on Article 27, 'in which minorities or indigenous groups have a right to the protection of traditional activities such as hunting, fishing or reindeer husbandry, and that all measures must be taken to ensure the effective participation of members of minority communities in decisions which affect them. The participation of members of indigenous communities in decision-making and its importance in ensuring the sustainability of their culture and their way of life is also addressed in a range of Concluding Observations issued by the HRC, for example, with regard to Sweden, Venezuela, and Mexico.

Increasingly, participation rights, such as those we have referred to, are being interpreted not merely as a right to consultation but as a right to consent. In 2002, the Inter-American Court of Human Rights (IACtHR) ruled on the importance of consent and the implied need for prior participation in decision-making regarding indigenous peoples and their land in Awas Tingni Indigenous Community of Mayagna v. the State of Nicaragua. Finding that Nicaragua had violated the right to property, judicial protection and due process of law, by granting logging concessions on the lands of indigenous peoples without taking steps to title and demarcate those lands, the IACtHR held that:

> 'The State of Nicaragua is actively responsible for violations of the right to property, embodied in Article 21 of the Convention, by granting a concession to the company SOLCARSA to carry out road construction work and logging exploitation on the Awas Tingni lands, without the consent of the Awas Tingni Community.'

While this was the first case regarding indigenous people to be heard by the Inter-American Court, the Inter-American Commission on Human Rights in its capacity to consider petitions has examined allegations against governments for the violation of the rights of indigenous peoples. The submission regarding the Huaorani in Ecuador listed the ills of 'development' to which this indigenous group had been exposed, including colonization, land speculation and dispossession, logging, disease epidemics and displacement from traditional territories.

The Commission's recommendations addressed, inter alia, access to information and participation in relevant decision-making processes, interpreting this to mean:

> ' ... that the State take measures necessary to ensure the meaningful and effective participation of indigenous representatives in the decision-making processes about development and other issues which affect them and their cultural survival. "Meaningful" in this sense necessarily implies that indigenous representatives have full access to information which will facilitate their participation.'

In addition, the underlying principle of 'respect for the inherent dignity of the person' - and as such the right to life and physical integrity - was recognized by the Commission as a key right at issue in the process of development. The Commission's conclusion reflected an appreciation of the right to development which entails a process and form of development that respects all human rights when they observed that 'the norms of the Inter-American system neither prevent nor discourage development; rather, they require that development take place under conditions that respect and ensure the human rights of the individuals concerned'.

In the concluding recommendations on indigenous issues in its 1999 Report of the State of Human Rights in Colombia, the Inter-American Commission remarked that it expected the state to ensure that processes of development did not 'cause irreparable harm to the religious, economic or cultural identity and rights of indigenous communities'. In the same report the Commission referred specifically to the right to development,

> 'in the sense of future development of their social groups, their culture, and improvement of their own quality of life, in accordance with their cultural and social systems and the life plans they devise or carry out as peoples, and their development in terms of their inter-cultural relationship with national development'.

Just as in the DRD, the IACHR has defined the right to development as providing an improvement in well-being. This reflects an appreciation of the right to development as a right to a particular process of development which has as its aim the constant improvement of all people. Increasingly, the right to development understood as a legal right to a particular process of development, is being addressed in international judicial fora, and international and, regional standards and jurisprudence are elaborating its scope. The full range of international human rights standards, including those elaborated specifically to protect the rights of minorities and indigenous peoples, must be consistently respected in development.

The right to development builds on the coordination of these standards and requires not only that they are consistently applied by states acting at the national level and by the international community of states, but that their interdependence is reflected in the process of development. The interdependence of rights in a process of development aims to ensure that the realization or improvement of one right is not achieved at the cost of another's deterioration. As such, the right to development is not an aggregate of existing rights but a distinct right, in which the rights of minorities and indigenous peoples, including their effective participation in all stages of the development process, as well as access to its benefits, are essential to its fulfilment. The application of the principle of non-discrimination and the implementation of special measures, where required, is also of central importance, because discrimination against minorities and indigenous peoples dramatically hinders their development.

Detailing the rights of minorities and indigenous peoples within the realization of the right to development serves also to illustrate how the right to development is violated, and thus the relevance of treating the right to development in a comprehensive manner in which all rights are integral to it. Consequently, protecting and promoting the rights of minorities and indigenous peoples in any development process, and ensuring their ability to develop according to their values and in line with their human rights, imposes on states obligations not only of result, but of conduct.

Right to Development is a Right of States

Under international human rights law right-holders are individuals, or individuals owed rights collectively or as groups with regard to rights which only a group can claim. Within the right to development the right-holders are the collective of individuals in a given state as well as groups within the collective, as is the case for minorities and indigenous peoples. People are the subjects of international human rights law.

While individuals cannot assert their right to the process of development individually, they are nonetheless right-holders and certainly beneficiaries. With regard to the right to development, states acting at the international level as duty-bearers play an essential role in fulfilling obligations of international cooperation in order to assist in the realization of the right.

States acting nationally within the existing inter-state system are the entity through which the international component of the right is asserted. The role of developing states in asserting the right to development of their people internationally does not, however, render the right to development a right of states, as some commentators and representatives of several developing states insist on arguing.

Indeed, the debate on the right to development began with the developing countries propounding that the right to development was distinct from civil, political, economic, social and cultural rights and instead should be understood as a right of developing countries seeking to build a new international economic order. Bedjaoui is among those who claim that the right to development is a right of states. He defends the view that the right to development is primarily a right belonging to developing states in claiming their entitlement 'to receive a fair share of what belongs to all', although he recognizes that the beneficiaries should be individuals, as well as the state.

The DRD offers a different interpretation, casting the right to development as a human right at the centre of which is 'the constant improvement and ... well-being of the entire population and of all individuals ... [aimed at] conditions favourable to the development of peoples and individuals ... [and] [c]onfirming that the right to development is an inalienable human right'. The primary concern of those who defend the right to development as a right of states is to extend the human rights principles of equality, non-discrimination, participation and accountability, as well as democratic decision-making, to international relations. This, it is felt, would facilitate the development of their countries thwarted by the unequal relationships of the international economic systems that govern trade and finance.

While developing countries emphasize the need for equity and participation in international relations, in the early debates of the 1970s this was not matched by equivalent attention given to their domestic obligations, a problem that persists, as is apparent in many of the exchanges in the Working Group on the Right to Development. Although there is little doubt that it is reasonable for developing states to expect equitable treatment that mirrors universally agreed human rights standards within the scope of their international interactions, in order for the right to development of people or groups to be fulfilled, representation must be established as genuine and democratic. The need for legitimate democratic structures is part of the right to development, which, as the DRD makes clear, includes respect for civil and political rights.

The duty placed upon states to cooperate with each other in ensuring development and in eliminating obstacles to development is meaningful only if the benefits of that cooperation further the rights of people to develop. This is critical to advancing the rights of minorities and indigenous peoples who, because of discrimination and marginalization, are less likely to benefit from the fulfilment of any obligations at the international level when this has a positive impact at the domestic level. Since in many cases they have little or no access to any form of political influence or public participation, overall development of a country may not contribute to their ability to develop. Respecting existing standards that pertain to minorities and indigenous peoples, redressing discrimination, ensuring participation, as well as assessing the impact of development activities, are part of what is required in realizing the right to development.

To suggest the right belongs to the state is to fail to fully comprehend the implications of the nature of human rights, whose beneficiaries are individuals for whom mechanisms must exist to ensure that their rights are protected, and that any benefits derived of international cooperation are accrued accordingly. The views of some detractors notwithstanding, there is now a general consensus that the right to development is a human right. The right to development as a human right was reaffirmed, inter alia, in the Vienna Declaration and Programme of Action adopted by consensus by 171 states at the World Conference on Human Rights in 1993.

A consensus document, elaborated and adopted by the states of the world community, reflects a strong endorsement of its content, indeed there is support for the view that consensus is replacing consent as a basis of international legal obligation. Article 10 of the Vienna -Declaration and Programme of Action states, inter alias 'The World Conference on Human Rights reaffirms the right to development, as established in the Declaration on the Right to Development, as a universal and inalienable right and an integral part of fundamental human rights. Its recognition and acceptance as a human right, at least from the adoption of the DRD onwards, implies the existence of a binary relationship between right-holders and duty-bearers - where there are rights there are duties.

Now if humans are the right-holders, who are the dutybearers of the right to development? The answer is that the duty-bearers are both the state and the international community of states. It is at both these levels that the obligation to realize the human right to development exists. As international law is still a system that operates within an inter-state paradigm, at the international level it is for the state to claim the right to development from the international community on behalf of its people, and therefore it follows that it is for the state to deliver the right to development to the people, within a framework that respects existing human rights standards. Despite the prospect that international law may be gradually transforming itself into a law of the worldwide community of human beings and transcending its inter-state basis, the machinery does not exist as yet for allowing people to demand that the international community put their right to development into effect.

Within the framework of international human rights law, rights and obligations, and thus accountability in the right to development, goes beyond inter-state accountability to respond to the accountability of the state or the international community of states, to the people who are meant to benefit from a process of development. However, no mechanism currently exists to assess compliance with the principles enumerated in the DRD.

While it is beyond the scope of this chapter to consider systems whereby states could be held accountable for violations of the right to development, including the rights of minorities and indigenous peoples, the Committee on Economic, Social and Cultural Rights is providing guidance in terms of the content of obligations under the ICESCR, both nationally and internationally.

An optional protocol allowing for communications under the ICESCR could contribute to strengthening accountability, as do the views of the Human Rights Committee in relation to Article 27. Domestic courts have also adjudicated on economic, social and cultural rights, and an international mechanism to enforce the right to development, including the particular process it entails, could complement the contribution being made by judicial and quasi-judicial bodies at the national and international levels.

So while the international community of states has human rights obligations to all people, the fulfilment of these obligations is often made possible through the state. When certain states assert that the right to development is a right of states, their argument can only be understood as another way of remarking on its role as a vehicle in the realization of the human right to development.

Although a state may need to claim the right to development from the international community before it can be realized by the people to whom it is owed, this does not make the right to development a right of states. It simply reflects the role of the state in an inter-state system. The government may be the agent through which the right can be vindicated; however, it will be acting in a secondary capacity, rather than as the holder of the rights.

So while there may be situations in which the state can claim the human right on behalf of people and groups, the condition of this claim must be that a procedure is established for the delivery of the human right in question. As previously mentioned, this procedure must be democratic and representative in order to ensure that the rights of individuals and of groups, including those of minorities and indigenous peoples, are met in the processes and in the outcomes. Obiora provides a cogent summary:

> 'Where LDCs [Least Developed Countries] become the subject of the right to development at the international level, their citizens and subjects are endowed with the right at the national level as individuals and/or as members of relevant ... groups. In this mode, development constitutes a collective process and

> the individual, while not able to assert the right per se, may claim the establishment of conditions necessary for her or his development in interaction with others. In turn the state becomes the plenipotentiary or international dimension of peoples ... '

Developing states' drive to participate as equals in the international economic order and to claim this prerogative in relation to the international community, in order to allow for their viable and sustainable economic development, is by no means without merit, and is reflected in the DRD. The Preamble confirms that 'the right to development is an inalienable human right and that the equality of opportunity for development is a prerogative both of nations and of individuals who make up nations'. The reference to the prerogative of nations recognizes the international dimension of the right to development and hence the implications of international cooperation on the ability of certain states to fulfil the right.

As right-holders it is human beings who are owed the rights, including the right to international cooperation, even though these may have to be asserted by their state. States do have rights (and obligations) under international law; they do not, however, have rights under international human rights law beyond that which facilitates the realization of the human rights of people. Article 2(3) of the DRD provides that

> 'States have the right and the duty to formulate appropriate national development policies that aim at the constant improvement of the well-being of the entire population and of all individuals, on the basis of their active, free and meaningful participation in development and in the fair distribution of the benefits resulting there from'.

The formulation implies that the state can assert the right of its people to development against other states and the international community. In the current globalized world Article 2(3) can indeed be interpreted as a developing state's need for international cooperation because of individual states' increasing loss of autonomy, a loss that characterizes the contemporary global economy. Hence, the ability of the state to fulfil its domestic obligations, including the duty to formulate appropriate policies to deliver the right to development, may be constrained by the actions of the international community.

In light of this reasoning, the interpretation of the right referred to in Article 2(3) is that the right of states is the 'right to develop human rights-based development policies in the interests of their people' made possible, where necessary, through international cooperation. The role of the state, then, is not as a holder of the right to development but as a vehicle through which the right can be realized by its people and as primary duty-bearer.

The international community of states, for its part, has an obligation to cooperate in order to enable the realization of the right and to contribute to the ability of the developing state to fulfil the right. Perhaps Keba Mbaye, former Vice-President of the International Court of justice and among the first advocates of a right to development, best explained the distinction when he wrote:

> Admittedly, it is usually States, as representatives ... that exercise the [human] rights accorded to [individuals considered jointly]. But it in no way alters the basic legal fact that these rights are accorded to peoples and nations ... The State itself plays the role of the equivalent of legal trustee.'

The 'right', then, 'is exercisable by the state against those with the power to deny or constrain the capacity of the state to formulate national development policies that benefit the people within the state'. While this is consistent with the role of the state as an agent of the people, it presupposes that the state is representing the interests of the people and their ability to realize their right to development - which necessarily includes their effective participation in the elaboration and implementation of any development policy or programme, a right central to the protection of the rights of minorities and indigenous peoples. Should the recipient state be unable or unwilling to represent its people in accordance with accepted international standards, it should necessarily forfeit its 'right to formulate appropriate national policies'.

International human rights law places constraints on a nation's sovereignty and, as a result, along with international law, the notion of sovereignty has evolved and has long since ceased to suggest the allowing of a state's unlimited power over its people. While effective and legitimate states may provide the best means of ensuring rights, the notion of 'sovereignty as responsibility' in both internal functions and external duties has redrawn the acceptable scope of the definition of sovereignty.

Under international human rights law, states are the primary duty-bearer (although by no means the only duty-bearer). By establishing an international human rights regime in the aftermath of the Second World War, states sacrificed a part of their sovereignty in order to allow for external assessment and regulation of the degree to which they ensure the promotion and protection of human rights, both within their jurisdictions and wherever their activities, or activities of any other agent falling within their jurisdiction, would have an impact on human rights.

States are consequently subject to the law of international human rights, their role being that of duty-bearer and not direct beneficiary of the rights. While states have the duty to formulate development policies (under the condition of aiming to improve the well-being of all people, including their full participation, and giving effect to the fair distribution of resulting benefits), in a globalized world states can also be said to have a right exercisable against the international community, because they face constraints that can be removed only by the cooperation of the international community; for example, through market access, debt relief, and the redesigning of structural adjustment. Finally, it should be noted that global cooperation can take many forms and is not limited to financial assistance. .

International obligations include the requirement that states acting singly respect the enjoyment of human rights in other countries, and acting collectively as part of international organizations, take due account of human rights. In this respect, international cooperation could include: meeting commitments provided for in international environmental treaties, the creation of patent laws that are more equitable than those which currently hinder access to medicine in less affluent countries, and other institutional reforms to the global economy.

6

Draft Declaration on the Rights of Indigenous Peoples

Annex 1

Draft declaration as agreed upon by the members of the working group at its eleventh session

Affirming that indigenous peoples are equal in dignity and rights to all other peoples, while recognizing the rights of all peoples to be different, to consider themselves different, and to be respected as such,

Affirming also that all peoples contribute to the diversity and richness of all civilizations and cultures, which constitute a common heritage of humankind,

Affirming further that all doctrines, polices and practices based on or advocating superiority of peoples or individuals on the basis of national origin, racial, religious, ethnic or cultural differences are racist, scientifically false, legally invalid, morally condemnable and socially unjust,

Reaffirming also that indigenous peoples, in the exercise of their rights, should be free from discrimination of any kind,

Concerned that indigenous peoples have been deprived of their human rights and fundamental freedoms, resulting, inter alia, in their colonization and the dispossession of their lands, territories and resources, thus preventing them from exercising, in particular, their right to development in accordance with their own needs and interests,

Recognizing the urgent need to respect and promote the rights and characteristics of indigenous peoples, especially their rights to their lands, territories and resources, which derive from their political, economic and social structures and from their cultures, spiritual traditions, histories and philosophies,

Welcoming the fact that indigenous peoples are organizing themselves for political, economic, and social and cultural enhancement and in order to bring an end to all forms of discrimination and oppression wherever they occur,

Convinced that control by indigenous peoples over developments affecting them and their lands, territories and resources will enable them to maintain and strengthen their institutions, cultures and traditions, and to promote their development in accordance with their aspirations and needs,

Recognizing also that respect for indigenous knowledge, cultures and traditional practices contributes to sustainable and equitable development and proper management of the environment,

Emphasizing the need for demilitarization of the lands and territories of indigenous peoples, which will contribute to peace, economic and social progress and development, understanding and friendly relations among nations and peoples of the world,

Recognizing in particular the right of indigenous families and communities to retain shared responsibility for the upbringing, training, education and well-being of their children,

Recognizing also that indigenous peoples have the right freely to determine their relationships with States in a spirit of coexistence, mutual benefit and full respect,

Considering that treaties, agreements and other arrangements between States and indigenous peoples are properly matters of international concern and responsibility,

Acknowledging that the Charter of United Nations, the International Covenant on Economic, Social and Cultural Rights and the International Covenant on Civil and political Rights affirm the fundamental importance of the right of self-determination of all peoples, by virtue of which they freely determine their political status and freely pursue their economic, social and cultural development,

Bearing in mind that nothing in this Declaration may be used to deny any peoples their right of self-determination,

Encouraging States to comply with and effectively implement all international instruments, in particular those relating to human rights, as they apply to indigenous peoples, in consultation and cooperation with the people concerned,

Emphasizing that the United Nations has an important and continuing role to play in promoting and protecting the rights of indigenous peoples,

Believing that this Declaration is a further important step forward for the recognition, promotion and protection of the rights and freedoms of indigenous peoples and in the development of relevant activities of the United Nations system in this field,

Solemnly proclaims the following United Nations Declaration on the Rights of Indigenous Peoples:

Part I

Article 1.

Indigenous peoples have the right to the full and effective enjoyment of all of the human rights and fundamental freedoms which are recognized in the Charter of the United Nations and in the human rights law;

Article 2.

Indigenous individuals and peoples are free and equal to all other individuals and peoples in dignity and rights, and have the right to be free from any kind of adverse discrimination, in particular that based on their indigenous origin or identity;

Article 3.

Indigenous people have the right of self-determination. By virtue of that right they freely determine their political status and freely pursue their economic, social and cultural development;

Article 4.

Indigenous peoples have the right to maintain and strengthen their distinct political, economic, social and cultural characteristics, as well as their legal systems, while retaining their rights to participate fully, if they so choose, in the political, economic, social and cultural life of the State;

Article 5.

Every Indigenous person has the right to belong to a nationality;

Part II

Article 6.

No Genecide Indigenous peoples have the collective right to live in freedom, peace and security as distinct peoples and to full guarantees against genocide or any other act of violence, including the removal of indigenous children from their families and communities under any pretext.

Article 7.

Indigenous peoples have the collective and individual right not to be subject to ethnocide and cultural genocide, including the prevention of and redress for:

(a) Any action which has the aim or effect of depriving them of their integrity as distinct peoples, or of their cultural values or identities;

(b) Any action which has the aim or effect of dispossessing them of their lands, territories or resources;

(c) Any form of population transfer which has the aim or effect of violating or undermining any of their rights;

(d) Any form of assimilation or integration by other cultures or ways of life imposed on them by legislative, administrative or other measures;

(e) Any form of propoganda directed against them;

Article 8.

Indigenous peoples have the collective and individual right to maintain and develop their distinct identities and characteristics, including the right to identify themselves as indigenous and to be recognized as such;

Article 9.

Indigenous peoples and individuals have the right to belong to an indigenous community or nation, in accordance with the traditions and customs of the community or nation concerned. No disadvantage of any kind may arise from the exercise of such a right;

Article 10.

Indigenous peoples shall not be forced from their lands or territories. No relocation shall take place without the free and informed consent of the indigenous peoples concerned and after agreement on just and fair compensation and, where possible, with the option of return;,

Article 11.

Indigenous peoples have the right to special protection and security in periods of armed conflict.

States shall observe international standards, in particular the Fourth Geneva Convention of 1949, for the protection of civilian populations in circumstances of emergency and armed conflict, and shall not:

(a) Recruit indigenous individuals against their will in the armed forces and, in particular, for use against other indigenous peoples;

(b) Recruit indigenous children into the armed forces under any circumstances;

(c) Force indigenous individuals to abandon their lands, territories or means of subsistence, or relocate them in special centers for military purposes;

(d) Force indigenous individuals to work for military purposes under any discriminary conditions;

Part III

Article 12.

Indigenous peoples have the right to practice and revitalize their cultural traditions and customs. This includes the right to maintain, protect and develop the past, present and future manifestations of their cultures, such as archaeological and historical sites, artifacts, designs, ceremonies, technologies and visual and performing arts and literature, as well as the right to restitution of cultural, intellectual, religious and spiritual property taken without their free and informed consent or in violation of their laws, traditions and customs;

Article 13.

Indigenous peoples have the right to manifest, practice, develop and teach their spiritual and religious traditions, customs and ceremonies; the right to maintain, protect, and have access in privacy to their religious and cultural sites; the right to use and control of ceremonial objects; and the right to repatriation of human remains.

States shall take effective measures, in conjunction with the indigenous peoples concerned, to ensure that indigenous sacred places, including burial sites, be preserved, respected and protected;

Article 14.

Indigenous peoples have the right to revitalize, use, develop and transmit to future generations their histories, languages, oral traditions, philosophies, writing systems and literatures, and to designate and retain their own names for communities, places and persons.

States shall take effective measures, especially whenever any right of indigenous peoples may be affected, to ensure this right and to ensure that they can understand and be understood in political, legal and administrative proceedings where necessary through the provision of interpretation or by other appropriate means;

Part IV

Article 15.

Indigenous children have the right to all levels and forms of education of the State. All indigenous peoples also have this right and the right to establish and control their educational systems and institutions providing education in their own languages, in a manner appropriate to their cultural methods of teaching and learning.

Indigenous children living outside their communities have the right to be provided access to education in their own culture and language.

Article 16.

Indigenous peoples have the right to have the dignity and diversity of their cultures, traditions, histories and aspirations appropriately reflected in all forms of education and public information.

States shall take effective measures, in consultation with the indigenous peoples concerned, to eliminate all prejudice and discrimination and to promote tolerance, understanding and good relations among indigenous peoples and all segments of society;

Article 17.

Indigenous people have the right to establish their own languages. They also have the right to equal access to all forms of non-indigenous media.

States shall take effective measures to ensure that State-owned media duly reflect indigenous cultural diversity;

Article 18.

Indigenous peoples have the right to enjoy fully all rights established under international labour law and national labour legislation.

Indigenous individuals have the right not to be subjected to any discriminatory conditions of labour, inter alia, employment and salary;

Part V

Article 19.

Indigenous peoples have the right to participate fully, if they so choose, at all levels of decision-making in matters which may affect their rights, lives and destinies through representatives chosen by themselves in accordance with their own procedures as well as to maintain and develop their own indigenous decision-making institutions;

Article 20.

Indigenous peoples have the right to participate fully, if they so choose, through procedures determined by them, in devising legislative or administrative measures that may affect them.

States shall obtain the free and informed consent of the peoples concerned before adopting and implementing such measures;

Article 21.

Indigenous people have the right to maintain and develop their political, economic and social systems, to be secure in the enjoyment of their own means of subsistence and development, and to engage freely in all their traditional and other economic activities. Indigenous peoples who have been deprived of their means of subsistence and development are entitled to just and fair compensation;

Article 22.

Indigenous people have the right to special measures for immediate effective and continuing improvement of their economic and social conditions, including in the areas of employment, vocational training and retraining, housing, sanitation, health and social security.

Particular attention shall be paid to the rights and special needs of indigenous elders, women, youth, children and disabled persons;

Article 23.

Indigenous people have the right to determine and develop priorities and strategies for exercising their right to development. In particular, indigenous people have the right to determine and develop all health, housing and other economic and social programmes affecting them and, as far as possible, to administer such programmes through their own institutions;

Article 24.

They also have the right to access, without any discrimination, to all medical institutions, health services and medical care;

Part VI

Article 25.

Indigenous peoples have the right to maintain and strengthen their distinctive spiritual and material relationship with the lands, territories, waters and coastal seas and other resources which they have traditionally owned or otherwise occupied or used, and to uphold their responsibilities to future generations in this regard;

Article 26.

Indigenous peoples have the right to own, develop, control and use the lands and territories, including to total environment of the lands, air, waters, coastal seas, sea-ice, flora and fauna and other resources which they have traditionally owned or otherwise occupied or used. This includes the right to the full recognition of their laws, traditions and customs, land-tenure systems and institutions for the development and management of resources, and the right to effective measures by States to prevent any interference with, alienation of or encoachment upon these rights;

Article 27.

Indigenous peoples have the right to the resititution of the lands, territories and resources which they have traditionally owned or otherwise occupied or used, and which have been confiscated, occupied, used or damaged without their free and informed consent. Where this is not possible, they have the right to just and fair compensation. Unless otherwise freely agreed upon by the peoples concerned, compensation shall take the form of lands, territories and resources equal in quality, size and legal status.

Article 28.

Indigenous peoples have the right to the conservation, restoration and protection of the total environment and production capacity of their lands, territories and resources, as well as to the assistance for this purpose from States and through international cooperation. Military activities shall not take place in the lands and territories of indigenous peoples, unless otherwise freely agreed upon by the peoples concerned.

States shall take effective measure to ensure, as needed, that programmes for monitoring, maintaining and restoring health of indigenous peoples, as developed and implemented by the peoples affected by such materials, are duly implemented;

Article 29.

Indigenous peoples are entitled to the recognition of the full ownership, control and protection of their cultural and intellectual property.

They have the right to special measures to control, develop and protect their sciences, technologies and cultural manifestations, including human and other genetic resources, seeds, medicines, knowledge of properties of fauna and flora, oral traditions, literatures, designs and visual and performing arts;

Article 30.

Indigenous peoples have the right to determine and develop priorities and strategies for the development or use of their lands, territories and other resources, including the right to require that States obtain their free and informed consent prior to the approval of any project affecting their lands, territories and other resources, particularly in connection with the development, utilization or exploitation of mineral, water or other resources. Pursuant to agreements with the indigenous peoples concerned, just and fair compensation shall be provided for any such activities and measures taken to mitigate adverse environmental, economic, social, cultural or spiritual impact;

Part VII

Article 31.

Indigenous peoples, as a specific form of exercising their right to self determination, have the right to autonomy or self-government in matters relating to their internal and local affairs, including culture, religion, education, information, media, health, housing, employment, social welfare, economic activities, land and resource management, environment and entry by non-members, as well as ways and means for financing these autonomous functions.

Article 32.

Indigenous peoples have the collective right to determine their own citizenship in accordance with their customs and traditions. Indigenous citizenship does not impair the right of indigenous individuals to obtain citizenship of the States in which they live.

Indigenous peoples have the right to determine the structures and to select the membership of their institutions in accordance with their own procedures.

Article 33.

Indigenous peoples have the right to promote, develop and maintain their institutional structures and their distinctive juridical customs, traditions, procedures and practices, in accordance with internationally recognized human right standards.

Article 34.

Indigenous peoples have the collective right to determine the responsibilities of individuals to their communities.

Article 35.

Indigenous peoples, in particular those divided by international borders, have the right to maintain and develop contacts, relations and cooperation, including activities for spiritual, cultural, political, economic and social purposes, with other peoples across the borders.

States shall take effective measures to ensure the exercise and implementation of this right.

Article 36.

Indigenous peoples have the right to the recognition, observance and enforcement of treaties, agreements and other constructive arrangements concluded with States or their successors, according to their original spirit and intent, and to have States honour and respect such treaties, agreements and other constructive arrangements. Conflicts and disputes which cannot otherwise be settled should be submitted to competent international bodies agreed to by all parties concerned;

Part VIII

Article 37.

States shall take effective and appropriate measures, in consultation with the indigenous peoples concerned, to give full effect to the provisions of this Declaration. The rights recognized herein shall be adopted and included in national legislation in such a manner that indigenous peoples can avail themselves of such rights in practice.

Article 38.

Indigenous people have the right to have access to adequate financial and technicial assistance, from States and through international cooperation, to pursue freely their political, economic, social, cultural and spiritual development and for the enjoyment of the rights and freedoms recognized in this Declaration.

Article 39.

Indigenous peoples have the right to have access to and prompt decision through mutually acceptable and fair procedures for the resolution of conflicts and disputes with the states, as well as to effective remedies for all infringements of their individual and collective rights. Such a decision shall take into consideration the customs, traditions, rules and legal systems of the indigenous peoples concerned.

Article 40.

The organs and specialized agencies of the United Nations system and other intergovernmental organizations shall contribute to the full realization of the provisions of this Declaration through the mobilization, inter alia , of financial cooperation and technical assistance. Ways and means of ensuring participation of indigenous peoples on issues affecting them shall be established.

Article 41.

The United Nations shall take the necessary steps to ensure the implementation of this Declaration including the creation of a body at the highest level with special competence in this field and with the direct participation of indigenous peoples. All United Nations bodies shall promote respect for and full application of the provisions of this Declaration.

Part IX

Article 42.

The rights recognized herein constitute the minimum standards for the survival, dignity and well-being of the indigenous peoples of the world.

Article 43.

All the rights and freedoms recognized herein are equally garanteed to male and female indigenous individuals.

Article 44.

Nothing in this Declaration may be construed as diminishing or extinguishing or future rights of indigenous peoples may have or acquire.

Article 45.

Nothing in this Declaration may be interpreted as implying for any State, group or person any right to engage in any activity or to perform any act contrary to the Charter of the United Nations.

7

International Obligations to Protect the Rights of Indigenous People

While the term 'the right to development' is not explicitly mentioned in the UN Charter, the Universal Declaration of Human Rights (UDHR) or the two international human rights Covenants, the principles enshrined in the Declaration on the Right to Development (DRD) are rooted in the provisions of those fundamental documents. One of the objectives of the international community of states as articulated in the Charter is to 'promote social progress and better standards of life'. This provides the context for the purpose of the UN in which Member States are, inter alia, 'to achieve international co-operation in solving international problems of an economic, social, cultural or humanitarian nature, and in promoting and encouraging respect for human rights and fundamental freedoms for all without distinction as to race, sex, language, or religion'.

The UDHR, in addition to providing for a range of fundamental human rights, recognizes the importance of 'national effort and international cooperation' in the realization for every individual of 'economic, social and cultural rights indispensable for his dignity and the free development of his personality'. This seminal declaration also refers to the entitlement of everyone 'to a social and international order in which the rights and freedoms set forth in [the] Declaration can be fully realized'. The Covenants, in addition to codifying many human rights, also recognize the importance of international cooperation in their realization. Moreover, the Committee on Economic, Social and Cultural Rights has explicitly referred to the importance of, inter alia, the DRD and 'the need for States parties to take full account of [it]'. The process that moves a General Assembly declaration from perhaps 'provid[ing] evidence of the state of the law and also the meaning of texts, and ha[ving] considerable legal significance', to attaining full normative maturity is typically determined by a host of factors, but the fact that the underlying logic informing the DRD is firmly established in international law can only serve to enhance its normative force. The application of a range of criteria, applied on a case-by-case basis, tends to determine whether the principles enshrined in a given declaration are 'law'.

International agreements may take many forms and hence the particular title given to an international agreement by itself does not determine its legal effect. However, it has been remarked that while 'the title alone cannot change the nature of a resolution, [but] its sub-stantive content - whether it declares or recommends - is significant'. Thus it is argued that the fact that the right to development was enshrined in a declaration, and further a declaration of the General Assembly, which is representative of the world community, 'gives rise to reasonable expectations ... that there is an obligation on States to fulfil those obligations'. Among the key factors recognized as important in interpreting the effect or force of a declaration is the intent of the parties.

Intent can be determined, to provide one example, by the use of language: for instance, whether it is mandatory or hortatory. The mandatory nature of the language of the DRD, exemplified in Article 1, which states that 'the right to development is an inalienable human right' and then refers to the 'entitlement of every human person and all peoples', is such, it has been argued, that it 'leaves little scope for debate as to whether the intention of the General Assembly was to declare the existence of a legally guaranteed right to development'. The degree to which a declaration is seen to enshrine basic values generally shared by the international community-'community values, community needs and community expectations'- is also relevant in interpreting its effect.

The purpose of achieving international co-operation in solving international problems and in promoting respect for human rights, as found in the UN Charter among its purposes, is cited in the first preambular paragraph of the DRD, and recognition of the entitlement of everyone to a national and international order in which their human rights can be realized as per the UDHR is reaffirmed in the third preambular paragraph of the DRD. These assertions provide the framework through which the operative paragraphs of the DRD should be interpreted. In this way, the DRD can be understood as enshrining and elaborating values of the international community.

In addition to the duty of states to cooperate, the reference in the DRD to, inter alia, the right to self-determination, sovereignty over natural resources, and international peace and security, reflects 'a reasonable relationship with existing principles of international law' - another applicable criterion in determining the effect of General Assembly resolutions. The number of votes and the voting patterns are also considered important factors in measuring the weight of a resolution. While abstentions have been considered by some as a negative vote and by others as an affirmative vote, the better view may be 'to treat abstentions, as a general rule, as acquiescence'. It is significant in this regard that the DRD was adopted in 1986 with only one state having cast a vote against it and six abstentions. In relation to the DRD, the apposite view may be that where the declaration has the

> 'intent to declare law, whether customary, general principles or instant, spontaneous or new law, and the resolution is adopted

> by a unanimous or nearly unanimous vote or by genuine consensus, there is a presumption that the rules and principles embodied in the declaration are law'.

At a minimum, 'a vote in favour of a resolution infers that the state will act according to its terms, even if it is not legally bound to do so'. The degree to which implementation procedures are established, reflective of a 'continued solidarity and determination by a large group of states to see a Resolution implemented', can be a factor in the consideration of the effect of declarations.' Implementation procedures can include gathering of information by the UN Secretariat, or the calling of reports from Member States, as well as more elaborate machinery such as the establishment of a committee.

Commitment to the promotion and implementation of the right to development is reflected by, for example: the fact that a new Branch within the Office of the High Commissioner for Human Rights was established, ' .... the primary responsibilities of which would include the promotion and protection of the right to development'; the establishment by the UN Commission on Human Rights of an open-ended Working Group on the Right to Development as a follow-up mechanism aimed at furthering methods by which the right to development may be implemented, and to report on the progress of said implementation; and the appointment by the Commission of an Independent Expert on the Right to Development,

> 'in view of the urgent need to make further progress towards the realization of the right to development as elaborated in the Declaration on the Right to Development ... [and] to present to the working group on the right to development at each of its sessions, a study on the current state of progress in the implementation of the right to development'.

These mechanisms reflect the importance placed on the right to development as provided for in the DRD. The normative status of the right to development has been reinforced in the annual resolutions of the General Assembly and the

Commission on Human Rights and in declarations adopted at representative world conferences, including the 1992 Rio Conference on Environment and Development, 1993 Vienna World Conference on Human Rights, the 1995 World Summit for Social Development, 1995 Fourth World Conference on Women, 2000 Millennium Summit, 2001 World Conference on Racism, Racial Discrimination, Xenophobia and Related Intolerance, and the 2002 World Summit on Sustainable Development. The fulfilment of the criteria outlined above may provide but a starting point for the consideration of the normative force of the DRD.

However, categorizing a human right as law does not depend on whether or not the level of protection of that right in many countries remains problematic, or on whether or not the machinery for its protection in most cases remains embryonic, or that there are still important areas of uncertainty about the content and application of those rights. As we hope to have illustrated, the international community fully recognizes a right to development and one which is integrally linked to the realization of all human rights, sustainable development and international economic equity. Therefore, even widespread examples of non-compliance do not negate the existence of the norm. While it is perhaps premature to suggest that the DRD can be said to be binding in the strictest sense, national and international obligations that appear throughout the DRD are also reflected in treaties and have thus been accepted as binding at a minimum, on States parties to those treaties.

The process described in the DRD essentially provides a consistent method of implementing those obligations by addressing the need to have human rights reflected throughout international and national processes that respect the notion of progressive realization and are sustainable over time. The duty-bearers of the right to development are both the state acting at the national level and the international community of states acting individually or collectively, and a balance is to be struck between duties entailing international cooperation and those requiring domestic implementation. States acting at the international level have obligations to realize the former and the state domestically is responsible to give effect to the latter.

At the national level, the right to development implies a need for an enabling environment, which includes arrangements to ensure good governance. Good governance refers to effective systems of governance by the state, including, for example, an accountable government, and one that takes action against corruption as well as ensuring respect for human rights and access to justice. An enabling national environment also requires: a legal and regulatory framework that enables minorities and indigenous peoples to organize and to be heard, without which they cannot be assured of non-discrimination in development; 'active, free and meaningful participation'; 'popular participation in all spheres ... of development'; and the 'fair distribution of the benefits' of development.

In fact, quite the opposite is likely unless discrimination against minorities and indigenous peoples is addressed, including in the distribution of resources, and unless participation rights are respected. Exclusion from decision-making can lead to their further marginalization in processes of national development, and increases the risk that outcomes of development violate, inter alia, their economic and cultural rights, such as those linked to sustainable agricultural practices and food security, as well as rights regarding minority languages in education and the expression and development of their customs.

National ownership of the development process, as well as regional plans such as the New Partnership for Africa's Development (NEPAD), only contribute to development understood as a human right within systems that mainstream and prioritize human rights, including those of groups traditionally excluded from the collective development of (a people in) a state or region. Without good governance and the related concepts of respect for human rights and social justice, any policies and programmes aimed at development will remain unfulfilled, both in terms of incorporating a rights-based approach to development and in terms of contributing to the realization of the right to development. In sum, it is impossible to adequately address human rights obligations without proper governance structures.

Efforts at the national level, however, could be limited by the non-implementation of obligations at the international level, broadly referred to as international cooperation. In principle, international cooperation, including international assistance, refers to the requirement that all actors refrain from inhibiting the realization of human rights, and chat those states in a position to assist, take measures to remove obstacles that impede the realization of human rights.

The exact content of these obligations of international cooperation are not yet definitively drawn, but adjusting the rules of operation of the existing trading and financial institutions and intellectual property protection to address the need for an equitable international economic system of multilateral trade, finance and investment is largely accepted as essential, particularly where there is a direct correlation to the promotion and protection of human rights.

The same could be said for ensuring that all bilateral and multilateral decision-making processes are fair, equitable, transparent and sensitive to the needs of developing states, including their marginalized groups; that the commercial activities for which a state has direct responsibility conform to international human rights standards; and that states take adequate measures to ensure that overseas operations of companies headquartered in their jurisdiction do nor subvert the international human rights obligations of either the home or the host state. International cooperation could also be understood to comprise: ensuring that, in accordance with the UN target, development assistance is equal to no less than 0.7 per cent of a country's GDP; that enhanced programmes for debt relief are implemented; and that market access is facilitated.

The implementation of the obligation of international cooperation may include, but is not limited to, the international transfer of resources. Other methods by which this obligation could be met is through, for example, supplying technology and creating new international mechanisms to meet the specific requirements of the developing countries. Equally, measures that could be understood as forming part of a state's obligations of international cooperation include ensuring that the appropriate people have an understanding of, and respect for, human rights obligations and the commitments undertaken in the form of the Millennium Development Goals: those responsible for foreign affairs; those in finance and trade who represent the state in international negotiations; and state representatives who are responsible for the policies and projects of the Bretton Woods institutions.

This under-standing of human rights includes those that pertain to minority and indigenous peoples as well as women, who are often excluded from development processes. At the international level, developing states also have obligations of international cooperation and these could include: ensuring that marginalized groups have a greater voice in international fora; addressing the need to enhance the negotiating capacity of the state in relation to its dealings with transnational corporations, including through the establishment of adequate and appropriate regulatory frameworks for the private sector; adhering to international human rights obligations, with careful attention to also ensuring that international processes and outcomes of development meet the conceptions of development as articulated by minorities and indigenous peoples; and refraining from concluding any international agreement that is inconsistent with its international human rights obligations as owed to people in its jurisdiction.

So, while the primary responsibility lies with the state at the national level, states acting at the international level are to ensure that their actions do not inhibit the ability of other states to fulfil their obligations; that they enable other states to implement rights nationally and regionally; and that their actions and decisions fully respect their existing human rights obligations and do not threaten their ability to implement them domestically. When international cooperation is considered in light of the type of human rights violations it is meant to avert, it becomes clearer why recognition and protection of the group rights of minorities and indigenous peoples within the right to development is helpful. While the beneficiary of the right to development is the individual, protecting indigenous economic production systems, recognition of lands, territories and resources, and traditional knowledge and lifestyles, as well accessing participation rights that will ensure linguistic and religious rights in the development process, are rights of the group within the collective process of (state) development.

All these rights relate to the expression of their identities as distinct minority and indigenous communities and it is these communities that will need to exercise their rights. Globalization has largely limited the ability of states to act effectively ut singuli in an era of unprecedented inter-dependence, and this reinforces the scope and need for effective international cooperation. Article 3(1)(2)(3), Article 4(1)(2), Article 6(1) and Article 10 of the DRD all reflect the international component of the right to development. The DRD recognizes the need for a global approach to development to complement national action, and thus international cooperation, perhaps conceived as a form of affirmative action in favour of developing countries, can be understood as an essential component of the realization of the right to development.

Within the right to development, all this is intended to contribute to processes and outcomes of development which strengthen human rights protection and promotion through a rights-based application, and which aim at greater capability and freedom for people in order that they may develop in ways that are meaningful to them. A two-tiered system of duty-bearers has been referred to by the Committee on Economic, Social and Cultural Rights when clarifying the nature of States parties' obligations as per Article 2(1) of ICESCR. For example, the Committee notes that 'the phrase "to the maximum of its available resources" was intended by the drafters of the Covenant to refer to both the resources existing within a State and those available from the international community through international cooperation and assistance'.

The Committee goes on to remind States parties that the obligation to cooperate internationally in facilitating the full realization of the relevant rights contained in ICESCR is further stressed by specific provisions in the Covenant: those contained in Article 11 on the adequate standard of living, including adequate food, clothing and housing and the continuous improvement of living conditions; those in Article 15 on the right to take part in cultural life and the right to enjoy the benefits of scientific progress; in Article 22 on international technical assistance; and in Article 23 on international action, which should be understood to include methods such as the conclusion of conventions and the adoption of recommendations. In a subsequent General Comment on the right to free primary education, the nature of the obligation to cooperate internationally was further elaborated when the Committee stressed that: 'Where a State party is clearly lacking in the financial resources and/or expertise required to "work out and adopt" a detailed plan, the international community had a clear obligation to assist.

In view of the importance of the right to development as a comprehensive right in which all human rights and freedoms can be realized, and given that its fulfilment is integrally linked to an international system that takes into account the interdependence of nations, the implication is that all states have a legal interest in its protection. The right to development may be understood as imposing upon states an obligation *ergo omnes*- an obligation owed towards all people. While unequal international divisions have been a permanent feature over the ages, the right to development has gained in currency as interdependence moves with unprecedented speed and repercussions in an era of globalization, and the concept of universal and indivisible rights has become evermore entrenched.

As many of the causes inhibiting the exercising of the right to development are global, so too must be the solutions - and not out of charity or thoughtfulness but as a matter of meeting legal obligations, because the satisfaction of the needs of people is an inalienable right, with corresponding obligations. The UN Working Group on Indigenous Populations noted this point when they remarked that the DRD provides for a shift in development thinking from '"development as charity" or "good intentions" to "development as a human right" that includes corresponding obligations. This challenges States to ensure that there is a paradigm shift from indigenous policies based on welfare models to policies based on rights.'

In the realization of the right to development, as with all human rights, the primary obligation rests with the state. In the right to development, development policies and programmes as central elements of the development process are for the state to design and implement. The international community has obligations to cooperate to enable the state to carry out its obligations, and while it can reprimand or sanction the state for its failure to meet its obligations, it is far more difficult for the international community to implement a development policy for the state.

However, in the event that a state fails to uphold its human rights obligations in the process of realizing the right to development - for example, those that protect and promote the rights of minorities and indigenous peoples - the international community may indeed have an obligation to step in, just as the international community has recognized the need for humanitarian intervention in the affairs of a state when there is a major violation of civil and political rights. It may be necessary to intervene with sanctions or other international measures, including ensuring that civil society actors, such as non-governmental organizations and trade unions, play key, if not primary, roles in arrangements 'related to international cooperation, if there is gross violation of the right to development by a state.

An intricate and multi-layered system of obligations necessary for the realization of human rights was foreseen in Article 28 of the UDHR, which established the principle that respect for human rights is not about narrowly focused obligations limited to relations between individuals and their states, but rather it is a multifaceted system of obligations which attach themselves to all societal relations at the national and international levels.

International Co-operation in the Right to Development

Article 3(1) of the Declaration on the Right to Development (DRD) makes clear that states have the primary responsibility for the creation of national and international conditions favourable to the realization of the right to development. While this includes all necessary measures at the national level for the realization of the right to development as reflected in DRD Article 8, the Declaration at Article 3(3) also recognizes the duty of all states to cooperate with each other in ensuring development and eliminating obstacles to development. This is followed by Article 4(1) which refers to the duty of all states to take steps individually and collectively to formulate international development policies. Then, at Article 4(4), the DRD unambiguously accepts that effective international cooperation is essential '[a]s a complement to the efforts of developing countries [and] in providing these countries with appropriate means and facilities to foster their comprehensive development'.

The DRD also calls upon states to cooperate in promoting, encouraging and strengthening universal respect for human rights and fundamental freedoms for all . However, the role of international cooperation of states in facilitating the right to development is not derived uniquely from the Declaration itself but may be considered as an imperative of the UN Charter. That development falls not only to states acting nationally but also to the international community of states to address can be seen in the Charter's Preamble, Article 1(3), and Article 55. Article 1 outlines the purposes of the UN; central among these, as Article 1(3) attests, is 'international co-operation in solving international problems of an economic, social, cultural or humanitarian character, and in promoting and encouraging respect for human rights and fundamental freedoms for all ...'.

Article 55 is the first article in the chapter of the Charter entitled 'International Economic and Social Co-operation'. This Article recognizes that peaceful and friendly relations among nations can only be based on equal rights and self-determination and hence it outlines that the UN shall promote, inter alia, higher standards of living, conditions of economic and social progress and development, solutions of international economic, social and health-related problems and universal respect for, and observance of, human rights and fundamental freedoms for all.

Significantly, Article 56 then states: All Members pledge themselves to take joint and separate action in co-operation with the Organization for the achievement of the purposes set forth in Article 55'. Thus, it has been remarked that '[t]he Charter itself provides ... an obligation of member states in [the] field [human rights]. It sets forth not only a "principle" but contains, in Article 56, the pledge of all members to take joint and separate action in cooperation with the organization for the achievement of the purposes set forth in Article 55.'

There is authoritative support, including from the International Court of Justice (ICJ), resolutions of the General

Assembly and the writings of scholars, for the position that the UN Charter imposes binding obligations in the area of human rights on every Member State, reinforced by the mandatory obligation implied in Article 55 and a distinct 'element of a legal duty in the undertaking' expressed in Article 56. Moreover, the General Assembly in its resolutions has repeatedly referred to the responsibilities and obligations which devolve upon it under Articles 55 and 56 and which place on it the duty to cooperate in the promotion of development specifically. Citing a string of resolutions, including the DRD, Brownlie asserts that:

> 'The United Nations Charter, in Chapters IX and X, recognizes the urgent need to deal with economic and social problems, and certain of its provisions create binding obligations for governments to maintain human rights. There is probably also a collective duty of member states to take responsible action to create reasonable living standards both for their own peoples and for those of other states.'

The Committee on Economic, Social and Cultural Rights (CESCR) emphatically endorsed the existence of an obligation to cooperate internationally in the protection of human rights including in development when it stated in its General Comment No. 3:

> 'The Committee wishes to emphasize that in accordance with Articles 55 and 56 of the Charter of the United Nations, with well-established principles of international law, and with the provisions of the Covenant itself, international cooperation for development and thus for the realization of economic, social and cultural rights is an obligation of all States. It is particularly incumbent upon those States which are in a position to assist others in this regard. The Committee notes in particular the importance of the Declaration on the Right to Development adopted by the General Assembly in its resolution 41/128 of 4 December 1986 and the need for States parties to take full account of all the principles recognized herein. It emphasizes that, in the absence of an active programme of international assistance and co-operation on the part of all those States that

are in a position to undertake one, the full realization of economic, social and cultural rights will remain an unfulfilled aspiration in many countries ... '

Following on from the UN Charter, the normative requirements to cooperate internationally in the protection and promotion of human rights can be found in Article 28 of the UDHR, in both International Covenants, and in the UN Convention on the Rights of the Child. CESCR has also explicitly highlighted the obligations of States parties to people outside their jurisdiction with regard to the right to health and the right to food. In the context of the right to health, the Committee stated:

'To comply with their international obligations in relation to article 2(1), States parties have to respect the enjoyment of the right to health in other countries, and to prevent third parties from violating the right in other countries, if they are able to influence these third parties by way of legal or political means, in accordance with the Charter of the United Nations and applicable international law. Depending on the availability of resources, States should facilitate access to essential facilities, goods and services in other countries, wherever possible and provide the necessary aid when required ...'

In interpreting the term 'the right of everyone' in Article 12 of the ICESCR, Judge Weeramanty in his dissenting opinion in the Advisory Opinion of the International Court of justice on the Legality of the Use by a State of Nuclear Weapons in Armed Conflict, having first quoted Article 12 by which 'States parties to the present Covenant recognize the right of everyone to the highest attainable standard of physical and mental health', went on to proclaim:

'It will be noted here that the recognition by States of the right to health is ... that they recognize the right of "everyone" and not merely of their own subjects. Consequently each state is under an obligation to respect the right to health of all members of the international community'

With regard to the right to food, CESCR highlighted the obligation of states to cooperate internationally, as well as the need for States parties to ensure the right to food in countries other than their own, as part of implementing that obligation. Referring to the UN Charter and the standards adopted in the Declaration of the World Food Summit of 1996 in the fulfilment of the rights enshrined in the ICESCR, the Committee affirmed:

> 'In the spirit of Article 56 of the Charter of the United Nations, the specific provisions contained in articles 11, 2.1, and 23 of the Covenant and the Rome Declaration of the World Food Summit, States parties should recognize the essential role of international cooperation and comply with their commitment to take joint and separate action to achieve the full realization of the right to adequate food. In implementing this commitment, States parties should take steps to respect the enjoyment of the right to food in other countries, to protect that right, to facilitate access to food and to provide the necessary aid when required ...'

DRD's call for international cooperation in the realization of the right to development provides an authoritative interpretation and elaboration of the principles of the UN Charter, and as such binds all states. This obligation is further strengthened and its scope elaborated by human rights jurisprudence in this and related areas. While the Charter did not explicitly define the human rights and fundamental freedoms to which it referred, it did both outline the purposes behind its creation, including international cooperation in the solving of international problems and the promotion of human rights, and provide the structure by which the content was expected to be elaborated.

Moreover, although at one time there may have been some debate as to whether the human rights provisions of the Charter were sufficiently clear and precise to give rise to specific obligations for Member States, in the decades since the birth of the UN, universal standards have been elaborated in a range of treaties and declarations providing the Charter with subsequent normative content and hence providing additional substance to the obligations that underscore its purposes and pledges. Indeed, the ICJ has accepted that the provisions of the Charter contain binding obligations and that they may be interpreted in light of subsequent human rights instruments adopted by the United Nations.

Although recognition of the role that international cooperation plays in the creation of an enabling environment, in which all people can be free from want and be able to fully develop, has always been implicit in international human rights instruments, the DRD clearly recognized development as a human right, with all that implies in terms of rights and duties.

The DRD has also added scope to the normative requirements in this area of human rights, including a reiteration of the imperative of international cooperation. Since the adoption of the DRD, the role of the international community in cooperating in the realization of the right to development has been reinforced in subsequent resolutions and declarations adopted at representative world conferences, including in the 1993 Vienna Declaration and Programme of Action of the World Conference on Human Rights. The normative status of the right to development as a right existing within an international law of cooperation should be beyond doubt. The international system premised on co-existence has evolved as the need for cooperation has intensified as a result of interdependence.

As Wolfgang Friedmann explains in his renowned work entitled *The Changing Structure of International Law,* we have shifted along the continuum from an outdated international law of coexistence of the 17th and 18th centuries,, where the primary objective of international law was to impose passive obligations of abstention on sovereign states, to the international law of cooperation of the 20th and 21st centuries, which provides the modalities of their co-operation, in the form of positive obligations, to realize common values and achieve common ends. Recognizing that core obligations must be read in conjunction with more contemporary instruments, the sanctioning of the right to development by the international community of states has placed us clearly within the ambit of 'the international law of cooperation', a law which 'takes into consideration the specific conditions of each State and doses its rights and obligations accordingly'.

The recognition of any human right implies the need to identify duty-bearers. In the right to development, as with any human right, states in which the right-holders are situated have the primary responsibility to deliver those rights. The state has the duty to implement policies and measures that enable the rights to be enjoyed.

For some rights, the state acting at the national level may be the only duty-bearer if it can adopt measures that are sufficient to realize those rights - which assumes that other states are refraining from acts that would impede this. However, with regard to the right to development, international cooperation, manifested in a range of ways as described in the previous section, is intimately bound up with the ability of states to fulfil the right to development of their people.

For minorities and indigenous peoples, cooperation at the international level in the realization of the right to development implies: equal and non-discriminatory participation in the global economy; assurances that decisions related to globalization and their effects, including through international trade and large-scale public or private industrial interests, do not impede or violate their particular rights; and that development takes place in a climate that fosters and does not further limit their ability to develop in line with their conception of development.

While there is no agreement among states that there exists an obligation to cooperate internationally in the realization of the right to development, few states disagree that an international enabling environment is required to meet the requirements of a right to development. And the content of the international obligation to cooperate in relation to specific human rights, most notably with regard to economic, social and cultural rights, has been, and continues to be elaborated, not least of all by the CESCR. It is widely accepted that human rights obligations generally, are required to be 'respected, protected and fulfilled' by states nationally. The obligation to 'respect' human rights refers to an obligation of abstention by the state and all its organs and agents from doing anything that violates human rights or undermines the realization of those rights.

The obligation to 'protect' human rights requires that states and their agents take the measures necessary to prevent any individual or entity from violating human rights. The obligation to 'fulfil' requires that measures be taken to ensure the realisation of, human rights. With regard to international cooperation in the realization of economic, social and cultural rights, the CESCR considers States parties to have an international obligation to respect and protect the rights of people in other countries. A similar minimum threshold can be applied to the scope of international cooperation in relation to the right to development. States acting at the international level should ensure that their actions and decisions do not inhibit the respect for and protection of the right to development of all people. However, as the right to development is understood as requiring an international enabling environment which entails elaborating a notion of shared responsibility for its realization, a minimum obligation also to assist in fulfilling this right could be said to apply equally.

Principles of Self-Determination and Sovereignty over Natural Resources

The principles of self-determination and of permanent sovereignty over natural resources are accepted principles of jus cogens. Jus cogens are rules that proscribe conduct that is regarded as fundamentally unacceptable by the international society of states. They form part of a body of peremptory norms having the highest rank in international law: 'a peremptory norm of general international law is a norm accepted and recognized by the international community of States as a whole as a norm from which no derogation is permitted and which can be modified only by a subsequent norm of general international law having the same character'. The right to self-determination is both a right unto itself and a constituent element of the right to development, as is the principle of permanent sovereignty over natural resources which is a right unto itself, and also forms a part of the right of self-determination, as well as to development.

As affirmed in Article 1(2) of the DRD, the right to development implies the full realization of the right of peoples to self-determination, which includes the exercise of their inalienable right to full sovereignty over their natural resources. The principle of self-determination was first codified in the UN Charter, followed by a reference to the right of self-determination in treaty form as found in the two human rights Covenants. The right of 'peoples and nations to permanent sovereignty over their natural wealth and resources in the interest of national development' was affirmed in the 1962 General Assembly Declaration on Permanent Sovereignty over Natural Resources and restated in the two human rights Covenants in the form of the right of peoples to 'freely dispose of their natural wealth and resources ... [and that a people not] be deprived of its own means of subsistence'.

As the voices of developing states breaking away from colonial domination gained strength within the UN, the right to self-determination was the platform on which they made their calls for freedom. The independence of the colonized states allowed for a degree of political self-determination; this, however, was not matched by economic self-determination of the states nor necessarily recognition or subsequent realization of the right to self-determination of peoples found within the states. With the evolution of international human rights law, particularly as it relates to indigenous peoples, these rights can now be understood as being owed both to the state, and to peoples and groups within the state in different forms, notwithstanding that there may have been a time when self-determination and sovereignty over natural resources were seen as being owed exclusively to the state.'

The right to development can only be realized if self-determination, an inviolable principle of international law, is realized at the same time. The DRD correlates the two by including several direct and implied references of the right of self-determination in its Preamble and it refers to the right twice in the operative paragraphs. In the preambular paragraphs, the Declaration recalls the ICCPR and ICESCR generally and then, in preambular paragraph 6, explicitly reaffirms the language of common Article 1(1) of the two Covenants, recalling 'the right of peoples to self-determination, by virtue of which they have the right to freely determine their political status and to pursue their economic, social and cultural development'.

In the following paragraph, the DRD refers with added mindfulness, to the principle stated in common Article 1(2) of the Covenants, namely, 'the right of peoples to exercise ... full and complete sovereignty over all their natural wealth and resources'. Among the operative paragraphs of the DRD, second only to Article 1(1) which asserts that the right to development is an inalienable human right, is the explicit reference to the relationship between the right to development and the right to self-determination. It states:

> 'The human right to development also implies the full realization of the right of peoples to self-determination, which includes, subject to the relevant provisions of both International Covenants on Human Rights, the exercise of their inalienable right to full sovereignty over their natural wealth and resources.'

Furthermore, in Article 5 of the DRD it is recognized that, inter alia, 'refusal to recognize the fundamental right of peoples to self-determination' is a bar to their ability to exercise their right to development. The right of peoples to sovereignty over their natural wealth and resources has been shown by the Human Rights Committee to include:

> 'a particular aspect of the economic content of the right to self-determination, namely the right of peoples, for their own ends, freely to "dispose of their natural wealth and resources without prejudice to any obligations arising out of international economic cooperation, based upon the principle of mutual benefit, and international law. In no case may a people be deprived of its own means of subsistence."'

The HRC then elaborates on the content of Article 1(2) by explaining: 'This right entails corresponding duties for all States and for the international community'. Significantly, in defining the scope of the right to self- determination, including sovereignty over natural wealth and resources, the HRC has recognized that obligations States parties may have under international economic law are to be weighed against their human rights obligations related to self-determination, both at the national level and in their international affairs as members of the international community.

The implication is such that multilateral and bilateral decisions, actions and agreements are not to infringe the right to self-determination of peoples. The international dimension related to this right specifically includes an obligation upon States parties to actively facilitate the realization of the right to self-determination of peoples found within other states, regardless of whether or not the state within which those people are found are afforded the protection of the rights under the Covenant. Notably, the Committee has adopted the view that:

> 'Paragraph 3 [Article 1] ... is particularly important in that it imposes specific obligations on States parties, not only in

> relation to their own peoples but vis-a-vis all peoples which have not been able to exercise or have been deprived of the possibility of exercising their right to self-determination ... The obligations exist irrespective of whether a people entitled to self-determination depends on a State party to the Covenant or not. It follows that all States parties to the Covenant should take positive action to facilitate realization of and respect for the rights of peoples to self-determination.'

Therefore, the international community of states has a duty to cooperate, not only in respecting the right to self-determination of all peoples (abstaining from violative practices), and in protecting it (regulating the activities of third parties), but also by taking legislative, administrative, budgetary and judicial measures in order that the right is fulfilled. The scope of the obligation in relation to self-determination and sovereignty over natural resources would apply when they are considered as rights unto themselves, and as part of the right to development. Self-determination is a right close to the hearts of indigenous peoples, as well as minorities.

Self-determination within the right to development addresses a right of 'self-determined development'. It is the freedom to pursue economic, social, cultural and political development, as the Covenants make clear. It is a right that facilitates the enjoyment by minorities and indigenous peoples of the right to their cultural identities, and their ability to determine their own economic, social and political system through democratic institutions and actions. It is about sustainable and equitable use of natural resources in a manner that fully and completely integrates the range of rights provided to indigenous peoples with regard to their lands, territories and resources, their values, traditions and economic, religious and spiritual relationships to their land, and that respects the rights of minorities to the traditional lands and territories they inhabit.

Self-determination within the right to development is thus linked to the right to be recognized as minority or indigenous community and as such to meaningfully participate as a group and thus influence any decisions that affect them or the regions in which they live. In line with the HRC's elaboration of the right to self-determination under the ICCPR, and in so far as it might be concluded that its interpretation informs the scope of the jus cogens principle, which applies to all states, the right to self-determination can be understood as imposing obligations not only on states acting at the national level, but on all states in their interactions at the international level, with regard to all people everywhere.

Moreover, the obligation imposes on states the duty not only to refrain from actions that might infringe the ability of people to realize their right to self-determination but to take positive action in seeing the right fulfilled. Here the onus 'to act' initially also imposes an obligation of conduct upon states at the international level. It is to the consideration of obligations of conduct and obligations of result that we will now turn.

Obligations of Conduct and of Result

The right to development entails a right to a particular process of development, which incorporates all human rights and as such expands the capabilities and freedoms of people to realize what they value. The notion that the right to development entails a right to a particular process of development is consistent with the language employed in the DRD. The second preambular paragraph states:

> 'Recognizing that development is a comprehensive economic, social, cultural and political process which aims at the constant improvement of the well-being of the entire population and of all individuals on the basis of their active, free and meaningful participation in development and in the fair distribution of benefits resulting therefrom, [...].'

Similar language describing national development policies aimed at the 'constant improvement of the well-being of the entire population ...' is found in Article 2(3). The reference to the 'constant improvement of the well-being' can be understood as referring to both to the 'progressive realisation' element of achieving the right to development while simultaneously calling for precise policy formulations that lead to a properly defined process of 'improvement' and a properly identified concept of 'well-being'.

In the work of the Independent Expert it is spelled out that '[t]he outcomes of development as well as the way in which the outcomes are realized constitute the process of development regarded as a human right'. The distinction is that:

> 'the right to that process is ... a programme or plan executed over time maintaining consistency and sustainability, with phased realization of the targets, and that programme is expected, with a high probability, to lead to the realization of all those outcomes'.

The right to this process thus entails commitments to pursue certain policies with the aim of achieving certain results in a manner that contributes to the realization of all human rights and to the fulfilment of the right to development. Human rights law establishes a binary relationship between right-holders and duty-bearers. As has been observed elsewhere, it is precisely this binary relation which distinguishes human rights from the general valuing of freedom that exists without a correlated obligation to help bring about that freedom. While human rights may vary as to the degree of precision that their normative and operational content invites, the minimum entitlement has a corresponding action required of the duty-bearer, the absence of which is to be considered a violation of that right.

The International Law Commission (ILC) has referred in the course of its work to 'obligations of conduct and obligations of result' - terms which have gained currency in international law. Obligations of conduct are referred to as 'best efforts obligations', whereas obligations of result are 'tantamount to guarantees of outcome'. The applicability of obligations of conduct and of result on states - domestically and with regard to international cooperation in the progressive realization of economic, social and cultural rights - has been recognized by the CESCR. According to the ICESCR Article 2(1), States parties are to ' ... undertake steps, individually and through international assistance and cooperation ... to the maximum of its available resources, with a view to achieving progressively the full realization of the rights recognized in the present Covenant ...'.

In its elaboration of the content of this provision, the CESCR explicitly states that '[t]hose obligations include both what may be termed (following the work of the International Law Commission) obligations of conduct and obligations of result'. A similar reference can be found in the Maastricht Guidelines on the Violations of Economic, Social and Cultural Rights. The ILC itself has also specifically recognized the applicability of the terms in relation to the provisions of ICESCR, stating:

> An instance of a case where the distinction was of value ... was provided by article 2, paragraph 1 [which addresses nature of States parties' obligations] of the International Covenant on Economic, Social and Cultural Rights, which contained a delicate mix of obligations of conduct and obligations of result.

Thus, as Alston and Quinn have noted, the undertaking 'to take steps' - language that appears throughout the ICESCR - is akin to assuming an obligation of conduct.

The ILC explains that the initial distinction in international law was borrowed from French law in which the obligations of result tend to be stronger than that of conduct, in that 'the mere fact of non-materialization of the result constitutes a violation of the obligation, rather than an obligation to make a bone fide effort with a view to achieving the result, but without guaranteeing its materialization'. In the work of the ILC on the subject, however, the obligations of conduct tend to be more stringent than the obligation of result.

The obligation to put in place a process for the progressive realization of rights may therefore invite more rigorous requirements than those entailing an immediate result. In the words of CESCR with regard to economic, social and cultural rights, 'the principal obligation [is] to take steps to achieve progressively the full realization of the right ... it [i]mposes an obligation to move as expeditiously as possible towards the goal and '[s]uch steps should be deliberate, concrete and targeted as clearly as possible towards meeting the obligations ...' Since obligations of result imply obligations of conduct (of action, policy, etc.) the distinctions may be equally applicable to civil and political rights as to economic, social and cultural rights. To varying degrees the promotion and protection of rights will require conduct on the part of the state which may include the adoption and implementation of plans and policies as well as the allocation of financial resources in order to realize human rights.

The conduct may entail training the police force in order to minimize the like-lihood of violations of the prohibition of non-discrimination or of torture or degrading treatment in the performance of their responsibilities, or the implementation of a plan of action to reduce infant, child and maternal mortality. Yet while civil and political rights also require conduct on the part of the state, unlike economic, social and cultural rights, they most often impose obligations that require immediate results. Thus while obligations of conduct and of result may be applied to all, rights, it is the particular right being addressed that will determine whether the more stringent requirement is placed on conduct or on result.

Obligations of conduct for rights that may entail progressive realization requires action 'reasonably calculated' to realize the enjoyment of a particular right. While the achievement of the result is the ultimate aim in all cases, in certain cases these policies or measures can produce the results with near certainty, in other cases with probability-which must have the maximum likelihood of producing the result. Certainly, then, with regard to the right to development, which entails a right to a process that necessarily includes different variables and agents and for which therefore there may be less control over the outcome, the obligation of conduct, aimed at the process of realizing the right, can be understood as imposing a more stringent obligation than that of result.

However, this does not suggest that states have anything less than human rights obligations of result, which include meeting internationally set targets to satisfy detailed substantive standards. Targets include, for example, those related to poverty reduction, universal primary education, reduction in child and maternal mortality rates, and strategies for sustainable development to levels agreed in the UN Millennium Declaration. While there remains an international legal obligation to produce results, obligations of conduct show that along the way to reaching those results there are rights and hence obligations that need to be met.

With regard to the right to development, which not only entails both immediate and progressive elements in its process of realization but also imposes explicit obligations at both the national and international levels, the distinction between obligations of conduct and those of result can be a useful one, in that it prescribes certain conduct even if the outcome remains uncertain. It is through the meeting of obligations of conduct that progressive realization, where necessary, is implemented and responsibility and accountability is attributed. Culpability for the failure to achieve results can be linked to the degree to which the fulfilment of conduct has been planned and implemented. While these classifications are not a substitute for the interpretation and application of the primary norm itself, both are important in determining whether a breach of the right to development has occurred.

At the national level, obligations of conduct include: the effective allocation and utilization of resources; representative participation, including that of women, minorities and indigenous peoples; transparency in decision-making processes; the adoption of sustainable policies and programmes that reflect prior representative consultation; and the establishment of an enabling legal, political, economic and social environment.

At the international level, where an enabling environment is equally important, obligations of conduct include: international cooperation in the realization of the right to development, such as ensuring participatory international multilateral trading and financial systems that are equitable and that respect existing human rights and environmental standards; meeting international development commitments; and effective regulation of multinational corporations headquartered in the jurisdiction of a given state.

The importance of obligations of conduct in the realization of a right that requires action at both the national level and international level cannot be overstated. The global character of the modern world has largely limited the possibility of any single state to put in place a process for the fulfilment of the right to development.

The domestic implementation of the right to development cannot be pursued in isolation, only in cooperation and, therefore, meeting obligations of conduct at the national and international levels is a prerequisite to the realization of the right to development. In determining whether obligations have been met at the national level, various factors need to be considered, including distinguishing inability from unwillingness on the part of the state, the degree to which the rights of marginalized groups are being protected in development, and the degree to which their rights are being realized so that they may have the opportunity to develop.

Other factors in determining whether states, nationally or internationally, are fulfilling their obligations include: assessing the failure of states to sufficiently regulate (acts of omission) the activities of third parties including individuals, groups or corporations; assessing the failure of states through acts of commission; and assessing the failure of states to take into account their legal obligations, including in relation to the specific rights of minorities and indigenous peoples, when entering into bilateral or multilateral agreements with other states, international organizations and other entities such as multinational corporations.

Just as the realization of the right to development imposes duties on both the state acting at the national level and the international community of states acting singly or collectively, obligations of conduct and of result exist for both the developing state and the international community of states. The cooperation between the international community and the developing state functions in tandem, because the right to a process for the realization of the right to development imposes obligations of conduct and of result on both duty-bearers. However, the primary responsibility for the creation of conditions, favourable to the development of people lies with their state. The obligation to produce results rests principally at the national level.

The methods of meeting obligations of conduct in a particular context will depend on who the specific rightholders are. Minorities and indigenous peoples are recognized in international law as having specific characteristics and rights and therefore the method of meeting obligations will be different, because the policies that are necessary to fulfil those rights will have to be designed in accordance with established international law elaborated to protect their rights. For example, the right to education is part of the right to development; however, the mere provision of physical infrastructure and an overall increase in access to education in a given country provides no guarantees that education will be accessible to minorities or indigenous peoples who suffer from discrimination and exclusion.

Furthermore, if minority rights are not respected in the process of fulfilling the right to education, rights related to learning or being instructed in their mothertongue may not be met and thus will not contribute to the ability of minorities to 'express their characteristics and to develop their culture, language, religion, traditions and customs', or to ensure that indigenous children 'are taught to read and write in their own indigenous language'.

Similarly, fulfilling the right to food as part of the particular process of the right to development would, for example, need to be consistent with the ability of indigenous peoples to secure food through traditional methods and with respect for their right to practise their own culture. Equally, the impact of multilateral treaties, such as the Agreement on Trade-Related Aspects of Intellectual Property Rights (TRIPS) under the World Trade Organization, would need to be weighed against the ability of states to fulfil their obligations related to the rights of, inter alia, indigenous peoples within the right to development.

Generally, recognizing the existence of minority and indigenous communities, addressing discrimination against them and providing for their meaningful participation in decisions that affect them, would also be essential to fulfilling obligations of conduct. Thus, while the result of conduct is the fulfilment of the right to development, which all individuals including those belonging to minorities and indigenous communities would be entitled to enjoy, minorities and indigenous peoples are also entitled to obligations of conduct or a set of policies necessary to achieve those results. These policies may differ according to both the duty-holders - states acting nationally or internationally -and the right-holders - in this case such as for minorities and indigenous peoples.

With regard to the right to development, the fulfilment of obligations of result is directly dependent on obligations of conduct being met, however these two types of obligations cannot be separated out and there is not necessarily a clear dividing line between them. Significantly, obligations of conduct are no less binding than obligations of result and, as the ILC has clarified, a failure to exercise due diligence in meeting the legal obligations of conduct could trigger responsibility, including a failure to take action in the protection of human rights. In fact the ILC has recognized that a failure of a state to take the necessary steps to avoid a breach is enough to be considered as breach of the obligation.

Whether or not the threat was realized as a result of the inaction is not the deciding factor. This suggests a clear endorsement of the acceptance of a right to a process whereby conduct in itself, regardless of whether or not the outcome is achieved and regardless of whether or not the conduct (or failure to act) can be determined to have had a negative impact on the fulfilment of the obligation of result, can be deemed a violation of the primary right.

Likewise, in the right to development, the obligation of result is not discharged if the right to a particular process was not respected in reaching the outcome. Therefore the failure to respect, protect and fulfil the rights of, inter alia, minorities and indigenous peoples within the process of realizing the right to development, is a breach of the obligations related to their rights, and of the obligations that correspond to the right to development.

Human Rights Obligations of Multilateral Institutions

States acting at the international level are individually and collectively bound by human rights obligations, including the obligation to cooperate internationally in the protection of human rights. Additionally, within the scope of operations of organizations that are made up of states, there is an obligation that rights are respected where those organizations may have an impact on them. To these ends, states are obliged to uphold human rights when they are supporting or participating in the work undertaken by international financial institutions (IFIs), such as the World Bank and the International Monetary Fund (IMF), and as part of the international trade regime under the auspices of the World Trade Organization (WTO), where those activities risk violating human rights, inhibit the ability of states to meet their human rights obligations, or threaten the ability of people to realize their rights, including the rights of vulnerable groups most prone to having their rights undermined.

Given the impact of multilateral organizations on human rights protection, the scope and nature of their human rights obligations are recognized as being of critical importance and are increasingly the subject of attention and analysis. Although detailed consideration of this important area cannot be fully addressed here, it is nonetheless important to include a brief overview as to possible sources of applicable legal obligations, given the considerable impact of the activities of the IFIs and the international trade regime on human rights generally, and on the right to development specifically. Today there are over 100 multilateral and bilateral treaties on the protection of human rights.

As a result of the UN Charter, the Universal Declaration of Human Rights, the Vienna Declaration on Human Rights, as well as numerous other UN instruments, all 191 Member States of the UN are committed to respect fundamental and inalienable human rights as part of general international law. Additionally, most states recognize human rights in their respective national constitutional laws.

Recognition of the sanctity of human rights has thus undoubtedly become part of the 'general principles of international law recognized by civilized nations' as per the Statute of the International Court of justice (ICJ). Furthermore, there is strong support for the position that respect for human rights constitutes an obligation erga omnes and as customary international law imposes obligations on all states towards the international community as a whole for their protection.

Recognizing the international obligation to respect human rights as erga omnes, the International Law Institute has emphasized that this obligation is incumbent on every state in relation to the international community as a whole and that every state has a legal interest in the protection of them, and thus that '[t]his obligation further implies a duty of solidarity among all states to ensure as rapidly as possible the effective protection of human rights throughout the world'.

Beyond agreed principles of customary international law, the shortlist of fundamental human rights required as a minimum to uphold said obligation erga omnes can be found in the International Bill of Human Rights. The obligation erga omnes to respect human rights would bind, at a minimum, not only states but all international legal persons, including therefore the multilateral institutions (MLIs). This would be in addition to obligations derived of other sources.

The primacy of human rights is derived from the inalienable jus cogens nature of the obligation to respect core human rights. Their universal recognition in both national and international law reinforces their inalienable character and recognition of their legal primacy. Further, in the case of conflict between the Charter obligations and the obligation of UN Member States under any other international agreements, the Charter makes clear that it shall prevail. This of course would consist of promoting higher standards of living and conditions of economic and social progress, and solutions of international economic and social problems as well as universal respect for, and observance of, human rights and fundamental freedoms for all without distinction. These obligations are to be achieved through the joint and separate action of the Member States.

World Bank and the International Monetary Fund

The scope of the activities of international financial institutions such as the World Bank and the IMF may have implications for the realization of all human rights for self-determination, the observance of civil and political rights, the ability of people within developing countries to realize their economic, social and cultural rights and their right to development. The mandates of the two institutions differ, in that the World Bank is a development agency engaged in project lending and sectoral activities, whereas the IMF is a monetary agency meant to provide financial assistance to its members to overcome balance of-payments problems, and hence any approach to ensure that human rights obligations are met in the execution of their mandates will probably invite different considerations.

However, with regard to the focus of our assessment, their institutional structures are very similar and may therefore invite similar appraisal regarding the nature of their obligations under international law. A recent study on the specific sources of obligations of the World Bank and the IMF shows that their obligations derive from the international legal personality of the institution, their status as Specialized Agencies of the UN, and the fact chat their members are states with human rights obligations.

As international legal persons IFIs are bound by the regular sources of international law - treaties to which they have acceded, customary international law, including pre-emptory norms of jus cogens, and general principles of international law. With the exception of treaty-based obligations, these obligations pertain to the World Bank and the IMF without any need for their consent.

While IFIs are not parry to international human rights conventions (nor can they be), and therefore, as a general rule, are not directly bound, the international organization as an international legal person is subject to the rules of international law, including conventional (where they have consented), and customary rules and principles of general international law. This is implicit in the approach taken in the Reparations for Injuries case, in which the ICJ found that an international organization is 'a subject of international law and capable of possessing international rights and duties'. In a subsequent Advisory Opinion, the ICJ explained that:

> 'International organizations are subjects of international law and, as such, are bound by any obligations incumbent upon them under general rules of international law, under their constitutions or under international agreements to which they are parry.'

Customary international law of which the 'the principles and rules concerning basic rights of the human person' form a part, as well as general principles of international law derived from the UDHR and the international human rights Covenants, represent minimum standards for all people and all nations and provide sufficient human rights standards upon which the World Bank and IMF can measure the degree to which they are adhering.

While it is not uncommon for representatives of the IFIs to claim that they are bound only by the scope of their mandates as stated in their constituent instruments, any legitimate pursuit of mandated objectives should be brought in line with international human rights norms. This might require limiting or redesigning the actions of the organization, but it is not to say that amendments of the objectives of the international organization will necessarily be required.

That international organizations, not having envisioned human rights as part of their mandates when they were founded 50 years ago, would apply human rights standards today is to be expected. International law is not static and is meant to be interpreted in light of contemporary circumstances. Not least, in order to meet the changing needs and expectations of its member states, one would assume that any intergovernmental organization would have to adequately incorporate human rights into its policies where its existing methods of work or policies risk violating human rights. In sum, as provided in Bowett's Law of International Institutions

> 'What this means in practise is that the organisation should, in the conduct of its activities, be assumed to be subject to rules of customary international law, including rules of jus cogens, which may be relevant to the conduct of its activities. In our

> view this would include, for example, rules of customary law relating to matters such as the protection of fundamental human rights [and] the protection of the environment ...'

Skogly, in her comprehensive work on the subject, concludes that at a minimum the World Bank and IMF are under an obligation to respect human rights through their policies, and possibly to protect human rights. 'However, the crucial point is that the two institutions are responsible for the effects of their own projects and programmes and for the actors involved in them. This could be understood as entailing due vigilance in order to ensure that their actions do not have a negative impact on the human rights situations in any country with which they are engaged and to ensure that they 'neither undermine[s] the ability of other subjects, including [its] members, to faithfully fulfill their international obligations nor facilitate or assist violation of those obligations', this lacer point having particular relevance for borrowing members of the IFIs.

The rights and duties of the World Bank and IMF as subjects of international law are separate from and in addition to those of its Member States. While the full range of obligations - to respect, protect and fulfil human rights -attach themselves to states, human rights standards reflected in general principles of international law should also be understood to bind the organizations, despite the position the organizations themselves may choose to defend. The position that intergovernmental organizations as interstate institutions are bound by the generally accepted standards of the world community, as articulated in, for example, the UDHR and the Covenants, has received recent authoritative endorsement:

> 'This view appears unimpeachable . ... It has been suggested that, for example, the World Bank is not subject to general international norms for the protection of fundamental human rights. In our view that conclusion is without merit, on legal or polity grounds, even if it may be the case that certain bodies charged with reviewing the legality of acts of the World Bank, such as its Inspection Panel, are not permitted to have recourse

> to such law in determining whether the Bank is acting in compliance with its obligations.'

It is accepted that international organizations are responsible under international law for breaches of international norms binding upon them. As maintained, this would include fundamental human rights. The World Bank and the IMF are Specialized Agencies of the UN, having entered into Relationship Agreements with the UN in accordance with Articles 57 and 63 of the UN Charter.

Although the agreements specifically refer to the independent status of the Bank and the Fund, it has been suggested that this status is limited to the UN's ability to direct the work of the two institutions, and does not provide for "a legal independence" in terms of not being bound by the general principles and purposes of the Charter'. Moreover, 'specialised agencies ... are meant to complement the action of the UN in more technical fields, while sharing the same overall objectives as the UN itself'.

Article 57 states that the specialized agencies are 'brought into relationship with the United Nations in accordance with the provisions of Article 63', and hence, 'the two institutions are under an obligation to operate within the principles and the purposes of the United Nations Charter, of which the respect for human rights is a fundamental part' as is international cooperation in the realization of development. Additionally, subsequent human rights instruments refer to the role of Specialized Agencies, as can be seen in Article 9 of the Minorities Declaration, which states: 'The specialized agencies and other organizations of the United Nations system shall contribute to the full realization of the rights and principles sec forth in the present Declaration, within their respective fields of competence.'

Similarly, the UN Draft Declaration on the Rights of Indigenous Peoples recognizes the role of Specialized Agencies and other intergovernmental organizations in the realization of the rights of indigenous peoples, including in relation to financial cooperation, technical assistance and, significantly, with regard to their right to participate in issues affecting them - rights specifically provided for in other instruments. In the case of ICESCR, the Committee has confirmed the role of the Specialized Agencies, in particular the international lending agencies, in relation to 'international assistance' as provided for in Articles 2(1) and 22 with specific mention of the impact and role of UN agencies and their need to ensure protection of economic, social and cultural rights with regard to debt burden and adjustment measures.

With regard to the right to adequate food, the right to education, and the right to health, CESCR has referred specifically to the role of the World Bank and IMF and its impact on the protection of the rights in relation to lending policies and credit agreements, and in international measures to deal with debt crisis, and structural adjustment. The World Bank and the IMF are bound to uphold human rights as a result of their international legal personality and their status as UN Specialized Agencies, the content of the obligations being of both a substantive and a procedural nature, and of conduct and of result. Another ground for upholding human rights within the work undertaken by the Bank and the Fund is the fact that the institutions are composed of states that have human rights obligations born of conventions, custom and general principles of international law.

The majority of member states of the IFIs have ratified the major human rights conventions and are thereby bound to respect, protect and fulfil their human rights obligations, including when entering into bilateral agreements with other states but also through their actions in international organizations. CESCR, for example, has made clear that should the state fail to take into account its legal obligations when entering into bilateral or multilateral agreements, with other states or international organizations, it is in breach of its human rights obligations under the Covenant. Significantly, it should be noted that the terms of the Covenant do not limit the duty to cooperate internationally to cooperation with other States parties or with states in general.

The duty is general and should include cooperation with international organizations as well as cooperation within international organizations. Where States parties are entering into agreements with another State parry to the Covenant, there is a further duty not to induce them to breach the obligations they have undertaken under the Covenant by adopting measures inconsistent with those obligations. Furthermore, and significantly, as UN Member States, all states have pledged themselves to promote respect for human rights and fundamental freedoms, both individually and through joint action and to uphold the purposes of the UN, including achieving international cooperation in solving, inter alia, international economic problems and in the promotion of human rights.

In accordance with Article 103 of the Charter, states' obligations under the Charter take precedence over other international law obligations. These commitments should be reflected in their undertakings as members of IFIs. CESCR has drawn attention to this on several occasions, noting with regard to the right to health that:

> '... States parties have an obligation to ensure that their actions as members of international organizations take due account of the right to health. Accordingly, States parties which are members of international financial institutions, notably the International Monetary Fund, the World Bank and the regional development banks, should pay greater attention to the protection to the right to health in influencing lending policies, credit agreements and international measures of these institutions.'

The Committee makes a similar point with regard to the right to food, and in its Concluding Observations on states' reports. As has been previously indicated, the Declaration on the Right to Development places considerable emphasis on the duty of states to cooperate in the realization of the right. This specifically includes taking steps 'individually and collectively to formulate international development policies with a view to facilitating the full realization of the right to development'. The joint action of states to cooperate in the protection of human rights is also a pledge of UN' Member States as codified in the Charter. As some of the most powerful formulations of development policies occur through the collective decisions of states as members of the World Bank and IMF, it falls to the states to uphold their human rights obligations in relation to the execution of their collective decisions as members of the IFIs - a point to which we will return.

The World Trade Organization

Any failure to integrate human rights into the international trade regime undermines the obligations of states, inter alia, to progressively realize economic, social and cultural rights in accordance with the ICESCR, and engage in the process of development as per the DRD. It severely limits the extent to which people are able to shape the policies of their governments, an element central to the right to development. The argument propounded by WTO representatives, claiming that human rights and the obligations of a state to the people within its jurisdiction does not fall within the mandate of an interstate multilateral trading system, are highly dubious on a range of legal grounds.

Just as with the World Bank and IMF, the VITO, as an organization with international legal personality, is bound by the regular sources of international law: treaties to which they have acceded, customary international law, including preemptory norms of jus cogens, and general principles of international law. Further, all WTO members are UN Member States bound by the provisions of the Charter (as elaborated in subsequent instruments), thereby having undertaken to uphold the purposes of the Charter, including international cooperation in the protection of human rights and fundamental freedoms. Also, according to Article 103 of the UN Charter, the obligations of Member States under the Charter shall prevail in the event of conflicting obligations under other international agreements.

Article 103 places obligations on its Member States to promote respect for human rights and fundamental freedoms, the elaboration of which is provided for in the UDHR, human rights treaties and general international law. Individual Member States will also be bound by their customary and conventional human rights obligations, as well as the law of treaties, both with regard to their involvement in the specialized committees, working groups and working parties dealing with individual agreements of the organization, as well as when working on other areas such as development and the environment.

Consistent with the law of treaties, and the view of the ICJ, the VITO has recognized its obligations to interpret WTO law in light of international law; indeed, according to Article 3 of the WTO Dispute Settlement Understanding (DSU) it is required 'to clarify the existing provision of those agreements in accordance with customary rules of interpretation of public international law'. Howse and Mutua, international legal experts on trade and ' human rights respectively, observe that:

> '[I]t would [thus] appear, that in the event of a conflict between a human rights obligation, particularly one that is universally recognized, and a commitment ensuing from international treaty law, the former prevails or the latter must be interpreted to be consistent with the former. The GATT and other WTO agreements are treaties which would be subject to such obligations and interpretation. Human rights norms should always be taken into account when interpreting international trade and investment obligations ... [t]rade law is basically treaty law. Its interpretation must be taken into account and be consistent with the hierarchy of norms in international law, reflecting for instance the status of some human rights as pre-emptory norms, ergo omnes.'

The obligation to protect human rights may form part of customary international law, and thus any interpretation of WTO law is to respect this obligation and be consistent with it. Where a particular human right is a norm of jus cogens, it must be given primacy, as 'rules of jus cogens trump all other international rules of general international law, and are therefore in the first rank in the hierarchy of the law of nations'. It may also be relevant to consider the international legal principle which holds that states cannot hide behind the organization when their activities cause damage to the interests of other states or organizations.

Where the interests of other states, or indeed other organizations to which they belong, such as the UN, commit them to promoting respect for human rights, general international law provides criteria according to which an organization may be held to be unlawful in conception and objects; additionally, particular acts in the law may be void if they are contrary to a principle of jus cogens.

While the WTO Agreement actually sets out free trade not as an end in itself but as related to the fulfilment of basic human values, including the improvement of living standards for all people and sustainable development and therefore cannot prima facie be considered as being founded on basic principles that violate human rights, the question remains as to whether human rights are violated in the execution of its mandate, despite the professed scope of its objectives.

The Preamble of the WTO Agreement establishes the framework for the entire WTO system in which free trade has been proclaimed as an objective of the system of the fulfilment of basic human values. Additionally, the preambular reference to raising standards of living and ensuring full employment and a large and steadily growing volume of real income elucidates the objective that human development and well-being is a central concern of the trade regime under the WTO, a position that was accepted in full in the statement by the WTO representative at the UN Working Group on the Right to Development when he claimed that the WTO shared the same objectives for development as those set out in the UN Charter and the Universal Declaration of Human Rights.

The reference to the fulfilment of human values and related aims in the WTO Agreement begs the question as to the legitimacy of subsequent WTO treaties - often felt by civil society actors to undermine these founding objectives - despite the fact that they are ostensibly created with the fulfilment of human development and well-being as among their objectives. Intergovernmental organizations such as the WTO and the Bretton Woods institutions are essentially creatures of the international legal system. They cannot therefore be deemed to be exempt from fundamental principles of international law such as the obligation to respect universal human rights.

Decisions taken by organizations, as well as agreements undertaken by their Member States, including those reflected in trade law, should be interpreted and evolve in a manner consistent with the hierarchy of norms in international law generally, which would include, at a minimum and in addition to conventional obligations where they exist, many basic human rights that have the status of custom, general principles or ergo omnes obligations. It would also include the minimum rights enumerated in the International Bill of Human Rights which may be understood as providing the content of an erga omnes obligation to respect human rights. These non-conventional sources of international law would bind all international legal persons, including intergovernmental organizations and states - which includes those states that have not ratified, and therefore are not bound by, a given human rights treaty.

While actual control, guarantee or agency would need to be established in order to challenge the accepted convention that the organizations themselves are the only subjects that may be held liable for the consequences of the wrongful acts of the organization to the exclusion of their Member States, the members of international organizations may be said to be under an obligation of 'due diligence' which compels them to make sure that the transfer of competences to the organization does not allow them to avoid their responsibilities under international law.

As emphasized on several occasions by the European Commission and European Court of Human Rights, including in the recent Matthews case, the Court remarked that the European Convention on Human Rights 'does not exclude the transfer of competences to international organizations provided that the Convention rights continue to be "secured". Member States' responsibility therefore continues even after such a transfer.' Significantly, as this ruling has shown, there are situations where:

> '[M]embers of international organisations may be responsible not for the consequences of the tatter's illegal acts, but for their own participation in that act, or for their failure to ensure that the powers they have transferred to an organisation have been exercised in conformity with their own international obligations.'

Such transfer of powers applied within an organization where their use is not exercised consistently with international human rights standards should also pertain to decision-making powers. The World Bank, IMF and WTO function according to collective decision-making by their representative organs, the decisions of which are taken by weighted voting in the case of the World Bank and IMF- and on the principle of one-country, one-vote in the WTO.

Despite acceptance of the formal process of decision-making by simple majority in the WTO, in practice, decisions are taken by consensus. However, although each country in principle has a vote and a right equal to that of any other country, the vast majority of developing countries are left out of the negotiations and 'consultations', which in fact are known to determine the decisions. This concern was voiced by certain states at the Working Group on the Right to Development in calling for developing countries to be given 'the possibility to participate in general [in a range of aspects related to international trade], and in particular to be given a more important role in discussions at the WTO'.

As a result of these forms of decision-making, might there be different responsibilities imposed on various states depending on their degree of influence on the collective decisions of an organization? The possible attribution of weighted responsibility to match weighted votes presents a further consideration beyond the broader proposition by UN experts Oloko-Onyango and Udagama, in their recent study on globalization and human rights in which they submit:

> 'In the case of decisions made collectively, one cannot disaggregate such actions and attribute them to individual member States. Member States are then obliged to discharge their obligations undertaken qua members pursuant to those collective decisions, and will be held individually responsible under international law for the breach thereof.'

Multilateral institutions play a vital role in the ability to hinder, or if they so choose, positively influence, the likelihood of minorities and indigenous peoples to realize their right to development. Regardless of the fact that their mandates do not, per se, refer to human rights protection and promotion as falling within the scope of their undertakings, the fact is that the decisions and actions of states, through their membership in these organizations, have a severe impact on, and often transgress, entrenched human rights norms. Too often, the capacity of minority and indigenous peoples to shape the policies of their governments, the competence of governments to fulfil their human rights obligations and the ability of minority and indigenous peoples to live free from violations of their right to development, are directly affected by the enterprise of these organizations.

States determine the policies of global actors, including the World Bank, the IMF and the WTO and some of the most powerful formulations of development policies - and in the case of the WTO, influential agreements with an impact on development emanate from them. This engagement triggers responsibility in the area of human rights. At a meeting convened in 2001 by Minority Rights Group International and the UN Working Group on Minorities, representatives of minority and indigenous peoples' organizations issued a range of recommendations in relation to minority rights and development. Respecting human rights standards, including with regard to redressing discrimination and ensuring participation, were felt to be crucial to furthering the protection of the rights of minority and indigenous peoples in development.

Assessing the impact of development programmes and projects to ensure that future plans do not violate their rights, strengthening their capacity to contribute to decision-making and allowing for their free, full and informed consent in matters that affect them, and ensuring the effective regulation of national and transnational corporations in order to secure respect for their identities and cultures, were all central to their demands. In a recent 'Dialogue Paper by Indigenous Peoples' submitted to the Commission on Sustainable Development, the WTO TRIPS Agreement and the WTO Agreement on Agriculture were noted as posing a serious threat to their cultural rights and their right to health, among others.

Indigenous peoples remarked further on their grave concern that compliance with WTO agreements, combined with the trade and investment regimes promoted by the World Bank and IMF, is undermining national legislation and regulations that protect the environment. Recognition by multilateral institutions, and by states as members of them, of their human rights obligations is the first step to addressing and reversing violations that stem from their activities.

8

Protection of Indegenous Peoples Under ILO Convention

Since 1919, the International Labour Organisation (ILO) has assigned an important place to human rights in its fields of competence. The organization has been a principal inspiration of the universal and regional texts relating economic and social rights, and to certain civil rights and political rights. This is especially true in connection with the protection of indigenous peoples. The ILO became active in this field long before the United Nations.

Concerning indigenous peoples the ILO made an important contribution in awakening public interest in that problem. And the ILO is still a pacemaker in the field, as the Convention No. 169 shows. But there is no doubt about a certain competition between the ILO and UN activities in that field. Some experts criticize the ILO, that the Convention 107 on indigenous populations had been a dead letter for many years.

One can ask what the advantage of an international convention for the protection of indigenous peoples is. After the experiences of these peoples, it seems understandable that they feel a need for the greatest possible protection of their human rights and their rights as peoples, in particular with a certain international law personality. From the standpoint of international law it is also obvious that one cannot speak of problems of discrimination of certain groups without mentioning the fate of indigenous peoples. History had demonstrated that indigenous rights cannot be left only to the national legal order. Their claims are ten-fold:

— physical survival;
— cultural survival and cultural identity;
— sovereignty;
— self-determination;
— self-government;
— land-rights;
— control over their land and its resources;
— compensation;
— non-discrimination;
— affirmative action.

Some of these claims have been recognized by the ILO Conventions. The importance for the theory and practice of international law of that development is that indigenous peoples have a limited capacity as subjects of international law.

ILO Convention No. 107 of 1957

The interest of the ILO in the problems of indigenous peoples resulted from the fact that individuals belonging to indigenous people were very often the victims of prejudices which led to gross exploitation in the labour market. The background has been the lack of appropriate education and vocational training of these individuals as well as a massive discrimination by the ruling societies in the relevant states. This has been the outcome of a historical process of conquest, penetration and marginalization of traditional indigenous societies. The discrimination was accompanied by attitudes of superiority among the Europeans. The result was a gradual destruction of the material and spiritual basis for the maintenance of indigenous societies. Many of indigenous individuals had been deprived of their land and natural resources and had nowhere to go. Therefore, these individuals had very often no other alternative but to accept employment under the worst conditions.

From the perspective of the competence of the ILO there was a task of elimination of discrimination and of integration of indigenous "populations" into the societies of the concerned member States. The result of these considerations was the adoption of Convention No. 107, the Convention on Indigenous and Tribal Populations. This was for a long time the only universal Convention which dealt exclusively with the rights of indigenous populations.

The aim of this Convention was the adoption of general international standards for the protection of indigenous populations, the improvement of their living and working conditions and "their progressive integration into their respective national communities".

The main idea of the document was, therefore, that governments undertake measures not only to protect but also to progressively integrate the indigenous populations into the wider societies (Article 2).

The authors of the Convention, however, saw some limits of this integration. It should not be a form of "artificial assimilation" (Article 2, paragraph 2 c). The limits were the respect of:

— the cultural and religious values;
— the forms of social control existing among these populations; and
— the nature of the problems which face them both as groups and as individuals when they undergo social and economic change.

The intention of a "moderate integration" becomes very obvious when reading Article 4 b of the Convention. According to that provision, the governments shall take into account "the danger involved in disrupting the values and institutions of the said populations unless they can be replaced by appropriate substitutes which the groups concerned are willing to accept."

Without any doubt, this Convention was a considerable success in directing international public opinion towards the often dramatic problems faced by indigenous populations. Also from the standpoint of international law, which is primarily a law of the relations between sovereign states, this Convention was a further step for the creation of a human rights protection system not only for the individuals but also for collective human rights.

However, for various reasons the Convention won only limited support. Typical is the case of Norway, a country with its own indigenous people within its territory:

> "When the question of accession was taken up in Norway in 1958, the government, with the support of the Storting, was of the opinion that there were no population groups in Norway such as those dealt with in the treaty, and that there was therefore no reason to go into the question of Norwegian ratification. The Convention has not been subsequently ratified by any of the other Nordic countries either."

Although the Convention had been ratified by 27 States by the end of 1981, the effects were rather poor. This cannot be a surprise, because many concerned states - like Norway - hesitated to participate. But this is perhaps not the most important reason. More important seems to be the general problem of the relationship between a state and the protection of human rights in general vis-à-vis the individual and especially vis-à-vis groups. Eide describes the situation very convincing:

> "We live in a world composed of states. The role of the state in regard to its inhabitants varies considerably from one political system to another. But everywhere it is, to some extent, Janus-faced. It has two faces. Some see the good face of the state, as a

> protector, a mediator and at times as an instrument of welfare. Those who experience the state in this way, consider it to be 'their' state, a state which they influence and utilize to solve common problems. But some also see the bad face of the state. They see it as an instrument for control and repression, of socialization into the dominant values of society. They see it as an agency of the strong against the weak, and those who see it this way do not consider the state to be 'theirs', even though they must accept to live under the sway of its authority."

Especially the indigenous peoples have the experience of the "bad face" of the state. This is primarily a consequence of their understanding of the function and the task of a "state", which was established without their support in "their" territories. This tension becomes obvious in the impressive Declaration of the Indigenous People of the Dene, which provides a typical example of their standpoint:

> "The Dene find themselves as a part of a country. That country is Canada. But the government of Canada is not the government of the Dene. This government was not the choice of the Dene, they were imposed upon the Dene."

Therefore it was clear that the indigenous peoples were not interested in integration in such a "state". However, a great number of them were integrated or assimilated in societies against their will, sometimes with military force and political pressure. In cases where treaties between indigenous peoples and the colonizers exist, they were very often violated and broken. One of the most complicated tasks for every codification in this field "is the consideration of methods of protection and guaranteeing the respect for these rights of indigenous peoples as well as to develop systems for interfacing between nation-states and the indigenous peoples' institutions."

Challenge of the Revision of Convention No. 107

In the 1980s the problem of the revision of Convention No. 107 appeared on the agenda of the ILO. This was due to two developments. The first was the very active work and the important influence of non-governmental organizations of indigenous peoples, working at the national and international level:

> "Indigenous NGOs have major advantages in dealing with mechanisms of the international fora: first, they possess an enormous moral and ethical imperative; second, the process involved in international fora operate dynamically over relatively long periods of time as do traditional forms of decision making; and third, the necessary capacity for compromise and eventual consensus is well established in indigenous traditions."

The second development was the new understanding of the right of self-determination after the process of decolonization and elaboration of the 1970 Declaration on Friendly Relations. This document provides a cornerstone of the modern approach to the concept of self-determination. After this it became clear, that "integration should be the result of the freely expressed wishes of the territory's peoples acting with full knowledge of the change in their status, their wishes having been expressed through informed and democratic processes impartially conducted and based on universal adult suffrage. The United Nations could, when it deems it necessary, supervise these procedures."

Closely connected with this understanding of the principle of self-determination was the international engagement in the struggle against discrimination. On several occasions the UN General Assembly commented in connection with its struggle against discrimination also upon on the well being and prosperity of indigenous peoples. It shows the growing interest of the community of States in this subject that the UN Sub-Commission on Prevention of Discrimination and Protection of Minorities appointed José R. Martinez Cobo as Special Rapporteur for a Study of the Problem of Discrimination against Indigenous Populations in the early 1970s. This study, completed in 1983, is an important overview

of the national and international situation of indigenous peoples.

In the light of these developments in the 1970s it was clear for the ILO that there was a need for a modernization of some of the aspects of the Convention No. 107 which deal with self-determination, integration and prohibition of discrimination. On the other hand, some of the original articles have been reinforced by these developments:

> "While the Convention has been criticized for its emphasis on integration and assimilation, it contains significant provisions, for example Article 11 which stipulates that '(t)he right of ownership, collective or individual, of the members of the populations concerned over the lands which these populations traditionally occupy shall be recognized.'"

The World Council of Indigenous Peoples (WCIP) played a leading role in initiating the revision. During its Third Assembly, held in Canberra in April 1981, WCIP presented a draft. The basic approaches were fundamentally different from the ILO idea of integration. This became clear with the wording of Article 1:

> "All peoples have the right to self-determination. By virtue of that right indigenous peoples may freely determine their political status and freely pursue their economic, social and cultural development."

Article 3 goes on as follows:

> "One manner in which the right of self-determination can be realized is by the free determination of an Indigenous People to associate their territories and institutions with one or more states in a manner involving free association, regional autonomy, home rule or associate statehood as self governing unite. Indigenous People may freely determine to enter into such relationships and to alter those relationships after they have been established."

This draft has been a challenge for the traditional understanding of international law as a law which deals primarily with the relationship between sovereign states. On the other hand this proposal was of a certain influence for the modernization of the ILO itself. The Organization became aware that its integrationist approach was unacceptable to the indigenous peoples.

Under this impression the cooperation with the UN Working Group on Indigenous Populations was intensified. This Working Group was proposed by the UN Sub-Commission on Prevention of Discrimination and Protection of Minoritiesand was created in 1982 with the following mandate:

> "—review developments pertaining to the promotion and protection of human rights and fundamental freedoms of indigenous populations, including information requested by the Secretary-General annually from governments, specialized agencies, regional inter-governmental organizations and non-governmental organizations in consultative status, particularly those of indigenous peoples, to analyze such materials, and to submit conclusions to the Sub-Commission, bearing in mind the report of the Special Rapporteur of the Sub-Commission;
>
> —give special attention to the evolution of standards concerning the rights of indigenous populations, taking account of both the similarities and the differences in the situations and aspirations of indigenous populations throughout the world."

The Working Group was at this time drafting a Universal Declaration of Indigenous Rights, which was strongly influenced by the developments in the ILO. However, it also played an active role in the process of revision. But the legal difference between the tasks of the two bodies must be emphasized: A declaration should include general goals and objectives, but a convention is a legal instrument which creates binding obligations for the ratifying states.

In general, the international standard-setting concerning indigenous peoples has been a very slow process; but nevertheless, there is such a process. This process is going on in different organs and organizations of the UN system, but it is a process with a high degree of unity. There is no conflict between either the procedures or the substance of the ILO Convention and the standards which the UN intends to adopt. The ILO standards are "designed to be minimum standards, in the sense that they are intended to establish a floor under the rights of indigenous and tribal peoples and, in particular, to establish a basis for government conduct in relations to them."

Convention No. 169 on Indigenous and Tribal Peoples

The revision of the Convention No. 107 began in 1986. After a meeting of experts the ILO decided to start this process. It was finished in 1989. In all the debates the NGOs of indigenous peoples took part. Nevertheless there were a lot of criticism concerning the procedure of drafting by these organizations:

> "...the results of the ILO initiative to update Convention No.107 (1957) by means of a new instrument (i.e. Convention No. 169) were received by a number of indigenous organizations with dismay and bitterness stemming from what they considered the very much restricted nature of their participation in the deliberations at the Conference and from actual contents of the new Convention."

On the other hand, the result of the codification process has been accepted by the community of states with success: the vote for the adoption was 128 to 1 (Netherlands) and 49 abstentions. This seems important, because other activities in this sphere "are received with apprehension by some Governments, which regret what in their view is undue attention to matters of relatively minor overall importance and pertaining, after all, to their domestic jurisdiction."

These contradictions become understandable in connection with the main points of discussion.

A. "Peoples" versus "Populations" and "Minorities"

The most important and obvious difference one can note is that the Convention No. 169 refers to peoples and not to populations like the Convention 107. The legal consequences of this change are important. From the point of view of international law it should be emphasized that a population has nearly no juridical significance in international law. In general it is a group of individuals which may be of relevance for the domestic law of a state. An exception may be a population which consists of ethnic or religious groups of at least several thousand individuals, established over a long period of time in a particular area and which is affected by expulsion and transfer.

"Peoples" is a term which is often used in international law, but there is no definition of that expression. In the case of indigenous peoples the description of their character as a people is rather clear:

> "Indigenous communities, peoples and nations are those which, having a historical continuity with pre-invasion and pre-colonial societies that developed on their territories, consider themselves distinct from other sectors of the societies now prevailing in those territories, or part of them. They form at present non-dominant sectors of society and are determined to preserve, develop and transmit to future generations their ancestral territories, and their ethnic identity, as a basis of their ethnic identity, in accordance with their own cultural patterns, social institutions and legal system."

In the practical definition great importance has been attached to objective elements (ancestry, culture, language etc.) and subjective elements (self-identification and acceptance).

The consequences of the acceptance of the character of peoples for the indigenous are far-reaching. Peoples have the right to self-determination. This right is one of the basic principles of international law:

> "The rights of important groups such become particularly prominent in connection with the principle or rights, of self-determination, vi., the right of cohesive national groups ("people") to choose for themselves a form of political organization and their relation to other groups. The choice may be independence as a state, association with other groups in a federal state, or autonomy or assimilation in a unitary state."

The definition of the right to self-determination makes understandable that the discussion over the term "peoples" versus "population" was extensive. There was also no doubt, that the opposition to the term "peoples" emanates from the fear of the states that if indigenous peoples were recognized as peoples they would assert their own right to self-determination. This right is a human right which is applicable to all peoples, as it is included in both UN Human Rights Covenants:

> "All peoples have the rights to self-determination. By virtue of that right they freely determine their political status and freely pursue their economic, social and cultural development.".

Because of these far-reaching consequences some states considered indigenous peoples as "ethnic minorities" and dealt with them in accordance with Article 27 of the International Convenant on Civil and Political Rights. This Article reads:

> "In those States in which ethnic, religious or linguistic minorities exist, persons belonging to such minorities shall not be denied the right, in community with the other members of their group, to enjoy their own culture, to profess and practice their own religion, or to use their own language."

The wording of Article 27 shows that international law does not treat minorities as entities. Instead the rights are given to individuals. The contradiction is obvious, because these rights can only be practiced together with other individuals belonging to the same group. The background of this contradiction has been that the community of states hesitated to give minorities an international personality:

> "Such international personality, it was feared, might have given a minority the capacity to vindicate its rights before a competent international institution."

Especially under these conditions Article 27 does not meet the needs of indigenous peoples. It is true that indigenous peoples are not always in a minority position. In some countries, indeed, "they may constitute the majority, so while it is appropriate to discuss them here they may only be minorities in the sociological sense of the term." It should also be mentioned that Article 27 represents an international minimum standard, which is only indirectly relevant to the indigenous situation. The Working Group identified the following points as important:

— the right to land and other natural resources, including the right to water resources;

— the right to autonomy and self-government including their own legal systems and their own customary law.

These rights are collective in nature. It is true that the development of a theory of collective human rights is not yet very advanced. But this cannot mean that the enjoyment of these rights by the indigenous peoples may be reflected. Thus, Falk is right when writing:

> " ...we cannot approach the challenge of the relationship with indigenous people as long as it remains an abstraction that can be lumped with other categories of injustice. Instead it has a specific history or series of histories, that is bound up with our modernizing, development civilization. Unless that history is acknowledged and understood, it will be very difficult to make an appropriate response."

The acceptance of these collective human rights of indigenous peoples is one of the acts of "understanding".

Doubtless the recognition of the collective character of indigenous rights by the using of the term "peoples" represents an important success for the protection of indigenous rights and an existing development in international law. But the success is bigger in theory than in practice, because the ILO added as a result of the fear of self-determination a qualifier to the term "peoples". Article 1 paragraph 3 reads:

> "The use of the term 'peoples' in this convention shall not be construed as having any implications as regards the rights which may attach to the term under international law."

Therefore there has been a necessity to explain this understanding of self-determination. Obviously it is used similar to some domestic legal orders, e.g. in Canada. The already-mentioned Declaration of the Dene is illustrative:

> "What we the Dene are struggling for is the recognition of the Dene Nation by the governments and peoples of the world. And while there are realities we are forced to submit to such as the existence of a country called Canada, we insist on the right to self-determination as a distinct people and the recognition of the Dene Nation ....What we seek then is independence and self-determination within the country of Canada. This is what we mean when we call for a just land settlement of the Dene Nation."

This Declaration makes clear that there is a need to demystify the concept of self-determination in connection with the indigenous peoples. In this case it does "not mean statehood or independence or any sort of secession," but rather "self-development."

It should be underlined that the positions of the indigenous peoples vary greatly from country to country. However, in general it seems - and the ILO Convention supports this view - that there is a strong connection between the aspirations of indigenous peoples and concepts of autonomy:

"Autonomy and self-government are determined primarily by the degree of actual as well as formal independence enjoyed by the autonomous entity in its political decision-making process. Generally autonomy is understood to refer to independence of action on the internal or domestic level, as foreign affairs and defence normally are in the hands of the central or national government, but occasionally power to conclude international agreements concerning cultural or economic matters also may reside with the autonomous entity."

In the light of many problems with separatist movements in the whole world the concept of autonomy is of primary importance. The solution of the ILO seems therefore reasonable. It is regrettable that representatives of indigenous peoples do not share this opinion and consider the ILO Convention as a failure to recognize the indigenous world view:

"In Convention 169, the term 'peoples' has been qualified to have no significance in international law. We do not accept this decision of the ILO. We still maintain our right to call ourselves people. Furthermore, we have the right to self-determination to determine our own international status."

B. The Rights of Indigenous Peoples

The Convention contains a comprehensive catalogue of the rights of indigenous peoples. The starting point is Article 2, a kind of general clause of the whole document:

> "Governments shall have the responsibility for developing, with the participation of the peoples concerned, coordinated and systematic action to protect the rights of these peoples and to guarantee respect for their integrity."

Article 2 creates obligations of the government, primarily enabling the participation of indigenous peoples in the development of human rights protection. It is clear from the

text that there is a need for positive action on the part of the States. The aim of this activity is formulated in sub-paragraph 2(c), "to eliminate socioeconomic gaps that may exist between indigenous and other members of the national community."

This obligation is a consequence of the principle of non-discrimination, which sometimes means to undertake affirmative action measures to overcome consequences of former discrimination. But the demand of non-discrimination, equality under the law and equal protection of the law are not particular to indigenous peoples. There are many reasons for the position that non-discrimination is a principle of customary international law with ius cogens character.

This principle is emphasized and developed in the UN Charter, the Universal Declaration of Human Rights and the International Covenants on Human Rights. The most notable expression of this principle one can find in the UN International Convention on the Elimination of All Forms of Racial Discrimination. It is interesting, that the participating States of that Convention explain in their state reports to the Committee on the Elimination of Racial Discrimination (CERD) their policy concerning indigenous peoples.

The reports show that it is very common to protect indigenous peoples by the principle of non-discrimination. Therefore the criticism of some representatives of indigenous organizations, who fear a new kind of assimilation, seems to be a misunderstanding:

> "First, it is assumed that we want to be on an equal footing with the non-indigenous peoples; secondly, that the national laws and regulations constitute the proper system to ensure our rights; and thirdly, that our status within the socioeconomic order is one which we find a need to correct. This last assumption carries with it the racial prejudice that our lifestyle is inferior and unacceptable by implying a need to abandon our lifestyle to adopt the non-indigenous socio-economic system."

That these fears in connection with this norm of the Convention are without any basis becomes obvious with the wording of Article 4, paragraph 2:

> "Such special measures shall not be contrary to the freely-expressed wishes of the peoples concerned."

It is in this sense, that Article 6 provides:

> "1. In applying the provisions of this convention, governments shall: (a) consult the peoples concerned, through appropriate procedures and in particular through their representative institutions, whenever consideration is being given to legislative or administrative measures which may affect them directly."

The underlying idea of the rule is that of cooperation between all concerned groups in society. However, the meaning of the term "consult" from the legal point of view is not that clear. The explanation of the Convention is that "consultation" shall be undertaken "in good faith and in a form appropriate to the circumstances, with the objective of achieving agreement or consent to the to the proposed measures."

The practice shows that the content of the term "consultation" is very often not satisfying. One can expect, at least, that it involves discussion between the parties in an attempt to reach an understanding. But the reality is different. Venne mentioned an example:

> "In Canada, the federal government customarily will mail letters to the chiefs, notifying them of new administrative or legislative changes, often without allowing them enough time to conduct an appropriate and thorough analysis of these changes. If the chiefs do not answer these letters within a certain limit, the government proceeds. When we complain about these changes, we are told that the letter itself was the only form of consultation."

It is important for indigenous peoples to have the right to decide their own priorities for the process of development as

it affects their lives (Article 7) and to retain their own customs and institutions.

Part II deals with the land. This issue has long been a principal claim of indigenous peoples. The developments in the last decades - the integration of the world system of production and consumption - have increased the pressure on the remaining land of indigenous peoples.

> "Since the Second World War the number of incursions into indigenous peoples land has escalated worldwide. Once thought of as barren wastelands of little economic and political value, indigenous territories have now been identified as areas of vital national and even international importance ...With no untroubled or unconverted regions to retreat to, the native inhabitants have been forced to accept these invasions reluctantly, or else fight back."

Considering also the special relationship between indigenous peoples and the land - the land is for such peoples not merely a possession and a means of production, but part of the spiritual life and therefore connected with many "deep-seated implications" - it is understandable that this problem is of primary importance. Articles 13 and 14 recognize the land rights of indigenous peoples. Problems may be raised in relationship to the subsoil resources. Governments "shall establish or maintain procedures through they shall consult these peoples" in cases of exploitation. This norm is indeed not very exact: indigenous representatives reflect it as "truly shameful", because it enshrines the "concept of terra nullus".

ILO's Convention No. 169 Concerning Indigenous and Tribal Peoples in Independent Countries

The General Conference of the International Labour Organisation, Having been convened at Geneva by the Governing Body of the International Labour Office, and having met in its 76th Session on 7 June 1989, and

Noting the international standards contained in the Indigenous and Tribal Populations Convention and Recommendation, 1957, and

Recalling the terms of the Universal Declaration of Human Rights, the International Covenant on Economic, Social and Cultural Rights, the International Covenant on Civil and Political Rights, and the many international instruments on the prevention of discrimination, and

Considering that the developments which have taken place in international law since 1957, as well as developments in the situation of indigenous and tribal peoples in all regions of the world, have made it appropriate to adopt new international standards on the subject with a view to removing the assimilationist orientation of the earlier standards, and

Recognising the aspirations of these peoples to exercise control over their own institutions, ways of life and economic development and to maintain and develop their identities, languages and religions, within the framework of the States in which they live, and

Noting that in many parts of the world these peoples are unable to enjoy their fundamental human rights to the same degree as the rest of the population of the States within which they live, and that their laws, values, customs and perspectives have often been eroded, and

Calling attention to the distinctive contributions of indigenous and tribal peoples to the cultural diversity and social and ecological harmony of humankind and to international co-operation and understanding, and

Noting that the following provisions have been framed with the cooperation of the United Nations, the Food and Agriculture Organisation of the United Nations, the United Nations Educational, Scientific and Cultural Organisation and the World Health Organisation, as well as of the Inter-American Indian Institute, at appropriate Levels and in their respective fields, and that it is proposed to continue this co-

operation in promoting and securing the application of these provisions, and

Having decided upon the adoption of certain proposals with regard to the partial revision of the Indigenous and Tribal Populations Convention, 1957 (No. 107), which is the fourth item on the agenda of the session and

Having determined that these proposals shall take the form of an international Convention revising the Indigenous and Tribal Populations Convention, 1957;

adopts this twenty-seventh day of June of the year one thousand nine hundred and eighty-nine, the following Convention, which may be cited as the Indigenous and Tribal Peoples Convention, 1989;

Part I. General Policy

Article 1

1. This Convention applies to:

   (a) tribal peoples in independent countries whose social, cultural and economic conditions distinguish them from other sections of the national community and whose status is regulated wholly or partially by their own customs or traditions or by special laws or regulations;

   (b) peoples in independent countries who are regarded as indigenous on account of their descent from the populations which inhabited the country, or a geographical region to which the country belongs, at the time of conquest or colonisation or the establishment of present state boundaries and who irrespective of their legal status, retain some or all of their own social, economic, cultural and political institutions.

2. Self-identification as indigenous or tribal shall be regarded as a fundamental criterion for determining the groups to which the provisions of this Convention apply.
3. The use of the term "peoples" in this Convention shall not be construed as having any implications as regards the rights which may attach to the term under international law.

Article 2

1. Governments shall have the responsibility for developing, with the participation of the peoples concerned, co-ordinated and systematic action to protect the rights of these peoples and to guarantee respect for their integrity.
2. Such action shall include measures for:
   (a) ensuring that members of these peoples benefit on an equal footing from the rights and opportunities which national laws and regulations grant to other members of the population;
   (b) promoting the full realisation of the social, economic and cultural rights of these peoples with respect for their social and cultural identity, their customs and traditions and their institutions;
   (c) assisting the members of the peoples concerned to eliminate socio-economic gaps that may exist between indigenous and other members of the national community, in a manner compatible with their aspirations and ways of life.

Article 3

1. Indigenous and tribal peoples shall enjoy the full measure of human rights and fundamental freedoms without hindrance or discrimination. The provisions of the Convention shall be applied without discrimination to male and female members of these peoples.

2. No form of force or coercion shall be used in violation of the human rights and fundamental freedoms of the peoples concerned, including the rights contained in this Convention.

Article 4

1. Special measures shall be adopted as appropriate for safeguarding the persons, institutions, property, labour, cultures and environment of the peoples concerned.
2. Such special measures shall not be contrary to the freely-expressed wishes of the peoples concerned.
3. Enjoyment of the general rights of citizenship, without discrimination shall not be prejudiced in any way by such special measures.

Article 5

1. In applying the provisions of this Convention:
   (a) the social, cultural, religious and spiritual values and practices of these peoples shall be recognised and protected, and due account shall be taken of the nature of the problems which face them both as groups and as individuals;
   (b) the integrity of the values, practices and institutions of these peoples shall be respected;
   (c) policies aimed at mitigating the difficulties experienced by these, peoples in facing new conditions of life and work shall be adopted, with the participation and co-operation of the peoples affected.

Article 6

1. In applying the provisions of this Convention, governments shall:
   (a) consult the peoples concerned, through appropriate procedures and in particular through their

representative institutions, whenever consideration is being given to legislative or administrative measures which may affect them directly;

(b) establish means by which these peoples can freely participate, to at least the same extent as other sectors of the population, at all levels of decision-making in elective institutions and administrative and other bodies responsible for policies and programmes which concern them;

(c) establish means for the full development of these peoples' own institutions and initiatives, and in appropriate cases provide the resources necessary for this purpose.

2. The consultations carried out in application of this Convention shall be undertaken, in good faith and in a form appropriate to the circumstances, with the objective of achieving agreement or consent to the proposed measures.

Article 7

1. The peoples concerned shall have the right to decide their own priorities for the process of development as it affects their lives, beliefs, institutions and spiritual well-being and the lands they occupy or otherwise use, and to exercise control, to the extent possible, over their own economic, social and cultural development. In addition, they shall participate in the formulation, implementation and evaluation of plans and programmes for national and regional development which may affect them directly.

2. The improvement of the conditions of life and work and levels of health and education of the peoples concerned, with their participation and cooperation, shall be a matter of priority in plans for the overall economic development of areas they inhabit. Special projects for development of the areas in question shall also be so designed as to promote such improvement.

3. Governments shall ensure that, whenever appropriate, studies are carried out, in co-operation with the peoples concerned, to assess the social, spiritual, cultural and environmental impact on them of planned development activities. The results of these studies shall be considered as fundamental criteria for the implementation of these activities.

4. Governments shall take measures, in co-operation with the peoples concerned, to protect and preserve the environment of the territories they inhabit.

Article 8

1. In applying national laws and regulations to the peoples concerned, due regard shall be had to their customs or customary laws.

2. These peoples shall have the right to retain their own customs and institutions, where these are not incompatible with fundamental rights defined by the national legal system and with internationally recognised human rights. Procedures shall be established, whenever necessary, to resolve conflicts which may arise in the application of this principle.

3. The application of paragraphs 1 and 2 of this Article shall not prevent members of these peoples from exercising the rights granted to all citizens and from assuming the corresponding duties.

Article 9

1. To the extent compatible with the national legal system and internationally recognised human rights, the methods customarily practised by the peoples concerned for dealing with offences committed by their members shall be respected.

2. The customs of these peoples in regard to penal matters shall be taken into consideration by the authorities and courts dealing with such cases.

Article 10

1. In imposing penalties laid down by general law on members of these peoples account shall be taken of their economic, social and cultural characteristics.
2. Preference shall be given to methods of punishment other than confinement in prison.

Article 11

The exaction from members of the peoples concerned of compulsory personal services in any form, whether paid or unpaid, shall be prohibited and punishable by law, except in cases prescribed by law for all citizens.

Article 12

The peoples concerned shall be safeguarded against the abuse of their rights and shall be able to take legal proceedings, either individually or through their representative bodies, for the effective protection of these rights. Measures shall be taken to ensure that members of these peoples can understand and be understood in legal proceedings, where necessary through the provision of interpretation or by other effective means.

PART II. LAND

Article 13

1. In applying the provisions of this Part of the Convention governments shall respect the special importance for the cultures and spiritual values of the peoples concerned of their relationship with the lands or territories, or both as applicable, which they occupy or otherwise use, and in particular the collective aspects of this relationship.
2. The use of the term "lands' in Articles 15 and 16 shall include the concept of territories, which covers the total environment of the areas which the peoples concerned occupy or otherwise use.

Article 14

1. The rights of ownership and possession of the peoples concerned over the lands which they traditionally occupy shall be recognised. In addition, measures shall be taken in appropriate cases to safeguard the right of the peoples concerned to use lands not exclusively occupied by them, but to which they have traditionally had access for their subsistence and traditional activities. Particular attention shall be paid to the situation of nomadic peoples and shifting cultivators in this respect.
2. Governments shall take steps as necessary to identify the lands which the peoples concerned traditionally occupy, and to guarantee effective protection of their rights of ownership and possession.
3. Adequate procedures shall be established within the national legal system to resolve land claims by the peoples concerned.

Article 15

1. The rights of the peoples concerned to the natural resources pertaining to their lands shall be specially safeguarded. These rights include the right of these peoples to participate in the use, management and conservation of these resources.
2. In cases in which the State retains the ownership of mineral or subsurface resources or rights to other resources pertaining to lands, governments shall establish or maintain procedures through which they shall consult these peoples, with a view to ascertaining whether and to what degree their interests would be prejudiced, before undertaking or permitting any programmes for the exploration or exploitation of such resources pertaining to their lands. The peoples concerned shall wherever possible participate in the benefits of such activities, and shall receive fair compensation for any damages which they may sustain as a result of such activities.

Article 16

1. Subject to the following paragraphs of this Article, the peoples concerned shall not be removed from the lands which they occupy.
2. Where the relocation of these peoples is considered necessary as an exceptional measure, such relocation shall take place only with their free and informed consent. Where their consent cannot be obtained, such relocation shall take place only following appropriate procedures established by national laws and regulations, including public inquiries where appropriate, which provide the opportunity for effective representation of the peoples concerned.
3. Whenever possible, these peoples shall have the right to return to their traditional lands, as soon as the grounds for relocation cease to exist.
4. When such return is not possible, as determined by agreement or, in the absence of such agreement, through appropriate procedures, these peoples shall be provided in all possible cases with lands of quality and legal status at least equal to that of the lands previously occupied by them, suitable to provide for their present needs and future development. Where the peoples concerned express a preference for compensation in money or in kind, they shall be so compensated under appropriate guarantees.
5. Persons thus relocated shall be fully compensated for any resulting loss or injury.

Article 17

1. Procedures established by the peoples concerned for the transmission of rights among members of these peoples shall be respected.

2. The peoples concerned shall be consulted whenever consideration is being given to their capacity to alienate their lands or otherwise transmit their rights outside their own community.

3. Persons not belonging to these peoples shall be prevented from taking advantage of their customs or of lack of understanding of the laws on the part of their members to secure the ownership, possession or use of land belonging to them

Article 18

Adequate penalties shall be established by law for unauthorised intrusion upon, or use of, the lands of the peoples concerned, and governments shall take measures to prevent such offences

Article 19

National agrarian programmes shall secure to the peoples concerned treatment equivalent to that accorded to other sectors of the population with regard to:

(a) the provision of more land for these peoples when they have not the area necessary for providing the essentials f a normal existence, or for any possible increase in their numbers;

(b) the provision of the means required to promote the development of the lands which these peoples already possess.

PART III. RECRUITMENT AND CONDITIONS OF EMPLOYMENT

Article 20

1. Governments shall, within the framework of national laws and regulations, and in co-operation with the peoples concerned, adopt special measures to ensure the

effective protection with regard to recruitment and conditions of employment of workers belonging to these peoples, to the extent that they are not effectively protected by laws applicable to workers in general.

2. Governments shall do everything possible to prevent any discrimination between workers belonging to the peoples concerned and other workers, in particular as regards:

   (a) admission to employment, including skilled employment, as well as measures for promotion and advancement;

   (6) equal remuneration for work of equal value;

   (c) medical and social assistance, occupational safety and health, all social security benefits and any other occupationally related benefits, and housing;

   (d) the right of association and freedom for all lawful trade union activities, and the right to conclude collective agreements with employers or employers' organisations.

3. The measurers taken shall include measures to ensure:

   (a) that workers belonging to the peoples concerned, including seasonal, casual and migrant workers in agricultural and other employment, as well as those employed by labour contractors, enjoy the protection afforded by national law and practice to other such workers in the same sectors, and that they are fully informed of their rights under labour legislation and of the means of redress available to them;

   (b) that workers belonging to these peoples are not subjected to working conditions hazardous to their health, in particular through exposure to pesticides or other toxic substances;

   (c) that workers belonging to these peoples are not subjected to coercive recruitment systems, including bonded labour and other forms of debt servitude;

(d) that workers belonging to these peoples enjoy equal opportunities and equal treatment in employment for men and women, and protection from sexual harassment.

4. Particular attention shall be paid to the establishment of adequate labour inspection services in areas where workers belonging to the peoples concerned undertake wage employment, in order to ensure compliance with the provisions of this part of this Convention.

PART IV. VOCATION TRAINING, HANDICRAFTS AND RURAL INDUSTRIES

Article 21

Members of the peoples concerned shall enjoy opportunities at least equal to those of other citizens in respect of vocational training measures.

Article 22

1. Measures shall be taken to promote the voluntary participation of members of the peoples concerned in vocational training programmes of general application.

2. Whenever existing programmes of vocational training of general application do not meet the special needs of the peoples concerned, governments shall, with the participation of these peoples, ensure the provision of special training programmes and facilities

3. Any special training programmes shall be based on the economic environment, social and cultural conditions and practical needs of the peoples concerned. Any studies made in this connection shall be carried out in co-operation with these peoples, who shall be consulted on the organisation and operation of such programmes Where feasible, these peoples shall progressively assume

responsibility for the organisation and operation of such special training programmes, if they so decide.

Article 23

1. Handicrafts, rural and community-based industries, and subsistence economy and traditional activities of the peoples concerned, such as hunting, fishing, trapping and gathering, shall be recognised as important factors in the maintenance of their cultures and in their economic self-reliance and development. Governments shall, with the participation of these people and whenever appropriate, ensure that these activities are strengthened and promoted.
2. Upon the request of the peoples concerned, appropriate technical and financial assistance shall be provided wherever possible, taking into account the traditional technologies and cultural characteristics of these peoples, as well as the importance of sustainable and equitable development

PART V. SOCIAL SECURITY AND HEALTH

Article 24

Social security schemes shall be extended progressively to cover the peoples concerned, and applied without discrimination against them.

Article 25

1. Governments shall ensure that adequate health services are made available to the peoples concerned, or shall provide them with resources to allow them to design and deliver such services under their own responsibility and control, so that they may enjoy the highest attainable standard of physical and mental health

2. Health services shall, to the extent possible, be community-based. These services shall be planned and administered in co-operation with the peoples concerned and take into account their economic, geographic, social and cultural conditions as well as their traditional preventive care, healing practices and medicines

3. The health care system shall give preference to the training and employment of local community health workers, and focus on primary health care while maintaining strong links with other levels of health care services.

4. The provision of such health services shall be co-ordinated with other social, economic and cultural measures in the country.

PART VI. EDUCATION AND MEANS OF COMMUNICATION

Article 26

Measures shall be taken to ensure that members of the peoples concerned have the opportunity to acquire education at all levels on at least an equal footing with the rest of the national community.

Article 27

1. Education programmes and services for the peoples concerned shall be developed and implemented in co-operation with them to address their special needs, and shall incorporate their histories, their knowledge and technologies, their value systems and their further social, economic and cultural aspirations.

2. The competent authority shall ensure the training of members of these peoples and their involvement in the formulation and implementation of education programmes, with a view to the progressive transfer of responsibility for the conduct of these programmes to these peoples as appropriate.

3. In addition, governments shall recognise the right of these peoples to establish their own educational institutions and facilities, provided that such institutions meet minimum standards established by the competent authority in consultation with these peoples. Appropriate resources shall be provided for this purpose.

Article 28

1. Children belonging to the peoples concerned shall, wherever practicable, be taught to read and write in their own indigenous language or in the language most commonly used by the group to which they belong. When this is not practicable, the competent authorities shall undertake consultations with these peoples with a view to the adoption of measures to achieve this objective.
2. Adequate measures shall be taken to ensure that these peoples have the opportunity to attain fluency in the national language or in one of the official languages of the country.
3. Measures shall be taken to preserve and promote the development and practice of the indigenous languages of the peoples concerned.

Article 29

The imparting of general knowledge and skills that will help children belonging to the peoples concerned to participate fully and on all equal footing in their own community and in the national community shall be an aim of education for these peoples.

Article 30

1. Governments shall adopt measures appropriate to the traditions and cultures of the peoples concerned, to make known to them their rights and duties, especially in

regard to labour, economic opportunities, education and health matters, social welfare and their rights deriving from this Convention.

2. If necessary, this shall be done by means of written translations and through the use of mass communications in the languages of these peoples.

Article 31

Educational measures shall be taken among all sections of the national community, and particularly among those that are in most direct contact with the peoples concerned, with the object of eliminating prejudices that they may harbour in respect of these peoples. To this end, efforts shall be made to ensure that history textbooks and other educational materials provide a fair, accurate and informative portrayal of the societies and cultures of these peoples.

PART VII. CONTACTS AND CO-OPERATIONS ACROSS BORDERS

Article 32

Governments shall take appropriate measures, including by means of international agreements, to facilitate contacts and co-operation between indigenous arid tribal peoples across borders, including activities in the economic, social, cultural, spiritual and environmental fields.

PART VIII. ADMINISTRATION

Article 33

1. The governmental authority responsible for the matters covered in this Convention shall ensure that agencies or other appropriate mechanisms exist to administer the programmes affecting the peoples concerned, and shall ensure that they have the means necessary for the proper fulfilment of the functions assigned to them.

2. These programmes shall include:
   (a) the planning, co-ordination, execution and evaluation, in co-operation with the peoples concerned, of the measures provided for in this Convention;
   (b) the proposing of legislative and other measures to the competent authorities and supervision of the application of the measures taken, in co-operation with the peoples concerned.

Part IX. General Provisions

Article 34

The nature and scope of the measures to be taken to give effect to this Convention shall be determined in a flexible manner, having regard to the conditions characteristic of each country.

Article 35

The Application of the provisions of this Convention shall not adversely affect rights and benefits of the peoples concerned pursuant to other Conventions and Recommendations, international instruments, treaties, or national laws, awards, custom or agreements.

Article 36

This Convention revises the Indigenous and Tribal Populations Convention, 1957.

Bibliography

Anderson, Robert S. and Walter Huber, *The Hour of the Fox: Tropical forests, The World Bank, and Indigenous People in Central India*. Seattle: University of Washington Press, 1988.

Bailey, F.G., *Tribe, Caste and Nation*. Bombay: Oxford University Press, 1960.

Baral, Lok Raj, *The Relevance and Application of Human Rights to Development*. Human Rights Quarterly 3(3):31-36, 1981.

Colchester, Marcus and Christian Erni, "From Principles to Practice: Indigenous Peoples and Protected Areas in South and Southeast Asia", *IWGIA Document No. 97*. Copenhagen: International Work Group for Indigenous Affairs, 1999.

Department of Environment and Forests, "Environmental Aspects of Narmada Sagar and Sardar Sarovar Multi-Purpose Projects", New Delhi: Government of India, Department of Environment and Forests, 1987.

Dube, S.C., *Tribal Heritage of India, Vol. 1*. New Delhi: Vikas Publishing House, 1977.

Ghurye, G.S., *The Aborigines—So Called—and Their Future*. poona, India: Gokhale Institute of Politics and Economics, 1943.

Ghuryw, G.S., *The Scheduled Tribes of India*. New Brunswick, New Jersey: Transaction Publishers, 1980.

Grigson, W.V., *The Challenge of Backwardness: Some Notes and Papers on Tribals and Depressed Classes Policy, with Special*

Reference to Hyderabad State. Hyderabad, India: Government Press, 1947.

Vidyarthi, L.P., "Rise of Anthropology in India: A Social Science Orientation". *Vol. 1, The Tribal Dimension*. Atlantic Highlands, New Jersey: Humanities Press, 1976.

von Furer-Haimendorf, Christoph, *Tribes of India: The Struggle for Survival*. Berkeley: University of California Press, 1982.

Weber, Thomas, *Hugging the Trees: The Story of the Chipko Movement*. Delhi: Viking, 1985.

Index

HUMAN RIGHTS OF INDIGENOUS PEOPLES

HUMAN RIGHTS OF INDIGENOUS PEOPLES

(In 2 Volumes)

Volume 2
(Comparative Analysis of Indigenous Peoples)

Editor
Aman Gupta

ISHA

ISHA BOOKS

Delhi-110033

Human Rights of Indigenous Peoples
(Comparative Analysis of Indigenous People)

Rs. 1800 (Set)
Rs. 900 (Each Volume)

ISBN : 81-8205-205-X (Set)
ISBN : 81-8205-276-9 (Vol. 1)

Published in 2005 in India by
Isha Books
D-43, Prithviraj Road,
Adarsh Nagar, Delhi - 110033
e-mail : ishabooks@hotmail.com

Laser Typesetting at : Global Printers, New Delhi
Printed at : Chawla Offset Press, Delhi

Contents

Preface

According to United Nations indigenous communities, peoples and nations are those which, having a historical continuity with pre-invasion and pre-colonial societies that developed on their territories, consider themselves distinct from other sectors of the societies now prevailing in those territories, or parts of them. They form at present non-dominant sectors of society and are determined to preserve, develop and transmit to future generations their ancestral territories, and their ethnic identity as the basis of their continued existence as peoples, in accordance with their own cultural patterns, social institutions and legal systems.

Despite the diversity of indigenous peoples, they share common problems and issues in dealing with the prevailing, or invading, society. The cultures of indigenous peoples are being lost and that indigenous peoples suffer both discrimination and pressure to assimilate into their surrounding societies. This is borne out by the fact that the lands and cultures of nearly all of the peoples are under threat. It is important for the human species as a whole to preserve a wide range of cultural diversity as possible, and that the protection of indigenous cultures is vital to this enterprise.

This book analytically evaluates the living conditions, socioeconomic development and survival challenges of indigenous peoples around the world. It looks at the historical, cultural, and legal background to the position of indigenous peoples in a range of different cultures. The book elaborately describes who and what indigenous peoples actually are, and looks at their position in the light of the development of international law. It also considers their legal position, and their economic, social and cultural rights in respect of various laws and conventions passed on a national and international scale throughout the world. The book will universally appeal to all readers related· to the issues of indigenous peoples and will also useful for scholars of sociology and anthropology.

Editor

1

Indigenous People and Ethnic Invasion

Indigenous people and their communities have an historical relationship with their lands and are generally descendants of the original inhabitants of such lands. Indigenous people and their communities represent a significant percentage of the global population. They have developed over many generations a holistic traditional scientific knowledge of their lands, natural resources and environment. Indigenous people and their communities shall enjoy the full measure of human rights and fundamental freedoms without hindrance or discrimination. Their ability to participate fully in sustainable development practices on their lands has tended to be limited as a result of factors of an economic, social and historical nature.

In view of the interrelationship between the natural environment and its sustainable development and the cultural, social, economic and physical well-being of indigenous people, national and international efforts to implement environmentally sound and sustainable development should recognize, accommodate, promote and strengthen the role of indigenous people and their communities. Some of the goals inherent in the objectives and activities of Agenda 21 Declaration on Environment and Development programme area are already contained in such international legal instruments as the ILO Indigenous and Tribal Peoples

Convention and are being incorporated into the draft universal declaration on indigenous rights, being prepared by the United Nations working group on indigenous populations. The International Year for the World's Indigenous People, proclaimed by the General Assembly in its resolution 45/164 of 18 December 1990, presents a timely opportunity to mobilize further international technical and financial cooperation.

In full partnership with indigenous people and their communities, Governments and, where appropriate, intergovernmental organizations should aim at fulfilling the following objectives:

(a) Establishment of a process to empower indigenous people and their communities through measures that include:

— Adoption or strengthening of appropriate policies and/or legal instruments at the national level;

— Recognition that the lands of indigenous people and their communities should be protected from activities that are environmentally unsound or that the indigenous people concerned consider to be socially and culturally inappropriate;

— Recognition of their values, traditional knowledge and resource management practices with a view to promoting environmentally sound and sustainable development;

— Recognition that traditional and direct dependence on renewable resources and ecosystems, including sustainable harvesting, continues to be essential to the cultural, economic and physical well-being of indigenous people and their communities;

— Development and strengthening of national dispute-resolution arrangements in relation to settlement of land and resource-management concerns;

— Support for alternative environmentally sound means of production to ensure a range of choices on how to improve their quality of life so that they effectively participate in sustainable development;

— Enhancement of capacity-building for indigenous communities, based on the adaptation and exchange of traditional experience, knowledge and resource-management practices, to ensure their sustainable development;

(b) Establishment, where appropriate, of arrangements to strengthen the active participation of indigenous people and their communities in the national formulation of policies, laws and programmes relating to resource management and other development processes that may affect them, and their initiation of proposals for such policies and programmes;

(c) Involvement of indigenous people and their communities at the national and local levels in resource management and conservation strategies and other relevant programmes established to support and review sustainable development strategies, such as those suggested in other programme areas of Agenda 21.

Some indigenous people and their communities may require, in accordance with national legislation, greater control over their lands, self-management of their resources, participation in development decisions affecting them, including, where appropriate, participation in the establishment or management of protected areas. The following are some of the specific measures which Governments could take:

(a) Consider the ratification and application of existing international conventions relevant to indigenous people and their communities (where not yet done) and provide support for the adoption by the General Assembly of a declaration on indigenous rights;

(b) Adopt or strengthen appropriate policies and/or legal instruments that will protect indigenous intellectual and cultural property and the right to preserve customary and administrative systems and practices.

United Nations organizations and other international development and finance organizations and Governments should, drawing on the active participation of indigenous people and their communities, as appropriate, take the following measures, inter alia, to incorporate their values, views and knowledge, including the unique contribution of indigenous women, in resource management and other policies and programmes that may affect them:

(a) Appoint a special focal point within each international organization, and organize annual interorganizational coordination meetings in consultation with Governments and indigenous organizations, as appropriate, and develop a procedure within and between operational agencies for assisting Governments in ensuring the coherent and coordinated incorporation of the views of indigenous people in the design and implementation of policies and programmes. Under this procedure, indigenous people and their communities should be informed and consulted and allowed to participate in national decision-making, in particular regarding regional and international cooperative efforts. In addition, these policies and programmes should take fully into account strategies based on local indigenous initiatives;

(b) Provide technical and financial assistance for capacity-building programmes to support the sustainable self-development of indigenous people and their communities;

(c) Strengthen research and education programmes aimed at:

— Achieving a better understanding of indigenous people's knowledge and management experience related to the environment, and applying this to contemporary development challenges;

— Increasing the efficiency of indigenous people's resource management systems, for example, by promoting the adaptation and dissemination of suitable technological innovations;

(d) Contribute to the endeavours of indigenous people and their communities in resource management and conservation strategies and other programme areas of Agenda 21, including programmes to collect, analyse and use data and other information in support of sustainable development projects.

Governments, in full partnership with indigenous people and their communities should, where appropriate:

(a) Develop or strengthen national arrangements to consult with indigenous people and their communities with a view to reflecting their needs and incorporating their values and traditional and other knowledge and practices in national policies and programmes in the field of natural resource management and conservation and other development programmes affecting them;

(b) Cooperate at the regional level, where appropriate, to address common indigenous issues with a view to recognizing and strengthening their participation in sustainable development.

Means of Implementation

Financing and cost evaluation: The Conference secretariat has estimated the average total annual cost of implementing the activities of this programme to be about $3 million on grant or concessional terms. These are indicative and order-of-magnitude estimates only and have not been reviewed by Governments. Actual costs and financial terms, including any that are non-concessional, will depend upon, inter alia, the specific strategies and programmes Governments decide upon for implementation.

Legal and administrative frameworks: Governments should incorporate, in collaboration with the indigenous people affected, the rights and responsibilities of indigenous people and their communities in the legislation of each country, suitable to the country's specific situation. Developing countries may require technical assistance to implement these activities.

Human resource development: International development agencies and Governments should commit financial and other resources to education and training for indigenous people and their communities to develop their capacities to achieve their sustainable self-development, and to contribute to and participate in sustainable and equitable development at the national level. Particular attention should be given to strengthening the role of indigenous women.

Indigenous People in Bangladesh

The "Chittagong Hill Tracts" (CHTs), sandwiched between the Arakan hills of Burma and the North East India is a part of south east Bangladesh. Covering an area of 5,093 square miles or 10 per cent of the total land area of Bangladesh, the CHTs is the homeland of ten different ethnic nationalities namely the Chakma, Marma, Tripura, Khiyang, Lushai, Khumi, Chak, Murung, Bowm and Pankoo for the last few centuries. They are collectively known as Jumma, a pejorative term used by the Chittagonian Bangalees, for their shifting cultivation or Jum cultivation.

The Jumma peoples belong to Tibeto-Burma linguistic group and distinctly differ in culture, religion, customs, death and birth rites and above all, notion of life from the mainstream Bengali muslim population of Bangladesh. The Chakmas, Marmas, Chaks, Murungs and Khumis profess Buddhism; the Tripuras believe in Hinduism; and the Lushais, Bowms, Pankhoos and Khiyangs practice Christianity. The British East India Company brought the CHTs under its control in 1787 after defeating the tribal kings and the region was made a tributary state. In 1860, the CHTs were brought under direct administrative control of the British India.

The British promulgated the Chittagong Hill Tracts Frontier Police Regulation in 1881 and the Chittagong Hill Tracts 1900 Regulation. The roots of the CHTs crisis lies with the fact that the hill peoples of the CHTs have not been provided the opportunity to express their opinion through a referendum or a similar exercise whether to be a part of India or Pakistan, or remain status quo of being "Excluded" both from India and Pakistan in 1947. New Delhi and Karachi arbitrarily decided the fate of the Chittagong Hill Tracts without the consent of the hill peoples.

Despite the Jummas being 98.5% of the total population and non-muslim, the CHTs were awarded to Pakistan. The relationship between the Bengali muslim majority and the hill peoples minority has been marked by suspicion, exploitation and conflict. The Government of Pakistan gradually abrogated the constitutional safeguards and finally, the construction of the Kaptai Hydro Electric Project submerged 40% of the total cultivable land area and displaced 100,000 Jummas. Little compensation was paid and displaced Jummas were not properly rehabilitated.

In 1972, after Bangladesh independence the Jumma people demanded autonomy with self-legislature, retention of the CHTs 1900 Regulation, continuation of the three Chiefs offices, constitutional guarantee against amendment of the regulations and a ban on the influx of the settlers. Prime Minister, Sheikh Mujibur Rahman declined to oblige, stating that the Jummas were Bengalees. It was clear that extreme Bengali nationalist were not willing to accommodate the Jumma peoples within the Bangladeshi society. The Bengali nationalists wanted the hill peoples to identify as Bengalis.

The Chittagong Hill Tracts problem is a creation of the extreme Bengali nationalists who refuse to recognize the distinct identity of the indigenous Jumma peoples. In order to destroy their distinct identity, Bangladesh Government abrogated the constitutional safeguards enjoyed by them since 1860. Indeed, the demands of the Jummas are nothing new but restoration of the constitutional safeguards they enjoyed since the British period. After the assassination of Sheikh Mujibur Rahman on 15 August 1975 and proscription of political activities under Political Parties Regulations Ordinance, 1976, the Jana Samhati Samiti, the political party of the Jummas, having no other option went underground in 1976. It was the beginning of the decade long armed struggle in the CHTs.

The Government of Bangladesh in order to suppress the Jana Samhati Samiti and its armed wing, Shanti Bahinis, militarized the CHTs. Militarisation was followed by the Planned Population Transfer of 500,000 illegal Bengali settlers from the plain areas of Bangladesh. The Bangladesh army and illegal settlers resorted to systematic massacres, land grabbing, dispossession, arbitrary arrests, torture, detention, and extrajudicial killings of the Jummas with impunity. Thousands of Jummas fled in 1979, 1981 and 1984 to seek refuge in India to escape from massacres. After bilateral discussions, the Government of India forcibly repatriated them. No international agencies were allowed to monitor the repatriation process.

In 1985, the military government of Bangladesh and the Jana Samhati Samiti attempted to resolve the CHTs crisis through negotiation. After the Government of Bangladesh rejected the Five Points Charter of Demands of the JSS, the dialogue broke down. It resulted renewed armed conflict between the Shanti Bahinis and the Bangladesh army. Around 60,000 indigenous Jumma peoples fled to India to seek refuge in 1986. As international scrutiny increased and the Jumma refugees showed no sign of voluntary return, President Ershad in an attempt to improve its international image unilaterally passed Local District Council Acts for Rangamati, Khagrachari and Bandarban district on 28 February 1989.

On 10 August 1992, the JSS declared unilateral cease-fire with the Government of Bangladesh. The dialogue initiated by the Bangladesh National Party Government in November 1992 continued till the Awami League came to power after the completion of the term by the Bangladesh National Party which lost in the general elections in June 1996. The JSS continued the cease-fire as the Jumma refugees gradually returned to India under the duress of the Government of India. On 2 December 1997, the Jana Samhati Samiti signed the CHTs Peace Agreement with the Government of Bangladesh and accepted the same Hill District Councils imposed by General Ershad with few amendments, which brought the basic semblance of democracy.

Although, the CHTs Peace Agreement envisages a Regional Council with no executive powers, none of the Five Points Charter of Demands of the JSS like autonomy with self legislature, withdrawal of illegal settlers, withdrawal of the security forces, guarantee for land rights etc were accepted. The CHTs Peace Agreement was a consequence of the increasing approximation of the relationship between New Delhi and Dhaka. The Agreement consequently paved the way for return of the remaining 43,000 Jumma refugees Jumma refugees between December 1997 and February 1998.

Illegal Bengali settlers

The United Nations Sub-Commission on Prevention of Discrimination and Protection of Minorities elaborates the definition of population transfer in the following way: "The term transfer implies in the act of moving a population... The State's role may be actives or passive but nonetheless contributes to the systematic, coercive and deliberate nature of the movement of population into or out of an area.... the State's role may involve financial subsidies, planning, public information, military action, recruitment of settlers, legislation or other judicial action, recruitment of settlers, legislation or other judicial action, and even the administration of justice. Population transfer has been conducted with the effect or purpose of altering the demographic composition of a territory in accordance with policy objectives or prevailing ideology, particularly when that ideology or policy asserts the dominance of a certain group over another."

Before the disguise invasion of the plain settlers between 1979 and 1985, the Chittagong Hill Tracts was exclusively a land of the indigenous Jumma peoples. The Chittagong Hill Tracts 1900 Regulation prohibits settlement of plains people into the Chittagong Hill Tracts without the consent of the indigenous hillmen. Article 52 of the Chittagong Hill Tracts 1900 Regulation provides:

"Article 52. Immigration into the Hill Tracts:

a) Save as hereinafter provided, no person other a Chakma, Mogh or a member of any hill tribe indigenous to the Chittagong Hill Tracts, the Lushai Hill, the Arakan Hill Tracts, or the State of Tripura shall enter or reside within the Chittagong Hill Tracts unless he is in possession of a permit granted by the Deputy Commissioner at his discretion.

d) No permit shall be valid for more than twelve months from the date of its grant.

   i) Every person required by this rule to be in possession of a permit shall be bound to produce it on the demand of any Government officer, headman, Karbari or Bazar Chaudhuri, and on his failure to produce such permit such government officer, headman, Karbari or Bazar Choudhuri shall arrest him and forward him without delay to the nearest police officer or Magistrate."

This particular provision of the CHTs 1900 Regulation protected the indigenous peoples of the CHTs and there was no land alienation during the British colonial period. However, after the independence from British, successive governments sought to undermine the 1900 Regulation. Pakistan Government played passive role to allow settlement of Bengali settlers into the Chittagong Hill Tracts. In the early 1950s, Pakistan Government settled "several hundred muslim families for settlement in the Chittagong Hill Tracts. These muslim families were settled in Naniachar area of Chengi valley and Longudu area of Kassalong valley".

In 1963, about 15,000 Bengali muslims were settled at Tabalchari Union, Belchari Union, Ramgarh Union, and Manikchari Union under present Khagrachari district and Alikadam Union and Lama union under present Bandarban district. The Jummas resented against such settlement and Pakistan Government stopped settlement of Bengali muslim families. After the Bangladesh Liberation War in 1971, about 50,000 Bengali immigrants were settled in the Feni valley, which caused resentment in the area. But like the previous settlements in the CHTs, the Government did not withdraw them and resentment gradually subsided. These two known cases of settlement of non-hillmen into the CHT are, however, insignificant in comparison to what was to follow in 1980s.

After Political Parties Regulations Ordinance, 1976, banned all political activities, the Jana Samhati Samiti had little option to press for demand for autonomy. The JSS was also banned, as its activities were perceived as anti-national. It went underground and started guerilla warfare in 1976 onwards to press the demands of autonomy. As the conflict intensified and military failed to eradicate the Shanti Bahinis, the Bangladesh Government of general Ziaur Rahman decided in 1979 to illegally transfer thousands of plain settlers into the CHTs in clear violation of domestic laws governing the CHTs and customary international law.

The policy of settlement stemming from the highest political level is undeniably for politico-military purposes. Firstly, Bengali settlements in the interior of the district are considered to be effective counter checks on the insurgent movement by way of their counter-intelligence and supply of auxiliary military support to the Bangladesh army. Secondly, a policy of increased Bengali settlement "under the aegis of the government" can ultimately turn the local hill people into a minority group on their "own" soil - thereby solving the political problem arising out of the hill people being the majority of the population. Thirdly, the settlement of Bengali settlers could gradually destroy the last bastion of distinct ethnic groups and turn Bangladesh into a homogenous country.

In mid 1979, President Ziaur Rahman decided to settle 30,000 Bengali muslim families in the following year. A sum of 60 million Takas was allocated to the scheme. And the blueprint to resolve the Chittagong Hill Tracts problems by exterminating the indigenous Jumma people was finalised. The district commissioner headed the district committee and sub-divisional officers the sub-divisional committees. The Committees appointed agents from among the Bengali settlers and assigned them to contact landless Bengalis willing to settle in the CHTs. They were not hard to find and from February 1980 truckloads of poor Bengali families poured into the CHTs attracted by the inducement of the Government to provide five acres of land, 3600 Takas and provisions to each new settler family. According to the United States Agency for International Development (USAID) in 1980, the Bangladesh Government decided to resettle 100,000 Bengali muslim settlers in the first phase of this scheme.

The Population in the CHTs was 125,000 in 1901, 154,000 in 1921, 173,000 in 1931, 213 in 1931, 247,000 in 1941, 288,000 in 1951, 385,000 in 1961, 508,000 in 1974, 751,000 in 1981 and 968,000 in 1991 excluding the floating population. The increasing trend in the Bengali muslim population in the CHTs after 1947 reveals consistent infringement of the CHTs 1900 Regulation. According to census figures, in 1941 the muslim population was 2.94 per cent of the total population of the CHTs and it has risen to 6.29 in 1951, 11.77 in 1961, 22.83 in 1974 35.18 in 1981 and 49% in 1991.

Although, there is no estimate, unconfirmed reports states that around 500,000 Bengali plainsmen were settled into the CHTs. The settlers were allotted five acres of hill land or four acres of mixed land or 2.5 acres of wet rice land. They were provided free transport, food and protection. Most of the settlers were given identity cards and food rations, cattle, roof tins and illegal title deeds to lands. However, the land allotment varied in different areas. In Rangamati district, district land registers and information from headmen show that at Adarakchara mouza, under Langadu than a, families of settlers received between 1.5 to 4 acres of class III (hillside) land.

At Barunachari mouza within Barkal thana, each settler family received title deeds to not less than 1.25 acres and not more than 2.25 acres of class III land. At Gorasthan mouza, the highest allocation was 4.73 acre and the lowest was about 1 acre, in both cases being class II (gently sloping) land. At Bhushanchara mouza and across the river in Maodang mouza, the average allocation was 3 acres of class II (gently sloping) land. Then again, at Choto Merung and Bara Merung mouzas in Dighinala thana within Khagrachari district, the extent of allocation varied a great deal, but it is alleged that here, even class I lands, i.e., non-submergible flat lands suitable for intensive plough cultivation, were allotted to the settlers.

According to the UN Special Rapporteur on the human rights dimensions of population transfer including implantation of settlers, Awn Shawhat Al-Khasawneh, "The first duty that international law demands from a wrongdoing State is cessation of the wrongful act if its is of a continuing character. However, compliance with such a duty does not in itself relieve the wrongdoing State of its responsibility. Hence, in addition reparation may also be demanded". There was no public announcement of the start of the Population Transfer of Bengali settlers.

The Government of Bangladesh views the resettlement as necessary for the overall development of the country in view of the undeniable problem of population pressure and land resources. A representative of the Bangladesh diplomatic mission Geneva in a statement before the Working Group on Indigenous Peoples on 12 August 1983 said, "The people of Bangladesh have to share the available resources in an equitable manner within severe economic constraints well known to the international community". However, according to 1981 Census, the Chittagong Hill Tracts, the average size of farm holding in the CHTs was 4.9 acres in comparison to 3.5 acres nationally.

The Patuakhali district had the highest average land holding of 6.2 acres per family followed by 4.8 acres in Dinajpur district, 4.6 in Khustia district, 4.3 acres in Khulna district, 4.1 acres in Pubna, Rajshahi and Jessore district and 4 acres in Sylhet district. Comilla and Chittagong District had lowest rate of land holding respectively 2.0 acres and 2.7 acres. If the intention of the Government was to "share the available resources in an equitable manner", the Government would have resorted to similar sponsored population transfer into the Patuakhali district, followed by Chittagong Hill Tracts, Dinajpur, Khulna, Pubna, Rajshahi, Jessore and Sylhet district etc. The fact that there was no such population transfer in other districts except in the Chittagong Hill Tracts shows that it was a racist measure "to destroy the ethnic identity of the indigenous Jumma peoples".

Under the Constitution of Bangladesh, there is no absolute right to freedom of movement. Article 36 of the Constitution of Bangladesh states, "Subject to any reasonable restrictions imposed by law in the public interest, every citizen shall have the right to move freely throughout Bangladesh, to reside and settle in any place therein and to leave and re-enter Bangladesh". Notwithstanding the restrictions imposed by the Chittagong Hill Tracts 1900 Regulation for movement of plain settlers into the CHTs, Government of Bangladesh settled the Bengali settlers by providing incentives and not by exercising the right to freedom of movement. The Government of Bangladesh in order to hide its racist policies now attempts to give a "perverted interpretation" of the right to freedom of movement.

Implimenting of the Population Transfer Programmes

The Population Transfer of Bengali settlers had serious effects on the social, political, economic and cultural rights of the indigenous Jumma peoples. It has created tremendous pressure on lands and structural violence in the hill tracts. The latter permeated the whole CHTs and threatens the cultural identity of the Jumma population.

The Chittagong Hill Tracts had serious cultivable land crisis, the Bangladesh Government promised to provide 2.5 acres of paddyland, 5 acres of hilly land and 4 acres of gently sloping land to each settler family from the plains. The CHTs was already overpopulated in the 1960s after inundation of 54,000 acres of the best arable land in the CHTs. Around 25% of the total population of the CHTs were already displaced in the 1960s thereby creating severe land shortage. Before the construction of the Kaptai Hydro-Electric Project, the Chittagong Hill Tracts had 32,59,520 acres of land, out of which 130,000 acres were cultivable land. However, with inundation of 54,000 acres of land, cultivable land in the CHTs was only 76,000 acres. Obviously, the intention of the Government of Bangladesh was to encourage land grabbing by the illegal settlers.

Now the indigenous CHT population is taken to be 508,199 or about 100,000 families or so, according to 1974 census, each family could be provided with 3.7 acres which was even less than the minimum 5 acres each CHT family was entitled to, under an amendment to rule 34 of the CHT Manual made by the Pakistan government in 1971. This shows that not only plough lands, mixed as well as hilly lands were equally inadequate for the CHT residents before the arrival of the Bengali settlers. The government settlement scheme was clearly racist considering the fact there was available only about 3.7 acres of mixed and hilly land and about 1 or 1.3 acres of paddy land.

Despite protest and strong opposition of the tribals, the government have taken up programme of rehabilitating 100,000 families from other districts of the country in the CHTs." This is excluding the number of people trickled into the CHTs since 1985. Even if the Bengali settlers into the CHTs were 100,000 families, it would require whopping 250,000 acres (100,000 families x 2.5 acres) of paddy land; 500,000 acres (100,000 families x 5 acres) of hilly land and 400,000 acres (100,000 families x 4) of mixed lands to fulfill the promises to the illegal settlers.

The Chittagong Hill Tracts simply does not have the capacity to bear the presence of the illegal settlers. The land crisis in the Chittagong Hill Tracts is further reflected from the fact that 91.28% of the total land area in the CHTs is under the control of the Government of Bangladesh. The District Councils and Regional Council only control a mere 8.72% of the total area of the CHTs. In addition to these Reserve Forest, the Government of Bangladesh has been occupying large amount of land for creation of new Reserve Forest, construction of military camps etc.

Land Grabbing

The immediate effect of the planned population transfer was organized massacre of the Jummas. It was only after the illegal settlers came into the CHTs, the conflict took a communal overtone. The military resorted to indiscriminate killings, destruction of village after village to vacate the lands and hand them over to the illegal settlers, destruction of temples, rape, etc. Consequently, the Jummas had to seek refuge in 1977, 1979, 1981, 1984, 1986, 1989 and 1992 to escape from organized massacres perpetrated by the illegal settlers and Bangladesh security forces to occupy their lands. Between 1986 and 1992, 72,000 Jummas had to seek refuge in Tripura State of India in 1986. Most of the victims of atrocities by the security forces or the illegal settlers have come from rural areas where the lands are fertile and plough cultivation is possible. They are targeted simply because they belong to a different ethnic minority. This is aimed at pushing the hill peoples into the more interior areas where plough based cultivation is not possible and to occupy the lands of the Jumma peoples.

In areas where Jumma people refused to move out of their traditional villages, they were forcibly relocated in "Strategic Hamlets" - a counter insurgency model village implemented by the Chittagong Hill Tracts Development Board (CHTDB). The illegal settlers were not interested in bumpy land. They were interested in paddy lands. The paddy lands were available in the Chengi, Mayoni, Feni and Kassalong valleys and in some of the areas of submerged shores of the Kaptai lake. Small holdings of paddyland are also available at Manikchari and Guimara Unions, east bank tributaries of Feni valley, narrow valley of the west of Rangamati town, scattered valleys south of Chandragona town, around Bandarban town and Matamuhari valleys north of Alikadam town.

However, most of these potentially best agricultural lands are located in the Northern valleys of Chengi, Mayoni, Kassalong and Feni. Consequently ".... most of the current ethnic conflicts (between the natives and the Bengalees), as well as clashes between Shanti Bahini guerrillas and the Bangladesh army and the government sponsored Bengalee settlement programmes are located in the potentially best agricultural lands." The Government of Bangladesh and its authorities gave the lands of the Jummas to the illegal settlers as khas lands and encouraged the illegal settlers to grab the lands. "When the poor and helpless people of the CHTs approach the law enforcing authorities for justice they are driven out by mercilessly with beatings, harassment and filthy abuses".

A large number of Bengalis were apparently displaced. However, the army had other insidious plans to resettle these

Bengali settlers in Mogban mouza under Rangamati Thana on about 500 acres of land on which 100 Chakma families had been resettled in a Joutha Khamar (Collective Farm) set up by the Chittagong Hill Tracts Development Board. Each of these Chakma families has been allotted 5 acres of land, which were processed, by the mouza headman and the Sub-Divisional Officer. Twenty years later, they were still waiting the Deputy Commissioner's approval.

The Chakma families protested through the local authorities to the army against the resettlement of the Bengalis. However, the army went ahead and resettled the Bengalis in December 1995 and January 1994, ousting the Chakma families without any compensation. The Ministry of Environment and Forest issued on 4 January 1992 and published in the Bangladesh Gazette on 21 May 1992 to create a Reserved Forest amounting to more than 175,000 acres in all districts of the CHTs. After a large-scale protest against these plans, the Government stopped the process of creating Reserved Forest. However, the Government of Bangladesh has not so far canceled the project. Thousands of Jummas will be displaced if the project is implemented.

It is a well-planned conspiracy of the Government of Bangladesh to take control of more land of the Jumma peoples of the CHTs. Article 26 of the CHTs Treaty signed on 2 December 1997 provides:

> "Clause 64 will be amended as follows:
>
> a) Whatever exists in the currently prevailing laws, without prior permission of the parishad, no lands, including leasable khas lands in the district, can be leased out, sold, purchased or transferred.
> However, it will not be applicable in case of the reserved forest, Kaptai Hydroelectricity Project area, Betbunia Satellite Station area, state-owned industrial enterprises and lands recorded in the name of the government.

By invoking the above clause, the Government of Bangladesh could take 'control of these socalled "Reserved Forest areas".

Under the Forest Act, the Government could declare any tracts of land as Reserved Forest without the consent of the affected people.

Most of the lands allotted to the illegal settlers were not khas lands. Most of these lands were owned and possessed by the indigenous Jumma peoples and consisted of paddy lands. The indigenous people of the CHT have a collective right over all lands within the CHT as they have been in occupation of these lands for hundreds of years. Their customary rights to land have been explicitly and implicitly recognized by the CHT Manual of 1900.

If a particular plot of land in the CHT, whether homestead, jum land, grazing land, fringeland or village forest is not registered in the name of any individual or individuals, it is not technically khas land with the same meaning as in other districts of Bangladesh which are regulated by the Bengal Tenancy Acts which do not apply to the CHT. The Government may regulate the use of these khas lands (and grant settlements, leases, etc.) but only through a certain process involving consultation with the Chiefs and headmen and sufficient notice to the affected people to put forward their case.

In cases where these lands are already occupied, e.g., the homesteads recognized by rule 50(1), they can only be 'resumed' by the government on payment of compensation in accordance with rules 50(3)(b) and 50(4) of the CHT Manual and section 4 of the CHT Land Acquisition Regulation of 1958. It is clear that the lands owned by the Jummas individually (such as homesteads and fringelands) or communally (such as forest, jum and grazing lands) did not and do not required to be registered their titles or other rights or to provide any documentation to establish or prove their rights over such lands. The report of the Jumma Refugees Welfare Association also shows that thousands of acres of lands despite having land titles by the indigenous Jummas were taken away by the illegal settlers.

The Government of Bangladesh moved an amendment into the Section 34(1) of the CHTs 1900 Regulation to justify the population transfer as it prohibited settlement of outsiders into the CHTs. The amendment to Section 34(1) of the CHT 1900 Regulation removed the provision, which required the prior approval of the Board of Revenue before settlement of 'outsiders'. However, the wording of the amended rule 34(1) is absolutely clear that it envisages the settlement of lands to 'hillmen' and 'non-hillmen residents' only; and only allows long-term leases to non-residents in a very restricted manner.

Surveys in various areas in Rangamati district show that the settlers in these areas were only allotted class III lands - theoretically for 'grove' plantations. But many such allotments also included within their boundaries class l and class II lands (plain/plough lands) which were owned by and were being cultivated by the indigenous Jumma people before the settlers arrived there. Under the secret memoranda, the illegal settlers were to receive 'paddy lands' (classes I and II) and 'mixed lands' (class II) lands as well. The illegal settlers do not fall into the category of 'industrialists'; they were the landless people.

Similarly, land granted to the settlers were not for 'industrial purposes' or for plantations on a 'commercial basis'. Hence the settlements certainly do not fall into exceptions even with a very liberal interpretation of sub-rules 1(b) and 1(c) of rule 34 of the CHTs 1900 Regulation. Now, the only way nonresidents could be granted land within the CHT for residential purposes was (a) if it was a long-term lease; (b) if the non-residents were 'deserving persons'; (c) if they paid 100 per cent salami (license/lease fee) and (d) if they paid the annual land tax at the rate of one-half per cent of market value of the land.

Furthermore, the grants of land for residential purposes of 1979-80s did not satisfy the other conditions mentioned in sub-rule (d) because there are no known cases where the settlers were paid, or were asked to pay, any salami or assessed the special rate of rent. In the surveyed areas of Rangamati district mentioned above, the settlers were asked to pay only Taka 1.00 or Taka 2.00 per acre as annual land tax. Therefore, these settlements were clearly not of the category provided for by sub-rule (c) of rule 34. Moreover, the settlers were given fee simple grants, i.e., grants in perpetuity, and not long leases, although leases were the only type of land grant allowed by the concerned sub-rule.

Nevertheless, even if it were conceded, for the sake of argument, that the grant of homestead plots to the settlers was valid, that would still leave the grants for the agricultural and horticultural lands of classes I, II and III (paddy land, plain and bumpy land) illegal and irregular and outside the narrow ambit of sub-rules 1(b) and 1(c) of rule 34. In other words, the settlement programme of 1979-1980s was illegal even according to the amended version of rule 34(1) of 1979. In addition to the above, there are other provisions in rule 34, for example, the provisions of sub-rule 13, which tend to make the interpretation of the entire rule 34 quite restrictive when it comes to the question of non-residents acquiring land rights in the CHTs. Sub-rule 13 of rule 34, which remained unaffected by the 1979 amendment (which only amended the old sub-rule (1) clearly forbids the inheritance of CHT land by non-residents of the CHT except in exceptional circumstances deserving equitable considerations.

Thus clearly, where even inheritance of CHT land by non-residents was, and is, disallowed except in exceptional circumstances, the matter of grants of settlements/leases to non-residents must certainly also be interpreted restrictively, in the light of other provisions of rule 34 and other provisions of the CHT Manual. According to another interpretation of the amendment of 1979, it can be said that this amendment actually amended the rule 34 that subsisted before 16 September 1971 and not the rule 34 that was introduced in 1971. The 1971 amendment was not valid at the date of the 1979 amendment in accordance with a government notification which held that all laws passed by the occupation Pakistani Government from 26 March, 1971 to 15 December, 1971 were to be deemed to be null and void.

If this were the legal position, it would lead to ridiculous results because the 1979 amendment would in that case have amended only a tiny portion of the old rule 34 - i.e., only sub-rule 1 from among fourteen subrules - as it subsisted prior to 16 September 1971. In such a situation, the overwhelming weight of the provisions of the amendment of 1979 in conjunction with the remaining portions of the older rule 34 (i.e., sub-rule 2 and onwards) would clearly rule out settlement of land in the CHT to non-residents, especially due to sub-rule 14 of the old rule 34 prior to 1971 which held that " Nothing in these rules, or any grant, lease or contract under which land is held in the Hill Tracts shall operate to increase the existing number of non-hillmen lessees (emphasis added) in respect of any holding or to permit the inheritance of any Hill Tracts land by non-residents of the district express with the express consent of the Deputy Commissioner who in giving his consent shall have regard to the principles of equity and as far as may be to the rights of plainsmen which but for this rule would be operative.

An appeal from the orders of the Deputy Commissioner shall lie to the Commissioner". In the circumstances, there is little room to argue that principles of equity would have favoured settlement of lands to non-residents without first satisfying the needs of landless CHT residents both indigenous and ethnic Bengalis especially those displaced earlier by the Kaptai Dam or by other government projects. Secondly, the settlement programme violated rule 39 of the CHT Manual which obliged the government's representative in the CHT, the deputy commissioners, to consult the Chiefs of the CHT on important matters affecting the administration of the CHT. The settlement of tens of thousands of non-residents within the three chiefs' administrative and revenue circles was certainly an important administrative matter. But none of them had been consulted. Similarly, no other indigenous leaders of any importance are known to have been consulted by the government on the above matter.

Thirdly, it violated the long-standing practice whereby settlements and leases were granted only after consulting the headmen of the administrative and revenue units called mouzas. Fourthly, the settlements of 1979-80s violated the collective land rights of the indigenous people in the instances where their common jum lands and forests were settled out to non-residents. Since the indigenous peoples' collective rights over their common lands were based on indigenous law, customs and usages known only to the chiefs, headmen, karbaries and other elders, the indigenous officials, especially the headmen, were always by convention consulted prior to the grant of such lands to any persons those who were using and occupying the same. These officials were not consulted at all. Fifthly, it violated the private property rights of thousands of indigenous people since they were the rightful legal owners of the concerned lands in accordance with rules 34 and 50 of the CHT Manual and prevailing customs, conventions, practices and usages.

Under Article 32 of the Constitution of Bangladesh states "Subject to any restrictions imposed by law, every citizen shall have the right to acquire, hold, transfer or otherwise dispose of property and no property shall be compulsorily acquired, nationalized or requisitioned save by authority of law". In numerous cases, the indigenous landowners' registered lands were re-allotted to the settlers without the same lands being first acquired by the authorities in accordance with the concerned regulation on land acquisition, i.e., the CHT Land Acquisition Regulation of 1958, or by canceling their leases in accordance with rules 34(5) or 34(6) of the CHT Manual, if at all, or by resuming these lands in accordance with rule 50(3) and rule 50(4) of the CHT Manual.

Thus the grant of lease/settlement deeds to thousands of settlers during the subsistence of the earlier leases/settlements amounted to a deprivation of the indigenous owners' lands other than in accordance with law. Furthermore, according to a fundamental principle of Bangladeshi law, namely, the principle of natural justice, no action may be taken against any person to deprive him of his or her rights, interests and legitimate expectations without providing him or her a reasonable opportunity of putting forward his case. Since the dispossessed indigenous owners and occupiers of CHT land received no such opportunity, the settlement programme also violated the principle of natural justice.

Negative Impact of the Jumma Economy

"Typically, tribal and other land based people displaced from their habitat can suffer a severe reduction in food sources commensurate with the net loss of land. This phenomenon has been reported as pandemic, and social science analysts have observed that almost universally, governments fail to pay proper attention to how relocatees are going to make a living after removal. For land based peoples who have been forced from their lands and community, their readjustment to life is uncertain". The economy of the CHTs is completely dominated by the Bengalis and this is reflected in all spheres of trade, commerce, fishing, government contracts, employment, operation of marketing centres, transport and communication, industry and factory, retail and wholesale business, exports and imports, timber and firewood business, fruit and vegetable marketing, banking, insurance, credit and cooperative societies and nearly two thirds of the agricultural sectors.

The explosion of 500,000 illegal settlers made the situation worse for the Jummas. The indigenous Jumma people have gradually changed their mode of production from Jum cultivation to more intensive and more productive plough cultivation on the very small amount of plain and gently sloping (bumpy') lands available in the river valleys. A large number of the Jumma people were displaced once before by the Kaptai dam and had reclaimed these lands with hard toil and monetary investments. Unfortunately, it was these most valuable and rarely-procurable plough lands, and not hillside lands, which were appropriated by the illegal settlers. The land grabbing hence had tremendous effect on the economy of the Jumma people.

Thousands of Jumma refugees had to seek refuge in Indian State of Tripura and Mizoram. Between 1977 and 1992, at least 125,000 individual Jummas had to cross international border. A large majority of them did not get back their lands as they were taken over by the illegal settlers. Similarly, around 50,000 Jummas were internally displaced and moved into cluster villages, model villages etc. A large majority of them too lost their lands to the illegal settlers. Since they have not got back their lands, their economy has completely broken down. They constitute about 35% of the total indigenous Jumma population.

Under the Bangladesh regime, developments have been predominantly establishment oriented of both a civil and political nature. The roads and highways have been extended to the furthest point of the hill people's villages. Buildings, barracks and communication networks have been constructed with the help of foreign aid. This type of entirely state sponsored development inevitably ensured not only deployment of thousands of soldiers but also employment of hundreds of workers and employees- almost all from outside the hill tracts. The Chittagong Hill Tracts Development Board (CHTDB), established in 1976 had been playing an instrumental role in bringing about socio-economic and political transformation in the Chittagong hill tracts in favour of the Bangladesh Government. The schemes implemented under CHTDB projects have invariably worsened the economic conditions of the hill peoples.

Under the model villages programmes, the Jummas were moved from their traditional villages to model villages as a counter insurgency measure and to vacate their villages in order to settle illegal settlers. In some cases, Jummas from several villages were put into one model village. After they were moved into model villages, they do not have any right to freedom of movement. "No one is allowed to move without the permission of the military. It has crippled their economy as their livelihood depends on free movement to tend their crops in often far-off fields. People are forced to risk their lives in order to survive. Anyone if found in places off-limits by the army is suspected of links with the Shanti Bahini and may be summarily shot or taken into custody and tortured."

The Bazar development programmes also only benefited the Bengalis who control the trade in the CHTs. It is estimated that the illegal settlers are enjoying 99% of the business and trade facilities. Around 2% Jummas who are working in support of the military gets permit for timber business, rice business etc. Expansion of industrial and other income generating activities also could not provide a different picture: "only 40 Hillman got jobs in the Chandraghona Paper mills where the total working force is 6000".

During the Bangladesh National Party rule (1991-96), there are almost clandestine ban on employment of the Indigenous Jumma peoples. Consequently, the unemployment rate is increasing and the Jummas do not enjoy the benefits accrued from the resources in the Chittagong Hill Tracts. As the US State Department's Country Report on Human Rights Practices states, "Religious minorities are in practice disadvantaged in such areas as access to jobs and political office. Selection boards in the government services are often without minority group representations".

Right to Self-Determination

Common Article 1.1 of the International Covenant on Civil and Political Rights and International Covenant on Economic, Social and Cultural Rights states, "All peoples have the right of self-determination. By virtue of that right they freely determine their political status and freely pursue their economic, social and cultural development." The right to self-determination has been argued to be a process rather than one particular outcome. It consists off a "bundle of rights" from which, depending on the specific situation experienced by that people, a variety of rights can be chosen for its implementation. The exercise of the right to self-determination involves a range of political options, ranging from mere self-identification to self-government and secession or independent statehood.

"Policies and practices of population transfer may be aimed specifically at denying a meaningful implementation of the right to self-determination, for instance, by altering the relevant unit of self-determination through demographic manipulation, or policies which have that effect. Instances include the implantation of settlers and settlements in occupied or disputed territories and the concurrent, induced dispersal of the original inhabitants, changing the demographic compositions of the territory to extend control or annex the territory, thereby undermining a legitimate exercise of self-determination by its people." states the UN Special Rapporteurs on the human rights dimensions of population transfer, including implantation of settlers.

The core content of the right to self-determination encompasses the right to exist as a people and safeguards the cultural and political continuation of groups. However, the population transfer contributes to the destruction of a distinct identity and impairs a people's ability to determine their own destiny as a people. "The forced removal of people away from their traditional lands, or the implantation of settlers without the consent of the original inhabitants into whose territories they are being moved, for instance, are instrumental to assimilationist policies and constitute obvious breaches of the minimum guarantee which the right to self-determination is accepted as conferring: the right of a people to "freely determine" its destiny."

The Government of Bangladesh completely undermined the political institutions and traditional system of governance of the Jummas. They have been integrated or nearly assimilated into a centrally controlled system. The voice of the indigenous peoples has seldom been acknowledged. The Government of Bangladesh sought to provide autonomy to the Chittagong Hill Tracts to allow the Jummas exercise the right of self-determination through the Hill District Councils Act of 1989 and presently under the CHTs Peace Treaty of 2 December 1997. However, it is clear that such institutions have lost their meaning from the Jumma perspective, as the illegal Bengali settlers constitute more than 50% of the total population of the CHTs. Since they have been recognized as residents of the CHTs, at least one third of the seats are reserved for them.

In addition, the Government of Bangladesh has taken measures to take over political control. In 1995 the Government divided Latiban Union into two: Latiban and Ultachari. The Ultachari Union has 2700 Bengali votes and only 1100 Jumma voters. Considering the Divide and Rule Policy adopted by the Government of Bangaldesh with the 10 ethnic groups of the CHTs, it is easy for the illegal Bengali settlers to control the political institutions which seek to provide exercise of the right of self determination. There, there is no mechanism to check continuing infiltration of the illegal settlers. If the trickling of settlers is not checked, the indigenous Jumma peoples will be reduced to an insignificant minority in their ancestral homeland.

Given the high rate of population growth amongst the illegal settlers who are illiterate and government's lack of family planning programmes, within a decade the Jummas would not be able to elect their representatives in the Parliament. The illegal settlers will defeat any Jumma candidate espousing the cause of the Jummas. Hence, the presence of the illegal settlers completely impairs the right of self-determination of the indigenous Jumma peoples of the CHTs.

Religious Freedom

The influx of 500,000 settlers who are muslims, the right to religious freedom of the Jummas has been under serious attacks. In a situation where the Islamic fundamentalists exploit the religious sentiments of the majority settlers, the religious freedom of the Jummas have been under serious threat.

The Government of Bangladesh has sponsored religious conversion in the CHTs. In the military controlled areas Muslim young women are being married to local youths after converting them to Islam. Similarly, Jumma women after being converted are married to Bengali youths and even security personnel. Al-Rabita is the main Islamic missionary organization in the region. Backed by the military, it is entrusted with the task of Islamisation of the CHTs. It has an Islamic centre at Alikadam. It has offices in Rangamati and Longudu where it also maintains a hospital. In addition to these the security forces and the settlers destroyed many temples and statues.

On 6 December 1995, soldiers from the 4th Field Artillery Group at Kacchaptalu army camp under Bandarban district searched Nathakgiri Buddha Vihar and Liragaon Buddha Vihara of Kacchaptalu Mouza for Shanti Bahini members. When the army did not find anything, they interrogated the monks and desecrated the Buddha statues. On 25 June 1995, Lt Firdous of the Kachuchari army camp entered the Janaindra Buddhist temple without any reason and desecrated the Buddha Vihar. After he did not find anything, he broke the pot and abused Rev Amritananda and threatened to assault him. Mr Sappya Chakma (18 years), S/o- Nidmani Chakma and Mr Dhanarash Chakma (28 years), S/o - Dhudhukhang Chakma who were engaged in the temple work were also beaten up by Lt Firdous.

On 15 February 1994, two Buddhist monks, Rev Gaindhama and Daeing Moaoima went to the market at Bandarban to buy some fresh vegetables. The seller, an illegal settler, started taunting the monks by using filthy languages. When the monks protested, around 10 illegal settlers attacked the monks and they were mercilessly beaten and became unconscious. Despite protest, no action was taken. The Jammat-I-Islam works very actively with the military in CHT. The number of mosques and madrasahs (Islamic education school) is steadily increasing in the area. The following will make it clear.

Year	Mosques	Madrasahs
1961	40	2
1974	200	20
1981	592	35
1991	650	37

Apart from instances of proselytization, there have been many reported incidents of religious persecution in the form of violation and destruction of religious places of the Hill people by the military.

Communal Harmony

The aggressive behaviour of the illegal Bengali settlers has contributed to a climate of violence and intolerance in the CHTs. Backed by the military and civil administration, the illegal settlers attack the Jummas with slightest provocation and sometimes without any provocation. Consequently, the indigenous Jumma peoples virtually live on the edges with engineered riots looming large over the head. Apart from being physically present, the military is also in total control of the administration of CHT. At the political level there is no freedom of expression or right of association. The local people require the permission of military authorities to arrange and hold meetings and get-togethers.

This permission is required even in instances of religious ceremonies. The Local Government Council for the CHT which has been put forward by the Bengali elite as the 'solution' to the CHT issue is the brainchild of the military and does not alter the army-dominated power structure in the area. Local newspapers require the permission of military authorities for their publication and news items and articles published in these papers have to conform to the requisites of the state. The military has also set up several organisations of the Bengali settlers community in the CHT, like the Bengali Krishak Sramik Kalyan Parishad (Bengali farmers and workers association) and the Parbattya Gano Parishad (PGP, Council of Hill Peoples), CHT Peace and Coordination Council.

One of the serious problems of Bengali settlers has been increased in forced and consensual inter-marriages between the Bengalis and the indigenous Jumma people. There is no problem in such inter-marriages. However, it poses a threat to the cultural and religious identity of the indigenous Jumma peoples. Under the Islamic law, inter-marriage between the indigenous Jummas and Bengalis is only possible if the indigenous person is converted to Islam. The Jummas because of the conflict expressed resentment against inter-marriages with Bengalis.

Crimes Against Women

"In the construction of a nationalist cause rape has always played a central role for women as child bearers are considered important for the biological continuation of a nation; rape therefore is used systematically as a deliberate tactic to destroy or damage the enemy. In the CHT too, rape has been inflicted upon the Hill women by Bengali security personnel and Bengali settlers". There has been unprecedented increase in violence against women in the Chittagong Hill Tracts since the arrival of the illegal settlers. The illegal settlers and the security forces targeted the Jumma women.

The Hill Watch Human Rights Forum has reported that between January 1991 and June 1992, a total number of 47 Jumma women were raped by the Bangladeshi security forces.

According to Hill Women's Federation, there have been five reported cases of rape in 1993, four in 1994 and twelve in 1995. However, Hill Women Federation maintains that because of the social taboos and fear of reprisals, many do not report rape cases. It was also found that over 94 per cent of the rape cases of Hill Women were committed by security personnel. Over 40 per cent of the victims were women under eighteen years of age.

Ethnic Cleansing

The Bangladesh security forces and the settlers have reportedly killed "hundreds if not thousands" of Jumma peoples in systematic genocides and organized communal riots. The successive massacres of the Jummas were in reprisals of Shanti Bahini attacks on the security forces in the late 70s and the illegal settlers in the early eighties. There was not a single massacre where the illegal Bengali settlers were not involved. It was only after arrival of the settlers that the first major massacre took place at Kalampati in 1980.

The attacks on individual Jummas have been endemic. Hundreds of Jummas have also disappeared or been extrajudicially executed after being abducted by members of security forces, paramilitary forces, Village Defence Personnel and civilian vigilantes in the last one and half decades. Some of the victims are arbitrarily arrested as suspected "Shanti Bahini" insurgents in combing operations. Most of those who were killed had been brutally tortured, as were the few who survived abduction or disappearance and who could escape. In the last 25 years, hundreds of indigenous Jumma peoples were killed by the security forces and illegal settlers. The Government of Bangladesh provided impunity to the security forces and tacitly gave license to kill.

Jumma Refugee Influx

The first refugee influx was reported in the Indian media as early as 1977. Around 4,000 Jumma refugees crossed over to Indian State of Tripura. They were repatriated after bilateral discussions with the Bangladesh Government from March 1978 onwards. It was reported that the then Indian Prime Minister, Mr Morarji Desai wanted them to push back but the Tripura State Government did not agree. Around 25,000 refugees took shelter in Tripura when the innocent tribals were attacked by the army and the settlers at Tabalchari and Feni areas of the Chittagong Hill Tracts on 19 September 1981.

Many Jummas died on their way to Tripura, some of them were drowned while swimming the Feni river into Tripura. Hundreds of children died in the refugee camps in Tripura of measles and gastric disorders. They were repatriated forcibly after flag meetings between the Border Security Force (BSF) personnel and the Bangladesh Rifles. "India forcibly repatriated them to Bangladesh" says the Chittagong Hill Tracts Commission. These refugees took shelter after the Bhusan Chara Massacre in 1984. President Ershad visited the spot after the massacre. These refugees had crossed the border for the third time. They were forcibly repatriated by the Indian security forces. Curfew was imposed in the camps on the morning of 29 January 1986 so that no one could flee. They were tied around their necks and backs, dragged to the boats where the Bangladesh Rifles were waiting.

The same refugees crossed the border to seek refuge in Tripura in 1986 after the Panchari-Khagrachari-Dighinala massacres. Around 60,000 Jummas took refuge. They were followed by more refugees after the Longudu massacre on 4 May 1989. More than 13,000 Jummas sought refuge. The Logang Massacre on 10 April 1992 brought an additional 3,000 refugees. The Indian Government refused to register these refugees, thereby refusing refuge. In 1994, about 5,000 Jumma refugees returned "under duress" to the Chittagong Hill Tracts after bilateral discussions between India and Bangladesh. Following the return of this first refugee group in February 1994, human rights groups in Dhaka, Bangladesh conducted a survey indicating that 37 percent of the 42 families interviewed had not reclaimed their original lands.

The Jumma Refugee Welfare Association reported that more than 103 families had still not received the land they originally left. The Returnee Jumma Refugees 16 Points Implementation Committee states that out of the 1027 families consisting of 5186 individual refugees, 25 returnee Jummas refugees who had earlier been employed in various Government jobs were not reinstated in their previous jobs, 134 returnee Jumma refugee families could not settle in their own lands due to the misappropriation of their lands by the security forces and Bengali illegal settlers and 79 families were not given back their lands as it was under forcible occupation of the illegal settlers from the plains. The Bangladesh Government also registered false cases against 23 returnee refugees.

In March-April 1997, another 6708 individual refugees consisting of 1247 families were repatriated. Out of these refugees, 604 families did not get back their lands back which are under the occupation of either army camp or illegal settlers and 25 refugees are still living in transit camps. The Government of Bangladesh shows no signs of rehabilitating the Jumma refugees. Although 43,000 Jumma refugees have returned after the signing of the CHTs Peace Agreement on 2 December 1997, a large majority of the refugee continue to live in makeshift camps or houses. A large majority of the Jumma refugees could not get back their lands and hence could not return to their houses. On the other hand, the Government is yet to set up a Land Commission under the CHTs Peace Agreement.

Racial Discrimination

Bangladesh has a large number of Adivasisor indigenous peoples, who are distinctly different from the mainstream Bengali muslim population in their culture, religion, tradition, customs etc. The indigenous peoples are scattered in hilly parts of Bangladesh, mainly in the districts of Rangpur, Dinajpur, Rajshahi, Mymensingh, Syllet and the Chittagong Hill Tracts (CHTs) consisting of Kharachari, Rangmati and Bandarban district. In addition to the Jummas, there are Hajongs, Khasis, Garos, Santhals, Oraons, Rajbangshis, Manipuris etc in other districts. They face entrenched societal discrimination and suffer from discriminatory policies of the Government.

The delegation of the Government of Bangladesh stated before the CERD Committee in August 1992 that "All the domestic and external policies and actions of Bangladesh were non-racial. In international relations, Bangladesh had always stood against all forms of racial discrimination. It condemned the racist minority Government of South Africa and maintained no diplomatic, political, economic or cultural links with it". There is no doubt that Bangladesh has been vocal on racial discrimination against the former apartheid regime in South Africa. However, there is there is a divergence between its inherently racist domestic and international policies.

Internationally, the Government of Bangladesh opposed the settlement of Jews settlers in the Occupied Arab Territories and sponsored many resolutions like resolution No 1992/2A and 2B at the 48th Session of the United Nations Commission on Human Rights in 1992. At domestic level, Bangladesh Government sponsored "Planned Population Transfer" of over half a million Bengali settlers into the CHTs and continues to encourage such settlement. The Government of Bangladesh demanded withdrawal of Jews settlers for peaceful resolution of the Palestine crisis, yet not a single of Bengali settlers have been withdrawn from the CHTs. "Issues of private preferences and problems of an essentially integrative nature did not come within the definition of racial discrimination under the Convention.

In Bangladesh, there were some residual problems of socio-political integration, as in most States." further stated the delegation of Bangladesh to the CERD Committee.

"Integration" has long been an alibi for many Governments for forcible assimilation of the distinct ethnic, racial, cultural or religious groups. Ethnic cleansing through transmigration, militarisation, rape of women, massacres with impunity, land grabbing and other human rights abuses are not "essentially integrative nature" but "essentially segregative nature". The problems of the indigenous Jumma peoples of CHTs is not "some residual problems of socio-political integration".

None of the settlements of the illegal settlers took place on hilly lands with steep slopes - which are so common all around the CHT. The settlement took place in the valley areas which contained plain and gently sloping lands suitable for intensive plough agriculture. Moreover, the settlers were settled only in those valley regions which were populated by indigenous people and not in the valley areas inhabited by non-indigenous Bengali people. It was a clear case of racial discrimination.

The settlement of the Bengali settlers in the CHT was clear violation of Article 28 of the Bangladesh Constitution. Article 28.1 of Bangladesh Constitution states "The State shall not discriminate against any citizen on the grounds only of religion, race, caste, sex or place of birth". Although, the CHTs had serious lack of land crisis, the Government sponsored population transfer including implantation of 500,000 illegal settlers simply because the CHTs is inhabited the different ethnic group of people.

Some indigenous Chakma farmers who were displaced by the Kaptai Dam, who had re-claimed farmlands from hill and marsh areas from within deforested portions of Reserved Forest areas near Mainimukh in Rangamati district. They had consistently been demanding from the 1960s that these lands now comprising of Amtali mouza, Gadachara mouza, Gulshakhali mouza and Kalapakojya mouza in Longadu thana be de-reserved for their benefit. Repeated appeals failed to evoke any response. Yet, the same lands which were not de-reserved for the indigenous farmers who were released by the

Forest Department for formal settlement to settlers from the plains districts after the Chakma farmers had been evicted from those lands. The survey officials and the district authorities were of the same race and religion as the settlers.

The Government of Bangladesh has ratified the International Labour Organization (ILO)'s Convention on Indigenous and Tribal Populations (Convention No. 107) of 1957 and hence the convention is part of Bangladeshi law. The Convention includes the following provisions.

Article 11: The right of ownership, collective or individual, of the members of the populations concerned over the lands, which these populations traditionally occupy, shall be recognised.

Article 13(1): Procedures for the transmission of rights of ownership and use of land which are established by the customs of the populations concerned shall be respected, within the framework of national laws and resolutions, in so far as they satisfy the needs of these populations and do not hinder their economic and social development.

Article 13(2): Arrangements shall be made to prevent persons who are not members of the populations concerned from taking advantage of these customs or lack of understanding of the laws on the part of the members of these populations to secure the ownership or use of lands belonging to such members.

The above provisions make it clear that it is the responsibility of the government not only to recognise the collective and individual rights of the indigenous (and tribal') persons over lands traditionally occupied by them but to actually prevent these lands from being taken over by non-tribal and non-indigenous persons. In the circumstances, the grant of settlement of lands occupied (and owned) by the indigenous people to the non-indigenous settlers of 1979-80s and the failure to prevent the dispossession of the indigenous people's lands to the non-indigenous settlers is a clear breach of this Convention.

Population Transfer and International Law

The earliest explicit mention of population transfer in an international legal document was the recognition of "forced resettlements" as a war crime in the Allied Declaration on German War Crimes, adopted by representatives of the nine occupied countries, exiled in London, in 1942. It stated, inter alia: "With respect to the fact that Germany, from the beginning of the present conflict, has erected regimes of terror in the occupied territories... characterized in particular by... mass expulsions"

The International Military Tribunal (IMT) Charter introduced into international law the notions of crimes against the peace, war crimes and crimes against humanity. It defined "war crimes" as follows:

> "Murder, ill-treatment or deportation to slave labour or for any other purpose of civilian population of or in occupied territory..."

Article 6 (c) of the Charter defined "crimes against humanity as:

> "Murder, extermination, enslavement, deportation and other inhumane acts committed against any civilian population before or during the war... in execution of or in connection with any crime within the jurisdiction of the Tribunal..."

It is clear that the Nuremberg judgment held that population transfers and colonization in occupied territory constituted both a war crime and a crime against humanity, and that deportation of persons was illegal.

Article 49 of the Geneva Convention Relative to the Protection of Civilian Persons in Time of War states, "The occupying Power shall not deport or transfer parts of its own civilian population into the territory it occupies". While Governments deny the "occupation of particular region" and the applicability of the Fourth Geneva Convention, the issues that prompted the Fourth Geneva Conventions transcend the issue of "occupation". The intention of the Fourth Geneva Convention is to prevent the abuse of human rights, and consequently the issue of historical sovereignty is irrelevant to the prohibition of the transfer of population transfer. According to International Commission of Jurists: "Much of the Convention, including Article 49, is declaratory of the pre-existing international law and such provisions in the Convention should be recognized as being of universal applicability and binding".

Article 49 of the Geneva Convention Relative to the Protection of Civilian Persons in Time of War further states: "Individual or mass forcible transfers, as well as deportations of protected persons from occupied territory... are prohibited, regardless of their motive". The prohibition is absolute, apart from the exceptions stipulated in paragraph 2, which authorizes the Occupying Power to evacuate an occupied territory wholly or partly, but only if "the security of the population or imperative military reasons so demanded".

"Although Article 49 was drafted with the intention to prohibit and thereby prevent population transfers in times of armed conflict, at the same time it sanctions such transfers when imperative military reasons so demands. Through inclusion of the exception clause based on imperative military reasons, the principles contained in article 49 can just as easily be used to give forced removals a legal basis as to protect the rights of potential relocatees. The breadth with which "imperative military reasons" could be interpreted leaves doubt as to the de facto protection this article might provide. None the less, the basic guarantee contained in this provision is the clear and unambiguous prohibition of individual and mass forcible transfers."

In situations of non-international armed conflict, a prohibition of population transfers could be inferred from Common Article 3 to all the Geneva Conventions of 1949.

Although the Common Article 3 does not explicitly mention population transfer as such it enshrines a minimum humanitarian standard of treatment for protected persons, including the prohibition of "violence to life and person" and "outrages upon personal dignity, in particular humiliating and degrading treatment".

In 1977, two Additional Protocols were added to the Geneva Conventions of 1949. Additional Protocol I supplements the protection in situations of international conflict by extending its application to include situations "of armed conflict in which people are fighting against colonial domination and alien occupation and against racist regimes in the exercise of their right of self-determination". Protection against practices of population transfer is further extended by article 85 of Protocol I, which, inter alia, provides in paragraph 4 that:

> "In addition to the grave breaches defined in the preceding paragraphs and in the Conventions, the following shall be regarded as grave breaches of this Protocol, when committed willfully and in violation of the Conventions or Protocol:
>
> (a) the transfer by the Occupying Power of its own civilian population into the territory it occupies, or the deportation or transfer of all parts of the population of the occupied territory within or outside of this territory, in violation of article 49 of the Fourth [Civilians'] Convention."

Article 85, paragraph 5 of Protocol I provides that "grave breaches of these instruments shall be regarded as war crimes". Additional Protocol II to the Geneva Conventions applies in particular situations of internal conflict. Article 17 of the Additional Protocol II provides that:

> "The displacement of the civilian population shall not be ordered for reasons related to the conflict unless the security of the civilians involved or imperative military reasons so demand."

The wording of this provision is based on article 49 of the Civilians Convention. Its inclusion fills the gap in protection against forced displacement in non-international armed conflicts, a situation in which the need for such protection is particularly acute.

Article 17 of Protocol II provides that no displacement shall take place for reasons related to the conflict, leaving open the possibility that transfer may be imperative in certain cases of epidemic or natural disaster, such as floods or earthquakes. However, imperative military reasons cannot be justified by political motives. For example, it would be prohibited to move a population in order to exercise more effective control over a dissident ethnic group.

The preamble of the Convention on the Non-Applicability of Statutory Limitations to War Crimes and Crimes Against Humanity provides:

> "Recalling resolutions of the General Assembly of the United Nations 3 (I) 13 February 1946 and 170 (II) of 31 October 1947 on the extradition and punishment of war criminals, resolution 9595 (I) of 11 December 1946 affirming the principles of international law recognized by the Charter of the International Military Tribunal, Nurnberg, and the judgement of the Tribunal, and resolutions 2184(XXI) of 12 December 1996 and 2202 (XXI) of 16 December 1996 which expressly condemned as crimes against humanity the violation of the economic and political rights of the indigenous(emphasis ours) population on the one hand and the policies of apartheid on the other,"

The Convention on the Non-Applicability of Statutory Limitations to War Crimes and Crimes Against Humanity is relevant to the legal discussion concerning population transfers as it extends the concept of war crimes and crimes against humanity as defined by the Charter of the Nuremberg Tribunal. It also embodies the principle that no statutory limitations shall apply to the crimes referred to in the Convention, "irrespective of the date of their commission". In accordance with article 1 (b) of the Convention the following acts are to be included as crimes against humanity:

"Crimes against humanity whether committed in time of war or in nay time of peace as they are defined in the Charter of International Military Tribunal, Nurnberg, of 8 August 1945 and confirmed by resolutions 3(I) 11 December 1946 of the General Assembly of the United Nations, eviction by armed attack or occupation and inhumane acts resulting from the policy of apartheid, and the crime of genocide as defined in the 1948 Convention on the Prevention and Punishment of the Crime of Genocide, even if such acts do not constitute a violation of the domestic law of the country in which they were committed."

Article 1 (b) specifies that crimes against humanity may be committed "in time of war or in time of peace". Thus its delinks from the ambiguity of article 6 (c) of the Charter of the Nuremberg Tribunal, which could be interpreted as not extending to the same category of crimes committed in time of peace not followed by war.

The concept of crimes against humanity led to the adoption in 1948 of the Convention on the Prevention and the Punishment of the Crime of Genocide (the Genocide Convention). Its main purpose was to make genocide a crime under international law. In its Advisory Opinion, the International Court of Justice stated that "the principles underlying this Convention are principles which are recognized by civilized nations as binding on States, even without any conventional obligation". Although the Convention does not prohibit population transfers per se, its relevance to practices of population transfer becomes obvious when one considers its definition of genocide.

In Article 2, genocide is defined as including:

"any of the following acts committed with the intent to destroy, in whole or in part, a national, ethnic, racial or religious group as such:

(a) Killing members of the group;

(b) Causing serious bodily or mental harm to members of the group;

(c) Deliberately inflicting on the group conditions of life calculated to bring about its physical destruction in whole or in part;

(d) Imposing measures to prevent births within the group;

(e) Forcibly transferring children of the group to another group".

The prohibition of genocide is linked to right of peoples to physical existence. However, population transfer and implantation of settlers may threaten the physical existence of a people. In addition to removal of the indigenous Jumma peoples from their homeland, there was a clear pattern of killings of the Jummas in the CHTs at genocidal proportion. In addition, the change in the demographic composition threatens the identity of the Jummas.

The Special Rapporteurs on the human rights dimensions of population transfer and implantation of settlers stated "For specific policies and practices of population transfer to constitute genocide under the Convention, in addition to the destructive effects of the transfer, the intent of the Government or other actor "to destroy, in whole or in part, a national ethnic, racial or religious group as such" must be sufficiently proved. The governmental intent required to raise the level of an act to genocide will vary, depending on circumstances."

The Special Rapporteur further add, "But even when governmental participation in population transfers is insidious and merely takes the form of encouragement or inducement, it can contain enough governmental authority to raise the consequences for a subject population to the level of genocide. Awareness of the destructive effects-of the transfer on the affected group, concurrent with continued governmental involvement or failure to undertake action to terminate the transfer, would render ineffective a Government's claim to lack of intend".

2

Indigenous People and their Relationship to Land

There are an enormous number of problems and issues relating to indigenous land rights. Indigenous peoples have fundamental issue of their relationship to their homelands. Indigenous peoples have explained that, because of the profound relationship that indigenous peoples have to their lands, territories and resources, there is a need for a different conceptual framework to understand this relationship and a need for recognition of the cultural differences that exist. Indigenous peoples have urged the world community to attach positive value to this distinct relationship.

It is difficult to separate one indigenous concept from another. The relationship with the land and all living things is at the core of indigenous societies. For example, the land tenure system, known as Kipat, of the Limbu indigenous people of Nepal provides a means of belonging to a place and to a distinctive community - the one not separable from the other. Kipat defines them as a "tribe". According to one authority, Kipat "is fused with and articulates the culture and any assault on Kipat is seen as a threat to the very existence of the Limbu as a separate community within the society". Indigenous peoples have emphasized that the spiritual and material foundations of their cultural identities are sustained by their unique relationships to their traditional territories.

Professor James sake Henderson attempts to illustrate this distinct relationship and conceptual framework by stating that "the Aboriginal vision of property was ecological space that creates our consciousness, not an ideological construct or fungible resource... Their vision is of different realms enfolded into a sacred space... It is fundamental to their identity, personality and humanity... the notion of self does not end with their flesh, but continues with the reach of their senses into the land". Such a relationship manifests itself in the elements of indigenous peoples' cultures, such as language. For example, an Inuit elder tried to articulate this relationship by stating that "our language contains an intricate knowledge of the Arctic that we have seen no others demonstrate".

For a number of different reasons, the international community has begun to respond to indigenous peoples in the context of a new philosophy and world perspective with respect to land, territory and resources. New standards are being devised based, in part, upon the values that have been expressed by indigenous peoples and which are consistent with indigenous peoples' perspectives and philosophies about their relationships to their lands, territories and resources. Policy and direction within the Sub-Commission and other United Nation bodies in regard to the relationship of indigenous peoples with their lands, territories and resources have been shaped by the conclusions, proposals and recommendations of Special Rapporteur José R. Martínez Cobo, in volume V of the Study of the Problem of Discrimination Against Indigenous Populations. They generally reflect indigenous peoples' articulation of this distinct relationship. Mr. Martínez Cobo states:

"It is essential to know and understand the deeply spiritual special relationship between indigenous peoples and their land as basic to their existence as such and to all their beliefs, customs, traditions and culture." For such peoples, the land is not merely a possession and a means of production. The entire relationship between the spiritual life of indigenous peoples and Mother Earth, and their land, has a great many deep-seated implications. Their land is not a commodity which can be acquired, but a material element to be enjoyed freely.

Further examples of the recognition of this special relationship include the specific reference to "the special importance for the cultures and spiritual values of the peoples concerned of their relationship with the lands or territories, or both as applicable, which they occupy or otherwise use, and in particular the collective aspects of this relationship", in article 13 of the International Labour Organization Convention (No. 169) Concerning Indigenous and Tribal Peoples in Independent Countries.

The distinctive nature of indigenous peoples' relationship to lands is also referred to in the draft United Nations declaration on the rights of indigenous peoples, in both preambular and operative paragraphs. In particular, article 25 states: "Indigenous peoples have the right to maintain and strengthen their distinctive spiritual and material relationship with the lands territories, waters and coastal seas and other resources which they have traditionally owned or otherwise occupied or used, and to uphold their responsibilities to future generations in this regard." Finally, the proposed American Declaration on the Rights of Indigenous Peoples, drafted by the Inter-American Commission on Human Rights and now under consideration by the Permanent Council of the Organization of American States, contains the following preambular language:

"The States,

— Recognizing the respect for the environment accorded by the cultures of indigenous peoples of the Americas, and considering the special relationship between the indigenous peoples and the environment, lands, resources and territories on which they live and their natural resources.

— Recognizing that in many indigenous cultures, traditional collective systems for control and use of land and territory and resources, including bodies of water and coastal areas, are a necessary condition for their survival, social organization, development and their individual and collective well-being..."

Each of these examples underscores a number of elements that are unique to indigenous peoples:

(i) a profound relationship exists between indigenous peoples and their lands, territories and resources;

(ii) this relationship has various social, cultural, spiritual, economic and political dimensions and responsibilities;

(iii) the collective dimension of this relationship is significant; and

(iv) the intergenerational aspect of such a relationship is also crucial to indigenous peoples' identity, survival and cultural viability.

Impacts of Doctrines of Dispossession

The gradual deterioration of indigenous societies can be traced to the non-recognition of the profound relationship that indigenous peoples have to their lands, territories and resources, as well as the lack of recognition of other fundamental human rights. The natural order of life for indigenous peoples has been and continues to be threatened by a different order, one which is no longer dictated by the natural environment and the indigenous peoples' relationship to it. Indigenous societies in a number of countries are in a state of rapid deterioration and change due in large part to the denial of the rights of the indigenous peoples to lands, territories and resources.

The colonization of indigenous territories has affected indigenous peoples in a number of ways. Demographic deterioration occurred through maltreatment, enslavement, suicide, punishment for resistance, warfare, malnutrition due to destruction of the natural environment or over-exploitation of natural resources, disease and outright extermination. Rodolfo Stavenhagen states that "the entire population of the Americas decreased by 95 per cent in the century and a half following the first encounter". The intent to convert indigenous peoples to Christianity and bring them under the "sovereignty" of foreign monarchs created widespread havoc, despite some early attempts at "friendly treatment".

With population decline came the destruction of the traditional social order, due to the efforts of missionaries and Western attitudes towards the divisions of labour and of gender, among others. The introduction of the practice of attaching a monetary value to things and of buying and selling things previously considered non-merchantable, including land, added the stress of an economic environment quite opposite to the traditional economic order of most indigenous communities. These concepts were all alien to the collective social organization of indigenous communities.

The factual accounts relating to the dispossession and expropriation of indigenous peoples' lands are too varied. There is much to be learned from indigenous peoples worldwide about the methods and legal doctrines used to dispossess them. At present, however, it is of critical importance to underscore the cultural biases that contributed to the conceptual framework constructed to legitimize colonization and the various methods used to dispossess indigenous peoples and expropriate their lands, territories and resources. It is safe to say that the attitudes, doctrines and policies developed to justify the taking of lands from indigenous peoples were and continue to be largely driven by the economic agendas of States.

The early theorists who espoused a "naturalist" framework were the first to tackle the difficult question of the place of indigenous peoples within modern international law and, in particular, indigenous peoples as rightful owners of their lands, territories and resources. "Naturalist" constructions were founded upon the notion of a higher authority and divine reason, and rooted in morality. An important feature of the "naturalist" view was the principle of the equality of all human beings. This principle had an important place in the articulation of the application of natural law to the "Indians" of the New World.

Early naturalists actually advocated on behalf of the Indians against imperial and papal authority with regard to the assertions of Spanish ownership, use and exploitation of Indian lands and resources, which were based upon the doctrines of conquest and discovery. They argued that Indian peoples did in fact have rights to the land, and some went one step further by addressing, in the context of the laws of war, the rights and capacity of Indian nations and peoples to enter into treaty relations although they were "strangers to the true religion". In their construction, if Indian peoples were in fact human beings and equal, they would have "just cause" to wage war against the invaders. However, unless conquest followed a just war, Indians could not unilaterally be dispossessed of their lands or deprived of their autonomous existence.

Such prescriptions for the European encounters with indigenous peoples were building blocks for a system of principles and rules governing encounters among all peoples of the world. Subsequent theorists continued during the early nineteenth century to include non-European aboriginal peoples among the subjects of what came to be known as the "law of nations" and later, "international law".

Hence, early theorists did address the question of the rights of Indian peoples in the framework of natural law, albeit without their participation or knowledge. Nonetheless, such theorists believed that natural law had the capacity to respond to the rights and interests of the indigenous peoples of the Americas. Whatever protection the early law of nations afforded indigenous peoples, it was not enough to stop the forces of colonization and empire as they extended throughout the globe. Theorists eventually modified the law of nations to reflect, and hence legitimize, a state of affairs that subjugated indigenous peoples. International law remains primarily concerned with the rights and duties of European and similarly "civilized" States and has its source principally in the positive, consensual acts of those States.

Unfortunately, established Christian and other religious values became embedded in natural law and international law, undercutting any possibility for indigenous peoples' claims, rights and values to be advanced in the years following invasion. Indigenous peoples were commonly labelled "infidels" and "pagans" in natural law discourse. Discriminatory and racist attitudes are apparent in the terminology alone. Although natural law may have been more expansive in some respects, a very narrow concept began to emerge when the colonizing countries furthered their adventures into the Americas and elsewhere. Their perspectives and values began to subsume indigenous nations and peoples.

In most situations, it was only through rationalization and military domination that colonizers secured "ownership" of the lands, territories and resources of indigenous peoples. The territories of indigenous peoples in the Americas and elsewhere were taken through many means, but largely by military force. Where "just war" could not be waged, treaties sometimes were concluded. In regard to North America, Vine Deloria, Jr. wrote:

"Treaty-making was a feasible method of gaining a foothold on the continent without alarming the natives. Treating with the Indians, then, brought an air of civility and legitimacy to the white settlers' relations with the Indians and provoked no immediate retaliation by the tribes. Instead of the Indians being subjected to bondage or their lands merely seized through the use of force, which Spain eventually did, civility reigned in North America. Indian land and the rights to live in certain areas were purchased at formal treaty sessions."

What territory remained was diminished further by forcible or coerced removal, relocation and allotment. Many indigenous communities in North America were forced onto reservations. The severing of indigenous peoples from their lands and territories and the failure by States to recognize the social, cultural, spiritual and economic significance of land to indigenous peoples had both short- and long-term impacts on indigenous communities.

The doctrines of dispossession which emerged in the subsequent development of modern international law, particularly conquest, discovery and terra nullius, have all had untold adverse effects on indigenous peoples. Only recently has the international community begun to understand that such doctrines are illegitimate and racist. For example, while the Permanent Court of International Justice based its decision in the Eastern Greenland case of 1933 upon the same framework and attitudes, in 1975 the International Court of Justice ruled that the doctrine of terra nullius had been erroneously and invalidly applied against the tribal peoples of the Western Sahara.

The High Court of Australia in its 1992 decision in Mabo v. Queensland discussed the legal and other effects of the doctrine of terra nullius. The Court denounced the doctrine by concluding that this "unjust and discriminatory doctrine... can no longer be accepted". This decision gave rise to the Native Title Act, adopted by the Government of Australia in 1993, which established a framework and mechanism by which Aboriginal peoples in Australia could secure land rights.

To what extent the Government of Australia can continue to extinguish indigenous land title through legislation that discriminates against indigenous title is a matter of ongoing debate. The Committee on the Elimination of Racial Discrimination, on 18 March 1999, issued a decision finding that provisions in the 1998 Native Title Act Amendments extinguish or impair the exercise of indigenous title rights and interests and discriminate against native title holders.

Problems in Land Right

Failure of States to Ecognize the Existence of Indigenous Use, occupancy and ownership

This most fundamental and widespread problem is divided into two parts: the failure of States to recognize the existence of indigenous use, occupancy and ownership, and the failure of States to accord appropriate legal status, juridical capacity and other legal rights in connection with indigenous peoples' ownership of land.

Failure to recognize the existence of indigenous use, occupancy and ownership: Countries in many parts of the world are unaware of or ignore the fact that communities, tribes or nations of indigenous peoples inhabit and use areas of land and sea and have done so, in many cases, since time immemorial. These areas are typically far from the capitals and other urban areas of the country and typically countries regard these lands and resources as public or government lands. Although the indigenous people concerned regard themselves, with good reason, as owning the land and resources they occupy and use, the country itself, typically, disposes of the land and resources as if the indigenous people were not there.

In Belize, for example, 17 logging concessions were recently granted by the Government to foreign companies to cut timber in forests where Maya people have always lived and have relied on the forest for their subsistence. The San or Bushmen in certain African countries face, among other land problems, grave difficulties because of the lack of national legislation safeguarding their land use and tenure. In West Papua New Guinea (West Irian), the Government of Indonesia encouraged transmigration and settlement on lands where indigenous peoples have lived. This process has reportedly caused widespread dislocation of indigenous peoples, practically forcing many to live in other countries.

The indigenous peoples of the Philippines are squatters on their own lands, because the Philippine State claims ownership of some 62 per cent of the country's territory. The Indigenous Peoples Right Act of 1997 now provides a means for recognition of indigenous land rights. The usefulness of the Act deserves careful evaluation. Similar situations are reported in Indonesia, Thailand and India, and most African countries are reported to claim all forest lands. In Nicaragua, the Government planned an environmental preserve or park in complete disregard of the indigenous population living on that land. The Martínez Cobo study found that many countries with large indigenous populations nevertheless reported that no such peoples existed there. Although this situation has improved, the problem appears to continue.

The failure of States to accord appropriate legal status, appropriate juridical capacity and other legal rights: This problem is closely related to the one discussed above. Although States know that indigenous communities, nations or groups exist and have exclusive use and occupancy of an area, some States do not acknowledge that the indigenous peoples concerned have legal entitlement or rights to the land or resources. In some situations, the indigenous peoples are regarded as using the public or national lands at the sufferance of the Government.

The concept of aboriginal title and the relationship of this legal concept to the human rights of indigenous peoples is centrally important. In many countries, particularly those of the British Commonwealth, exclusive use and occupancy of land from time immemorial gives rise to aboriginal title, a title that is good against all but the Sovereign, that is, the Government of the State. Where aboriginal title is recognized, indigenous peoples have at least some legal right that can be asserted in the domestic legal system. However, aboriginal title is often subject to the illegitimate assumption of State power to extinguish such title, in contrast to the legal protection and rights that, in most countries, protect the land and property of citizens. This single fact probably accounts for the overwhelming majority of human rights problems affecting indigenous peoples.

Aboriginal title or the title of indigenous peoples is also, in many countries, more limited in its legal character and the rights that appertain to it and more limited in the legal protection accorded to that title as compared to other land titles. The land cannot be used in a manner that is irreconcilable with the nature of the claimants' attachment to that land. For example, land used as a hunting ground cannot be used so as to destroy its value as a hunting ground. Fair compensation is required for infringements of aboriginal title, but no clear principles for compensation were established in the decision.

In some countries, indigenous communities do not have the legal capacity to own land, or do not have the capacity to own land collectively. Where the indigenous people or group is not recognized as having juridical status or existence, it cannot hold title to lands or resources nor take legal action to protect those property interests. Many States that a generation ago denied such legal capacity to indigenous peoples have now made positive reforms, but further study of this problem is called for.

Discriminatory Laws and Policies

In those States that have developed a body of positive law and a body of jurisprudence in regard to indigenous peoples - and their number is increasing - the most significant problems appear to arise because of persistent discriminatory laws and legal doctrines that are applied to indigenous peoples and their lands and resources. The concept of aboriginal title, as discussed above, is itself discriminatory in that it provides only defective, vulnerable and inferior legal status for indigenous land and resource ownership. These discriminatory laws and legal doctrines deserve special attention because they appear to be so widespread, because they appear to be in violation of existing international human rights norms and because they appear to be relatively amenable to correction.

Laws regarding the extinguishment of indigenous peoples' land and resource rights: Practically all countries where indigenous peoples live assert the power to "extinguish" the land titles and rights of the indigenous peoples within their borders, without the consent of the indigenous peoples. The concept of extinguishment includes voluntary purchase and sale of title, but more commonly the term "extinguishment" is used to mean outright taking or expropriation, most often without just compensation. Like the concept of aboriginal title, extinguishment is a term that came into prominent use during the colonial period.

The problem of extinguishment is related to the concept of aboriginal title. The central defect of so-called aboriginal title is that it is, by definition, title that can be taken at will by the Sovereign - that is, by the colonial Government, or nowadays, by the State. Like aboriginal title, the practice of involuntary extinguishment of indigenous land rights is a relic of the colonial period. It appears that, in modern times, the practice of involuntary extinguishment of land titles without compensation is applied only to indigenous peoples. As such, it is discriminatory and unjust, to say the least, and deserving of close examination.

One particularly clear example of the problem of extinguishment is provided by the case of the Tee-Hit-Ton Indians v. United States. In this case the Supreme Court decided that the United States may (with limited exceptions) take or confiscate the land or property of an Indian tribe without due process of law and without paying just compensation, this despite the fact that the United States Constitution explicitly provides that the Government may not take property without due process of law and just compensation. The Supreme Court found that property held by aboriginal title, as most Indian land is, is not entitled to the constitutional protection that is accorded all other property.

The racially discriminatory nature of the Tee-Hit-Ton decision can be seen in the opinion, an extract of which follows:

"No case in this court has ever held that taking of Indian title or use by Congress required compensation. The American people have compassion for the descendants of those Indians who were deprived of their homes and hunting grounds by the drive of civilization. They seek to have the Indians share the benefits of our society as citizens of this Nation. Generous provision has been willingly made to allow tribes to recover for wrongs, as a matter of grace, not because of legal liability." Every American schoolboy knows that the savage tribes of this continent were deprived of their ancestral ranges by force and that, even when the Indians ceded millions of acres by treaty in return for blankets, food and trinkets, it was not a sale but the conquerors' will that deprived them of their land.

The legal doctrine created by this case continues to be the governing law on this matter in the United States today. The racially discriminatory character of the decision has not prevented this doctrine from being freely used by the courts and by the United States Congress in legislation, even in recent years. Indeed the Congress relied on this doctrine in 1971 when it extinguished all the land rights and claims of practically every one of the 226 indigenous nations and tribes in Alaska by adopting the Alaska Native Claims Settlement Act. The Act provided for transferring the land to profit-making corporations that were required to be created by the indigenous peoples and for paying a sum of money to each native corporation - a sum far less than the value of the land.

The Alaska native tribes themselves were paid nothing. The remaining lands of the territory that belonged to the tribes, or that had been claimed by them, were turned over to the State of Alaska and the United States. The Alaska native tribes never consented to the legislation. Because of the concepts of aboriginal title and extinguishment, and because of the related discriminatory legal doctrines, it was understood that the lands of these indigenous peoples could be taken outright, without payment or just compensation.

Indigenous representatives and experts have reported that many other countries have laws and policies similar to those of the United States in this regard. But the Constitution Act of 1982, section 35 (1), recognizes and affirms aboriginal and treaty rights. By reason of the Constitution Act of 1982, courts in Canada no longer acknowledge government power to "extinguish" aboriginal rights. Instead, the courts have decided that aboriginal rights, including aboriginal land title, are not absolute but may be "infringed" by the federal or provincial governments when the infringement is "justified" by the needs of the larger society.

In a recent case, Chief Justice Lamer of the Supreme Court of Canada wrote: "In my opinion, the development of agriculture, forestry, mining, and hydroelectric power, the general economic development of the interior of British Columbia, protection of the environment or endangered species, the building of infrastructure and the settlement of foreign populations to support those aims, are the kinds of objectives that are consistent with this purpose and, in principle, can justify the infringement of aboriginal title." It remains unclear whether this new requirement of "justification" will in fact provide greater protection to indigenous land rights than previous law. As noted above, it also remains doubtful whether the law accords an equal, non-discriminatory level of legal protection to indigenous property rights as compared to the property rights of others.

The High Court of Australia, in Mabo v. Queensland, ruled that the doctrine of terra nullius may not be applied to deny indigenous rights to land, but nonetheless confirmed the power of the Sovereign to extinguish native title. The Court held that native title may be extinguished, but only by legislation, by the alienation of land by the Crown or by the appropriation of the land by the Crown in a manner inconsistent with the continuation of native title. The Native Title Amendment Act, enacted in 1998, provided a number of means whereby native or indigenous title would be extinguished. The Act has been attacked as discriminatory in several respects:

— the amendments prefer the rights of non-native title holders over those of native title holders;

— they fail to provide native title holders with protection of the kind given to other landowners;

— they allow for discriminatory action by governments;

— they place barriers to the protection and recognition of native title; and

— they fail to provide for appropriately different treatment of unique aspects of Aboriginal culture.

Aboriginal and Torres Strait Islander Peoples and Australia's obligations under the United Nations Convention on the Elimination of all Forms of Racial Discrimination. The Committee on the Elimination of Racial Discrimination has found various provisions of the Act discriminatory:

"7. The Committee notes, in particular, four specific provisions that discriminate against indigenous title-holders under the newly amended Act. These include: the Act's 'validation' provisions; the 'confirmation of extinguishment' provisions; the primary production upgrade provisions; and the restrictions concerning the right of indigenous title holders to negotiate non-indigenous land uses." "Validation" refers to validation of certain non-indigenous titles; the consequence of validation is the arbitrary extinguishment or impairment of affected native title and the loss of an opportunity to negotiate. "Confirmation of extinguishment" provisions refer to past acts of extinguishment.

A range of previously issued titles are deemed by the Act to extinguish native title permanently, whether or not such titles extinguish title at common law. "Primary production upgrade" provisions permit pastoral lease holders to apply to upgrade their rights to permit a broad range of higher intensity "primary production activities" without requirements of consultation or negotiation with affected native title holders.

The restrictions on the right of native title holders to negotiate mean that States and Territories are entitled to establish regimes for the grant of interests to mining companies and other developers on terms significantly less favourable to native title holders than before the amendments. The Committee found that the amended Act cannot be considered to be a special measure within the meaning of articles 1.4 and 2.2 of the Convention and expressed its concerns about Australia's compliance with articles 2 and 5 of the Convention.

Plenary power: Another discriminatory legal doctrine that appears to be widespread is the doctrine that States have practically unlimited power to control or regulate the use of indigenous lands, without regard for constitutional limits on governmental power that would otherwise be applicable. In the United States, this is known as the "plenary power doctrine" and it holds that the United States Congress may exercise virtually unlimited power over indigenous nations and tribes and their property. No other population or group is subject to such limitless and potentially abusive governmental power.

Treaty abrogation and land rights: Another example of discriminatory legal doctrines is the law in regard to treaties made with indigenous peoples. Treaties have been used, among other purposes, as mechanisms for gaining cessions of indigenous land and for ostensibly guaranteeing rights to the remaining lands held by the indigenous nation. The problem of discrimination arises when the State later abrogates or violates the treaty. In the typical case, the injured indigenous nation or tribe has no legal remedy against the State either in domestic law or under international law. The denial of any remedy under international law is inconsistent with the use of treaties as a legal mechanism and with the status of indigenous peoples as subjects of international law.

Thus, indigenous peoples appear to be unique in being denied legal remedies for violation of their rights, where the State abrogates or violates a treaty between the State and an indigenous nation, tribe or peoples. Certain States, including New Zealand and the United States, regard treaties as instruments of domestic law as well as international law and accordingly do not believe a remedy under international law is necessarily appropriate. The question, in such cases remains whether a just remedy is provided for treaty violation or abrogation, and whether the use of the treaty mechanism in domestic law is non-discriminatory.

Failure to Demarcate Lands

In terms of frequency and scope of complaints, the greatest single problem today for indigenous peoples is the failure of States to demarcate indigenous lands. Demarcation of lands is the formal process of identifying the actual locations and boundaries of indigenous lands or territories and physically marking those boundaries on the ground. Purely abstract or legal recognition of indigenous lands, territories or resources can be practically meaningless unless the physical identity of the property is determined and marked.

Some States, such as Brazil, have strong and very positive laws requiring demarcation of indigenous lands. Others, perhaps the majority, have no such laws. In States with laws requiring demarcation, the implementation and execution of those laws have been weak or absent. Where such laws are lacking or weak, problems arise because, not having demarcated indigenous land, the State cannot identify what is indigenous land and what is not. As a result there are conflicts with indigenous communities. Nicaragua and Belize present examples of this kind of situation.

An important case now before the Inter-American Court of Human Rights raises the issues of States' obligations to recognize and respect the lands, resources and territories of indigenous peoples, and States' obligations to demarcate those lands and territories. The case is that of the Mayagna indigenous community of Awas Tingni against Nicaragua; it was filed with the Court by the Inter-American Commission on Human Rights in June 1998.

The complaint is based on a petition filed by the community of Awas Tingni with the Inter-American Commission. The community of Awas Tingni alleged that the Government of Nicaragua had not met its legal obligations under the Nicaraguan Constitution and international law by failing to recognize and safeguard the community's rights to the lands that its members have traditionally occupied and used. Despite various efforts by the community of Awas Tingni to formally demarcate or achieve other specific legal recognition of its traditional lands, the community's use and occupancy of those lands became increasingly threatened. Rather than respond to Awas Tingni's requests that its land rights be respected, and without consulting with Awas Tingni, the Government of Nicaragua granted a concession to a Korean timber company to log lands (nearly 65,000 hectares) traditionally held by Awas Tingni.

The case before the Court asserts, among other things, that Nicaragua has a legal obligation to demarcate and respect the traditional lands of Awas Tingni by reason of article 21 of the American Convention on Human Rights ("Everyone has the right to the use and enjoyment of his property...") and article 27 of the International Covenant on Civil and Political Rights, which provides: "In those States where ethnic, religious or linguistic minorities exist, persons belonging to such minorities shall not be denied the right, in community with the other members of their group, to enjoy their own culture, to profess and practise their own religion, or to use their own language."

Nicaragua is a party to both the Convention and the Covenant. It is argued, with considerable authority, that traditional indigenous land tenure systems and patterns of land use are an aspect of culture that is protected by article 27 of the Covenant. This case is the first to raise indigenous land rights issues and the obligations of States to respect these rights. The decision of the Inter-American Court may have a far-reaching impact in determining the present scope of international legal obligations to respect and demarcate indigenous lands and resources under the American Convention and the International Covenant on Civil and Political Rights.

Failure to Enforce or Implement Laws Protecting

Some of the most grave situations, such as the massive invasion of Yanomami lands in Brazil and the resulting deaths of thousands of Yanomami Indians, came about in large part because of the State's failure to enforce existing laws. Even after demarcation of the Yanomami territory, the Government of Brazil has not devoted the resources necessary to prevent the illegal invasion of thousands of gold miners. Gold miners have recently been responsible in part for the unprecedented fires that have burned extensively within the Yanomami territory, destroying vast areas of forest and food crops. The fires caused widespread outbreaks of disease that resulted in the deaths of more than 100 Yanomami in 1998.

In other situations, indigenous peoples find they cannot protect their rights to lands and resources because they do not have effective recourse to the courts or other legal remedies. In the worst situations, violence, intimidation and corruption prevent effective legal action by or on behalf of indigenous peoples. This was reported, for example, concerning efforts by Macuxi Indian communities in Brazil to protect their lands. In December 1998, the Government of Brazil took a positive step towards remedying the situation by issuing a decision to proceed with demarcation of the Raposa Serra do Sul area in the northern state of Roraima. The area is home to the Macuxi, Wapixana, Ingariko and Taurepang Indian peoples.

Previously, the Inter-American Commission on Human Rights of the Organization of American States had visited the area and formally recommended that the Government of Brazil take steps to demarcate the Raposa. However, in the months following the Government's decision there have been widespread reports of an increase in acts of physical and political intimidation by gold miners and agriculturalists living in the area. Official demarcation of the Raposa Serra do Sul area still awaits ratification by the President of Brazil and there is still a considerable possibility that the area will be further reduced before demarcation begins.

In other settings, in various countries, there is sometimes no effective legal system to provide a remedy, or indigenous peoples cannot afford to pay for necessary professional legal representation, or they cannot use the language required by the courts or legal agencies, or they cannot travel to the courts or legal agencies, or they simply do not know that legal remedies may be available. As with other human rights, the poverty, geographical remoteness and cultural and linguistic differences of indigenous peoples create severe impediments to the protection of their land, territorial and resource rights.

Land Claims and Return of Lands

The long and painful history of the unjust and inhuman dispossession of indigenous peoples from their territories has resulted in many indigenous peoples having no land or resources or too little land and resources to sustain their communities and their cultures. This is by no means universally true, but for many indigenous peoples, their future will depend on acquiring the lands and resources needed for sustainable economic development and for a degree of self-sufficiency. The most severe problems exist in countries where there are no legal remedies and no legal or political mechanisms for addressing or resolving indigenous land claims. It is reported that in Nepal, for example, no such remedies or mechanisms are available to indigenous peoples, who have lost practically all their lands and resources.

A particular problem that has been repeatedly brought to the attention of the Commission on Human Rights and the Sub-Commission is the use or misuse of claim procedures to deprive indigenous peoples of their rights, or their claimed rights to land and resources. Numerous such problems have been reported by indigenous peoples in many countries. The problems may be summarized as follows: in some cases, an unauthorized or mistaken claim is made to a court or administrative body that the State has taken or paid an unfairly low price for an area of land originally owned by an indigenous people, whereas in fact, the land has not in fact been taken but is still owned by the indigenous people.

In other cases, the land has been taken but the indigenous people concerned does not want compensation but return of the land. These fraudulent or mistaken claims are sometimes, in effect, encouraged by legal provisions that permit a lawyer to earn a fee of as much as 10 per cent of the money award recovered. When such claims are taken to conclusion and an award of compensation is made, the payment of the award effectively extinguishes the indigenous title to the land in question. This has occurred even in situations where the Indian nation or tribe is still in possession of the land. Thus, these "claims" processes are depriving Indians of their lands.

The problems created by fraudulent and improper claims are aggravated by the lack of proper legal procedures in the claim process. Processes such as that of the now defunct Indian Claims Commission in the United States did not ensure that claimants had proper authority to act for the tribe concerned. Procedures did not give the tribes concerned proper notice or an opportunity to be heard. The Commission in more than one case permitted lawyers to act in direct opposition to their supposed or nominal client tribes and even permitted lawyers to carry on money compensation claims after the claimant tribes had dismissed the lawyers in an effort to stop the claims.

Although the Indian Claims Commission no longer exists, the cases that it handled and the problems it created continue. Some notable cases that remain unresolved are the Black Hills claim (in which the Sioux tribes have refused to accept the compensation awarded and seek a return of portions of the land) and the Western Shoshone case (in which the Western Shoshone tribes also refuse payment and seek a restoration of some of the land). In the latter case, some Western Shoshones have remained in possession of certain areas of the land supposedly taken by the United States and are resisting Government efforts to interfere with their use of the land. The extensive and disruptive problems relating to the Indian Claims Commission have been given scholarly attention. These problems have also been the subject of complaints to the United Nations and other bodies.

Many of the problems have been raised in a formal human rights complaint filed with the Inter-American Commission on Human Rights of the Organization of American States by two Western Shoshone Indian women on behalf of their Band. They assert that they are and have always been in possession of parts of the territory of the Western Shoshone Nation, an area recognized by the United States in the Treaty of Ruby Valley of 1863. They use the land for ranching, for religious purposes, for hunting and gathering, and other purposes.

The United States claims that it now owns nearly all the land at issue and that the Western Shoshone rights to the land were extinguished by the Indian Claims Commission process more than 15 years ago. The United States claims that these Western Shoshones are trespassing on the land, and the United States has taken various measures to remove them and their livestock. In recent years, the discovery of one of the largest gold ore bodies in North America on this land has led to even greater pressure on these Western Shoshone people, who oppose open-pit gold mining.

The complaint asserts that the United States has never lawfully extinguished the Western Shoshone title and that the Indian Claims Commission process was discriminatory and lacking in due process of law. The principal allegations are summarized as follows. It is alleged that the attorneys prosecuting the claim falsely stated and agreed that the land had been taken and Western Shoshone title extinguished long ago, when in fact it had not. The lawyers were permitted by the Commission to represent all Western Shoshones when in fact they did not. The Commission refused to permit any other Western Shoshone tribe or group to object or to be heard in the proceeding. The Commission entered its award, although by then not a single Western Shoshone tribe approved of the claim.

The United States Government encouraged and participated in the proceedings throughout. The Claims Commission award amounted to about $0.15 per acre for the land supposedly taken. The United States asserts that the complaint is inadmissable on various procedural grounds and on the ground that the facts do not constitute human rights violations. The Inter-American Commission requested the United States Government to stay its actions against the complainants pending the investigation of the facts by the Inter-American Commission.

It is apparent from the proceedings in this matter that the United States has ostensibly extinguished the rights of Western Shoshone Indians to a large area of their ancestral land without according the ordinary rights of due process of law and fair market compensation that would have been accorded to non-Indian landowners. This is the more notable because the land at issue had been recognized as Western Shoshone land by the United States in a treaty it signed with the Western Shoshones in 1863. The Indian Claims Commission process appears to have been lacking in fundamental fairness in many respects, particularly the failure to assure proper representation of the supposed claimants, the lack of notice and opportunity to be heard for other Western Shoshone parties, the failure to require proof of the supposed taking of the land, and the award of just a few cents per acre for the land at issue.

The Claims Commission process in this case, and reportedly in other cases as well, appears to violate the fundamental requirements of non-discrimination and equality before the law. In all events, this case seems to demonstrate that for any claim process to be effective in resolving indigenous land rights issues it must be fundamentally fair. The central legal problem in this case appears to be the doctrine, which has been discussed above, that the State can extinguish Indian or indigenous land rights without due process of law and without fair market compensation. This frankly discriminatory doctrine should be rejected by the United States and by all countries where it is found as a violation of existing human rights standards requiring equality before the law.

There have also been complaints about land claim mechanisms in other countries. In Canada, the process has been reported to be extremely time consuming. In New Zealand, anger has been expressed over allegedly unauthorized settlements of claims. In Australia, the provisions of the 1993 Native Title Act were drastically changed in 1998 to make native title claims significantly more difficult, particularly by providing a substantially higher threshold test for the registration of claims. These provisions have been found racially discriminatory.

Expropriation of Indigenous Lands for National Interests, Including Development

The legacy of colonialism is probably most acute in the area of expropriation of indigenous lands, territories and resources for national economic and development interests. In every part of the globe, indigenous peoples are being impeded from proceeding with their own forms of development consistent with their own values, perspectives and interests. The concentration of extensive legal, political and economic power in the State has contributed to the problem of development and indigenous peoples' rights to lands, territories and resources.

In the Malaysian province of Sarawak, on the island of Borneo, for example, some one fifth of the land is classified as

Native Customary Rights Land (and of this, only one tenth is titled to indigenous communities), but on this land the Government can override indigenous rights for timber concessions. In Indonesia it is reported that the Government purports to respect adat, or indigenous customary rights, unless the national interest is at stake; but economic development is equated with the national interest, and indigenous land rights are thus avoided. Moreover, the strict view of international law as solely the law of nations, and not of peoples or individuals, has furthered this narrow State-based approach to development. The notion of development can be linked directly to the affirmation of "permanent sovereignty over natural resources" and the rights of States to "freely utilize and exploit" their natural resources.

Much large-scale economic and industrial development has taken place without recognition of and respect for indigenous peoples' rights to lands, territories and resources. Economic development has been largely imposed from outside, with complete disregard for the right of indigenous peoples to participate in the control, implementation and benefits of development. For years, non-governmental organizations have been saying that indigenous peoples have been deprived of much or all of their land and that it has been turned over to commercial use or for development projects.

In addition, development projects designed to benefit or which affect indigenous peoples have been carried out without the peoples concerned being consulted. National economic development schemes not only dispossess indigenous peoples of their lands, but also convert indigenous peoples into cheap labourers for industry, because the exploitation of their lands and the environmental degradation have deprived them of their livelihood.

Even in areas where economic development has resulted in the transfer of lands to indigenous communities, they have been unable fully to control such development. Specific examples include the Alaska Native Claims Settlement Act of

1971 and the James Bay and Northern Quebec Agreement of 1975. Other forms of development accompanied by blatant human rights violations include the gold mining in Yanomami Indian territory. Oil and gas exploration and exploitation, geothermal energy development, mining, dam construction, logging, agriculture, ranching and other forms of economic activity ostensibly in the national interest have had an adverse impact both on indigenous peoples who have already suffered from contact and colonialism, and on indigenous peoples in areas long isolated. Often, development takes place without indigenous peoples' consent, consultation, participation or benefit.

Removal and Relocation

Removal of indigenous peoples from their lands and territories is both a historical and a contemporary problem worldwide. Removal of indigenous peoples from their lands and territories is considered by some States as an appropriate solution or a suitable means for "removing" a problem, whether it is done purportedly to protect indigenous peoples or to promote State interests in their lands, territories and resources. Such a policy must rather be acknowledged as at best a postponement of dealing with the real matter of accommodating the rights and interests of the indigenous peoples concerned.

Removal and relocation are so widespread that the international community has responded in the context of human rights standard-setting: article 16 of ILO Convention No. 169; article 10 of the draft United Nations declaration on the rights of indigenous peoples; article XVIII.6 of the proposed Inter-American declaration on the rights of indigenous peoples. In connection with the elaboration of these specific standards, the term "forced" removal has been used to describe the coercive and abusive actions taken by Governments, without the consent of indigenous peoples, to remove them from their land. Instances of removal include the removal and relocation of the Mushuau Innu from Davis Inlet to Nutak and the High Arctic relocation of Inuit by the Government of Canada, the relocation of Inuit in northern Greenland by the Government of Denmark, and the expulsion of Kiowa Indians from their land by ranchers, with no action being taken by the United States Government despite recognition of Indian ownership of the lands in 1996.

Indigenous peoples have characterized population transfers and forced relocation as a very serious problem. These involuntary transfers and relocations have meant the loss of traditional lands and traditional ways of life, with devastating consequences for the social and economic welfare of the communities concerned.

Other Government Programmes and Policies

There are a range of other government programmes and policies which must be noted because they have been widely used and abused to justify violating indigenous land rights. It appears that some States have been unaware of the baneful effects of such programmes and policies, which are briefly addressed below.

Allotment of land to individuals: Programmes of this sort divide commonly held indigenous land and allot land to individuals or families. These programmes invariably weaken the indigenous community, nation or people and usually result in the eventual loss of most or all of the land. The supposed advantages of permitting individuals to use their land as collateral for loans is in fact far outweighed by the almost inevitable loss of the land and the resulting overall decline in resources available to indigenous peoples. The experience of the Mapuche peoples in Chile during the 1970s and 1980s is a sorrowful example.

Settlement programmes: States often view indigenous peoples' territories as areas suitable for settlement by non-indigenous peoples - even though the resources in the area provide only a modest economy for the indigenous owners.

The results of such programmes appear to be even greater poverty and social unrest. The encouragement of settlement in the Chittagong Hill Tracts in Bangladesh is an example, and the problem has also been reported in South America.

State assumption of trust title: In certain countries, particularly in the Americas, States have created the legal notion that the State itself holds title to all or most indigenous lands and holds that title in trust for the various indigenous nations, tribes or peoples. This legal status for Indian land has been given scholarly attention in the United States. There are many problems with such systems of trust title. They are usually imposed without the indigenous peoples' consent. They often give to the State extensive power to control the use of the land and its resources.

The indigenous tribe or nation often has no adequate remedy for breach of the trust responsibility or abuse of the State's power to control or dispose of their lands and resources. The responsibility of the trustee, the State, is likely to be poorly defined and is likely to be in conflict with the State's other proprietary and governmental interests. Systems of trust title, depending upon the circumstances, may make indigenous ownership of land and resources a second-class legal right, and as such they are or can be racially discriminatory.

Loan programmes: Programmes that encourage using indigenous lands as collateral for loans are likely to result in the eventual loss of indigenous lands and resources. This appears to be due in part to the relative lack of economic power of most indigenous peoples, as a result of which almost any programme that makes indigenous lands or resources a commodity in the market place is likely to result in the loss of these resources to the indigenous peoples concerned. This is not to say that indigenous peoples should not participate in market economies, but they should do so on terms of fairness and equality.

Management of sacred and cultural sites by Governments: In many countries, particular sites or areas of land that are of great religious or cultural significance to indigenous peoples are now in the ownership of the State or a governmental subdivision of the State. This situation may present a special problem, even where title to the land is not contested, when they are managed in a way that prohibits or interferes with indigenous access or indigenous religious practices tied to the site.

Failure to protect the integrity of the environment of indigenous lands and territories: For analytical purposes it is useful to identify situations that involve deprivation of indigenous land rights through activities that destroy the integrity of the environment of indigenous peoples. The problems regarding environmental degradation and development illustrate the specific matter of State failure to protect the integrity of indigenous peoples' lands, territories and resources from both direct and indirect adverse impacts. Furthermore, this question relates to global environmental problems as well as national development initiatives.

One aspect of the problem is that indigenous peoples' territories and lands do not always follow State, provincial or other administrative boundaries. Indigenous peoples whose territories transcend State boundaries include many indigenous peoples in Central and South America, the Mohawk Nation in Canada and the United States, and the Inuit of the Russian Far East, the United States, Canada and Greenland. The diversity of interests, laws, policies and national development schemes in different jurisdictions can have direct adverse impacts upon the integrity of indigenous lands, territories and resources. States claiming jurisdiction or authority over territories often do not recognize the impacts that their policies will have outside their borders.

In addition, though Governments may initiate and require environmental impact assessments, too often indigenous peoples' perspectives and values are overlooked in State efforts to mitigate or minimize environmental degradation. Other failures to protect the integrity of indigenous lands, territories and resources include transboundary pollution, dumping of hazardous or toxic waste, ocean dumping, ozone layer depletion, militarization and diminishing supplies of fresh water.

The profound, highly complex and sensitive relationship that indigenous peoples have to their lands, territories and resources must be taken into account in protecting the integrity of their environment from degradation. Again it includes social, economic, cultural and spiritual dimensions which must not be overlooked in the present discussion. Cultures that have flourished as an integral part of the environment, cannot continue to tolerate disruption. The dependence of indigenous peoples upon the integrity of their lands, territories and resources remains a highly significant factor.

Internal Self- Determination

An important dimension in affirming indigenous land rights is the exercise of a measure of control over lands, territories and resources by indigenous peoples through their own institutions. Though rights to lands, territories and resources may be affirmed, the exercise of internal self-determination, in the form of control over and decision-making concerning development, use of natural resources, management and conservation measures, is often absent. For example, indigenous people may be free to carry out their traditional economic activities such as hunting, fishing, trapping, gathering or cultivating, but may be unable to control development that may diminish or destroy these activities.

Solutions for Land Issues and Problems

There are many positive and practical examples of advances worldwide regarding indigenous land rights. Most of these developments represent a change in philosophy, a slight retreat from the orientation which denied the rights of indigenous peoples towards a modern human rights programme that is beginning to embrace the values, perspectives and philosophies of indigenous peoples. However, no tidal change has taken place. Despite the advances and positive developments, urgent problems remain.

Positive measures may be divided into five groups:

(a) judicial mechanisms;

(b) mechanisms for negotiation;

(c) constitutional reform and framework legislation;

(d) indigenous peoples' initiatives; and

(e) human rights standards.

Judicial Mechanisms

Between the 1933 decision of the Permanent Court of International Justice (Eastern Greenland) and the Western Sahara decision of the International Court of Justice in 1975, it is clear that legal thought had evolved with regard to the place of indigenous peoples. The Marshall decisions of the United States Supreme Court have been interpreted as being both good and bad: good in the sense that Marshall insisted upon the recognition of Indian land rights and the right to self-government; however, Marshall's construction of these rights was within the framework of the doctrine of discovery.

An example of the mixed results or limitations of judicial mechanisms is the Mabo case in Australia. This decision was positive in that it denounced the doctrine of terra nullius. However, from the perspective of Aboriginal peoples in Australia, the decision did not remove all of the cultural biases, nor did it flesh out or fully examine the assumed State authority and power to determine the extent of indigenous land rights. Judges, like others, are likely to be fearful of the unknown cost of resolving these issues. Hence, there is an apparent tendency to ensure that openings for interpretation remain.

Pastoral leases cover vast areas of land and are essentially interests granted by government for the purpose of raising sheep, cattle or other animals. This case, combined with the Mabo decision, led to the enactment of the Native Title Amendment Act in 1998 exercised legislative power to extinguish indigenous or native title and thus practically negate most of the legal rights recognized by the Court. For a limited class of cases and a limited number of indigenous peoples, United States law provides a means for the return of indigenous lands. The Supreme Court has decided that the title to land taken in violation of a certain Act of Congress remains the property of the Indian owners.

However, practically no Indian lands have actually been returned by action of the United States courts. Numerous suits for the recovery of lands have been filed and in several cases negotiation and legislation have led to the return of significant areas of land to a few Indian tribes. Another example of a judicial or quasi-judicial mechanism is the Waitangi Tribunal in New Zealand, which is a statutory body created to address claims by Maori of breaches of the Treaty of Waitangi. The decisions of the Waitangi Tribunal have been credited with helping to resolve some long-standing Maori land grievances. However, there have also been criticisms and complaints based upon the Tribunal's limited power, as well as of some decisions and negotiated settlements reached in connection with cases before the Tribunal.

At present, it is safe to say that the use of judicial mechanisms may be risky because of the problem of different interpretive tools, the subjective and highly political nature of these State-chartered forums, and continuing cultural biases demonstrated by Governments. The mechanisms referred to above represent some examples of the judicial mechanisms which exist and have been employed. Governments and indigenous organizations will be called upon to supply further information about positive measures with regard to judicial mechanisms.

Mechanisms for Negotiation

Mechanisms for negotiation may allow for a broader set of issues, concepts and perspectives to explore the accommodation of indigenous peoples' rights to lands. They may also provide a greater opportunity for both sides to achieve or create genuine understanding and to engage in confidence-building. Negotiation, if undertaken with full respect for and recognition of the fundamental rights of indigenous peoples, can also contribute to ongoing and lasting political and legal relationships. Such an alternative may prove to be more constructive to both Governments and indigenous peoples, as well as others.

A recent example of the creation of an international mechanism for negotiation is the formation of the Arctic Council, which includes eight Arctic-rim States and representatives of the Association of Small Nations of the Russian North, the Nordic Saami Council and the Inuit Circumpolar Conference. The basic document of this new body also provides for the direct participation of other indigenous peoples' organizations from this geographic region. Though indigenous peoples are not entirely pleased with the few qualifications put into the document, they are nonetheless at the negotiating table and able to register their concerns relating to environmental and development matters.

Another international mechanism was the procedure that resulted in the negotiated peace agreements in Guatemala. Within this process, the United Nations played a role in the conclusion of the Agreement on the Identity and Rights of Indigenous Peoples. The Agreement includes far-reaching provisions on indigenous lands, restitution, acquisition of land and other measures.

In Canada, the British Columbia Treaty Commission was established by Canada, the Government of British Columbia and the First Nations Summit (an organization of indigenous First Nations), with a mandate to facilitate the negotiation of modern treaties in the province of British Columbia. The Commission consists of five commissioners: two nominated by the Summit, one nominated by each of the federal and provincial governments, and a Chief Commissioner chosen by all three principals. The Commission opened its doors in December 1993. As of October 1997, the Commission had accepted statements of intent to negotiate treaties from 51 First Nations (representing over 70 per cent of the First Nations in the province), had made annual funding allocations to First Nations for participation in negotiations and had declared 42 negotiation tables as ready.

According to the Government of Canada, as of May 1998, more than 30 framework agreements had been signed, and these First Nations had entered into "agreement-in-principle negotiations". Recent negotiated agreements include the Nunavut Agreement (creating a new territory in northern Canada) and a number of other agreements with First Nations in Canada. According to the Government, 12 comprehensive land claims agreements have been settled since the announcement of the Federal Government's comprehensive claims policy in 1973. The Nisga'a Treaty is the furthest along in the treaty-making process, having been approved by both the Nisga'a and the provincial parliament of British Columbia in 1999. The agreement recognizes Nisga'a rights to approximately 2,000 square kilometres of land and acknowledges their rights to self-government in that territory.

The Nisga'a Treaty is expected to set a precedent that will be used to resolve approximately 50 similar claims brought by Indian peoples in Canada. Upon its approval by the Federal Government of Canada, the Nisga'a Treaty will be the thirteenth land claim settled. The six most recently completed agreements are with the Yukon First Nations and include similar self-government agreements. The Federal Government has expressed its commitment to maintaining momentum on claims settlement and in 1998 reported participating in approximately 70 modern treaty negotiations. In its submission to the Special Rapporteur, the Government provided the following observations:

"Steady progress is being made. Settling claims does take time as it is important to get it right: treaties are solemn and legally-binding documents which are protected by the Constitution of Canada. It also takes time because negotiations are complex, involving many stakeholders and intersecting jurisdictions. In Canada, there are three parties at the table: the Federal Government, the provincial (or territorial) government, and the Aboriginal group. Separate federal-provincial discussions are required on many key aspects such as cost-sharing and jurisdictional arrangements, while a very wide range of lands and resources and self-government issues are on the table. Public and private legal interests must be dealt with fairly, and negotiations are often complicated by several Aboriginal groups claiming the same area."

The Government of Canada drew particular attention to negotiated settlements of land claims as a positive and practical measure for achieving desirable goals with respect to indigenous peoples' relationship to lands and resources. The Government pointed out in its submission: "Land settlements provide many opportunities, in that much can and has been done within the claims negotiation process to further the goals of Aboriginal people for a continuing relationship to lands and resources in their traditional territories. Land claims agreements in Canada have provided Aboriginal groups with rights and benefits which include:

— full ownership of certain lands in the area covered by the settlement; guaranteed wildlife harvesting rights;
— guaranteed participation in land, water, wildlife and environmental management throughout the settlement area (typically by membership on committees, boards or other decision-making bodies);
— financial compensation; resource revenue-sharing;
— specific measures to stimulate economic development; and

— a role in the management of heritage resources and national parks of the settlement area.

Co-management arrangements have reflected the principle of parity of membership between Aboriginal and government representatives; and have respected and incorporated the traditional knowledge of Aboriginal people, as well as scientific knowledge. "Financial benefits in settlement agreements can provide Aboriginal communities with much needed capital for investment and economic growth, while increased training and educational opportunities can contribute to self-sufficiency. Royalty sharing arrangements can provide an important ongoing source of revenue. In these and other ways, modern treaties provide an important springboard to economic and political growth."

The friendly settlement procedure of the Inter-American Commission on Human Rights has provided a context for the negotiation of indigenous land rights. When a human rights petition is filed with the Commission, the Commission has the competence, pursuant to the American Convention on Human Rights, to "place itself at the disposal of the parties concerned with a view to reaching a friendly settlement of the matter on the basis of respect for human rights recognized in the Convention". In March of 1998, the Commission announced the settlement of a land claim between the Government of Paraguay and the indigenous communities of Lamenxay and Riachito pursuant to an agreement to transfer a large area of land to the Indian claimants. This settlement is the first agreement in the inter-American human rights system which restores land rights to an indigenous community.

In another case, in February 1999, the Commission formally oversaw the beginning of formal negotiations between the Government of Belize and the Maya Indian people of southern Belize. The context of the negotiations is a long campaign by Maya leaders to secure recognition of their lands. These indigenous peoples had found themselves without any formal, legal rights to the lands where they have traditionally lived. The land is regarded by the Government as simply "public" land. Since 1993, the Government had secretly granted 17 logging concessions to log more than 500,000 acres of Maya land, and had granted oil and gas concessions covering practically the entire area, all without consultation with the Maya.

The Maya filed legal proceedings in the courts of Belize without success and in 1998 filed a petition with the Inter-American Commission on Human Rights asserting that the concessions and the failure to recognize Maya land rights were a violation of their human rights. Negotiations have just begun. The Government's willingness to negotiate under the auspices of the Inter-American Commission suggests that this may prove to be a useful and positive approach for resolving this land issue.

Finally, the substantive, constructive and formal dialogue at the international, national and local levels concerning international indigenous human rights standards may prove to be a fruitful method or mechanism for creating understanding about the values and perspectives of indigenous peoples. Such a process of education will be necessary for effective steps to be taken towards resolving long-standing conflicts and understanding the implications of accommodating the competing rights and interests of indigenous peoples and States.

Constitutional Reform and Framework Legislation

In certain countries, significant steps have been taken to recognize or secure indigenous land rights through specific legislation to return certain areas of land or through general, framework legislation to protect indigenous land or resolve indigenous land issues. A particularly notable example in recent years is the Constitution of Brazil, adopted in 1988. The Constitution incorporates significant provisions calling for the demarcation and protection of indigenous lands. The Native Title Act of 1993 in Australia is another example. In Canada, the Constitution Act of 1982, section 35, gives constitutional protection to then-existing aboriginal land rights; and land claim settlements, as treaties, are now similarly given constitutional protection.

Some countries have taken more specific action to return land to indigenous peoples or to recognize or respect indigenous land areas. Examples include the return of land to indigenous peoples in Argentina. Under constitutional reform laws of 1994, the Government has now returned almost 4 million acres to some of Argentina's 600,000 indigenous peoples and reportedly plans to hand over 988,400 more acres by 1999. In Colombia, similar return of land has taken place in recent years. Information about the success of these measures and the problems associated with them deserve close attention.

The Greenland Home Rule Act of November 1978 is probably one of the best examples of constructive framework legislation to accommodate the rights and aspirations of indigenous peoples. The rights of ownership to lands in Greenland have been arranged in a very distinct fashion, consistent with the Greenlandic Inuit land tenure systems. One significant feature of the Act is the granting to the Inuit of authority to make decisions concerning the use of the lands. In particular, with regard to development activities, the Greenland Home Rule Government, or Landsstyret, which is elected by the Parliament, has veto power over development activities.

Despite the failure of a referendum to approve the Charlottetown Accord, the constitutional debate in Canada allowed for the exploration of a more effective context for the realization of rights and principles that may guide relations between the Government and indigenous peoples. This process generated awareness and increased knowledge, through national debate, about the distinct rights and status of indigenous peoples in Canada. Again, though it did not respond sufficiently to such fundamental concerns as the need of indigenous peoples for an adequate land and resource base and the obligations of the State, the Accord provided for a constructive political and legal relationship, in the context of the Constitution, between indigenous peoples and the Government.

Indigenous Peoples' Initiatives

It must be noted that indigenous peoples themselves are initiating various projects and programmes with regard to their lands, territories and resources which contribute to the safeguarding and promotion of their rights. Examples include management and co-management of resources in Alaska and elsewhere. Indigenous peoples are also contributing to global and national environmental protection initiatives.

Indigenous peoples in certain countries have initiated mapping projects as a means for documenting and specifying their traditional land ownership and land use practices. This may prove to be an important means for creating broader awareness and understanding of indigenous land ownership and for creating a basis for eventual legal recognition and protection of these land and resource rights. In Belize, the mapping project of the Maya Indian people of the Toledo district resulted in the publication in 1998 of the Maya Atlas: The Struggle to Preserve Maya Land in Southern Belize, which is said to be the first indigenous-produced atlas in the world.

The Maya Atlas, produced by the Toledo Maya Cultural Council and the Toledo Alcaldes Association, documents the Mopan and Ke'kchi Maya's traditional and current use of their land and includes a unique description of Maya history, culture, land tenure and socio-economic activities. The Maya Atlas contains maps of every Maya village in southern Belize - each one hand drawn by Maya community researchers who interviewed every household in the village. The atlas is part of an effort to win legal protection for Maya land. Mapping by indigenous peoples as a means of clarifying land rights is also being done in other countries. The role of indigenous peoples in the Arctic Council, which primarily concerns itself with environmental protection and development in the Arctic, is another useful example in this respect.

Human Rights Standards and Mechanisms

The existing and emerging norms and minimum standards contained in the Rio Declaration, the Convention on Biological Diversity, ILO Convention No. 169, the proposed Organization of American States American declaration on the rights of indigenous peoples and the draft United Nations declaration on the rights of indigenous peoples should all be seen as a way to resolve the problems between States and indigenous peoples. The various mechanisms established for dealing with human rights complaints have been used to some extent by indigenous peoples.

In addition, the emerging human rights norms relating to the right to development, intergenerational rights, the right to peace and the right to a safe and healthy environment are areas in which indigenous peoples are beginning to influence old thinking and bring about the progressive development of standards that are more sensitive, responsive and useful to indigenous peoples and humankind generally. The conclusions of the Bruntdland report should not be omitted from this review of change and development of human rights standards.

Our Common Future, the report of the Bruntdland Commission, gave recognition to the unique situation of indigenous peoples: "The starting point for a just and humane policy for such groups is the recognition and protection of their traditional rights to land and other resources that sustain their way of life – rights they may define in terms that do not fit into standard legal systems. These groups' own institutions to regulate rights and obligations are crucial for maintaining harmony with nature and the environmental awareness characteristic of the traditional way of life. Hence the recognition of traditional rights must go hand in hand with measures to protect the local institutions that enforce responsibility in resource use. And this recognition must also give local communities a decisive voice in the decisions about resource use in their areas."

3

Indigenous Peoples and Human Rights

The creation of the United Nations provided an ideal forum for the development and adoption of international human rights instruments. Other instruments have been adopted at regional levels reflecting the particular human rights concerns of the region involved. Most States have also adopted constitutions and other laws that formally protect basic human rights. Often the language used by States is drawn directly from the international human rights instruments. International human rights law consists mainly of treaties and customs as well as declarations, guidelines and principles.

International Treaties

A treaty is an agreement by States to be bound by particular rules. International treaties have different designations, such as covenants, charters, protocols, conventions, accords and agreements. A treaty is legally binding on those States that have consented to be bound by the provisions of the treaty-in other words, those States that are party to the treaty. A State can become a party to a treaty by ratification or accession. Ratification is a State's formal expression of consent to be bound by a treaty. Only a State that has previously signed the treaty can ratify it. Ratification consists of two procedural acts:

on the domestic level, it requires approval by the appropriate constitutional organ. On the international level, the instrument of ratification is formally transmitted to the place where the instrument is held. That may be a State or an international organization, such as the United Nations.

Accession is the agreement to be bound by a treaty by a State that has not previously signed the instrument. States ratify treaties both before and after the treaty has entered into force. The same applies to accession. In order for most international treaties to be applied, other national laws must be adopted. In some States, treaties are superior to domestic law; in other States treaties are given Constitutional status; in yet other countries, only certain provisions of a treaty are incorporated into domestic law. In ratifying a treaty, a State may enter reservations to that treaty, indicating that, while it consents to be bound by most of the provisions, the State does not agree to be bound by certain specific provisions. However, a reservation may not defeat the object and purpose of the treaty. Moreover, States are bound by those treaty provisions that have become part of customary international law or are peremptory rules of international law, such as the prohibition against torture. Consult the leaflet on Human Rights Treaty Bodies and Indigenous Peoples to see how the treaty bodies can be used to protect indigenous rights.

Customary International Law

Customary international law is the term used to describe a general and consistent practice followed by States that derives from a sense of legal obligation. For example, while the Universal Declaration of Human Rights is not a binding treaty, some of its provisions have the character of customary international law in that they are consistently applied by States. Declarations, resolutions, etc. adopted by UN organs General norms of international law principles and practices to which most States would agree are often stated in declarations, proclamations, standard rules, guidelines, recommendations and principles. While they are not legally binding on States, they nevertheless represent a broad consensus of the international community and, therefore, have a strong moral force on the practice of States in their international relations. The value of such instruments rests in their recognition and acceptance by a large number of States. Even without binding legal effect, they may be seen as declaring principles widely accepted within the international community.

The obligation to protect, promote and ensure the enjoyment of human rights is the prime responsibility of States. Many human rights are owed by States to all people within their territories, while certain human rights are owed by a State to particular groups of people: for example, the right to vote in elections is only owed to citizens of a State. States are obligated to make sure that human rights are protected by both providing effective remedies for persons whose rights are violated and preventing human rights violations against persons within their territories. Under international law, the enjoyment of certain rights can be restricted in specific circumstances.

For example, if an individual is found guilty of a crime after a fair trial, a State may lawfully restrict a person's freedom of movement by imprisonment. Restrictions on civil and political rights may only be imposed if the limitation is determined by law, but only for the purposes of respecting the rights of others and meeting the just requirements of morality, public order and the general welfare in a democratic society. Economic, social and cultural rights may be limited by law, but only if the limitation is compatible with the nature of the rights and only to promote the general welfare in a democratic society. In a legitimate and declared state of emergency, States can take measures that limit or suspend the enjoyment of certain rights.

Such derogations are permitted only to the extent necessary for the situation and may never involve discrimination based on race, colour, gender, language, religion or social origin. Any derogation must be reported to the Secretary-General of the Untied Nations. However, in accordance with article 4, paragraph 3 of the International Covenant on Civil and Political Rights (ICCPR), certain human rights-those called non-derogable rights-may never be suspended or restricted, even in situations of war and armed conflict. These include the right to life, freedom from torture, freedom from enslavement or servitude, and freedom of thought, conscience and religion. During times of armed conflict when humanitarian law applies, human rights law is also still in force.

With the horrors of the Second World War in mind, the founders of the UN built into the organization's purposes and structures a strong emphasis on human rights. They believed that protecting human rights would provide freedom, justice and peace for all peoples. In its early years, the UN established basic human rights standards intended to serve all people and all nations. The organization has expanded the range of those standards throughout its existence.

Systems of UN Human Rights

It is useful to distinguish between those bodies and mechanisms of the UN human rights system that have been set up as a result of resolutions and decisions of the UN system and those that have been set up by legally binding human rights treaties. Those bodies of the former type are said to make up the charter-based system. The latter type make up the treaty-based system. The UN Charter allowed the UN to set up a number of bodies to discuss and take action on human rights questions and to draft new standards. The most important of these Charter-based bodies is the Commission on Human Rights (CHR), which meets for six weeks each year in Geneva, the Sub-Commission on the Promotion and Protections of Human Rights and the Third Committee of the General Assembly.

The most important body for indigenous peoples is the Working Group on Indigenous Populations (WGIP). The major international human rights treaties have special bodies to supervise governments' implementation of those treaties. The main function of these treaty bodies is to consider and comment on reports from governments on how they observe the treaties to which they are party. Some of these bodies consider complaints from individuals who allege that their governments have violated their rights. The Office of the High Commissioner for Human Rights, a permanent office staffed by UN officials and head quartered in Geneva, provides support for all the UN's activities in the field of human rights.

The Office is part of the UN's Secretariat and administers and coordinates the UN's human rights programme, organizes meetings, prepares studies and reports, and disseminates information and publications. The Office is headed by the High Commissioner, who is the UN's most senior official responsible for human rights issues. The High Commissioner has an important role in promoting human rights through the UN system.

The UN's first major achievement in the field of human rights was the General Assembly's adoption of the Universal Declaration of Human Rights in 1948. Members of the UN disputed the wording of the Universal Declaration at the time, but the declaration was finally adopted by consensus. The Universal Declaration is an eloquent and far-reaching description of the rights of all human beings. In addition, it gives individuals a place in international law that they had never had before. Many other human rights instruments are based on the Universal Declaration.

Fundamental Rights

— the right to equality and freedom from discrimination

— the right to life, liberty and personal security

— freedom from torture and degrading treatment

— the right to equality before the law
— the right to a fair trial
— the right to privacy
— freedom of belief and religion
— freedom of opinion
— freedom of peaceful assembly and association
— the right to participate in government
— the right to social security
— the right to work
— the right to adequate standards of living
— the right to education

The Universal Declaration of Human Rights, the UN drafted two treaties, called covenants, which contain provisions of the Universal Declaration and made them legally binding on countries that agreed to become parties to the covenants. The two covenants are the International Covenant on Civil and Political Rights (ICCPR) and the International Covenant on Economic, Social and Cultural Rights (ICESCR). They were adopted by the General Assembly in 1966, but did not enter into force until 1976, after a sufficient number of countries had agreed to become party to them.

Other instruments have specified how these rights apply to specific groups of people, such as women or children. New instruments, such as the Declaration on the Right to Development, have introduced concepts that had not been part of the thinking of the drafters of the 1948 Universal Declaration. Other important human rights treaties and declarations include:

— the Convention on the Prevention and Punishment of the Crime of Genocide the International Convention on the Elimination of All Forms of Racial Discrimination (CERD)

- the Convention Against Torture and Other Cruel, Inhuman or Degrading Treatment or Punishment (CAT)
- the Convention on the Elimination of All Forms of Discrimination against Women (CEDAW)
- the Convention on the Rights of the Child
- Convention 169 of the International Labour Organization concerning Indigenous and Tribal Peoples in Independent Countries (ILO 169)
- the Declaration on the Right to Development
- the Declaration on the Rights of Persons Belonging to National or Ethnic, Religious and Linguistic Minorities
- the Declaration on the Elimination of All Forms of Intolerance and of Discrimination Based on Religion or Belief .

There are many other human rights instruments. Work continues, though more slowly, on developing new standards. One of the most important new sets of standards for indigenous peoples is found in the draft Declaration on the Rights of Indigenous Peoples. Here explained the difference between legally binding instruments-treaties, covenants, conventions and protocols-and instruments that are not legally binding, but have morally persuasive force, such as declarations and principles. If you think that your rights are being violated in some way, it makes a difference whether the instrument that cites the right is, or is not, legally binding. If it is legally binding, such as the Convention on the Elimination of Racial Discrimination, it may be possible to express your concern to a UN treaty body.

The instrument that sets out the right is not legally binding, there is no treaty body that you can go to for assistance. Whether or not an instrument is legally binding will make a difference to your ability to take action. You need to know which legally binding instruments your country is a party to. If your country is a party to the complaints mechanisms that are provided for under the International Covenant on Civil and Political Rights, the Convention on the Elimination of All Forms of Racial Discrimination, or the Convention Against Torture , you may be able to lodge complaints. Even when there is no mechanism for submitting a complaint, as is true of the International Covenant on Economic, Social and Cultural Rights, and the Convention on the Rights of the Child, you can still provide information to the relevant treaty body alleging that your country is in breach of its legal obligations.

Table 1 sets out some of the instruments that are particularly relevant to indigenous peoples. It indicates which instruments are legally binding and which are not, and the range of actions available under each type of instrument, depending on whether or not your country is a party to the instrument in question. Government is violating rights found in nonbinding instruments, there is no official body to which you can appeal. Even when the draft Declaration on the Rights of Indigenous Peoples is finalized, it will not include a legally effective complaints mechanism. You will be able to draw national and international attention to violations of the Declaration, but the impact will be political rather than legal.

UN legislative bodies, such as the General Assembly, ECOSOC or the Commission on Human Rights, are similar to parliaments. Member States participate in discussions and may vote. These bodies consider issues of concern and formulate outcomes, which are then set out in what is called a resolution or decision. When a resolution is approved by a majority of voting members of a specific body, it is said to have been adopted. If all of the participating members approve the proposed outcome, a vote is not necessary and the resolution it is said to have been adopted by consensus . The writing, or drafting, of human rights standards can be a long and difficult process. The governments involved represent peoples from all parts of the world, with differing political, economic and

Table 1.Types of International Human Rights Instruments

Type of instrument	Name of instrument	Possibilities for Actions on violations
Legally-binding, *with* a complaints mechanism	- International Covenant on Civil and Political Rights - Convention on the Civil and Political Rights of Racial Discrimination - Convention Against Torture	- Complaints to a treaty body - Comment on or criticism of content of a report - Public criticism in UN or media over violations
Legally binding, but *no* complaints mechanism	- International Covenant on Economic, Social and Cultural Rights - Convention on the Rights of the Child - Convention on the Elimination of all forms of Discrimination Against Women	- Comment on or criticism of content of a report - Public criticism in UN or media over violations - NGO reports to the Committees
Not legally binding	- Universal Declaration of Human Rights - Other declarations - Draft Declaration on the Rights of Indigenous Peoples	- Public criticism in UN or media over violations

cultural systems. It is generally believed that for a human rights instrument to be effective, it should have the support of many governments.

Indigenous Peoples, Mining, and International Law

Upon Columbus arrival to the 'New World', existing legal doctrines were strained by the first contact with indigenous peoples in the Americas. In the enterprise of conquest and domination, two dimensions must be clearly separated: one, that of legal discourse and, second that of the lure for gold driving the process. Although these two dimensions are inextricably interrelated, they followed different paths, which explains the divergence between normative theory and on the ground history.

When Europeans arrived to Northern Africa and to the Americas, a highly sophisticated legal dialogue between the Pope and the Kings justified the enterprise of conquest. Several Papal Bulls, granted for the protection of the local indigenous populations and for the spread of Christianity and civilization among them, gave the Portuguese an effective monopoly over their newly established colonies in Northern Africa. These bulls built on centuries of legal and philosophical debate: from the crusades, through the question of investitures, to the status of Indians in the 'New World'.

This last topic burdened the Council of Burgos, early in the Spanish history of conquest, which tried to resolve whether it was legal to enslave Indians in the name of Christianity. The Dominican friars who had travelled to the Indies, like Montecinos and Bartolomé de las Casas, provided overwhelming evidence of the brutality that Spanish conquerors unleashed over the local indigenous populations, enslaving them and forcing them to work in the gold mines. Demographic deterioration occurred through maltreatment, enslavement, suicide, punishment for resistance, warfare, malnutrition due to destruction of the natural environment, and outright extermination. The figures are striking: the entire population of the Americas decreased by 95 per cent in the century and a half following the first encounter.

Francisco de Vittoria extended natural law reasoning to the international plane, arguing that all nations and all peoples of the earth were bound by the Ius Gentium. According to his theory, indigenous peoples had true dominion over their lands and could not be dispossessed without just cause. This statement of principle, which is often quoted as his great contribution to indigenous peoples land rights, is offset by his discussion on justifications for Spanish conquest. On this last plane, Vittoria argued that according to natural law, which in his conception is binding upon all peoples, Spaniards had the right to send missionaries, to trade, and to use communal Indian lands. Where Indians placed obstacles to the exercise of these international natural law rights, Spaniards would be justified in resorting to arms to defend their natural law rights.

In other regions of the world, international legal arguments followed different paths. For example, in Australia and other places, the legal doctrine of terra nullius was resorted to appropriate indigenous lands. According to this roman-law theory, lands that had no owner could be appropriated by nations manifesting such intention. Accordingly, a fictional representation of the world came about: lands were regarded empty or abandoned in spite of indigenous occupancy. The terra nullius doctrine was apparently set aside by the International Court of Justice in the 1975 Western Sahara Case, where the Court seemed to acknowledge the existence of a theory of international land tenure based on a non-European conception of title.

Nevertheless, despite finding that there were "legal ties of allegiance" and "some rights relating to the land", the ICJ still applied the European notion of acquisition of title as the exclusive criterion. Another legal theory utilized to deprive indigenous peoples of their lands was that of discovery.

According to this mode of land acquisition, in the context of European legal thought, a territory belonged to that nation that discovered it. Like terra nullius, this theory ignored previous occupancy of the land. Discovery, however, received only limited recognition by international adjudicatory bodies, which usually required that discovery as a symbolic act be followed by effective occupation.

The enterprise of conquest followed by Europeans in the 'New World' also took legal shape through international treaties concluded with local peoples. There was a multiplicity of treaties, which makes unitary categories impossible, but at least three modalities must be singled out. First, certain treaties provided for cession of indigenous lands to nations or even individuals. Other treaties contemplated the creation of a dual regime, granting the colonial power rights and duties relating to external government, but retaining indigenous autonomy over lands and affairs. The last category of interest here is made up of those treaties which settled borders or frontiers between the conquerors and indigenous peoples, and which thus demarcated spheres of sovereignty and jurisdiction.

These three categories of treaties produced different legal effects, which for the purpose of analysis may be reduced to two: (1) some treaties had the effect of depriving indigenous peoples of their lands and external self-determination. According to these legal arrangements, indigenous peoples either ceded their lands or became subject to the government of the occupying power, thus losing their international personality. In contrast, (2) treaties that settled boundaries had the effect of recognizing international personality to the indigenous communities that entered into them. In fact, in the legal practice of the European powers of the time, these boundary treaties were regarded of equal status with other treaties. These treaties provide further evidence that indigenous peoples were subjects of international law during the XV-XVIIIth centuries.

New International Society

During the XIXth century, European nation-states that had consolidated after the Westphalian break with the medieval era had entered into a new stage in the progressive development of their laws and customs. After Westphalia, the new sovereigns emphasized the consensual dimensions of international law, whereby the will and recognition of the state was the principal source of international law. Indeed, in struggling to set past theories aside, during the XIXth century international law was regarded as the law existing between civilized nations, that was, Christian European States. International law would admit as international subjects only European states and those entities recognized by European States. Accordingly, indigenous peoples were not recognized as sovereigns and/or civilized by the European states, and were thus marginalized from the international community.

The Cayuga Indians Arbitration of 1926 between the UK and the US provides evidence of this shift of the international legal system towards the exclusion of indigenous peoples. In this case, the tribunal concluded that the Cayuga Nation and the Cayuga as individuals had no status under international law. The Tribunal still held that general principles of equity, fair dealing and justice recognized by international law established that the Cayuga in Canada were entitled to receive the annuity covenanted with the State of New York in a 1795 treaty.

The political and legal principle of self-determination triggered a radical transformation in the international political landscape, witnessing the creation of a multitude of new states. The principle of Uti Possidetis Juris came to inform the demarcation of boundaries of the newly independent states. According to this principle, the colonial administrative boundaries at the time of independence would determine the frontiers of the new states. Clearly, the Uti Possidetis principle provided the new states with an accessible source of legitimacy and stability in the definition of their boundaries, thereby preventing conflict between them, as well as intervention by the colonial powers. At the same time, the principle transplanted the inequitable structures of colonial domination onto the indigenous occupants of lands, whose territories were again artificially separated by alien frontiers.

The ICJ has ignored indigenous title to land in several cases, including its recent 1994 decision on the Territorial Dispute between Libya and Chad over a tract of territory believed to contain uranium deposits. Another clear example of the application of the uti possidetis jurisis the Gulf of Fonseca case, where El Salvador drew the Chamber's attention to the potential conflict between claims based on Spanish documents and those on earlier rights of Indian Poblaciones. The Chamber held that, 95-6 It was the administrative boundaries between the Spanish colonial administrative units, not the boundaries between the Indian settlements as such, that were transformed by the operation of the uti possidetis juris, into international boundaries in 1821. The New International Economic Order (NIEO) was a process that sought to radically transform the anciéne international regime based on colonial domination, on natural resource plunder, and on inequitable production and consumption patterns into a more fair and just world order.

In the NIEO, developing nations would exercise complete sovereignty over their natural resources, as a means of recuperating the wealth that the powerful 'empires' had been exploiting within their boundaries. Consequently, the emphasis of the NIEO was placed on achieving external economic independence, recuperating control over their economic wealth, and implementing development schemes. However, the consequences that these restructuring processes brought about, particularly as they affected vulnerable local communities within the territories of new states, are not to be overlooked.

Culturally distinct groups from the dominant society were "expropriated" the natural resources on which their whole civilization had been erected along the centuries past. The NIEO was explicit: natural resources would now belong to the State, not to their traditional users. This new reality obviously created a conflict between the dominant society and marginalized groups; ultimately between the State and customary holders of native title to the natural resources. The paradox lies in that the new States wanted to liberate themselves from external powers, and in so doing, they oppressed communities that had been using the natural resources within their lands since times immemorial.

Emergence of Human Rights Standards

The emergence of human rights standards and supervisory machinery has transformed the structures of the international legal system. The sovereignty of the State has been qualified by the duty to protect and promote the rights of its citizens, now an issue of common concern to the international community and which thus escapes the domain of exclusive jurisdiction reserved for the State. This section will explore three angles of the human rights dimension of indigenous peoples lands: first, an outline of substantive rights, including the right to exist as distinct communities and self-determination. Subsequently, the framework of international legal instruments together with an outline of the institutional bodies that have been created to oversee the implementation of human rights norms.

Right to Existence

The right to exist of peoples has been elevated to the category of ius cogens in international law, whereby no international treaty may derogate from the obligation incumbent upon all members of the international community to prevent and punish the crime of genocide. Further, genocide has been recognized as an international crime which raises universal jurisdiction to prosecute their perpetrators. The 1948

International Convention on the Prevention and Punishment of the Crime of Genocide, passed unanimously by the United Nations General Assembly, establishes the elements of the crime of genocide. The definitions of the Genocide Convention were reproduced verbatim by the 1998 Rome Statute of the International Criminal Court, whose preamble recognizes that the cultures of all peoples are pieced together in a shared heritage and that this delicate mosaic may be shattered at any time.

In the interpretation of the elements of the crime of genocide, regard must be taken to these preambular ideas; as the International Court of Justice stated in the 1951 case concerning Reservations to the Genocide Convention, the principles underlying the Convention are principles which are recognized by civilized nations as binding on States, even without conventional obligation. It has been often said that the Genocide Convention deals only with the physical destruction of groups and not with cultural genocide or ethnocide; further, the convention requires specific intent to eliminate the group as such, in whole or in part. These two elements have been under question during the last decades, on the grounds that the close interrelationship between indigenous peoples and their lands renders the distinction between cultural and physical genocide artificial.

On this vein, it has been advanced that the cultural and physical dimensions of existence cannot be separated in the case of indigenous peoples, given the religious and material integration between indigenous peoples and their environment. Further, the 'direct intent' scienter standard has also been challenged as excessively narrow to encompass deliberate acts of environmental destruction that disguise behind the rhetoric of development and economic growth. On this point, it has been suggested that the 'aims and effect' standard would afford greater protection to indigenous peoples and their lands. The right to exist of peoples also means that they cannot be deprived of their means of subsistence. In the case of indigenous peoples, it has been argued that the right to their means of subsistence encompasses and protects their rivers, forests, seas, and other sources of livelihoods. Consequently, mining operations that pollute the rivers, open roads into the forests, and destroy local ecosystems would violate this fundamental human rights standard.

Right to Self-determination

The debate over the contours and applicability of the right to self-determination to indigenous peoples remains the most contested issue in the discussion of the United Nations draft declaration on the rights of indigenous peoples. In that debate, two dimensions of this right have been clearly delineated: one external as the right to international personality and/or to secede from existing states, and another internal as the right to autonomy over local affairs and government, including land and natural resources. From an international legal perspective self-determination is a collective right vested upon all peoples, which has been recognized by both the International Covenant on Economic, Social, and Cultural Rights and the International Covenant on Civil and Political Rights.

All peoples have the right of self-determination. By virtue of that right they freely determine their political status and freely pursue their economic, social and cultural development. It has been much discussed whether self-determination applies beyond the colonial context. It must be stressed that the formulation of the principle of self-determination in the United Nations Charter occurs in the context of the objectives of the organization, rather than in the context of decolonization. It must also be noted that United Nations General Assembly declarations and resolutions that address the issue of decolonization emphasize that the right to self-determination should not be used to disrupt the unity of the state or its territorial integrity.

Right to Equality

The right to equality and non-discrimination lies at the heart of international human rights law. Accordingly, racism is condemned in all its forms, a theme that was explored exhaustively during the recent 2001 Durban World Conference against Racism, Racial Discrimination, Xenophobia and Related Intolerance. The conference affirmed the importance attached to the values of solidarity, respect, tolerance, and multi-culturalism and recognized that indigenous peoples have been victims of discrimination for centuries. The conference also recognized the special relationship that indigenous peoples have with the land as the basis for their spiritual, physical, and cultural existence.

The International Convention on the Elimination of All Forms of Racial Discrimination (CERD) deals specifically with the problem of discrimination, and its supervisory body has received communications alleging violation of this right. Such is the case with Australia's 1998 Native Title Amendment Act, which allowed unilateral government extinguishment of native land rights. The Committee was of the view that this amendment act violated Australia's international responsibilities, and urged the government to suspend the Act's implementation. Significantly, the Committee affirmed that indigenous peoples' land rights are recognized in international law, and that the international community now understands that doctrines of dispossession are illegitimate and racist.

Universal Human Rights Convention

The seminal 1949 Universal Declaration on Human Rights, passed unanimously by the United Nations General Assembly and now accepted as international customary law, gave rise to the preparation and conclusion of the 1966 International Covenant on Economic, Social, and Cultural Rights (ICESCR) and the 1966 International Covenant on Civil and Political Rights (ICCPR). Both instruments contain provisions that may be interpreted to ensure protection to indigenous peoples' land rights, such as the right to religion, family, and cultural integrity. During several decades, it was argued that only civil and political rights belonged to the category of human rights, while economic, social, and cultural rights belonged to the realm of social aspirations.

The recent 1993 Vienna World Conference on Human Rights dispelled this argument by categorically affirming the interdependence of all human rights. In other words, the rhetoric of development and economic growth may not be utilized to justify violations and systematic denial of human rights, be it in their cultural or political dimensions. Recently, the debate has further expanded to encompass third-generation, solidarity rights, which are those vested in peoples, such as the rights to a healthy environment, to peace, and to self- determination, and which require solidarity at all levels of society for effective implementation.

Special note deserves the ICCPR formulation of the right to cultural integrity, which provides that persons belonging to ethnic minorities shall not be denied the right, in community with the other members of their group, to enjoy their own culture, to profess and practice their own religion, or to use their own language. The United Nations Human Rights Committee (HCR) is the treaty-based body entrusted with oversight of the ICCPR, including complaints against countries that have ratified the ICCPR First Optional Protocol alleging violation of protected rights. The HRC has stated in its General Comment on Article 27 that this provision extends to economic activity, where the activity is an essential element in the culture of an ethnic community.

The Committee has further stated that, Culture manifests itself in many forms, including a particular way of life associated with the use of land resources, especially in the case of indigenous peoples. The enjoyment of these rights may require positive measures of protection and measures to ensure the effective participation of members of minority communities in decisions which affect them. Examining a petition submitted by the Lubicon Lake Band of Cree, the Committee of Human Rights concluded that Canada had violated article 27 by allowing the provincial government of Alberta to grant leases for oil and gas exploration and timber development within the ancestral territory of the Lubicon Lake Band. The Committee also found that the natural resource development activity compounded historical inequities to threaten the way of life and culture of the Lubicon Lake Band. Then in the context of the Lansman cases, the Human Rights Committee addressed the specifics of mining projects in indigenous peoples lands.

There are several other international human rights treaties that deal with torture (CAT), gender discrimination (CEDAW), and children's rights (CRC). There is a supervisory committee for each of these treaties that monitors the way in which State parties are fulfilling their human rights obligations. In addition to receiving complaints from individuals (except ICESCR and CRC), the committees considers reports on how governments are implementing treaties. Although these reports open a space for leveraging progress towards implementation by encouraging openness and dialogue, the reporting system has many problems, including late submissions, lack of resources for evaluating reports, lack of publicity, and lack of influence of the Committees' comments and recommendations on governments.

Inter-American Human Rights System

The Inter-American Human Rights System has evolved over the latter half of the XXth Century to afford protection to indigenous peoples' rights to property, rights to family, right to judicial protection, among others. In the implementation of substantive standards contained in the 1947 American Declaration of the Rights and Duties of Man and in the 1969 American Convention on Human Rights, the Inter-American

Commission on Human Rights (IACHR) has played a fundamental role. Since it was established in 1959, the IACHR has contributed to the protection and promotion for the rights of indigenous peoples through on-site visits, country reports, friendly settlements, and individual petitions. In its 1997 Report on the Situation of Human Rights in Ecuador for example, the IAHCR observed that for indigenous peoples the continued utilization of traditional systems for the control and use of territory are essential to their survival, as well as to their individual and collective wellbeing.

Further, the IACHR observed that control over the land includes the capacity for providing the resources which sustain life and the geographical space necessary for the cultural and social reproduction of indigenous peoples. The IACHR has further elaborated a doctrine on the right to property in cases involving indigenous peoples' rights to lands. In 1985 for example, the IACHR recommended that the government of Brazil set and demarcate the boundaries of the Yanomami Park in the Amazonian Forest after finding, inter alia, that the authorization to exploit the resources of the subsoil of the Indian territories was the origin of massive human rights violations. The IACHR has also been instrumental in securing land rights to indigenous peoples by mediating friendly settlements, such is the 1998 agreement between the Enxet-Sanapana people and Paraguay.

Recently in 1998, the IACHR submitted the Awas Tingni case to Inter-American Court of Human Rights, alleging that Nicaragua had violated the indigenous community's right to property over their ancestral lands by granting a logging concession to a Korean timer corporation. In its 2001 Judgment, the Court considered that an evolutionary interpretation of international human rights instruments was warranted and found that the Convention protects the right to property of the members of indigenous communities over their communal lands. The Court also found that Nicaragua violated the Convention by failing to demarcate indigenous lands and by granting concessions for the exploitation of resources within these lands.

Among indigenous peoples there exists a community tradition over a communal form of collective property over the land, in the sense that title to land is not held by an individual but by the group and its community. Indigenous peoples have the right to live freely in their own territories, right which is based solely upon their existence; the close relationship that indigenous peoples maintain with the land must be recognized and comprehended as the fundamental basis of their cultures, their spiritual lives, their integrity, and their economic subsistence. For indigenous communities, the relationship with the earth is not merely a question of possession and production, but a material and spiritual element that they must enjoy fully, including for preserving their cultural legacy and transmitting it to future generations.

The IACHR has also elaborated a doctrine on collective rights, which afford indigenous communities group rights over their lands. In this regard, the IACHR has taken the approach that individual and collective rights are not opposed but, rather, are part of the principle of full and effective enjoyment of human rights. This approach has inspired the draft declaration on the rights of indigenous peoples prepared by the IACHR for the OAS, after extensive consultations with indigenous peoples, and particularly those articles that deal with cultural, political, and economic rights. This draft declaration is currently under discussion by the political organs of the Organization of American States.

The United Nations first focused its attention formally on the problems of indigenous peoples in the context of its work against racism and discrimination. Indigenous peoples began lobbying the United Nations trough non-governmental organizations such as the World Council of Indigenous Peoples and the International Indian Treaty Council during the 1970s. Responding to the legitimacy of their demands and to studies initiated by the Sub-Commission on Prevention of

Discrimination and Protection of Minorities, in 1982 the United Nations Economic and Social Council (ECOSOC) established a working group and charged it with the task of elaborating a declaration on the rights of indigenous populations. In 1993, the Sub-Commission Working Group produced a draft declaration on the matter, which is now being considered by the United Nations Human Rights Commission.

Draft declaration

The draft declaration builds upon a decade of consultations with indigenous peoples, who have voiced their concerns during the annual meeting of the working group in Geneva and in other forums. The draft declaration formulated an array of collective rights, such as the right to maintain and develop their distinct cultural identities, and the right to participate fully in the affairs of the metropolitan State. The draft declaration also contains several provisions safeguarding indigenous peoples' land rights, such as for example the following provision, Indigenous peoples have the right to own, develop, control and use the lands and territories, including the total environment of the lands, air, waters, coastal seas, sea-ice, flora and fauna and other resources which they have traditionally owned or otherwise occupied and used. The declaration is categorical in its protection to indigenous peoples' right to remain on their lands. It explicitly states that, "indigenous peoples shall not be forcibly removed from their lands or territories. No relocation shall take place without the free and informed consent of the indigenous peoples concerned...". Still and all, notice must be flagged to the fact that the draft declaration remains a soft-law instrument, which provides evidence of emerging customary norms and duties.

Thematic Reports

The UN Sub-Commission has also produced several thematic reports on particular aspects of indigenous peoples' relations with the contemporary world order. The seminal report by Special Rapporteur Martinez Cobo of Ecuador on "The Problem of Discrimination against Indigenous Populations" was completed in 1984. He addressed the human rights issues raised by mining in indigenous peoples lands by stating that, "543. Where possible within the prevailing legal system, the resources of the subsoil of indigenous land also must be regarded as the exclusive property of indigenous communities. Where this is rendered impossible by the fact that the deposits in the subsoil are the preserve of the State, the state must allow full participation by indigenous communities in respect of: the granting of exploration and exploitation licenses; the profits generated by such operations; the procedures for determining damage caused and compensation payable to indigenous communities as a result of the exploitation of the resources of the subsoil of indigenous land and in the consideration of all consequences of such exploration and exploitation activities.

No mining whatsoever should be allowed on indigenous land without first negotiating an agreement with the indigenous peoples who will be affected by the mining, guaranteeing them a fair share of the revenue that may be obtained". Subsequent studies focused on treaties entered into by indigenous peoples, on indigenous peoples cultural heritage, and on indigenous peoples' right to permanent sovereignty over their natural resources. Recently in 2001, the final working paper on "Indigenous Peoples and their Relationship to Land" was presented by the Special Rapporteur Daes. The UN Human Rights Commission has taken stock of these studies, and in 2001 appointed Rodolfo Stavenhagen for a three-year period as Special Rapporteur on the Situation of Human Rights and Fundamental Freedoms of Indigenous Peoples.

After a series of meetings and discussion in the context of the Decade of Indigenous Peoples, in 2000 the ECOSOC established the Permanent Forum on Indigenous Issues. The Permanent Forum is expected to provide advice and recommendations to the ECOSOC on indigenous issues relating to economic and social development, culture, the environment, education, health, and human rights. The Permanent Forum is also expected to raise awareness and to prepare and disseminate information on indigenous issues. The Forum will be comprised of 16 experts (8 nominated by governments and 8 by the President of the ECOSOC) and is expected to meet for 10 days each year. It is proposed that it will hold its first session in New York from 6-17 May 2002.

International Labour Organization (ILO)

The International Labour Organization is the oldest of the specialized agencies of the UN system, as well as the most active in promoting the rights of indigenous peoples, particularly their social and economic rights. The ILO's has taken the lead in elaborating international standards, monitoring their implementation through periodic state reporting and 'representations' mechanisms, and facilitating technical cooperation programs. ILO Convention 169 stands as the only international treaty dealing with indigenous peoples and land rights. This instrument was concluded in 1989 and came to replace ILO Convention 107, which had focused on the goal of integration and assimilation rather than on the protection of indigenous peoples lands, culture, and distinctiveness. ILO 169 contains several procedural and substantive safeguards for indigenous peoples' rights over their lands, including for example Article 15, "the rights of the peoples concerned to the natural resources pertaining to their lands shall be specially safeguarded".

Further, property rights are specifically protected by ILO 169, which provides that the rights of ownership and possession of the peoples concerned over the lands which they traditionally occupy shall be recognized. ILO 169 also includes the obligation of States to consult with indigenous peoples even when natural resources remain under state ownership. The relevant provision reads as follows, In cases in which the

State retains the ownership of mineral or subsurface resources or rights to other resources pertaining to lands, governments shall establish or maintain procedures through which they shall consult these peoples, with a view of ascertaining whether and to what degree their interests would be prejudiced, before undertaking or permitting any programs for the exploration or exploitation of such resources pertaining to their lands.

ILO 169 ensures indigenous peoples' control over their lands, legal status, and development. It further guarantees their environment from harmful alien interference and provides for internal structures of community organization. The implementation of these minimum international standards by national constitutions and domestic legislation in a large number of countries is also evidence of emerging norms of international customary law. Article 24 of the ILO Constitution provides that a national or international employers' or workers' organization may submit a "representation" to the ILO on the grounds that a member State has failed to observe or has not satisfactorily ensured the application of a ratified Convention.

A tripartite committee will examine the representation and submit a report to the Governing Body for adoption, which may require that the government take specific measures to resolve the problem. This dispute settlement machinery has forged constructive alliances between workers' unions and indigenous peoples, whereby the latter have submitted representations providing evidence on the State's failure to comply with its international obligations. In the context of indigenous peoples' lands, cases have been brought by organizations from Denmark, Mexico, Bolivia, Colombia, Ecuador, and Peru. Finally, the ILO carries technical cooperation programs that promote the active participation of indigenous and tribal peoples at all levels of project implementation and decision-making, from design to evaluation. Other technical cooperation activities address the living and working conditions of indigenous peoples. These characteristics of the programs are thus varied and tailored to the specific needs of the communities under focus, and they have been implemented in South and Southeast Asia, Africa, and the Americas.

UN Development Programme (UNDP)

The UNDP promotes programs for sustainable human development and administers a number of special-purpose funds to the effect. Its engagement with indigenous peoples is extensive and has involved small grants programs, as well as regional and national programs. These programs have focused on poverty eradication, environmental conservation, conflict prevention and resolution, and cultural revitalization. Besides actual funding of projects, the UNDP has also opened forums where indigenous peoples have been invited to discuss issues of policy, such as the Civil Society Organization Advisory Committee and the Executive Board meetings. The Indigenous Knowledge Programme is another important initiative of UNDP and pursues the following objectives:

— participation of indigenous peoples in international conferences and process of their concern,

— conservation of indigenous knowledge through research on customary laws and traditional resource rights, and

— allocation of funding for indigenous self-help initiatives that address poverty reduction and organization-building at community level. This program has funded two projects in Asia and one in South America, but future implementation is yet to be decided by its Steering Committee.

The World Bank (IBRD) exercises important influence in the development of international standards, either by filling the regulatory vacuum of borrowing countries, either by pushing the implementation of what then crystallize as customary norms. In 1982, the IBRD issued Operational Manual

Statement 2. 34, the purpose of which was to protect the interests of 'indigenous groups' in bank financed development interventions. In 1991, the IBRD issued a revised Operational Directive (OD) 4. 20, which intended to expand the emphasis from protection towards participation in, and benefits from, bank-financed development projects. The IBRD has recently engaged in a wide review of all its ODs, in an effort to clarify existing binding safeguards policies, which would ultimately lead to greater compliance. It has been argued that the creation of the Inspection Panel in 1993 has triggered this process, given that only then did safeguard policies acquire teeth and enforceable meaning.

In any event, the conversion of directives to policies provides opportunities for strengthening the rights of potentially affected persons suffering from 'development' projects, but also opens windows through which existing safeguards may be watered-down, thereby reducing the level of protection to vulnerable persons, groups, and communities. The transformation process of OD 4. 20 into OP/BP 4. 10 has been structured upon global and regional consultations, of which the last round ends on 15 February 2002. After such date, the IBRD will comment and revise draft OP/BP 4. 10, with a view to submitting a final version for approval by the Board of Directors early 2002.. In spite of this formal engagement by the IBRD with relevant stake holders, draft OP/BP 4. 10 does not include many of the most important recommendations made by indigenous peoples in the first round of consultations, including: the right to prior and informed consent, indigenous monitoring of Bank projects, and fair 'mitigation' requirements. Other concerns raised by indigenous peoples throughout the consultation process, and concerning the new the draft policy, include:

— Requirements concerning Indigenous land and resource issues are not clear.

— Provisions for legal protections are now optional instead of mandatory.

— Provisions for peoples affected by protected areas are unclear.

— It allows for involuntary resettlement of indigenous peoples.

— It does not meet existing international human rights standards.

4

Indigenous People and Natural, Cultural and Intelluctual Resources

One of the most notable features of the contemporary international human rights regime has been the recognition of indigenous peoples as special subjects of concern. A discrete body of international human rights law upholding the collective rights of indigenous peoples has emerged and is rapidly developing. The modern indigenous rights movement gained momentum in the 1960s and 1970s, when indigenous peoples in the Americas, Australia, New Zealand, and other parts of the world began to draw increased attention to their demands for continued survival as distinct communities with historically based cultures, political institutions, and entitlements to land. These efforts led to a number of important international conferences and heightened attention from scholars and international nongovernmental organizations.

By the late 1970s, indigenous peoples' representatives began appearing before United Nations and other human rights bodies in increasing numbers and with increasing frequency, grounding their concerns on generally applicable human rights principles. Since that time, a steady stream of important developments and responses to the concerns of indigenous peoples has issued from the international human rights system. Indigenous peoples prompted the International Labour Organization (ILO) to discard

Convention No. 107's assimilationist bias, which reflected the 1950s era in which it was passed. The resulting new multilateral treaty —ILO Convention No. 169 of 1989— has been ratified and is now binding on several states in the Americas and elsewhere.

The establishment of the United Nations Working Group on Indigenous Populations in 1982 and the Working Group's promulgation of the Draft United Nations Declaration on the Rights of Indigenous Peoples, which is presently under review by the U.N. Commission on Human Rights, have focused even greater international attention on the protection of indigenous peoples' rights. New international standards concerning the rights of indigenous peoples have significantly influenced the work of several international human rights bodies and other international institutions. The U.N. Human Rights Committee and the U.N. Committee on the Elimination of Racial Discrimination now regularly apply the prevailing understandings of indigenous peoples' rights reflected in the newly articulated standards. They draw heavily on these understandings when they monitor human rights situations involving indigenous groups.

Even beyond the formal human rights process, the discourse of indigenous human rights now affects the lending processes of the World Bank, the Inter-American Development Bank, the European Union, and the domestic legislation and policies and judge-made law of states. All of these important developments reflect the ever-increasing interdependencies, ever-improving communications technologies, and burgeoning international institutions that characterize the contemporary international system and its human rights regime of norms and related procedures.

International and Domestic Legal Practice

The foregoing interpretations of relevant provisions of the

American instruments and applicable UN human rights treaties is reinforced by an increasingly well defined and consistent pattern of international and domestic legal practice that recognizes indigenous peoples' rights to lands and natural resources. Especially significant is the international practice associated with International Labour Organization Convention (No. 169) on Indigenous and Tribal Peoples, which has been ratified by several states in the Americas. A drafting committee that included thirty-nine states in addition to the worker and employee delegates that are part of the ILO developed the convention. It was adopted by the full conference of the ILO by an overwhelming majority of the voting delegates, including government deletates. At the domestic level, relevant practices include legislation, judicial decisions, and constitutional reforms that pronounce protections for indigenous land and resource rights.

Viewed comprehensively, applicable international practice incorporates and goes beyond the domain of existing treaty obligations for states within the Inter-American system. Taken together with relevant domestic legal practice, international practice gives rise to obligations of customary international law that apply more generally throughout the Inter-American system. As demonstrated by an expanding body of literature, it is evident that indigenous peoples have achieved a substantial level of international concern for their interests, and there is substantial movement toward a convergence of international opinion on the content of indigenous peoples' rights, including rights over lands and natural resources.

Developments toward consensus about the content of indigenous rights simultaneously give rise to expectations that the rights will be upheld, regardless of any formal act of assent to the articulated norms. The discourse of indigenous peoples and their rights has been part of multiple international institutions and conferences in response to demands made by indigenous groups over several years backed by an extensive record of justification. The pervasive assumption has been that the articulation of norms concerning indigenous peoples is an exercise in identifying standards of conduct that are required to uphold widely shared values of human dignity. The multilateral processes that build a common understanding of the content of indigenous peoples' rights, therefore, also build expectations of behavior in conformity with those rights.

Under modern legal theory, processes that generate consensus about indigenous peoples' rights build customary international law. As a general matter, norms of customary law arise when a preponderance of states and other authoritative actors converge upon a common understanding of the norms' content and generally expect future behavior in conformity with the norms. The traditional points of reference for determining the existence and contours of customary norms include the relevant patterns of actual conduct of state actors.

Today, however, actual state conduct is not the only or necessarily determinative indicia of customary norms. With the advent of modern inter-governmental institutions and enhanced communications media, states and other relevant actors increasingly engage in prescriptive dialogue. Especially in multilateral settings, explicit communication may itself bring about a convergence of understanding and expectation about rules, establishing in those rules a pull toward compliance, even in advance of a widespread corresponding pattern of physical conduct.

It is thus increasingly understood that explicit communication, of the sort that is reflected in the numerous international documents and decisions cited below, builds customary rules of international law. Conforming domestic laws and related practice reinforces such customary rules of international law. Non-conforming domestic practice undermines the apparent direction of the international norm-building only to the extent the international regime holds out and eventually accepts as legitimate the non-conformity.

Although international and domestic practice varies somewhat in its recognition and protection of indigenous peoples' land and resource rights, just as state practice varies in its treatment of property rights in general, it nonetheless entails a sufficiently uniform and widespread acceptance of core principles to constitute a norm of customary international law. The relevant practice of states and international institutions establishes that, as a matter of customary international law, states must recognize and protect indigenous peoples' rights to land and natural resources in connection with traditional or ancestral use and occupancy patterns. This new and emerging customary international law, along with treaty obligations arising from outside the Inter-American system, inform an understanding of the rights that are protected by the American Convention and American Declaration.

One of the most impressive achievements of the post World War II international system in protecting human rights has been the recognition of indigenous peoples as special subjects of concern. As part of this development, states and others acting through international institutions increasingly have affirmed the central importance of traditional lands and resources to the cultural survival of indigenous peoples. The requirement that states recognize and protect indigenous peoples' rights in their traditional lands is included in the Inter-American Charter of Social Guaranties, which was adopted by the General Assembly of the Organization of American States in 1948.

Article 39 of the Charter requires that states take "necessary measures... to give protection and assistance to the Indians, safeguarding their life, liberty, and property, preventing their extermination, shielding them from oppression and exploitation, protecting them from want and furnishing them with an adequate education." Further, the article recommends establishing "institutions or services" created specifically "to safeguard Indian lands, legalize their ownership thereof, and prevent the invasion of such lands by outsiders."

ILO Convention No. 107 of 1957 similarly recognized indigenous peoples' rights of ownership to the lands they traditionally occupied. Despite Convention No. 107's widely criticized—and now rejected – assimilationist bias in other respects, its recognition in 1957 of the right to collective land ownership by indigenous groups demonstrates the long-standing concern in international practice for protecting indigenous peoples' rights to their traditional lands.

ILO Convention No. 169 of 1989, a revision of Convention No. 107, is international law's most concrete manifestation of the growing recognition of indigenous peoples' rights to property in lands. Convention No. 169's land rights provisions are framed by article 13(1), which states:

In applying the provisions of this Part of the Convention governments shall respect the special importance for the cultures and spiritual values of the peoples concerned of their relationship with the lands or territories, or both as applicable, which they occupy or otherwise use, and in particular the collective aspects of this relationship. The Convention, which has been ratified by a significant number of American states, speaks specifically to the property rights of indigenous peoples: "The rights of ownership and possession of the peoples concerned over the lands which they traditionally occupy shall be recognized."

The growing acceptance in international practice of indigenous peoples' rights in land and natural resources is further evidenced by relevant provisions of the Proposed American Declaration on the Rights of Indigenous Peoples, prepared by the Inter-American Commission on Human

Rights in consultation with OAS member states and representatives of indigenous peoples. Emphasizing that such property rights originate from traditional patterns of land tenure, the Proposed Declaration also stipulates: "Nothing... shall be construed as limiting the right of indigenous peoples to attribute ownership within the community in accordance with their customs, traditions, uses and traditional practices, nor shall it affect any collective community rights over them."

The Draft United Nations Declaration on the Rights of Indigenous Peoples, developed by the United Nations Working Group on Indigenous Populations and approved by U.N. Sub-Commission on Prevention of Discrimination and Protection of Minorities, provides further evidence of the increasingly widespread international recognition of and respect for indigenous peoples' rights in lands and resources. The Draft U.N. Declaration was approved by the Sub-Commission after several years of discussions in which both states and indigenous peoples from throughout the world took part.

The Draft U.N. Declaration affirms: Indigenous peoples have the right to own, develop, control and use the lands and territories, including the total environment of the lands, air, waters, coastal seas, sea-ice, flora and fauna and other resources which they have traditionally owned or otherwise occupied or used. This includes the right to the full recognition of their laws, traditions and customs, land-tenure systems and institutions for the development and management of resources, and the right to effective measures by States to prevent any interference with, alienation of or encroachment upon these rights.

In addition to the many documents that articulate the above principles, examination of the active engagement of international human rights bodies demonstrates the broad acceptance of these principles in the realm of practice as well. The U.N. Human Rights Committee, the U.N.

Committee on the Elimination of Racial Discrimination, the relevant organs of the International Labour Organization, and the Inter-American Commission on Human Rights apply the prevailing understandings of indigenous peoples' land and resource rights when they monitor human rights situations where indigenous peoples are located and when they consider complaints brought by specific indigenous groups.

Every major international body that has considered indigenous peoples' rights during the past decade has acknowledged the crucial importance of lands and resources to the cultural survival of indigenous peoples and communities. They also have recognized the critical need for governments to respect and protect the varied and particular forms of land tenure defined and regarded as property by indigenous peoples themselves. In addition to the international human rights institutions, the World Bank and the European Union have pronounced and acted in favor of these rights.

Indigenous peoples and their rights over land and natural resources have been discussed at a multitude of international meetings and conferences sponsored by the U.N., the OAS, and other inter-governmental organizations during the last several years.

Protection of Cultural and Intellectual Resources

Indigenous cultural production presents particular cultural and social value to communities, which does not fall within the conventional protection regimes of intellectual property law. Beyond the interests of private property and the exercise of monopolies and exclusive rights that characterize the framework of intellectual property, cultural and intellectual activity presents not only economic benefits to peoples, but is also instrumental in the preservation of culture and community. In a technologically advancing world where information is a global currency, such rights are crucial to the survival of peoples. Indigenous people have the right to control their cultures in the interests of the continued preservation of their shared identity. Further, people have the right to own and receive economic benefits from the fruits of their knowledge and cultural labour.

For peoples, the rights to protect the cultural integrity of works, and to be attributed as the source of these works are fundamental cultural and intellectual property rights. Clearly, conventional intellectual property regimes do not accommodate on going cultural preservation in a model where private property rights and monopolies serve as the fundamental framework. Potential for protection is found through a reconsideration of cultural knowledge and a paradigmatic shift, whereby customary law is a necessary means for preserving intellectual interests through biological diversity and international obligations. The value of cultural property does not exist merely within the material and discrete form of that property, but in the exchange between individuals, that is, in the circulation and continuation of those intellectual resources within the local community.

Whilst the basis for litigation upon, and thereby enforcement of, intellectual property rights could be said to be a kind of exchange, in that the value is unrealised except in the copying or reproduction of the form, there is a fundamental difference in the object of protection in that exchange. Where there is a conflict between the two perspectives is in the integrity afforded to the material form in Western intellectual property law that must be preserved within that regime, primarily through litigious enforcement of exclusive rights to the exploitation of that form. That which is paramount in Indigenous cultural property is not the commodified form that is trespassed upon, through copying and infringement, but the cultural process that produced that form. Similarly, distinct from the individual 'authorship' rights protected in intellectual property law, the value in cultural and intellectual resources is realized in the communal practice of the culture as well as the differentiation and continuation of the community through the dissemination of those resources.

Generally speaking, however, the right to a particular design, cultural practice, ceremony, and so on is not merely a general communal right, but a measure of a particular individual's cultural circumstances within a particular community, and that individual's initiatory advancement and differentiation within that unique cultural community. Nevertheless, the particular piece of intellectual property, if it can be comprehended as such, is not anchored to a particular individual as in Western intellectual property law. Although individual creativity is not stressed in traditional communities, it would be wrong to jump to the extreme and suppose that designs are subject to a generalised communal right. Communities are internally differentiated to quite a high degree, and their members should not be seen as interchangeable units.

On any matter, some people are likely to have rights of a certain kind, others rights of another kind, and yet others no rights at all. The concepts of cultural and intellectual property are not individual rights as such, but rights to the practice of the culture and integrity of the individual as well as the differentiation and continuation of the community. Assimilation of the value of intellectual property within Western notions of property is an inadequate and often destructive means by which to protect traditional knowledge.

Intellectual property laws have been criticised for imposing preconceived, individualistic concepts upon the customary values and knowledge that are vested in the community. Similarly, international norms and the approach of individual human rights are also limited in value, in that they are inapplicable to the role of the artist in traditional Aboriginal culture. On the other hand, the "safekeeping" through the anthropological rendering of culture within museums and so on, is itself a commodification of culture which cannot understand and preserve it in the way that is unique to a particular community. The rights to the resources in that culture must therefore be specifically recognised and realised through means that somehow empower traditional communities to protect and manage those resources within the dominant legal paradigms.

Traditional Intellectual Property Rights

Under Western law, copyright is of limited duration, after the expiration of which the works enter the public domain. Similarly, the monopolies granted for patents are of limited duration. In contrast, interests in traditional culture and art work are integral to continuing cultures and exist in perpetuity. The notion of rendering that culture part of the public domain can often undermine the value of that culture to those groups. "Mythological events are not simply located in the distant past but are also in some sense seen to be part of a continuous present". Generally speaking, Western intellectual property rights are vested exclusively in the author or creator as an individual from whom the expression or invention originates. Thus, conventional intellectual property law may not recognise the claims of others, protected under customary law, which understands cultural identity as existing in the community.

Indigenous customary law and practice recognises nonexclusive rights, where property is shared amongst a continuing cultural community within which individuals are differentiated. Aboriginal customary law, which gave the artist an entitlement to represent a particular theme, differed markedly from the general body of Australian law which recognised copyright. The fact that a work drew upon custom and tradition for its basis meant that contemporary works produced by Aboriginal artists represented a novel continuation of their very own ancient culture. To acknowledge the full copyright of an individual artist would be to deny the contribution of continuing living folklore to the particular artistic work and would give rights which the person did not have under traditional law. A copyright given without the limitations of tribal custom, and without debt to any body of tradition which might otherwise encumber it, might enable the individual artist to give or refuse permission to the reproduction of a work beyond that which he would be entitled to give under traditional law.

Such nonexclusive rights were a particular feature of Australian Aboriginal law and were not readily compatible with the exclusive rights of copyright. Furthermore, whilst originality is a requirement of Western copyright, and novelty and inventiveness necessary to the protection of industrial property, customary practice emphasises a shared continuation and adaptation of ancestral heritage and preexisting cultural tradition. Consequently, ownership of traditional intellectual property is not defined as it is under the statutory regimes, but is disparate amongst groups and beyond the individual, raising issues regarding those authorised to use and grant permission to use such property, and the issue of potential harm to a group because of the community's inability to protect the knowledge or culture in that 'property' in any permanent sense. At the basis of Western intellectual property regimes is the granting of certain rights to an 'individual' to protect and use a work within the knowledge economy, in return for disclosure. For instance, a monopoly is granted in respect of a patent in return for the disclosure of the invention. Indigenous knowledge is often subject to a particular custom regarding the dissemination of parts of that knowledge and secret and sacred practices governing its disclosure.

Finally, intellectual property protection requires a material form and does not protect the "idea", except in the limited sense of confidential information and trade secrets, usually in the context of commercial value. Traditional cultural interests inhere in oral histories, agricultural and medicinal practices, dance, body painting, and methodologies, indeed in the very 'ideas' that continue to inform the cultures and to produce the 'material' expressions of those cultures. The public's ability to inspect the subject of protection, as in anthropological display, should not destroy the confidential nature of the information for the purposes of protection, as it might if the conventional law of trade secrets were applied.

These regimes for the protection of commercially sensitive information do not necessarily translate effectively to secret-sacred knowledge. Just as the courts rely on standard industry practice to find confidentiality in trade secrets, a similar reliance on indigenous cultural practices and customary law should be made relevant to the question of confidentiality in sacred-secret information and designs. The important rights that require protection for peoples are the knowledge or 'ideas' through which an individual's tribal identity and the continuity of those origins are sustained. Thus, a more culturally appropriate understanding of the traditional perspective of intellectual property in that heritage must acknowledge a property right in the practice and continuation of sacred designs beyond mere aesthetics.

There are 'property' in its most basic sense, the distinction between real and intellectual property having no significance in Aboriginal customary law. It is thus a property right, not just a mere idea, which is infringed when a sacred design is employed in an unauthorised way: an infringement as concrete as trespass in Anglo-Australian law. This affirms the significance of the recognition of native title by common law, despite its recent erosion by the Australian High Court, and the potential for recognition of sui generis intellectual property rights. Whilst artwork has been the subject of recent litigation under the Copyright Act, medical and agricultural knowledge and practice present similar problems. Nevertheless, there is strength in the recognition of artwork and artistic method as sensitive cultural information, in defiance of the conventional Western dichotomy of artistic expression as opposed to the academic and rational disciplines of law and science.

It is often a feature of the style of the artworks in question that the artist will encode into the artwork secret parts of "dreaming" that will be recognised and understood only by those who are initiated into the relevant ceremonies, or at least have a close knowledge of the cultural significance of the story. This adds to the risk of offending the traditional owners, through the reproduction of Aboriginal artwork, unless the reproduction is accurate in every respect and done with full and proper permission. For example, Others evidence was tendered that inaccurate reproductions cause deep offence because artworks are an important means of recording stories and culture and continuing that culture; the right to create such artworks and to use preexisting designs and totems was said to reside in the traditional custodians of the stories who act as fiduciary to the greater Indigenous community.

Thus, this easing of the strict disciplinary division that operates in Western culture must be extended to protection of 'industrial' property, that is, applications of scientific, agricultural, and medicinal knowledge. There is a real need for an understanding of the integration of cultural and scientific/medicinal practice in customary law, and therefore the mutualism in the relationship between cultural diversity and bio-diversity, as distinct from the very separate spheres of artistic expression and scientific or legal discipline in Western law. The judgment is significant for the implementation of sui generis legislation in the application of "systems" of practice in land holding to the finding of proprietorship in individual parcels of land. Thus, proprietorship in agricultural practices, for instance, might arise through evidence of customary law and adherence to that practice, and the significance of that knowledge to the integrity of the cultural group, rather than through conventional requirements for intellectual property rights that emphasise a 'personal property' with very little relevance to the way in which intellectual property operates in a traditional sense.

Codifying Customary Law

The Australian Law Reform Commission has warned against codifying customary law. "There would be a danger of imposing uniformity where none exists and of freezing Aboriginal practice at an arbitrary date". This issue arises because the practices and culture of Indigenous Australians are not predetermined but are necessarily informed by the on going living exercise of that culture. That is, rather than behaviours prescribed by cultural practice, the culture is living and evolving through its individual members in what is a more complex relationship than a simple "generalised communal right". Codification of customary law seems to presume a relocation of the power to legislative bodies, and of the communal practice of that law to the state institutions.

Nevertheless, legal recognition of the principles of that law, namely, its custody within a particular community and the authority and capacity of that community to act within a legal paradigm, not only confers the necessary authority to customary law but also protects that law, itself a traditional and intellectual community resource, from commodification within conventional legal discourse. Conventional legislative regimes of protection are hindered by the definition of what comes within it. For example, copyright law is an inadequate means of protection because of its limited duration, its attachment to individual authors and the material form, and its requirement of originality. Any attempt legislatively to define in advance which 'traditional' art works are protected and which are not would appear, therefore, to raise the danger of freezing Aboriginal art within the 'authentic', 'noble savage' category within which it has hither to been confined. In addition, the almost exclusive emphasis upon the work of individual, traditional owners of designs means that many forms of Aboriginal art are in danger of 'slipping through the net'.

Not receiving legislative protection or even consideration at all. Similarly, commercial adaptation of various forms of intellectual knowledge, whether it be painting or agricultural techniques, may attract protection under the Copyright Act 1968, or may be found sufficiently novel or inventive to be patentable under the Patents Act 1990. These regimes are limited in their ability to provide ongoing protection for intellectual property as cultural heritage, as well as unable to offer any protection against the appropriation of intellectual resources by individuals outside the traditional community. Rather than protecting the form, sui generis regimes must protect the community's potential to preserve its cultural diversity through the application of international norms to the management of its resources, cultural and biological, intellectual and social.

Cultural Diversity and Rights

The personal property nature of copyright has no real meaning for a good many Aboriginal people whose rights, it is hoped, can be protected. 'Personal property' may have no real meaning within customary law, as distinct from 'communal integrity', which has some sort of connection to the people within a particular community and the differentiation of that community. It may be understood by Western law as a kind of property right, albeit one that cannot be adequately monetarily compensated, not because it is of no value in the Western sense, but because it is one for which the value resists commodification in the economic sense. The loss cannot be compensated by money because it is the very practice of these cultures that ensures the integrity of the community and of the individuals within that particular community. Indeed, the loss of knowledge without regulation by the people is a loss not merely to, but of, the people themselves. It is almost analogical to the importance of bodily integrity.

Intellectual property law "grants economic rights which are individual rights and freely assignable, whereas the rights of peoples are collective in nature, being focused on cultural rights that are often qualified in terms of transmission". The value of these rights is often in the exchange of the property or knowledge itself, rather than discretely subsisting within the material form, as in conventional copyright law. In other words, the emphasis is on cultural rather than economic rights. Protection of intellectual resources is significant not only in the context of intellectual property in the conventional economic sense, but also to the integrity and autonomy of unique traditions. The potential for restricting the adaptation of artistic works, however, has been criticised as an affront to the principle of free speech. But such criticism is unsubstantial in its necessary reliance on free market rhetoric. Free speech is not absolute but must be protected, requiring support mechanisms in order for it to be sustained. In a free market model, so-called free speech would ultimately be determined by the dominant ideological structures.

The kind of protection that is sought by Australian communities is not a restriction upon free speech, but a necessary protection of cultural expression against the commodification of culture in a free market economy. Specific protection of intellectual property is a necessary protection of cultural diversity against the uniformity that would ultimately arise through unhindered free market economies. If access to protection was governed by the commercial potential of traditional knowledge alone, traditional knowledges outside this criterion would be lost. "A great deal of traditional knowledge has no commercial potential whatsoever, but this does not make it any less worthy of respect or protection". Indeed, the very act of commodification of Indigenous intellectual property through the application of conventional intellectual property regimes, neglects the fact that it is not only Indigenous ownership of that property that must be protected, but also the cultural integrity vested in that property.

Peoples have other relationships to cultural forms - trust, secrecy, guardianship, stewardship, initiation, sacralisation - and obligations to relatives, ancestors, spirits, and future generations which make models of access and ownership appear extremely impoverished. Such knowledge is not adequately understood as information, nor may its circulation be properly understood as speech. Therefore, it would perhaps be more appropriate to identify Indigenous property rights as rights in Indigenous cultural practice. This signifies the communal value of these knowledges and traditions without fore grounding the inadequate concept of property. Discussion that ascribes conventional economic models of copyright law to folklore, and patent law to folk varieties of plants, neglects the fact that it is often the very practice of that culture that is the object of protection.

Foregrounding intellectual and cultural practice may also overcome the debates surrounding protection of Indigenous knowledge through the patenting of 'common heritage'. There needs to be a fundamental shift in the way such protection is understood, indicating the need for the development of specific sui generis regimes. The protection of cultural diversity through the acknowledgment and protection of Indigenous customary practice is necessarily also the protection of biological diversity through the protection of ongoing sustainable use and management of the land. The interdependence of biological and cultural diversity challenges the view of environment as something without humans ... Existing biological and cultural diversity occurs predominately in humanised, cultural landscapes and seascapes inhabited by indigenous nations. With this in mind, possibly the most difficult protection issue is that of traditional medicinal, agricultural, and cultural practices. In such practices, it is not necessarily the material form for which protection is sought, but the right to continue to exercise these practices in the continuation of cultural integrity.

Bioprospecting

Until recently, the concept of appropriation was not in currency and indeed the concept of 'ownership' on the part of Indigenous people in their culture was not comprehended by Western discourse. Indigenous art, culture, and medicine were within the realm of scientific and anthropological endeavour and their 'collection' was authorised and justified in the service of 'science' and 'international understanding.' This anthropological scrutiny has been criticised by some commentators as yet another way in which the West has consumed, commodified, categorised and civilised that which has been threatening in its 'difference', reconciling it through its incorporation into Western arts and sciences.

Critics argue that imposing traditional Western concepts of intellectual property protection maintains the fundamental cultural distortion. "To represent the person as a creature of nature whose idyllic way of life has been cruelly destroyed is one way of confining the culture within a category created by the coloniser".

Genetic Resources

In the past, the 'collection' of wild genetic resources was facilitated by virtually free access, justified by the argument that these were global biological resources to benefit the whole of humankind and could not be restricted or comprehended in terms of geographical location. While the developed world exhausted genetic and natural resources through commercialisation and industrialisation, developing nations preserved their bio-diversity through traditional agricultural practices that continued their cultural heritage. Community-based farming and agriculture, both in the Indigenous Australian example and elsewhere in the world, has caused minimal impact and indeed has managed and preserved the bio-diversity of their local resources. On the other hand, outside exploitation is without the same long-term interdependence with the environment, and is unsustainable in that it is largely a harvest rather than a cultural management of resources.

The level of exploitation by outsiders without a long-term dependence on the local resource is often of another magnitude of impact and highly unsustainable Commercial operations extract the same products used by local people, but they generally exploit them for short-term profits without concern for long-term sustainability. Extraction of commercially valuable medicinal plants has also led to depletion or local extinction of populations of those species. In the collection of genetic resources, the benefits are enjoyed by Western multinational companies at the expense of developing countries, which, if uncompensated, receive no benefit for their conservation of bio-diversity and their sustainable farming practices. In 1990, about a quarter of the world's drugs were plant-derived, with a sales value of US$43bn.

Of these, about three quarters were 'discovered' by scientists because Indigenous peoples had previously used them, more often than not for the same purpose. Not a penny of that US$32bn found its way to Indigenous people - in 1990, or in any other year, when sales figures were comparable. In short, the knowledge of Indigenous and other traditional peoples -among the poorest, most disenfranchised on earth - has gone unacknowledged, unprotected and unrewarded. It has been appropriated with impunity, to make millions for industry. Indigenous people and a growing number of governments in Asia, Africa and Latin America are now calling this biopiracy, and are seeking redress.

In Australia, Europeans have published records of Aboriginal medicinal plant uses since early colonial times. New compendia are still being compiled and published, with no assured protection of Aboriginal sources. Furthermore, such interference with the local community structure canfracture the community through the interruption of traditional authorities and ethics and the depletion of local resources, "as a few entrepreneurs emerge and claim individual rights over what had been communal resources".

The ideology of biological resources as a global commodity, that authorised unfettered access of bioprospectors, was rejected by Costa Rica in the 1980s, albeit in a limited nationalistic sense. The creation of the Ministry of Natural Resources, Energy, and Mines (MIRENEM) in 1986 increased, at the parliamentary executive level, awareness and environmental concerns such that by the end of the 1980s, Costa Rica had ended the practice of allowing free and unlimited access to its wild genetic resources. With the establishment of a non-profit national bio-diversity institute, Instituto Nacional de Biodiversidad (INBio), and accompanying legislation allowing the government to use INBio as a means of regulating access, bioprospecting concessions were negotiated in return for compensation to the government. In 1991, a landmark agreement between INBio and the Merck pharmaceutical company attracted a great deal of attention. In 1991, INBio signed a landmark contract with the Merck pharmaceutical company.

INBio agreed to provide 10, 000 chemical samples from plants, animals, and soil to the pharmaceutical company, which would have the exclusive right to analyse these samples for two years. In consideration, Merck paid INBio US$1m and gave INBio US$130000 of scientific equipment. In addition, Merck agreed to pay INBio a royalty on worldwide sales of any pharmaceutical products refined from or based on a compound found in one of the provided chemical samples. Fifty percent of these royalties will be paid to Costa Rica's National Park Fund. In its payment of US$1m and $130000 of scientific equipment, as well as royalty payments of between 5% and 65% depending on the type of genetic material, this agreement represents an important departure from the common heritage of human logic. It renders the inequitable exploitation of the genetic resources of developing countries by multinational companies more difficult to sustain.

However, this arrangement reflected a national interest in the wild genetic resources of a developing country and did not directly involve any Indigenous knowledge providers, nor was compensation granted to the local Indigenous custodians of those resources. Nevertheless, it is arguable that the same principles are useful in confronting the difficult issues in adequate protection of Indigenous cultural and intellectual property in a developed nation, such as Australia. That is, the property interest, if it can be adequately described in that way, is vested with the people of a particular group, practising and continuing their knowledge. An Australian example is Amrad, a Victorian pharmaceutical company that has entered into a bioprospecting agreement with the Tiwi Land Council. As Indigenous intellectual property lawyer. Indigenous people should be aware of their intellectual and cultural property rights so that they can negotiate terms for sharing such knowledge.

Convention On Biological Diversity (CBD)

The CBD was an important product of the United Nations Conference on Environment and Development, or the "Earth Summit", held in Rio de Janeiro in 1992. The CBD, ratified by Australia in 1993, has 187 parties, thus providing potential for global coverage and important acknowledgment of Indigenous cultural and intellectual property rights. The significance of the CBD in creating protection for Indigenous intellectual property against the threat of bioprospecting is found in the unique relationship between cultural diversity and bio-diversity. The potential for protection is found through a reconsideration of cultural knowledge and a paradigmatic shift, whereby customary law is a necessary means by which to preserve intellectual interests through biological diversity. The CBD provides an important international framework for legislative recognition of Indigenous rights. Implementation of a sui generis regime created through consultation that is culturally appropriate and respectful of Indigenous cultures will offer both the necessary protection for cultural diversity and a significant foundation for biological diversity.

The Preamble explicitly recognises "the close and traditional dependence of many indigenous and local communities embodying traditional lifestyles on biological resources". It continues that it is desirable to share equitably the "benefits arising from the use of traditional knowledge, innovations and practices relevant to the conservation of biological diversity and the sustainable use of its components". There is an obligation placed upon contracting parties to preserve knowledge and practices of Indigenous communities, but this international obligation is limited by its subjection to national legislation. Dęspite no explicit recognition of communal property rights, the CBD is an important acknowledgement of community knowledge and provides the potential for the protection of knowledge and practices beyond that protected by existing intellectual property laws.

The subsistence of intellectual property rights in species or knowledge has been criticised, both by researchers and some Indigenous groups, as beyond ownership by anyone. Representatives from some Indigenous peoples' organizations to the 1992 UN Working Group on Indigenous People argued that no one should own knowledge or species and that no one has the right to profit from knowledge that could be shared for the benefit of all. However, this position recognises and depends upon traditional values that are, unfortunately, not appreciated in the wider developed world. In fact, Australian Indigenous people recognise the need for a separate Act that will protect their interests in cultural and traditional knowledges and practices and recognise their unique form of custodianship as distinct from conventional ownership. Many Indigenous Australians favour the introduction of specific legislation that acknowledges the unique nature of that which is to be protected.

With its emphasis on trade and an economic model of rights in intellectual property, the GATT-TRIPs agreement stipulates patents on microorganisms and plants, leaving the patenting of animals to the discretion of the signatories. TRIPs has been criticised for reinforcing private monopoly rights and privileging industrial innovations over informal, communal innovations. Where the TRIPs agreement is potentially significant for Indigenous people is Article 27(3), which refers to subject matters that may be excluded from patent ability and also raises the potential for introducing sui generis systems for protection. Whilst TRIPs and the CBD both emphasise protection of the Biotechnology industries, this agenda is explicit in the TRIPs agreement through the obligation upon signatories to pass intellectual property legislation over life forms. The CBD also emphasises intellectual property laws within which protection of Indigenous intellectual property conform or, at least, remain "subject to", but despite this it does explicitly acknowledge Indigenous communities. Notwithstanding the limitation posed by the deference to national sovereignty, there is potential for governments to enact specific legislation to protect traditional knowledge.

Cultural Diversity

Whilst international intellectual property protection may appear to provide solutions to domestic problems, the extent to which those regimes may merely serve a global market economy, ultimately compromising the protection of traditional knowledge, should not be underestimated. Globalisation, as it has been advocated, often seems to replace the old dictatorships of national elites with new dictatorships of international finance". Conventional intellectual property rights, as raised in the Doha 'development' round of trade negotiations in Qatar, November 2001, prioritise the commercial investment and return of producers, over the interests and access of users. The value of those rights is understood in the global market context of property in which knowledge becomes an increasingly expensive commodity.

If peoples are forced to relinquish their traditional customs and languages through, for example, assimilatory programmes which emphasise the conversion of their traditional economies based on biodiverse agricultural and hunter-gather ereco systems to cash economies based on monocultural systems of resource exploitation, then both cultural and biological diversity will suffer. The man date involves an instruction to the TRIPs Council to look at the relationship between TRIPs and the CBD and the issue of traditional knowledge, including issues of bio-piracy and the patenting of biotechnology derived from traditional biological resources and knowledge.

The Declaration also instructs the TRIPs Council to examine the protection of "tradition" and "folklore" in the context of this review, in relation to biotechnology. This review must occur with regard to the "development dimension", that is, in consideration of the particular interests of developing countries. Where the CBD presents an important resource for Indigenous rights in traditional knowledge is in its potential for realising the value in Indigenous intellectual resources beyond a simple and individualistic proprietary model within a global market economy. It provides for the articulation of a system of conservation of biological diversity as a universal heritage while also including an explicit acknowledgment of customary and Indigenous knowledge and technologies.

Therefore, counter to the global access argument, the CBD presents international support for the use of legislative regimes to protect Indigenous resources from appropriation, whilst creating legal and financial incentives for the conservation of these precious biological and cultural resources. Utilising the principles of the CBD, there is an important opportunity for legislative recognition of indigenous interests by devising a regime through consultation that is culturally appropriate. In respecting cultural diversity, there is a significant transformation in the means of protecting bio-diversity and an important outcome in the end.

Standards and Materials

The following compilation of standards and materials is

comprised of the most relevant portions of various legal instruments, draft legal instruments and other relevant materials. It contains only the main or most important legal materials that pertain to indigenous peoples and their relationships to land, territories and resources. The purpose of this compilation is to facilitate understanding of current international standards and of the draft principles contained in the draft United Nations declaration on the rights of indigenous peoples and the proposed Inter-American Declaration on the Rights of Indigenous Peoples.

Universal Declaration of Human Rights

Article 7

All are equal before the law and are entitled without any discrimination to equal protection of the law. All are entitled to equal protection against any discrimination in violation of this Declaration and against any incitement to such discrimination.

Article 17

1. Everyone has the right to own property alone as well as in association with others.

2. No one shall be arbitrarily deprived of his property.

International Convention on the Elimination of All Forms of Racial Discrimination

Article 5

In compliance with the fundamental obligations laid down in article 2 of this Convention, States Parties undertake to prohibit and to eliminate racial discrimination in all its forms and to guarantee the right of everyone, without distinction as to race, colour, or national or ethnic origin, to equality before the law, notably in the enjoyment of the following rights: (v) The right to own property alone as well as in association with others;

Committee on the Elimination of Racial Discrimination

General Recommendation XXIII (51) on the rights of indigenous peoples, adopted at the Committee's 1235th meeting, on 18 August 1997

1. In the practice of the Committee on the Elimination of Racial Discrimination, in particular in the examination of reports of States parties under article 9 of the International Convention on the Elimination of All Forms of Racial Discrimination, the situation of indigenous peoples has always been a matter of close attention and concern. In this respect the Committee has consistently affirmed that discrimination against indigenous peoples falls under the scope of the Convention and that all appropriate means must be taken to combat and eliminate such discrimination.

2. The Committee, noting that the General Assembly proclaimed the International Decade of the World's Indigenous People commencing on 10 December 1994, reaffirms that the provisions of the International Convention on the Elimination of All Forms of Racial Discrimination apply to indigenous peoples.

3. The Committee is conscious of the fact that in many regions of the world indigenous peoples have been, and are still being, discriminated against and deprived of their human rights and fundamental freedoms and in particular that they have lost their land and resources to colonists, commercial companies and State enterprises. Consequently the preservation of their culture and their historical identity has been and still is jeopardized.

4. The Committee calls in particular upon States parties to:

   (a) Recognize and respect indigenous distinct culture, history, language and way of life as an enrichment of the State's cultural identity and to promote its preservation;

(b) Ensure that members of indigenous peoples are free and equal in dignity and rights and free from any discrimination, in particular that based on indigenous origin or identity;

(c) Provide indigenous peoples with conditions allowing for a sustainable economic and social development compatible with their cultural characteristics;

(d) Ensure that members of indigenous peoples have equal rights in respect of effective participation in public life and that no decisions directly relating to their rights and interests are taken without their informed consent;

(e) Ensure that indigenous communities can exercise their rights to practise and revitalize their cultural traditions and customs and to preserve and to practise their languages.

5. The Committee especially calls upon States parties to recognize and protect the rights of indigenous peoples to own, develop, control and use their communal lands, territories and resources and, where they have been deprived of their lands and territories traditionally owned or otherwise inhabited or used without their free and informed consent, to take steps to return those lands and territories. Only when this is for factual reasons not possible, the right to restitution should be substituted by the right to just, fair and prompt compensation. Such compensation should as far as possible take the form of lands and territories.

6. The Committee further calls upon States parties with indigenous peoples in their territories to include in their periodic reports full information on the situation of such peoples, taking into account all relevant provisions of the Convention.

International Covenant on Civil and Political Rights

Article 27

In those States in which ethnic, religious or linguistic minorities exist, persons belonging to such minorities shall not be denied the right, in community with the other members of their group, to enjoy their own culture, to profess and practise their own religion, or to use their own language.

Human Rights Committee General Comment 23, Article 27 (fiftieth session, 1994)

3.2 The enjoyment of the rights to which article 27 relates does not prejudice the sovereignty and territorial integrity of a State party. At the same time, one or other aspect of the rights of individuals protected under that article - for example, to enjoy a particular culture - may consist in a way of life which is closely associated with territory and use of its resources. This may particularly be true of members of indigenous communities constituting a minority.

7. With regard to the exercise of the cultural rights protected under article 27, the Committee observes that culture manifests itself in many forms, including a particular way of life associated with the use of land resources, especially in the case of indigenous peoples. That right may include such traditional activities as fishing or hunting and the right to live in reserves protected by law. The enjoyment of those rights may require positive legal measures of protection and measures to ensure the effective participation of members of minority communities in decisions which affect them.

International Labour Organization Convention No. 169 concerning Indigenous and Tribal Peoples in Independent Countries (1989)

Article 4

1. Special measures shall be adopted as appropriate for

safeguarding the persons, institutions, property, labour, cultures and environment of the peoples concerned.

2. Such special measures shall not be contrary to the freely-expressed wishes of the peoples concerned.

3. Enjoyment of the general rights of citizenship, without discrimination, shall not be prejudiced in any way by such special measures.

Article 7

The peoples concerned shall have the right to decide their own priorities for the process of development as it affects their lives, beliefs, institutions and spiritual well-being and the lands they occupy or otherwise use, and to exercise control, to the extent possible, over their own economic, social and cultural development. In addition, they shall participate in the formulation, implementation and evaluation of plans and programmes for national and regional development which may affect them directly.

Article 13

1. In applying the provisions of this Part of the Convention Governments shall respect the special importance for the cultures and spiritual values of the peoples concerned of their relationship with the lands or territories, or both as applicable, which they occupy or otherwise use, and in particular the collective aspects of this relationship.

2. The use of the term lands in Articles 15 and 16 shall include the concept of territories, which covers the total environment of the areas which the peoples concerned occupy or otherwise use.

Article 14

1. The rights of ownership and possession of the peoples concerned over the lands which they traditionally occupy shall be recognized. In addition, measures shall be taken in appropriate cases to safeguard the right of the peoples concerned to use lands not exclusively occupied by them,

but to which they have traditionally had access for their subsistence and traditional activities. Particular attention shall be paid to the situation of nomadic peoples and shifting cultivators in this respect.

2. Governments shall take steps as necessary to identify the lands which the peoples concerned traditionally occupy, and to guarantee effective protection of their rights of ownership and possession.

3. Adequate procedures shall be established within the national legal system to resolve land claims by the peoples concerned.

Article 15

1. The rights of the peoples concerned to the natural resources pertaining to their lands shall be specially safeguarded. These rights include the right of these peoples to participate in the use, management and conservation of these resources.

2. In cases in which the State retains the ownership of mineral or sub-surface resources or rights to other resources pertaining to lands, Governments shall establish or maintain procedures through which they shall consult these peoples, with a view to ascertaining whether and to what degree their interests would be prejudiced, before undertaking or permitting any programmes for the exploration or exploitation of such resources pertaining to their lands. The peoples concerned shall wherever possible participate in the benefits of such activities, and shall receive fair compensation for any damages which they may sustain as a result of such activities.

Article 16

1. Subject to the following paragraphs of this Article, the peoples concerned shall not be removed from the lands which they occupy.

2. Where the relocation of these peoples is considered necessary as an exceptional measure, such relocation shall take place only with their free and informed consent. Where their consent cannot be obtained, such relocation shall take place only following appropriate procedures established by national laws and regulations, including public inquiries where appropriate, which provide the opportunity for effective representation of the peoples concerned.

3. Whenever possible, these peoples shall have the right to return to their traditional lands, as soon as the grounds for relocation cease to exist.

4. When such return is not possible, as determined by agreement or, in the absence of such agreement, through appropriate procedures, these peoples shall be provided in all possible cases with lands of quality and legal status at least equal to that of the lands previously occupied by them, suitable to provide for their present needs and future development. Where the peoples concerned express a preference for compensation in money or in kind, they shall be so compensated under appropriate guarantees.

5. Persons thus relocated shall be fully compensated for any resulting loss or injury.

Article 17

1. Procedures established by the peoples concerned for the transmission of land rights among members of these peoples shall be respected.

2. The peoples concerned shall be consulted whenever consideration is being given to their capacity to alienate their lands or otherwise transmit their rights outside their own community.

3. Persons not belonging to these peoples shall be prevented from taking advantage of their customs or of lack of

understanding of the laws on the part of their members to secure the ownership, possession or use of land belonging to them.

Article 18

Adequate penalties shall be established by law for unauthorized intrusion upon, or use of, the lands of the peoples concerned, and Governments shall take measures to prevent such offences.

Article 19

National agrarian programmes shall secure to the peoples concerned treatment equivalent to that accorded to other sectors of the population with regard to:

(a) The provision of more land for these peoples when they have not the area necessary for providing the essentials of a normal existence, or for any possible increase in their numbers;

(b) The provision of the means required to promote the development of the lands which these peoples already possess.

World Bank Operational Directive 4.20 (September 1991)

15. The development plan should be prepared in tandem with the preparation of the main investment. In many cases, proper protection of the rights of indigenous people will require the implementation of special project components that may lie outside the primary project's objectives. These components can include activities related to health and nutrition, productive infrastructure, linguistic and cultural preservation, entitlement to natural resources, and education. The project component for indigenous peoples development should include the following elements, as needed:

(a) Legal Framework... (ii) the ability of such groups to obtain access to and effectively use the legal system to defend their rights. Particular attention should be given to the rights of indigenous peoples to use and develop the lands that they occupy, to be protected against illegal intruders, and to have access to natural resources (such as forests, wildlife, and water) vital to their subsistence and reproduction.

(c) Land Tenure. When local legislation needs strengthening, the Bank should offer to advise and assist the borrower in establishing legal recognition of the customary or traditional land tenure systems of indigenous peoples. Where the traditional lands of indigenous peoples have been brought by law into the domain of the State and where it is inappropriate to convert traditional rights into those of legal ownership, alternative arrangements should be implemented to grant long-term, renewable rights of custodianship and use to indigenous peoples. These steps should be taken before the initiation of other planning steps that may be contingent on recognized land titles.

Preparation

17. If it is agreed in the IEPS meeting that special action is needed, the indigenous peoples development plan or project component should be developed during project preparation. As necessary, the Bank should assist the borrower in preparing terms of reference and should provide specialized technical assistance. Early involvement of anthropologists and local NGOs with expertise in matters related to indigenous peoples is a useful way to identify mechanisms for effective participation and local development opportunities. In a project that involves the land rights of indigenous peoples, the Bank should work with the borrower to

clarify the steps needed for putting land tenure on a regular footing as early as possible, since land disputes frequently lead to delays in executing measures that are contingent on proper land titles.

United Nations Draft Declaration on the Rights of Indigenous Peoples

Article 10: Indigenous peoples shall not be forcibly removed from their lands or territories. No relocation shall take place without the free and informed consent of the indigenous peoples concerned and after agreement on just and fair compensation and, where possible, with the option of return.

Article 12: Indigenous peoples have the right to practise and revitalize their cultural traditions and customs. This includes the right to maintain, protect and develop the past, present and future manifestations of their cultures, such as archaeological and historical sites, artifacts, designs, ceremonies, technologies and visual and performing arts and literature, as well as the right to the restitution of cultural, intellectual, religious and spiritual property taken without their free and informed consent or in violation of their laws, traditions and customs.

Article 13: Indigenous peoples have the right to manifest, practise, develop and teach their spiritual and religious traditions, customs and ceremonies; the right to maintain, protect, and have access in privacy to their religious and cultural sites; the right to the use and control of ceremonial objects; and the right to the repatriation of human remains. States shall take effective measures, in conjunction with the indigenous peoples concerned, to ensure that indigenous sacred places, including burial sites, are preserved, respected and protected.

Article 25: Indigenous peoples have the right to maintain and strengthen their distinctive spiritual and material relationship with the lands, territories, waters and coastal seas and other resources which they have traditionally owned or otherwise occupied or used, and to uphold their responsibilities to future generations in this regard.

Article 26: Indigenous peoples have the right to own, develop, control and use the lands and territories, including the total environment of the lands, air, waters, coastal seas, sea-ice, flora and fauna and other resources which they have traditionally owned or otherwise occupied or used. This includes the right to the full recognition of their laws, traditions and customs, land-tenure systems and institutions for the development and management of resources, and the right to effective measures by States to prevent any interference with, alienation of or encroachment upon these rights.

Article 27: Indigenous peoples have the right to the restitution of the lands, territories and resources which they have traditionally owned or otherwise occupied or used, and which have been confiscated, occupied, used or damaged without their free and informed consent. Where this is not possible, they have the right to just and fair compensation. Unless otherwise freely agreed upon by the peoples concerned, compensation shall take the form of lands, territories and resources equal in quality, size and legal status.

Article 28: Indigenous peoples have the right to the conservation, restoration and protection of the total environment and the productive capacity of their lands, territories and resources, as well as to assistance for this purpose from States and through international cooperation. Military activities shall not take place in the lands and territories of indigenous peoples, unless otherwise freely agreed upon by the peoples concerned.

States shall take effective measures to ensure that no storage or disposal of hazardous materials shall take place in the lands and territories of indigenous peoples. States shall also take effective measures to ensure, as needed, that programmes for monitoring, maintaining and restoring the health of indigenous peoples, as developed and implemented by the peoples affected by such materials, are duly implemented.

Article 29: Indigenous peoples are entitled to the recognition of the full ownership, control and protection of their cultural and intellectual property. They have the right to special measures to control, develop and protect their sciences, technologies and cultural manifestations, including human and other genetic resources, seeds, medicines, knowledge of the properties of fauna and flora, oral traditions, literatures, designs and visual and performing arts.

Article 30: Indigenous peoples have the right to determine and develop priorities and strategies for the development or use of their lands, territories and other resources, including the right to require that States obtain their free and informed consent prior to the approval of any project affecting their lands, territories and other resources, particularly in connection with the development, utilization or exploitation of mineral, water or other resources. Pursuant to agreement with the indigenous peoples concerned, just and fair compensation shall be provided for any such activities and measures taken to mitigate adverse environmental, economic, social, cultural or spiritual impact.

Proposed Inter-American Declaration on the Rights of Indigenous Peoples

Approved by the Inter-American Commission on Human Rights on 26 February 1997 Article VII.

Right to Cultural Integrity

1. Indigenous peoples have the right to their cultural integrity, and their historical and archeological heritage, which are important both for their survival as well as for the identity of their members.

2. Indigenous peoples are entitled to restitution in respect of the property of which they have been dispossessed, and where that is not possible, compensation on a basis not less favourable than the standard of international law.

3. The States shall recognize and respect indigenous ways of life, customs, traditions, forms of social, economic and political organization, institutions, practices, beliefs and values, use of dress, and languages.

Right to Environmental Protection

Article 13

1. Indigenous peoples have the right to a safe and healthy environment, which is an essential condition for the enjoyment of the right to life and collective well-being.

2. Indigenous peoples have the right to be informed of measures which will affect their environment, including information that ensures their effective participation in actions and policies that might affect it.

3. Indigenous peoples shall have the right to conserve, restore and protect their environment, and the productive capacity of their lands, territories and resources.

4. Indigenous peoples have the right to participate fully in formulating, planning, managing and applying governmental programmes of conservation of their lands, territories and resources.

5. Indigenous peoples have the right to assistance from their States for purposes of environmental protection, and may receive assistance from international organizations.

6. The States shall prohibit and punish, and shall impede jointly with the indigenous peoples, the introduction, abandonment, or deposit of radioactive materials or residues, toxic substances and garbage in contravention of legal provisions; as well as the production,

introduction, transportation, possession or use of chemical, biological and nuclear weapons in indigenous areas.

7. When a State declares an indigenous territory as protected area, any lands, territories and resources under potential or actual claim by indigenous peoples, conservation areas shall not be subject to any natural resource development without the informed consent and participation of the peoples concerned.

Rights to Land, Territories and Resources

Article 18

1. Indigenous peoples have the right to the legal recognition of their varied and specific forms and modalities of their control, ownership, use and enjoyment of territories and property.
2. Indigenous peoples have the right to the recognition of their property and ownership rights with respect to lands, territories and resources they have historically occupied, as well as to the use of those to which they have historically had access for their traditional activities and livelihood.
3. (i) Subject to 3.ii, where property and user rights of indigenous peoples arise from rights existing prior to the creation of those States, the States shall recognize the titles of indigenous peoples relative thereto as permanent, exclusive, inalienable, imprescriptible and indefeasible.

   (ii) Such titles may only be changed by mutual consent between the State and respective indigenous peoples when they have full knowledge and appreciation of the nature or attributes of such property.

   (iii) Nothing in 3.i shall be construed as limiting the right of indigenous peoples to attribute ownership within the community in accordance with their customs, traditions, uses and traditional practices, nor shall it affect any collective community rights over them.

4. Indigenous peoples have the right to an effective legal framework for the protection of their rights with respect to the natural resources on their lands, including the ability to use, manage, and conserve such resources; and with respect to traditional uses of their lands, interests in lands, and resources, such as subsistence.

5. In the event that ownership of the minerals or resources of the subsoil pertains to the State or that the State has rights over other resources on the lands, the Governments must establish or maintain procedures for the participation of the peoples concerned in determining whether the interests of these people would be adversely affected and to what extent, before undertaking or authorizing any programme for planning, prospecting or exploiting existing resources on their lands. The peoples concerned shall participate in the benefits of such activities, and shall receive compensation, on a basis not less favourable than the standard of international law for any loss which they may sustain as a result of such activities.

6. Unless exceptional and justified circumstances so warrant in the public interest, the States shall not transfer or relocate indigenous peoples without the free, genuine, public and informed consent of those peoples, but in all cases with prior compensation and prompt replacement of lands taken, which must be of similar or better quality and which must have the same legal status; and with guarantee of the right to return if the causes that gave rise to the displacement cease to exist.

7. Indigenous peoples have the right to the restitution of the lands, territories and resources which they have traditionally owned or otherwise occupied or used, and which have been confiscated, occupied, used or damaged,

or when restitution is not possible, the right to compensation on a basis not less favorable than the standard of international law.

8. The States shall take all measures, including the use of law enforcement mechanisms, to avert, prevent and punish, if applicable, any intrusion or use of those lands by unauthorized persons to take possession or make use of them. The States shall give maximum priority to the demarcation and recognition of properties and areas of indigenous use.

5

Indigenous People and Sustainable Development

Today, the processes of twentieth century globalization have decentered the state. Capital moves freely around the world with relatively little direction from states. Internet technologies create global networks without regard to national or internal boundaries. Cultural influences and images flow across state lines without regard to borders. More importantly, many of the problems and actors with which states now deal are not, or not solely, within a state's own territorial boundaries. The state itself is now subject to and affected by the same globalizing forces that are transforming business and other aspects of daily life.

The empirical realities of globalization and their effects on the state raise important interpretive questions concerning how should now think about and achieve success in various and continuous global competitions. Due to the unstable status of Taiwan as an entity in global society, non-governmental organizations are one kind of creative diplomatic strategies to make break through under the pressure from China government and the unfriendly atmosphere among snobbish states. To show the power of Taiwan and accomplish goals with realistic meaning in the severe competition of the era of globalization, it is important to keep flexible gesture and adapt flexible approaches.

Rights and Knowledge

Indigenous peoples needs strong foundation of knowledge indefinitely. Since 1980s the relationship between indigenous peoples and natural environment has become a matter of major global attention, especially those indigenous traditional traditional eco-knowledge they gained from the long-term interactions with local natural ecosystems. It's true that about 250, 000, 000 indigenous peoples are almost totally dependent on their lands as their only means of subsisting. Apart from the economic support, lands have been understood as the derivation providing for aboriginals' histories, legends, religious, ceremonies, cultures, and lives. Away from the lands and its trees, crops, flowers, streams, and mountains, which have bred and enriched aboriginal cultures, the aboriginal peoples would have lost the connections with the nature.

Further, the aboriginals are not aboriginals any more. This is also the reason why all the indigenous groups in the world have started to defend and fight for their land rights from the past century. Development projects, mining and forestry activities continue to displace indigenous peoples. These man- made works have resulted in substantial environmental damage - flora and fauna species have become extinct or endangered, unique ecosystems have been destroyed, and rivers and other water catchments have been heavily polluted. On the international stage, indigenous movements have also aroused big echoes across the world.

A number of research projects on indigenous-environment issues have contributed to the birth of various international declarations and agreements, such as "the 1972 United Nations Conference on the Human Environment in Stockholm", "International Labour Organization (ILO) Convention No. 169 of 1989 concerning Indigenous and Tribal Peoples". The United Nations Conference on Environment and Development (the Earth Summit), held in Brazil in 1992, represented a turning point in the promotion of indigenous peoples' rights relating to the environment. A number of legal instruments adopted at the Earth Summit, such as the Rio Declaration, Agenda 21 and the Convention on Biological Diversity, established international legal standards to protect indigenous peoples' rights to their traditional knowledge and practices in the area of environmental management and conservation.

In the international environmental arenas, should human beings continue developing at current rates, the world development would ultimately over burden natural environmental endurance and cause severe eco-plight and eco-crisis. Environmental Disasters such as oil spills, industrial accidents, and floods often cause grave human and ecological harm. They usually strike without warning and frequently capture the attention of the public and are prominently reported in the news media. In order to retrieve the global environmental exploitation and degradation caused by economic development, the United Nations had its first conference on the Human Environment in Stockholm in the year 1972, calling upon the public to protect our earth.

Since the United Nations Conference on Human Environment in Stockholm, environmental issues have made the surprising diversity ranging from global to local levels. In 1987, the concept of "sustainable development" drew the world's attention with the publication of Our Common Future, the report of the World Commission on Environmental and Development. Progress on developing the concepts of sustainable development has been rapid since the 1980s. The 1992 United Nations Conference on Environment and Development convened two decades after the Stockholm Conference as a follow-up thereto, addressed the more obviously divergent views of developed and developing countries towards environmental issues and sought to bridge these by the concept of "sustainable development". Briefly speaking, "sustainable development" has become contemporary globally-concerned subject of debate.

In Taiwan sustainable development is also the "so-called core spirit" of the indigenous policy. Despite the long existence of the aborigines of Taiwan, Taiwan Aborigines have suffered for a long time unequal and discriminatory from economic exploitation, social discrimination, political oppression and negligence of culture by external forces. Taiwan Aborigines are effectively encountering a crisis of racial extermination. The establishment of national parks has long been a matter of controversy between the government, Aboriginals and non-Aboriginal society. The government always justifies its actions by advocating the ideology of conservation and natural resource management.

However, the creation of national parks usually causes harm to local Aboriginal communities by the expropriation of their traditional lands and prohibitions on their traditions, practices and customs. Certainly, in its deeds and in the legislation it has introduced, the government has long recognized the importance of conservation. But, over the past 10 years, the cultural harm resulting from the government's policy of creating national parks has been a matter of public debate. It has been proven from an ecological perspective that most natural environments on the Earth's surface, which are not occupied and inhabited by indigenous communities, have been depleted and destroyed over the past several centuries. The ecosystem has been preserved only within traditional Aboriginal areas.

Because many traditional and indigenous societies live so close to nature, they have gained exceptional insights into how best to preserve and sustainable use the world's invaluable biological resources. For this reason increasing weight has been attached to the input of Aboriginal peoples in matters of environmental protection. This has lent some impetus to the idea of co- management of resources. Aboriginal peoples have historically been excluded from any meaningful input into how, where, when and why resource development occurs on their traditional territory. This exclusion has had a significant, negative economic and social impact on Aboriginal communities.

The reasons for advocating Aboriginal participation in the management and development of their traditional territories and surrounding resources, are compelling and have much to do with the fundamental value of maintaining the social validity of Aboriginal communities, so inextricably and historically tied to the land. For many Aboriginal communities, subsistence practices such as hunting, fishing and trapping on traditional territories relate more to issues of culture, lifestyle and identity than to questions of economy, although economic considerations cannot be minimized.

Around the world, community involvement in conserving the natural habitat, wildlife and bio-diversity is becoming the preferred method of conservation, marking a shift away from the top-down approach that has characterized such efforts in the last few decades. But there are still important roles for government agencies, such as the establishment of a basic legal framework and management of the overall ecosystem. In the process of establishing a legal framework, there are further concerns that need to be addressed by government-whether there has been as little infringement as possible in order to affect the desired result and whether the Aboriginal group in question has been consulted with respect to the conservation measures being implemented.

The realization of the comanagement agreement is usually carried out by way of negotiation and reconciliation among interested parties. Fundamentally, comanagement implies that each participant at the negotiating table has equal rights of participation and these can then be formally institutionalized in the co-management process. This situation, unfortunately, is not possible under the present circumstances in Taiwan. In fact, unless a drastic change occurs within the relationship between Aboriginal people and the government, comanagement will remain simply an empty promise.

Therefore, non-governmental organizations get their working space to play roles like medium between individual groups and the government. To achieve the consensus among the parties of different interests, it is important to use non-governmental organizations' role as the third party or section to balance any possible disputes.

Indigenous Peoples' Plan of Implementation on Sustainable Development

(Johannesburg, South Africa 02 September 2002)

Introduction

We, the representatives of Indigenous Peoples attending the World Summit on Sustainable Development, have defined this Plan of Implementation for the next decade, based on the Kimberley Declaration, as part of our contribution for achieving human and environmental sustainability in the world. The Plan of Implementation reflects the heart and mind of Indigenous Peoples as traditional caretakers of Mother Earth who, for many millennia, have developed and refined our sustainable societies.

Cosmovision and Spirituality

1. We will direct our energies and organizational strength to consolidate our collective values and principles which spring from the interrelation of the different forms of life in Nature. Therein lies our origin which we reaffirm by practicing our culture and spirituality.

2. We will strengthen the role of our elders and wise traditional authorities as the keepers of our traditional wisdom which embodies our spirituality and cosmovision as an alternative to the existing unsustainable cultural models.

3. We demand that the concept of cultural damage be incorporated to impact assessments as part of the legal instruments which will safeguard our cultural integrity against energy mega projects, mining, tourism, logging and other unsustainable activities.

Self-Determination and Territory

4. We will ensure the recognition, protection and respect for Indigenous Peoples' unqualified right to self-determination, which is the basic precondition to guarantee our ownership, permanent sovereignty, control and management of our lands, territories and natural resources. Any dialogue or partnership with Indigenous Peoples on sustainable development must be based on recognition, protection and respect for this fundamental principle.

5. We urge governments to establish specific legal frameworks, recognizing Indigenous Peoples' rights to self-determination, ancestral lands and territories and to adopt the Draft Declaration on the Rights of Indigenous Peoples as approved by the UN Working Group on Indigenous Populations and the UN Sub-Commission on the Protection and Promotion of Human Rights before the end of the United Nations International Decade of the World's Indigenous Peoples.

6. We continue to demand recognition of our land tenure systems and customary laws. We reaffirm our spiritual and cultural connection to our land and territories. We call for an immediate halt to all policies and law reforms that compromise our collective land tenure systems.

7. We will share experiences about our use and management systems of natural resources with other Indigenous Peoples, and promote exchanges between our Peoples.

8. We, the Indigenous Peoples, will further our global strategy for international policies, to influence and shape governmental programmes.

9. We will protect and strengthen our institutions, safeguarding customary laws and practices, which are the bases of sound sustainable management of our environment and territories.

10. We assert our rights to demarcate our traditional lands and territories with our full participation, and we request governments to agree on mechanisms with Indigenous Peoples for this purpose, respecting our right to collective ownership.

11. We urge governments to initiate a process of restitution of Indigenous Peoples' ancestral lands and territories, as a concrete way of furthering human and environmental sustainability.

Treaties

12. We urge the United Nations to promote the recognition, observance and enforcement of treaties, agreements and other constructive arrangements concluded between Indigenous Peoples and States, or their successors, according to their original spirit and intent, and to have States honour and implement such treaties, agreements and other constructive arrangements.

Children and Youth

13. We will nurture an environment of intergenerational support, thereby laying a strong foundation for future generations. We will take the responsibility to pass on our indigenous way of life to safeguard our pride and dignity as peoples.

14. We will support and strengthen indigenous youth organizations to be fully empowered with resources to initiate, enable and support continuous communications among indigenous youth to enable them to voice their concerns in the international arena.

15. We will continue to promote the participation of indigenous youth in the international, national and local decision making processes pertinent to our peoples.

16. We call for immediate measures to stop child labour, child sexual exploitation, child trafficking, child soldiers, execution of minors and all other exploitations and injustices against indigenous children.

Women

17. We reaffirm the rights of Indigenous women and their vital role in human, cultural and environmental sustainability; and we work towards fair and equitable access to land, resources, education and other social and welfare services. We will take deliberate steps to ensure that indigenous women participate in all levels of governance and leadership both locally, nationally and internationally.

18. Violence against indigenous women must be systematically addressed. We call for immediate measures against all forms of sexual exploitation, forced sterilization and trafficking of women.

19. We reaffirm the role of indigenous women as custodians of traditional knowledge, culture and the sustainable use of biological diversity.

Sacred Sites

20. We urge States, governments and civil society to work

in conjunction with Indigenous Peoples to ensure that Indigenous Peoples' sacred, ceremonial and culturally significant sites and areas are preserved, respected and protected from destructive or exploitative development. We will ensure our peoples' access to our sacred, burial, archeological and historical sites, including the unqualified right to restrict access to those sites.

Food Security

21. We will promote the conservation, sustainable use and management of our traditional foods and strengthen our own models, systems and networks of production and trade, urging States to guarantee the integrity of our biological habitats for this purpose.

22. We will work against technologies, policies, and legal regimes that violate Indigenous Peoples' rights to maintain our traditional knowledge, practices, seeds and other food related genetic resources.

23. We urge governments and international institutions to develop mechanisms to support Indigenous Peoples' own practices and institutions to ensure food sovereignty.

24. We call for an immediate moratorium on the development, cultivation and use of genetically modified seeds, plants, fish and other organisms, in order to protect human health, native seeds and other food related genetic resources, governments must declare

25. We will strengthen pastoralism, hunting and gathering as viable and sustainable economic systems that ensure food sovereignty, including government recognition, acceptance and support.

26. We will urge governments to work with Indigenous Peoples to stop the introduction of alien or invasive

species which threaten the health of our traditional territories and food sources.

Indigenous Knowledge and Intellectual Property Rights (IPR)

27. We commit ourselves to safeguard, protect and reaffirm the use of indigenous knowledge and practices, respecting the spiritual values and dimensions of such knowledge. We will strengthen our own initiatives for disseminating information, research, capacity building and the exchange of experiences on biological and cultural diversity among indigenous peoples.

28. We reaffirm and commit ourselves to protect indigenous knowledge systems and the diversity of life within our territories which are collective resources under our direct control and administration. We will work against any IPR regime that attempts to assert patents, copyrights, or trademark monopolies for products, data, or processes derived or originating from our knowledge. Genetic material, isolated genes, life forms or other natural processes must be excluded from IPR regimes.

29. We urge States and international organizations to recognize and respect the establishment and development of our own systems for the protection of indigenous knowledge; and to call for the immediate halt of all biopiracy activities.

30. We call on States and governments to respect the spirit of Article 8(j) of the Convention on Biological Diversity. We demand the annulment of agreements adopted under the Trade Related Aspects of Intellectual Property Rights (TRIPs) of the World Trade Organization (WTO) that compromise indigenous knowledge.

31. We strongly assert our right to full and effective participation in the national and international decision

making arenas on biodiversity and traditional knowledge, such as Convention on Biological Diversity (CBD), World Intellectual Property Organization (WIPO), UN Commission on Trade and Development (UNCTAD) and Andean Community of Nations (CAN).

Biodiversity

32. We call for the declaration of a moratorium on all activities related to human genetic diversity, specifically involving Indigenous Peoples, including access, sampling, testing, research and experimentation.
33. We demand that States establish mechanisms for returning all human, botanical and genome collections, and for providing complete and exact information of any past use of such collections to our peoples.
34. We demand the establishment of an international code of ethics on bioprospecting to avoid biopiracy and to ensure the respect of our cultural and intellectual heritage.
35. We will continue to participate actively in the full process of the Convention on Biological Diversity, through the International Indigenous Forum on Biodiversity, in order to defend and safeguard the biodiversity of our lands and territories, and we call for the coherence and consistency in the implementation of the different Rio instruments, with other local, national and regional instruments.
36. We will oppose biopiracy and the patenting of all life forms.
37. We call for constitutional and legislative recognition of our conservation and management of biodiversity, as inherent to the sovereignty of Indigenous Peoples.

Forests and Protected Areas

38. We demand that all legislation, policies or work programs on forests and protected areas guarantee and rigorously respect our lands and territories, rights, needs and benefits and recognize our full rights to control and manage our forests.

39. We will defend the cultural values and material integrity of our forests, promoting adequate policies for this defense, specifically we call for the declaration of a moratorium on any harmful economic activity, as well as on the granting of concessions for oil and timber exploitation or mining.

40. With regards to protected areas established on indigenous lands and territories, including wetlands, coasts and seas, States must transfer the territorial control, including the jurisdiction, administration and management over these areas to Indigenous Peoples.

Mining

41. We demand the declaration of a moratorium on mining activities until governments and corporations recognize and respect our fundamental rights to self-determination and to free, prior and informed consent on all forms of mining.

42. We demand comprehensive and participatory multi-criteria assessment of mining activities, which incorporates environmental, social, cultural and health impact assessments.

43. We urge governments to establish laws, rules and constitutional provisions that prohibit the confiscation of indigenous lands for mining activities. Indigenous lands and territories must not be included in the planning zones for mining.

Energy

44. We call for the declaration of governmental moratoria on the following activities:

    a. The expansion of and new exploration for the extraction of oil, natural gas and uranium and coal mining within or near indigenous lands and territories, especially in pristine areas and environmentally, socially, culturally and historically sensitive areas.

    b. The construction of large dams. Governments and multilateral institutions should utilize the framework proposed by the World Commission on Dams for an approach to development based on the recognition of rights and the assessment of risk.

    c. New nuclear power plants. We call for a phase-out and decommission of all nuclear power plants.

    d. The transportation and storage of radioactive waste on indigenous peoples' lands and territories. We firmly support the containment and monitoring of waste on-site for the duration of its radioactive life.

45. We will support and commit ourselves to promote the use of renewable energy sources to meet the energy needs of our peoples and communities. We will work towards the development of international mechanisms to support capacity building, financial mechanisms and technology transfer for our communities to address renewable clean energy development to promote sustainable development initiatives that embrace traditional knowledge.

46. We will demand that, in addition to environmental impact assessments on energy related activities, social, cultural and health impact assessments must be conducted, and we commit ourselves to participate actively in such impact assessments.

47. We will urge governments to establish laws, rules and constitutional provisions that prohibit the confiscation of indigenous lands for development energy related activities.

48. We will identify Government subsidies of unsustainable forms of energy and demand that such subsidies be phased out under a five year time frame.

Tourism

49. We will take responsibility for tourism activities we generate, that these are based on our own development strategies, incorporate the respect for our traditional values, ethics and human rights and conserve our natural and cultural heritage.

50. We invite governments to participate in our efforts to develop and apply norms, guidelines and regulations on the development of tourism, based on the principles of respect for our rights, the cultures and the integrity of ecosystems.

Fisheries, Marine and Coastal Resources

51. We will maintain and promote our traditional systems for the sustainable harvesting of marine resources.

52. We commit ourselves to maintain our marine and freshwater fisheries resources that many of our peoples depend upon, and we will fight against over fishing, waste and toxic dumping, as well as the impact of tourism, which affect the oceans, coasts and inland waters.

53. We will develop proposals for the protection and management of national and transboundary coastal areas and their biological resources, and we call on States to

incorporate these proposals into legal and policy frameworks.

54. We will promote the establishment of new quota regimes on an equal footing with other stakeholders, through national and international negotiations, based on our inalienable historical rights as resource owners and managers.

Water

55. We will demonstrate our power and our common interest to protect water and life, by building water alliances and networks worldwide.

56. We call for the creation of an International Regulatory Body to track the trade of water. We oppose and denounce the privatisation of water, as well as the diversion which affects the water resources of our territories.

57. We will demand the establishment of systems for restoration and compensation, to reestablish the integrity of water and ecosystems.

Climate Change

58. We urge the United States and all other countries which have not done so, to ratify and implement the Kyoto Protocol. We urge all countries to adopt equitable cross-sectoral strategies to halt the destruction of key carbon sequestration ecosystems.

59. We demand that the Kyoto Protocol raise the 5. 2% carbon dioxide reduction target and implement the recommendation from the UN Intergovernmental Panel on Climate Change (IPCC) that greenhouse gas emissions

be immediately reduced by 60% in order to stabilize global temperatures.

60. We renew our commitments to our practices and knowledge for minimizing the emission of greenhouse gases, and urge all countries to fulfill their commitments to reduce greenhouse gases emissions.

61. We oppose the implementation of carbon sinks and carbon-trading mechanisms in the Clean Development Mechanism (CDM) of the Kyoto Protocol and United Nations Framework Convention on Climate Change.

62. We urge the States to promote equitable cross-sectoral sociopolitical processes, based on an ecoregion approach, for the economic mitigation of natural disasters caused by climate change.

63. We will give priority to our own scientific and technical initiatives based on our traditional practices, which generate knowledge on production systems which have a minimal greenhouse effect.

64. We demand that Indigenous Peoples be accorded Special Status in the United Nations Framework Convention on Climate Change process.

65. We demand the creation of an Ad Hoc Open-Ended Inter-Sessional Working Group on Indigenous Peoples and Local Communities and Climate Change with the objective of studying and proposing timely, effective and adequate solutions to respond to the emergency situations caused by climate change affecting Indigenous Peoples and local communities.

66. We call upon all governments to implement Climate Impact Assessments which take into account indigenous knowledge systems and observations, as well as the full and equal participation of Indigenous Peoples in all aspects and stages of the assessment.

Health and Toxics

67. We will continue to utilize, strengthen and protect our traditional health systems within our communities. Our indigenous health systems, practices and traditional healers must be given due and equitable recognition. Our collective intellectual rights to our traditional medicines must be protected.

68. We demand financing and equitable partnerships for our own health programs, projects and initiatives.

69. We urge international institutions and governments to participate in the construction of a plural model of public health which validates our traditional knowledge, innovations and practices and healers.

70. We will cooperate to urgently establish all necessary measures to control new and resurgent diseases, such as HIV/AIDS, tuberculosis and malaria. Our traditional and customary institutions and laws should be recognized and strengthened to fight against these diseases.

71. We demand effective participation in the planning, implementation and monitoring of national and international health policies, programmes and services. We also demand that the national health systems provide treatments and vital medicines that are accessible, free of cost or at an affordable price.

72. We urge governments to recognize the particular vulnerability of indigenous children and pregnant and breast feeding women and take the necessary steps to protect them from being exposed to harmful environmental pollutants and conditions.

73. We call for an immediate halt to all polluting activities on indigenous lands and territories and the adoption of mechanisms to contain and monitor existing pollution and its effects on the environment, including the oceans,

and human health. We call for the immediate phasing out of leaded gasoline and other toxic substances.

74. We demand that industries and governments be accountable for the harms they have already caused to the environment and human health. We demand compensation and reparation for the destruction of the environment, including the oceans, and exposure to toxics.

75. We demand that governments expeditiously sign and ratify the Stockholm Convention on Persistent Organic Pollutants, the Rotterdam Convention on hazardous chemicals and pesticides; the Basel Convention and its 1995 ban on the export of hazardous wastes from OECD to non-OECD countries and the 1996 Protocol to the London Convention on ocean dumping.

Desertification

76. We call for the full and effective participation of Indigenous Peoples and local communities, especially those of Africa, in the negotiation and implementation process of the Convention to Combat Desertification. Therefore, we call for the necessary financial resources and equitable mechanisms that will enable us to substantially contribute to this Convention and related activities.

Education, Science, Technology and Communications

77. We will revitalize, strengthen and develop our traditional education institutions and systems for learning at all levels.

78. We will work towards changing the public and private education systems to recognize and teach the cultural

diversity of each country, taking into account the revision of curricula, restoration of historical truth, production of new teaching aids, and introduction of our languages.

79. We will promote capacity-building programmes in indigenous as well as non-indigenous societies on our rights and priorities for sustainable development, in order to strengthen the application of policies for cooperation with and amongst Indigenous Peoples.

80. We will strengthen our research, planning, conservation, use and management of indigenous lands, territories and natural resources using traditional knowledge and other appropriate technologies that respect our cultures and traditions.

81. We will continue strengthening our systems of and networks for information, communications and telecommunications and will request financial resources for these purposes.

82. We will promote networks for scientific and technical cooperation between Indigenous Peoples to strengthen our specialized and diversified learning and capacity building.

Security and Conflict Resolution

83. We will strengthen the capacity of our own indigenous systems of conflict resolution and reaffirm the role of our leaders and traditional authorities in resolving issues related to security and armed conflict such as rape, torture and all other forms of human rights violations. We will ensure that Indigenous Peoples' communities will not be used against each other to escalate armed conflict.

84. We demand the immediate demilitarization in and near indigenous lands and territories and a halt to human

rights violations against Indigenous Peoples. We urge States to resolve conflicts according to democratic principles and relevant international and humanitarian laws.

85. We urge governments to support the voluntary return of Indigenous Peoples, refugees and internally displaced peoples to their ancestral lands and territories. Rehabilitation efforts should address the specific interests of Indigenous Peoples.

Sustainable Livelihoods

86. We strongly reject all policies, including privatization, liberalization and structural adjustment programmes which do not recognize and respect Indigenous Peoples' rights. We strongly support the cancellation of the eternal debt of countries of the South which has resulted in adverse impacts on our cultures, lands and territories.

87. We urge States and the international community to develop specific instruments for the protection of Indigenous Peoples' natural, cultural, social and technological capital as a repository for our economy and the strengthening of indigenous development.

88. We request national governments and the international community to establish a legal framework that validates and enables the functioning of traditional and innovative collective economic models. These economic models should have access to mainstream financial mechanisms, including credit, and should enable trade or barter in goods and services relevant to Indigenous Peoples and our communities.

Corporate Accountability

89. We support the adoption of a legally binding Convention

on Corporate Accountability which upholds Indigenous Peoples' rights, including our free prior and informed consent to any activity of States or transnational corporations, which affects our land, territories or communities.

Governance

90. We demand Indigenous Peoples' full and effective participation at all stages and levels of decision making in programmes, policy and institutions promoting sustainable development.

91. We support the sustainable development models presented by the Arctic Council, which incorporate principles of genuine partnership between States and Indigenous Peoples, ecosystem approaches, collaboration between traditional and scientific knowledge and local, national and regional implementation plans.

92. We call for the inclusion of specific indicators of the situation of Indigenous Peoples in the assessment of the implementation of all levels of Agenda 21 and, in particular, of the progress on the implementation of Chapter 26 and 20 on the participation of Indigenous Peoples and Local Communities.

93. We demand and support the right to appoint our own governing structures. We reject so called "indigenous authorities" imposed at any level on our territories by the government, and used for implementing development models, whether sustainable or not.

Human Rights

94. In accordance with our values, we will take all necessary measures to promote human rights, including human

rights education among Indigenous Peoples and within our communities.

95. We call for the strengthening of the mandate of the Working Group on Indigenous Peoples under the African Commission on Human and Peoples Rights.

96. We will continue to participate in a constructive way in the processes, institutions and bodies of the United Nations and other multilateral organizations dedicated to Indigenous Peoples, such as the Permanent Forum on Indigenous Issues, the Working Group on Indigenous Populations and the Inter-American Commission on Human Rights of the Organization of American States.

97. We urge the United Nations to organize and convene a World Conference on Indigenous Peoples and Sustainable Development in the framework of the International Decade of the Indigenous Peoples of the World (1995-2004).

98. We urge the United Nations to declare the Second International Decade of the Indigenous Peoples of the World (2005-2014).

99. We urge governments to sign, ratify and implement the International Labour Organization Convention No. 169 on Indigenous and Tribal Peoples, in accordance with the wishes of the Indigenous Peoples in their respective countries.

100. We support the UN Permanent Forum on Indigenous Issues as a global focal point for promoting cooperation among States and Indigenous Peoples in the implementation of international policies, commitments and action plans on Indigenous Peoples and sustainable development. We will utilize the UN Permanent Forum on Indigenous Issues to monitor the fulfillment of this plan of implementation.

6

Indigenous Peoples and Native Americans

The problems of Native Americans can be seen in a larger context as the problem of all conquered indigenous peoples. Of the 115 nation-states on this planet, only about 70 of them were founded and are being maintained by the original inhabitants of that land. The rest, 45 nations or so, were built by outsiders who exterminated or tried to exterminate the indigenous, or original, population. The U.S. falls into this latter category.

Indigenous people are referred to as "Fourth World" as opposed to being Third World, which contains some outsider-built nations. About 50 nationalities belong to a group called the Unrepresented Nations and Peoples Organization (UNPO) which includes occupied nations, indigenous peoples, and oppressed minorities. Some indigenous peoples, like Native American Indians, also refer to themselves as "First World/ First Peoples".

Indigenous peoples are not allowed to have embassies, diplomats, or business representatives. They have no power to make trade agreements, collect tax revenue, enter into political alliances, or be involved in immigration. Investors and corporate firms have to be enticed to come in and set up business (a casino, for example) where it is hoped some of the revenue will stay in the community. What is more common, however, are business rip-offs and exploitation. No economic development is allowed at all unless the indigenous people own the land, which in most cases they don't because of unresolved legal battles or the land being held as a trust for them by some government entity. When land is held in trust (a "protectorate" arrangement), banks will not loan money on it, and the only thing to do is lease it out for development to the very same government entity that "protects" it for you. This ensures the exploitation of both land and human resources. The struggle of indigenous peoples is the struggle for sovereignty and the right to self-determination.

The United Nations has been at the forefront of the "indigenous peoples movement". It has been unable, however, to put together more than a 1994 draft Declaration on Indigenous Rights like it was able to do with the 1948 Universal Declaration of Human Rights. This isn't the place to go into international law, but you should know that the U.N. produces two types of documents: Declarations (which are unenforceable), and Conventions or Covenants (which are enforceable). The U.S., contrary to its popular image as the champion of human rights, doesn't really participate much in U.N. discussions on this, and in fact opposes declarations and conventions for indigenous peoples.

According to the Constitution, the U.S. Senate must also ratify all treaties that the U.N. ambassadors commit us to, and the Senate has taken a hard line against anything relating to "self-determination" that might imply the right of indigenous people, or any minority group, to secede from the union. The indigenous rights issue has also taken a backseat to the problem of genocide and creating an International Criminal Court (ICC) which they are right now (7/99) trying out on Yugoslavia. The ICC is separate from the International Court of Justice (ICJ) at The Hague, Netherlands which has existed since 1946.

The original tribal lands are the best way to understand the Native Americans. This is known as the "aboriginal lands" method. Although there is no such thing as a Native American "nation" (even though some tribes use that word to describe themselves), the "Seven Tribes" theory comes closest to describing one. Accordingly, there were:

(1) the Eastern hunter-gatherers, who first encountered the English;

(2) the Great Plains hunters, who first encountered the Spanish;

(3) the fishing societies of the Pacific Northwest;

(4) the seed gatherers of California;

(5) the shepherds and pueblos of Arizona and New Mexico;

(6) the desert societies of the American Southwest; and

(7) the Alaskan peoples, mainly the southernmost Aleuts and the northernmost former Eskimos, now known as Intuits.

Another method is to use linguistics, but it's important to note that Native American is not technically a racial classification. It's a political (ward of the state) designation. There have been attempts by the U.S. government to determine their racial makeup, but it's a controversial area in physical anthropology. Geneticists have uncovered five unique genetic features: earwax texture, organic compounds in urine, an Rh factor in the "blood quantum", fingerprint patterns, and the ability to taste the chemical phenylthiocar bamide. There is little or no scientific support for characteristics such as high cheekbones, reddish complexion, black hair, almond-shaped eyes, and little facial hair. The most promising lead for racial classification was the "blood quantum" approach, but the technique suffers from too much unreliability to be useful for scientific purposes.

The linguistics method is based on the assumption that Native Americans came across the Alaskan land bridge from Asia about 20,000 years ago. The "linguistic stock" method, as this approach is sometimes called, believes that there were twelve original tribes (the "Twelve Tribes" theory) based on linguistic similarities with the known history of Russian language characteristics. The puzzling thing is the Alaskan Eskimo peoples, who would have stayed closest to Russia, speak the least Russian-like language. Mayas, Aztecs, and Incas, who would have ventured further south, also don't fit any Asiatic patterns. Their glyphic language more closely resembles ancient Middle Eastern civilizations. The only way to adequately investigate what theory is true would require an enormous number of archeological digs. That's unlikely to happen anytime soon since Native Americans are already complaining about the desecration and highway construction over their ancestral gravesites.

As an ethnic group, Native Americans were once America's most visible minority. They were always seen in movies and on TV, and before that, on coins and in the form of wooden cigar store indians. They have become a bit less visible in recent years, and would prefer to see the remaining icons disappear. Indian nicknames (i.e., Redskins, Braves, Indians) are frequently used for athletic teams. No other ethnic group in America is used as a mascot. You may remember the flap over the Atlanta baseball team and the "tomahawk chop" which Native Americans saw as a demeaning and mocking gesture. In addition, Native Americans are widely used as logos for several major U.S. corporations (e.g., Butter, Tires, Carpeting, Automobiles), all without adequate consideration for their intellectual and cultural property rights. Their symbols, arts, and crafts have been widely counterfeited, and were one of the first to be replaced by "Made in Taiwan" items.

In1960 there were 523,591 Native Americans. The 1970 figures were 792,730. In 1980, it was 1.3 million. The 1990 Census had 1.9 million people reporting their race as full-blooded American Indian. The Bureau of Indian Affairs says there are 1.2 million card-carrying Indians. Another 7 million claimed partial Native American ancestry on their taxes. That's an astonishing 1 in every 35 Americans. The numbers can't be right, and there are no best estimates. There are approximately

557 different tribes or "bands" in the lower 48 states, at least 200 sizeable Alaskan villages, and 40,000 Native Hawaiians (they call themselves Kanaka Maoli and have already declared their independence from the U.S.) A "band" is a group of kinspeople who recognize a mutual assistance pact, joint economic obligations to one another, and share common rituals and celebrations. Members of a band who have accumulated surplus food or cash share it with other members whenever someone asks or even without asking. The band culture conflicts with many Eurocentric values.

About half of all Native Americans live in rural areas, despite popular belief, neither on or near any of the nation's 278 reservations (only 25% do). This makes them the most rural of any ethnic group in the U.S. The other half live in metropolitan areas. Oklahoma and California account for a sizeable majority. In metropolitan areas where a population cluster exists, the city is named (suburban areas included).

Legal Discrimination

Title 25 of the U.S. Code mentions the Bureau of Indian Affairs (originally a War Dept. agency, not in the Dept. of Interior) as the primary maker and enforcer of treaties and all other agreements with Native Americans. It's a complex piece of regulatory law controlling the lease, sale, and surrender of land as well as various programs for the health and welfare of Indians. The BIA also operates vast educational and law enforcement systems. It's exploitative control over the land-lease "protectorate" arrangement is often complained about. The U.S. Congress does, from time-to-time, talk about dismantling the costly BIA, but many Indians fear the consequence of abruptly ending a system they have become dependent on. The BIA also maintains the list of federally-recognized tribes (every year, about 20 new groups apply for approval), and this is sometimes used as a political tool.

During the Kennedy-Johnson administration, for example, about 100 tribes were stripped of their legal status ("terminated") as punishment for political activism. Federal recognition is the American equivalent of sovereignty. With it comes the power to form tribal governments, determine tribal membership, regulate and tax tribal property, regulate domestic relations and commerce, and establish law enforcement systems. There are about 60 tribes that are not recognized by the federal government, but are recognized by a state government.

Between 1785 and 1866, over 400 treaties were made with the Indians, and it is fairly well-known that every one of them were broken. Some typical scenarios involved taking back the land promised to them or not allowing the Indians to deal with trespassers themselves the way the treaties promised. Starting around 1985, some Indian tribes, like the Oneida, have won Supreme Court decisions giving them back their aboriginal lands, but because these actions would relocate thousands of white people and involve huge sections of states, the matter of enforcing it is anything but clear. The states have not cooperated, and the Tribes have resorted to suing white residents in the area.

Economic Discrimination

The main resource of Native Americans, their land, is leased out to corporations (for mining, waste dumping, ranching, farming, and gaming) by arrangement with the BIA who also control hiring for the migrant worker and regulatory jobs that come with these subsidized business incentive packages. Some 60% of all Native Americans work for the government in some capacity via these business-lease subsidy arrangements. In some cases, the regulatory work is white-collar, but in most cases, it's seasonal or low-paying government jobs that only provide a subsistence income. Indian "experts" constantly make economic decisions on what is good for Native

Americans. The average income is about 66% of that for whites, the lowest per capita income of any population group in the U.S.

Two major problems on reservations are unemployment and entrenched poverty. Native Americans there have a different attitude toward money and material possessions. They are able to survive without doing anything on account of the band culture and its mutual assistance, and they are used to free commodities, like food, water, and wood. No value is attached to the Eurocentric "keeping up with the Joneses", and therefore, most reservation dwellings are huts, shacks, or cabins. Native Americans tend to have lower-quality housing than whites. The Census Bureau reports that 5% of reservation homes don't even have bathrooms.

The (live) birth rates and life spans for Native Americans tend to be the smallest of all ethnic groups. Native Americans rarely live past age 70, and their suicide rates as well as infant mortality rates are double the national average. They are also twice as likely to be the victims of accidents (motor vehicle accidents, drownings, household injuries and/or fires). Problems with alcohol are the stuff of legends, but some experts say the Native American pattern most closely fits the "binge pattern" of white America. Some Indian tribes also value states of trance and euphoria, whether it's the Ghost Dance, the Native American Church and Peyote, or "speaking in tongues". There's a growing awareness within the Native American community that the more retreatist aspects of their lost culture need to be looked at more closely.

Educational Discrimination

It's not well known, but the BIA for years subsidized an educational program intended to alienate Native American youngsters from their parents. Starting in the 1800s and ending only in 1944, Morman missionaries were used to "kidnap" children and take them to Utah to get educated. Indian children were often rounded up at the age of 6 and not returned home until the age of 18. This kind of practice is more typical of totalitarian regimes, and is, in fact, referred to as an act of genocide in the 1948 U.N. Declaration of Human Rights. Since the U.S. stopped doing it, desegregation laws have forced Native American schoolchildren to compete in the same classrooms as white students, where cultural and language differences have ensured that Native American schoolchildren are the only minority group to have a steady decline in their scholastic achievement tests with advancement in grade.

It's not really known what the meaning of an education is to Native American culture. There's some suspicion that it's devalued. Take higher education, for example. Only 1% of all Native Americans have gone to college. Since 1978, there has been a movement toward the creation of tribal colleges. Currently, there are 24 of them in 11 states. Together, they only enroll about 5000 students. The U.S. Congress has authorized a subsidy of $6000 per student with additional promises to pay other operational costs. Former President Reagan was a strong critic of these subsidies, and before he left office, he succeeded in getting the student subsidy lowered. It's unknown what effect this had on the tribal colleges or their current condition today.

Criminal Justice Problems

Gambling invites organized crime, and in fact, can cause property crime 2% of the time. It may seem like a windfall right now for some Native American tribes, but it's not the best choice of industry. All gambling societies have inevitably brought on so much government intervention that, from the Indian point of view, you're right back at the economic dependency you started with. The Native American homicide (and suicide) rate is twice the national average. The rate of Indian arrests for crimes related to alcohol is many times the national average, and drunkenness seems to rise with migration to urban areas. Police officer and Native American contacts are volatile situations because there's a lot of baggage that both parties bring to the encounter.

Some tribal cultures view it as disrespectful to look someone in the eye for a long time, and aggressive verbal behavior is looked down upon by most tribes. Most Native Americans are also uncomfortable with being touched by strangers. English is a second language for some. White people should know that elders, or older people in the tribe, are always shown the upmost respect. Likewise, Native American parents can be extremely overly protective of their children, a fact that should be taken into consideration by juvenile workers.

Several studies on homelessness have found that this population consists of a disproportionate number of Native Americans. There's little trust in the American system, and especially the criminal justice system. Levels of cooperation may vary, and then there's the problem of "checkerboard" patterns of jurisdiction. Most police and court districts take in a part of the reservations, but there may be civil authorities or reservation laws which don't make the "bust" legal. Conflicts may erupt between Native Americans and other citizens over the issues of fishing rights and trespass/ suspected looting of sacred burial grounds.

Native Americans comprise about 5% of the prison population, an overrepresentation for a group that only makes up less than 1% of the U.S. population.

Discrimination against Northern Indigenous People

Socioeconomic conditions among indigenous people of the north have declined dramatically in recent years. In addition to long standing issues, there are new problems associated with high levels of unemployment, deteriorating living conditions, increased sickness and limited educational opportunities.These issues have long been discussed among indigenous peoples and many now believe that the only way to resolve these troubling issues is through direct negotiation with the Russian Government.

The directors and leaders of various social and public interest groups representing indigenous peoples of the north in the Russian Federation,

— in connection with the acceptance of the Russian Federation as a member of the European Council and with the adoption of the Charter of the European Council and General Agreement on Privileges and Immunities of the European Council and its protocols,

— the subsequent signing of the Convention on Defense of Human Rights and Basic Freedoms, November 04, 1950 and its protocols,

— the subsequent signing of the Ramok Convention for Defending National Minorities and the new obligations of the Russian Federation toward the indigenous peoples of the North resulting from these,

— accounting for the diminishing number of the peoples and the extreme climatic conditions of life in the Arctic,

— stating the devastating fact that in the last century Russia has lost such nationalities as Ain, Vod, Kamasinets, Kerek, Omok, and Yug,

— further stating the fact that such nationalities as the Aleut, Ket, Iganasan, Negidalets, Orok, Oroch, Tofalar, Enets, Yukagir are on the verge of extinction,

— noting the abuse of political rights of indigenous peoples: in the 1989-1991 period 18 indigenous representatives were seated in the Supreme Soviet (Parliament) of the USSR and RSFSR where they developed a code of law defending indigenous rights and interests; in 1995 only two deputies were elected to the Federal Assembly (Parliament) of Russia,

— further noting that the majority of the autonomous regions are no longer capable of defending the rights of indigenous peoples of the North and in the latest elections these regions experienced intense pressure from financial and industrial groups that promote interests not in keeping with the with issues facing indigenous people of the north,

— stating that article 69 of the new Russian Constitution does not "guarantee the rights of indigenous peoples" because normative acts have not been passed that provide for the representative needs of the peoples: "Basic Election Right Guarantees for Citizens of the Russian Federation," "Election of Deputies to the State Duma of the Federal Assembly of the Russian Federation," and Formation of the Council of the Federation of the Federal Assembly of the Russian Federation,

— noting that the Resolution Critical Economic and Cultural Condition of Indigenous Peoples of the North, Siberia and Far East, passed by the State Duma at its first meeting, was not followed up with appropriate action by the President or the Government of Russia while at the same time the Government remains indifferent to repeated appeals of the Association of Indigenous Peoples of the North on issues of the survival of these ethnic groups,

— underscoring that the Federal Law "Basis for the Legal Status of Indigenous Peoples of Russia" was passed twice in 1995 by the State Duma: the first time on July 21, and then, with the President's edits, on November 17th, and both times was tabled by the President of Russia, the guarantor of the Constitution, that the reform movement of President B.N. El'tsin that was optimistically supported by indigenous peoples of the North has not met these peoples' expectations,

— recognizing that the Russian Government lacks any kind of policy for the 29 endangered indigenous groups of the north that number 200,000 people, for whom the transition to a market economy is characterized by a total break down of traditional economic activities and way of life, an uncontrolled growth of unemployment and impoverishment, life threatening levels of crime and alcoholism that undermine traditional outlooks on life, sharp decline in the health of the peoples and death rates that are one and a half times the average in the country,

— expressing the will of the most socially unprotected and needy ethnic groups within Russia who have become outcasts on their own land, based upon the aforementioned facts on their political and economic situation,

— and address the President and Government of Russia as well as international organizations and individuals representing the interests of indigenous peoples with the appeal, and from the President and the Government of Russia, based on the fundamental rights of indigenous peoples to freedom, housing, food and education, demand the start of a negotiation process between the Government of the Russian Federation and indigenous peoples of the north as represented by its social organizations and movements in order to resolve fundamental issues essential to the survival and development of the peoples:

1. Procedures for direct compensation to organizations and indigenous enterprises compensation for the damage inflicted to the their lands and economic activities as a result of annexation and industrial development.
2. Direct licensing procedures that provide for the study of ways to develop coal / mineral deposits, production quotas and land tenure that guarantee traditional resource use and economic activities.
3. Creation of an economic development corporation for indigenous peoples of the north.
4. Negotiation procedures between the Russian Government and representatives of indigenous social organizations.

5. Creation, within the office of the President of the Russian Federation, of an fully empowered agency to advance the rights of indigenous peoples of the north.
6. Creation of a government fund to support indigenous peoples of the north.
7. Organization of a system of local, ethnic, self management bodies for peoples of the north.
8. Guaranteed minimum representation for people of the north in federal and regional representative bodies and executive branches.
9. Creation of a Department of the Arctic and appointment of a government ambassador to coordinate, at the international level, issues concerning the development of regions and peoples.
10. Federal Law "Basis for the Legal Status of Indigenous Peoples of Russia" and "Status for Peoples of the North."
11. Events marking in Russia the International Decade of Indigenous Peoples of the World 1995 - 2005.

Racism against Indigenous Peoples

Historians and academics agree that the colonization of the New World saw extreme expressions of racism - massacres, forced-march relocations, the "Indian wars", death by starvation and disease. Today, such practices would be called ethnic cleansing and genocide. What seems even more appalling for contemporary minds is that the subjugation of the native peoples of the New World was legally sanctioned. "Laws" of "discovery", "conquest" and "terra nullius" made up the "doctrines of dispossession", according to Erica Irene Daes, chairperson/rapporteur of the United Nations Working Group on Indigenous Populations, in a study on indigenous peoples and their relationship to land.

Specifically, in the fifteenth century, two Papal Bulls set the stage for European domination of the New World and Africa. Romanus Pontifex, issued by Pope Nicholas V to King Alfonso V of Portugal in 1452, declared war against all non-Christians throughout the world, and specifically sanctioned and promoted the conquest, colonization, and explcitation of non-Christian nations and their territories. Inter Caetera, issued by Pope Alexander VI in 1493 to the King and Queen of Spain following the voyage of Christopher Columbus to the island he called Hispaniola, officially established Christian dominion over the New World. It called for the subjugation of the native inhabitants and their territories, and divided all newly discovered or yet-to-be discovered lands into two - giving Spain rights of conquest and dominion over one side of the globe and Portugal over the other. The subsequent Treaty of Tordesillas re-divided the globe with the result that most Brazilians today speak Portuguese rather than Spanish, as in the rest of Latin America. The Papal Bulls have never been revoked, although indigenous representatives have asked the Vatican to consider doing so.

These "doctrines of discovery" provided the basis for both the "law of nations" and subsequent international law. Thus, they allowed Christian nations to claim "unoccupied lands" (terra nullius), or lands belonging to "heathens" or "pagans". In many parts of the world, these concepts later gave rise to the situation of many Native peoples in the today - dependent nations or wards of the State, whose ownership of their land could be revoked - or "extinguished" -- at any time by the Government. Indigenous leaders today contend that it is essentially discriminatory that native title does not confer the same privileges as ordinary title. According to Mick Dodson, an Australian Aboriginal lawyer, the concept of extinguishment "treats indigenous rights and interests in land as inferior to all other titles". According to indigenous law and custom, indigenous interests can only hold native title, and, according to the law put into place since then by the European immigrants, native title can be extinguished.

Today's Indigenous Peoples

The world's indigenous peoples - or "first peoples" - do not share the same story of colonization. In the New World, white European colonizers arrived and settled suddenly, with drastic results. The indigenous peoples were pushed aside and marginalized by the dominant descendents of Europeans. Some peoples have disappeared, or nearly so. Modern estimates place the 15th century, or pre-Columbus, population of North America at 10 to 12 million. By the 1890s, it had been reduced to approximately 300,000.

In parts of Latin America, the results were similar; in others, there are still majority indigenous populations. But even in those areas, indigenous people are often at a disadvantage. Indigenous peoples in Latin America still face the same obstacles as indigenous peoples elsewhere - primarily, separation from their lands. And that separation is usually based on distinctions originally deriving from race.

Old Indigenous Peoples

Among African peoples, there are clearly groups of peoples who have always lived where they are, who have struggled to maintain their culture, their language and their way of life, and who suffer problems similar to those of indigenous peoples everywhere, particularly when forcibly separated from their lands. These include poverty, marginalization, the loss of culture and language, and the subsequent problems of identity that often lead to social problems such as alcoholism and suicide. Because of these particular similarities, many people find it useful and suitable to consider such groups indigenous peoples.

The hunter-gatherer Forest Peoples (Pygmies) of the central African rainforests, comprising many groups, are threatened by conservation policies, logging, the spread of agriculture, and political upheavals and civil wars. They are usually at the bottom of the social structure. It is ironic that modern conservation policies intended to protect species of animals, not groups of humans, forbid many of these hunter-gatherers from hunting. Nomadic pastoralist peoples like the Maasai and Samburu of east Africa are struggling with the encroachment of farming and conservation into their areas. As they are limited to smaller and smaller spaces, it becomes more and more difficult for them to maintain their livestock, especially in difficult periods, such as times of drought. Increasingly, they are being forced to move to urban areas.

The San, or Bushmen, of southern Africa have in some cases disappeared, or nearly so, as they have lost or been driven from their traditional homelands. Large numbers remain in Namibia, but they are usually impoverished and unable to live their traditional way of life. Many of them, with nowhere to go, have simply stayed, and now find themselves poorly paid laborers on farms - made up of their traditional territory -- now owned by whites or by other Africans.

The Imazighen (Berbers) are the indigenous peoples of northern Africa and the Sahel. The best known Imazighen may be the Tuareg. Most Imazighen who have not been assimilated live in the mountains or the desert. In Mediterranean areas, they have become sedentary; those living in the desert are usually nomadic. Today they exist as small linguistic pockets, with few, if any, cultural protections. Activists are working to maintain their language and culture.

In Australia, Canada and the United States, one practice which has only been recognized as discriminatory and damaging in the second half of the 20th century is the forced removal of Native/Aboriginal children from their homes. In Australia, the practice focused on mixed-race Aboriginal children, who were forcibly taken from their parents and given to adoptive white families. These children usually grew up without the knowledge that they were in fact partly Aboriginal. Today they have been named the "Stolen Generation".

In the US and Canada, Native children were sent to the notorious residential schools, which persisted well into the latter part of the 20th century. Language, religion and cultural beliefs were often the objects of ridicule. Speaking native words was forbidden, and often earned physical punishment - to force a stubborn Indian child to learn to speak good English. Contact with parents and family was often discouraged, or even disallowed. In the worst examples, to discourage run-aways, children were told their parents had died, that there was no home to return to; or, vice versa, to discourage parental visits, families were told that their children had died. In an ironic twist, these falsehoods sometimes proved prophetic: there were cases where children did run away in mid-winter, dressed only in nightclothes, hoping to find their way home. Today it is assumed that they froze to death, as their parents have never been able to find them.

In an earlier age, these actions were defended as being in the "best interests" of the Indian/Aboriginal child, to improve her chances in the modern world. Assimilation was the goal. The value inherent in indigenous cultures and knowledge was not then recognized. In isolated areas, some residential schools attracted faculty and staff of the sort who prey on children. Extensive physical and sexual abuse has been documented. In North America, as the abuse has come to light, victims have been identified and there have been attempts to provide remedies and retribution.

The United Nations first focused its attention formally on the problems of indigenous peoples in the context of its work against racism and discrimination. In 1970, the Subcommission on Prevention and Discrimination and Protection of Minorities (a subsidiary body of the Commission on Human Rights) commissioned Special Rapporteur Martinez Cobo of Ecuador to undertake a study on "The Problem of Discrimination against Indigenous Populations". That monumental study, completed only in 1984, carefully documented modern discrimination against indigenous peoples and their precarious situation. His report catalogued the wide variety of laws in place to protect native peoples: some of these were discriminatory in concept, and others were routinely disregarded by the dominant community. It concluded that the continuous discrimination against indigenous peoples threatened their existence.

The report found that some governments denied that indigenous peoples existed within their borders. Others denied the existence of any kind of discrimination - in contradiction to the reality encountered. It described cases where the governmental authorities, when reporting on the situation of indigenous peoples, unwittingly betrayed their baldly discriminatory thinking.

The establishment of the United Nations Working Group on Indigenous Populations in 1982 was a direct result of the Cobo study. Consisting of five independent experts, the Working Group meets annually in Geneva, and, until now, has been the only arena in the United Nations system in which indigenous peoples could state their views. The United Nations International Decade of the World's Indigenous People has helped to focus efforts in the UN system on two primary goals: the creation of a Permanent Forum on Indigenous Issues, and the drafting of a declaration on the rights of indigenous peoples. The draft Declaration is still under consideration by the UN Commission on Human Rights.

The Economic and Social Council (ECOSOC), the UN Charter body to which the Commission on Human Rights reports, recently took steps to establish the Permanent Forum on Indigenous Issues, which will consist of eight governmental experts and eight indigenous representatives. Indigenous representatives will for the first time be allowed to address directly an official United Nations Charter body, ECOSOC. Due to growing concerns about the environment, the activity undertaken by the Working Group and other United Nations bodies and the advocacy work carried on by indigenous groups and non-governmental organizations, indigenous peoples worldwide are receiving increasing attention from their respective governments.

Countries such as Canada, Australia and the United States have focused efforts on settling land claims with indigenous groups and on achieving reconciliation for past injuries, including those done in the name of assimilation. In Scandinavia, the native Saami have established a parliamentary forum across their national borders. In Africa, indigenous groups have just begun to mobilize. In other areas, indigenous groups have taken strong positions in defiance of their governments. And in a first, a UN-brokered peace agreement in the civil war in Guatemala gave a specific role to indigenous peoples. But a lot has not been settled.

Native groups have made a great deal of progress in pursuing land claims, particularly in the Americas and Australia. Of particular note is Nunavut, Canada's newest and largest territory. The establishment of Nunavut represents a new level of indigenous self-determination in Canada. In response to the reports of widespread abuse in the residential school system, the Law Commission of Canada in 1996 published a report, "Restoring Dignity: Responding to Child Abuse in Canadian Institutions". In its research, the Commission found that, in addition to physical and sexual abuse, it was imperative to also consider the emotional, racial and cultural abuse.

Following the report, the Government of Canada announced a new programme "Gathering Strength - an Aboriginal Action Plan". It called for a renewed partnership with Aboriginal people based on recognizing past mistakes and injustices, the advancement of reconciliation, healing and renewal, and the building of a joint plan for the future. Unfortunately, it has become apparent that resolving such emotionally charged issues will take a great deal of time and commitment.

With over 6,000 lawsuits currently seeking reparations for physical and sexual abuse, the Churches who ran the schools for the Canadian Government and who are co-defendants in the suits report that they are facing almost certain bankruptcy. And a number of the victims of abuse have committed suicide. Elsewhere in North America, the United States is also in the process of settling many land claims. Some Indian Nations have successfully established a level of sovereignty. A few have established casinos that have become multi-billion dollars industries and that provide needed jobs to depressed areas - and not just to residents of the reservation.

In one particularly difficult case, the Federal Government has filed suit against New York State for illegally acquiring and selling land belonging to the Oneida Nation - land that is now occupied by thousands of upset American homeowners. While the Oneida Nation has insisted throughout that they have no intention of seizing anyone's land or evicting anyone, feelings have run very high. Death threats have been made.

The Cayugas, the Senecas, the Mohawks and the Onondagas - all Haudenosaunee, or members of the Iroquois Confederacy, along with the Oneida Nation - also have claims on property in New York State. Because the population of New York State is much more dense than in most other areas of "Indian country", these may prove difficult to resolve to everyone's mutual satisfaction. Pine Ridge Reservation, in South Dakota, is the poorest county in the United States of America. The midwestern states are also the site of more obvious racism against Native Americans. It has been commonly charged that there are two tiers of justce, one for Native Americans and another for "whites".

Native Americans say that crimes committed against them - including those resulting in death - receive only a cursory investigation, while crimes committed against "whites", allegedly committed by Native Americans, are fiercely prosecuted. And daily expressions of racism of the type long thought to exist only in memory still occur — but the apparent recipients are Native Americans. The segregated lunch counters of the South may no longer exist, but Native

Americans say they are not surprised when they are refused service in a coffee shop. Such experiences of Native Americans living in Indian Country, however, are not known to vast majority of American citizens.

7

Indigenous Peoples in Latin America and the Caribbean

Latin America is home to four hundred indigenous communities, composed of about 50 million people, the majority of whom suffer from various forms of discrimination due to their ethnocultural background and survive under marginalized conditions that contrast with the modern world around them. Their economic exclusion is based on general discrimination, similar to that experienced by the impoverished strata in rural and urban environments; however, their marginalization is intensified due to the intolerance and ethno-cultural discrimination existing in the national societies of the region.

The paradigm of economic globalization is sharpening the historical processes of social marginalization of the indigenous peoples. Meanwhile, in the cultural arena, a process of "homogenization" is beginning, which attempts to undermine the pluricultural identity of the continent, ignoring the fact that the construction of modern citizenship involves the challenge of reconciling the historical and cultural specific features of each community with world development and modernity.

However, the causes of the increase in indigenous exclusion and their current marginalization from the information society are not exclusively attributable to the unequal relations generated between the center and the periphery. Furthermore, the analysis must be focused on the internal dynamics of these societies and their forms of leadership, on gender relations and the migratory processes that define the differences between indigenous groups and individuals with respect to the educational level, ethnic awareness and acceptance of one's identity, possibilities for involvement in non-traditional activities and on the acceptance or rejection of the digital means of communication. In some cases, intellectuals, directors and indigenous organizations have seen the ICTs as a valuable opportunity to transcend the local level and achieve a regional, national and international presence.

Digital technology has rapidly and efficiently been appropriated and has the potential to strengthen their political-organizational and communication processes, as well as those of linguistic and cultural revitalization. Also, other indigenous sectors have criticized the ICTs as a new form of interference from the national society that attempts to add the communities to the established information consumption in order to serve the interests of others. To promote indigenous involvement in the information society, it is necessary to define proposals of innovation and reparatory social policies, which strengthen indigenous attempts to overcome the challenge of information marginalization. The strategies to achieve this end come from the native people who have achieved greater levels of community cohesion and representation, direct and legitimate, in second- and third-tier organizations.

In some cases, the non-indigenous political and civil societies start to support these processes, generally at the local level. However, as far as public policies are concerned, the consensus necessary to act in an integral and coordinated manner has not been reached. Such a consensus would join governmental forces with those of the international community and civil society associations, in order to stimulate the so-called "digital opportunity".

Challenges	Opportunities	Proposals
- Cultural prejudice of governmental agencies, NGOs and broad sectors of the national societies. - High levels of distrust within the indigenous communities with respect to the possible disruptive impact of the ICTs on cultural and social guidelines. - The gap between the cultural conception of time and space of the indigenous society and the global society. - Low levels of literacy and computer literacy of the indigenous peoples. - Intra-community processes that impede the appropriation of the ICTs. - High unemployment indices; weak indigenous economic base.	- The indigenous communities' historically successful appropriation of the global society's cultural goods. - Ascent of the ethnic movement to the continental level. - Existence of new types of leadership. - Rise of second- and third-tier organizations. - Greater recognition of the global society of the role of the indigenous peoples in the sustainability of development. - Increase of the international social sensitivity towards indigenous demands. - Experiences of economic, political, cultural and information self-management. - Increase in the educational level of the population,	- Reduction in the levels of prejudice and discrimination in the national societies, through specific communication strategies. - Promotion of favorable attitudes towards the ICTs in the indigenous population and leadership. - Implementation of specific access programs (short, medium and long-range), designed following integral diagnostics carried out with the active participation of the indigenous communities and respectful of their social, cultural and economic structures. - Articulation with long-range economic, social and cultural programs that involve strategic investment to provide

- Elevated costs of technological infrastructure, associated with geographical isolation and a lack of basic infrastructure services. - High levels of technological obsoleteness. - Absence of legal frameworks that facilitate access to credit lines and/or funding for technological programs. - Expansion of the ICTs according to market logic. - Concentrated production of hardware and software in a small nucleus of industrialized countries. - Predominance of English in the technological arena.	especially the migrants, leading to a significant number of indigenous professionals. - Greater acceptance of the incorporation of the gender equity approach. - Social experience accumulated starting from the effective appropriation of the ICTs by the people and organizations that independently manage the communication and information strategies. - Installed capacity in technical and human resources. - Experiences of e-involvement carried out through the model of shared access (telecenters). - Increase in social capital of the communities. - Increase in the technological incorporationof information literacy in basic education.	basic services (electricity, telephones, education) and promote the autonomous organization of the indigenous peoples. - Legal regulation of the participation of the private sector in such programs and support of the public sector when themarket cannot provide effective solutions to combat social inequality. - Implementation of long-range programs that permit intracommunity exploration to decide in what way the ICTs will be incorporated, on the premise that the indigenous communities can decide to use them in a different way than other groups of the national societies.

The current Virtual Workshop on Indigenous Involvement in the ICTs provides a space to deepen the conceptual debate and contribute to the development of a framework for action that facilitates indigenous access to the ICTs by serving as a vehicle of social transformation. The Virtual Workshop is a window of opportunity that adds proposals for an integrated course of action from a great diversity of criteria, experiences and cultural perspectives.

Digital Divide

The presence of the information society is producing a crucial transformation in the form in which people communicate with each other and organize themselves before the challenges of globalization. An important scenario is created in societies that require appropriate tools to promote their inclusion in modernity. For Latin America and the Caribbean, a region with profound economic and social inequalities, the transition toward the emerging paradigm of the information society could mean an unprecedented opportunity to incorporate new paths for development with equity of its citizens.

At the threshold of the new century, economic adjustment and globalization of the economy are producing profound technological, political, and socio-cultural restructuring that sharpens the differences between the sub-regions and marginalizes broad sectors of the population. In the long run, unequal development at the global level creates new dimensions that sharpen the poverty and exclusion within each social organization. In this sense, the international digital divide is directly associated with the preexisting socioeconomic conditions in Latin America; therefore, the internal digital divide in each of the countries increases the various types of exclusion experienced by the most underprivileged groups, among which the indigenous peoples form one of the sectors with the most extreme social lag.

If one maintains that the digital divide "should not be measured only by the possibility to utilize the latest communication technologies but, also, in terms of the capacity to process information and the ability to create mutually beneficial systems that can help improve the quality of life", it is possible to conceive the size of the abyss between the native populations' current position and their achieving an effective technological appropriation that can stimulate an agenda of development with equity.

In terms of ethno-cultural diversity, the Region has more than four hundred indigenous groups that are ethnically differentiated from each other and display a large variety of cultural manifestations; many of the countries are multi-ethnic and pluricultural. While some of the original populations have few members, many others exceed a quarter of a million and, in some cases, constitute a country's majority population. The total indigenous population of the continent is estimated to be 50 million. Most of these individuals are discriminated against because of their ethno-cultural identity and survive under conditions of economic and social marginalization, which creates ostensible contrasts between the modern world and the neglected settlement areas.

Latin America and the Caribbean make up one of the regions that still has not consolidated sufficient social forums for the debate, clarification, criticism, and expression of ethno-cultural demands, all of which will lead to the difficult root sustained by intercultural and inter-ethnic relations. These forums could unveil the reason of being, and have also paved the way to overcome these difficulties, instead of hiding them and appealing to the supposed benefits of forgetting or denying one's roots, or the proliferation of simple statements of tolerance which are always useful, but insufficient.

The Latin American states, supported in brave declarations in the latest world forums, legally recognize the equality of rights for all of their citizens, stating explicitly and emphasizing that this equality applies to members of all races and ethnic groups historically discriminated against. However, in their daily practices and routine behavior, actual societies, their governments and people promote an unequal treatment of the members of the native cultures. The contradictions between "legal" society and "real" society are part of the constitution of the modern states. While socioeconomic and political marginalization exist in the indigenous communities of the Region, current legislation regarding egalitarian integration will be nothing more than one of the emerging elements of these contradictions.

The equality of rights with actual inequality strengthens the discrimination hidden within society and tends to inhibit and demobilize the groups directly affected. The economic exclusion of the indigenous peoplesis based on the general discrimination that all impoverished strata of the city and countryside experience; however, because they belong to communities that have a different culture and history, they face another form of discrimination, namely intolerance and specific types of discrimination, based exclusively on their ethnic and cultural distinction.

The continuous social diffusion of a devaluating point of view of that which is "different" permeates all sectors of the national societies: the indigenous peoples are not only discriminated against by the most privileged sectors, which could be due to an inherited colonial ideology, but, also, by the non-indigenous members of their own social sector. This might be due to the poor, non-indigenous citizen's preference to identify himself culturally with the behavior of the hegemonic and privileged sectors, or because his contempt for the devaluated "other" confirms the existence of another "inferior" group on the social scale that allows him to obtain secondary benefits in possible public alliances and opportunities to accede to a greater social participation. The construction of modern citizenship, penetrated by tensions between the strengthening of the identities of the ethnic minorities and the cultural homogeneity proposed by the recent paradigms of modernity and globalization, implies assuming the challenge of reconciling the historicalcultural specific features of each community with development and modernity.

Challenges in the Third Millenium

In the last decades, the technification seen in some agricultural sectors has further marginalized the indigenous peoples in the production circuit. The movement of the smallholding economy towards a highly productive and self-sustainable agricultural one has been impeded by the scarcity of land and technical and credit abandonment. Environmental deterioration increased in many areas where indigenous peoples live, whose survival depends on the protection of renewable natural resources. For the majority of the native communities, land and its natural resources are considered "property" since they have to do with the habitat, or "living space". In no way are they considered "goods of exchange", as established in the rationality of extensive commercial exploitation. This contradiction produces new conflicts, greater impoverishment, and an increase in migration as well as in the sector's vulnerability.

Within the framework of an economic model that causes recurring, recessionary situations and restrictions on the labor market, indigenous marginalization is becoming worse. As a reduction in work opportunities increases competition, the unequal pressures on the job market become stratified by various types of discrimination. For example, the ethnocentric behaviors of the employers favor the applicants' belonging to the hegemonic social group over their professional qualifications; consequently, the average income of the total indigenous population, women and men, is less than that of the non-indigenous population, even in countries such as Chile.

Technological development and the growing incorporation of the national societies in the paradigm of the information society creates a serious domestic digital divide in each of the countries, in which the indigenous peoples form one of the sectors that is lagging the most in terms of access and appropriation. Their marginalization from the new information and communication technologies (ICTs) reinforces their limitations to become involved in a job market that has a growing need for them. However, for most indigenous peoples, the ICTs form part of the group of goods of the global society that they see as indispensable, destined for other, more socially privileged sectors, and from which they tend to experience an enormous distance in technical and, above all, cultural terms.

These recent phenomena, resulting from the new paradigm of economic globalization, add to the historical processes of social marginalization of the indigenous peoples. These processes are reproduced, activated and strengthened before each new act of exclusion, such as those that neoliberalism and its globalization model are producing in the Region. Also, exclusively in the cultural arena, the dissemination of an ideology-support of globalizing macroeconomic concepts stimulates a process of "homogenization", which undermines that pluricultural identity of the continent.

However, the causes of the increasing exclusion of the indigenous peoples and their current marginalization from the information society are not exclusively attributable to the unequal relations generated between the center and the periphery, between "backwardness and modernization." Furthermore, the level of analysis should be focused on the internal dynamics of the indigenous society, on their communities and leadership. Even though the socioeconomic lag of the indigenous peoples could be attributed to the deterioration of the peasant economies and the marginal-urban sectors, there are certain features of their socio-political and cultural dynamics that sharpen the aforementioned exclusion and bring awareness to various cultural behaviors, often opposing, which not only concern economic development, but also their degree of community cohesion and association with new technologies.

In order to start to define strategies that stimulate the participation of indigenous peoples in the basic codes of modernity, a more precise analysis highlights the internal differences existing in a population that, as a whole, is in an unfavorable position in terms of its access to goods and services. Such differences refer to longstanding inequities (by gender, social stratification, generation, etc.) and new cases of marginalization related to more recent population processes, such as the increase in migration for economic reasons and displacements provoked by border wars and regional and intra-community conflicts. The changing scenario to redefine the limits of ethnic entities establishes distances in the educational level, the conscience and acceptance of one's identity, the possibilities to obtain work in non-traditional activities and, in particular, the interaction with the digital means of information and communication.

In the first place, it should be mentioned that the gender inequities that impede women's development affect the quality of life and the well-being of the communities. For women, there is not an equal relation between physical and social reproduction and their access to productive, educational and communication resources; gender roles are assigned at an early age and are always prejudiced against women. Only a minimal percentage of women at an active age manage to enter the job market in the few populated centers. On average, they receive half the salary that men receive.

Scholastic desertion affects women in a different way than it affects men for reasons such as early pregnancy, involvement in domestic work or other economic factors for which the education of men is favored; girls are discriminated against in access to and continuation in the educational system. Also, the rights of indigenous women are continually violated. However, the problem is generally not approached from the scenario of multiple domination in which they find themselves, attending to socioeconomic, ethno-cultural and gender considerations. The interaction of these factors produces a complex set of inter-ethnic frictions and subordination of women. In cases such as those of the Tsotsil and Tseltal (Mexico), K'iche, Mam and Q'anjob'al (Guatemala), Quechuas and Aguaruna/Huambisa (Peru) women, the psychological effects of the violence suffered during armed confrontations and isolation create, with marked regularity, identity conflicts, dejection, depression and a strong deterioration of self-esteem. To this set of extreme submission and devaluation one adds the endemic and generalized phenomenon of illiteracy.

Therefore, the deruralization process of the youngest members of the communities tends to have a negative impact on the internal cohesion of the indigenous groups; in fact, the migratory movement affects and threatens the continuity of the ties of solidarity based on the kinship and reciprocity relations established in each culture. There are frequent rivalries between "those who left" and "those who stayed" in the communities, even though in neither case are strictly individual "options" concerned, but rather different survival strategies in a situation of shared impoverishment. In a context that is unfavorable for the economic survival of the families because it is based exclusively on agricultural production, land, a symbol-support of identity, is associated with each youth who assumes the mandate of his ancestors and continues working the plot of land of his parents and grandparents.

However, not all of them are chosen to maintain the "living space", that piece of land that offers a sense of ethnic belonging. It is also the place to which emigrants periodically return to mitigate their involuntary uprooting. The system of possession of the land-the smallholding and its subdivisions-is one of the principal causes provoking an expulsion of the residents; this expulsion, in turn, is increasing the indigenous presence in the periphery of big cities.

In their new locations, the migrants find themselves in continuous interaction with the nonindigenous society. This situation increases the phenomenon of discrimination and the inequality of opportunities for the indigenous peoples who recently arrived in the environment. Despite suffering from the consequences of the stigma of their native background, for most of them and, certainly, for the new generations born in the city, there are certain advantages to living in an urban environment. Some of these advantages are the acquisition of or improvement in Spanish as a second language, the possibility to study at various academic levels, employment opportunities that require higher qualifications, the stimulus of various forms of consumption through daily contact with the cultural offerings of the cities, means of mass communication and new information technologies, etc.

Some of the children of peasant origin who have had access to work opportunities, training, political and union experiences in the city are becoming the new generations of indigenous leaders. They have the behaviors and values of a culture in which one finds both features of an autochthonous cosmovision and a modernizing social point of view that is sometimes expressed in proposals for self-management starting from the recuperation of one's ethnicity. The conflicts between old and new leadership are numerous and make up a split that is comparable to that which the political parties or churches and religious sects have produced exogenously for decades.

In some cases, intellectuals, directors and indigenous organizations have seen the ICTs as a valuable opportunity for them to transcend the local level and achieve a regional, national and international presence. Digital technology has rapidly and efficiently been appropriated and has the potential to strengthen their political-organizational and communication processes, as well as those of linguistic and cultural revitalization, etc. The most well known and important case is that of the Zapatista Movement (EZLN) in Chiapas, Mexico, though there are numerous other experiences as well, from different angles and interests, that show the capacity to incorporate the ICTs and advance self-management. Also, other indigenous sectors have criticized the information technologies as a new form of interference from the national society that intends to add the communities to the established information consumption to serve the interests of others.

The existence of the aforementioned internal tensions is a critical aspect for the process of indigenous involvement in the information society. The role of leadership is very important because it influences the possibilities for the population's access; the ideological stance of the leaders regarding the worth of the ICTs determines whether they will be incorporated as cultural goods produced by the national society. Such differentiated positions are related to the long-term impact of the multiple, incomplete attempts for an equitable incorporation in the surrounding society; in other cases, they result from a conscious political will that denies a greater participation due to the fear of losing the ethnic and cultural specific features, as they do not recognize the fact that social integration is not incompatible with autonomy.

On the other hand, these particular expressions of ethnic resistance generally obscure the existence of opportunities that help the indigenous stakeholders to guide the modernization process, articulating it with the identifying characteristics of each native community.

Indigenous Peoples and ICTs

Until the present, no exhaustive studies have been carried out on the levels and paths of access, use and purposes of the indigenous peoples who have involved the ICTs in their daily activities. Census records do not show breakdowns by ethnic origin of the users. Those census records that have recently included this variable, such as in Chile, are currently being developed and their results will be available in 2003.

In some countries, like Mexico, Ecuador or Peru, there is an increasing number of indigenous peoples who have studied at the secondary or higher educational levels or who, due to their participation in social and political processes, are capable of self-managing communication and information strategies. Without a doubt, the presence of the individuals and organizations in the information systems, as well as the democratization of access to the ICTs, helps to modify the stigmatized image of the indigenous peoples that ethnic prejudice has established in the collective point of view. Furthermore, it promotes a diversity of discourses in a hegemonic global environment.

However, in terms of a broader participation of the population as a whole, few pilot programs are being designed or implemented for Internet access through the construction of community information centers, according to the shared access model. ECLAC's perspective places greater social significance on community or private proposals of this nature, which create opportunities for participation for the marginal sectors lacking access to the new technologies, than to the expansion of individual proprietorship of the means of communication. The most significant advances in this area have been made in the extreme north of Latin America. In 2003, the Monterrey Institute of Technology (Mexico) began the gradual installation of 500 telecenters in the communities of various linguistic groups of the country. These centers have been intended for the acquisition of reading and writing in Spanish through computerized learning methods.

However, the articulation between individual learning and collective training, which is the community's form of transmitting knowledge, is relative. There have been advances made in South America as well; in Columbia, the Inforcauca project, promoted by the International Center for Tropical Agricultural (CIAT) and the Universidad Autónoma de Occidente (UAO), with the financial support of the International Development Research Centre (IDRC) of Canada and the Rockefeller Foundation, have put into effect three community telecenters to facilitate the residents' access to information about the economy and sustainable management of natural resources.

In Chile, the Red de Información Comunitaria del Instituto de Informática Educacional of the Universidad de La Frontera, Temuco facilitates access to people and organizations of the region. Its homepage, available in Mapudungun, Spanish and English, has links to 21 communities with telecenters, serving as a connection between local and universal space. In the area northeast of the border between Ecuador and Colombia, the communities A´io Cofán, Siona and Secoya, members of the Amazonian Defense front, participate in the Community Networks project, which has three telecenters through trained community promotors.

In a first attempt for systematization, which requires greater evaluation and depth, it is possible to develop some categories that espouse the modes that the indigenous peoples have acquired in the information networks.

Involvement in the Information Society

In an analysis of the challenges that the native population faces regarding its involvement in the emerging paradigm of the information society, some central convergent aspects can be seen that result in their marginalization from the new technologies, concerning the rationalities and processes of the two different cultural worlds: global society and indigenous society. The strong root of cultural prejudice, which has already been indicated, carries particular significance when it exists in the key decision-making sectors within national societies. There are also aspects directly related to the information paradigm that influence and stimulate indigenous marginalization.

In the first place, the same mode of expansion acquired by the ICTs shows that it is oriented according to market logic;

this differs substantially from the cosmovision, which, though affected by the colonial process, still gives some meaning to the daily life of many of the indigenous communities of the Region. Concomitantly, the hegemony of technological production, concentrated in a small nucleus of industrialized countries and the predominance of the English language in the ICTs arena add barriers to the process of involvement of the indigenous communities.

The elevated costs of technological infrastructure in the indigenous areas are associated with the geographical isolation of the rural communities and the lack and/or deficiencies of basic infrastructure services. The absence of regulatory legal frameworks that facilitate funding opportunities is clear when the indigenous applicants lack titles of individual ownership of their plots of land. Also, the high levels of technological obsoleteness impose a fast rhythm of replacement that is far from the few opportunities for access to credit of a sector characterized by its weak economic base, while the rate of change impedes the community decision making processes. However, the central aspect of this tension might be related to the gap between the cultural conception of time and space of the indigenous society and the global society.

Within the indigenous society, in addition to the aforementioned intra-community processes that impede their information involvement, the blunt presence of illiteracy becomes a central obstacle that must quickly be overcome in order to democratize access to the ICTs. As Hilbert and Katz express, "the lack of education could be a crucial factor in the expansion of the digital divide. In debates on this issue, the fact that illiteracy is one of the fundamental barriers to participation in the information society tends to be avoided". However, one should remember that a person's illiteracy carries multiple capacities, the product of his life experiences and the transmission of knowledge through oral tradition.

However, even in the case of the indigenous peoples who have managed to achieve access to adequate educational levels, it is likely that this sector will also remain excluded from the information society. Control of the written code on the part of the potential users is a necessary, but insufficient, condition to stimulate the appropriation of the new technologies, promote information technology proficiency and the reduction of the digital divide. This observation highlights the importance attributed to the reduction of the cultural distance and the increase in the capacity of the ICTs to engage the users to participate the in linguistic and cultural contents; in this way, they can achieve an effective communication with other indigenous beneficiaries and support a more detailed study of their organizational processes.

Access to information organized according to the interests and needs of the indigenous users could contribute to a reduction in the levels of distrust of the communities and their forms of leadership, with respect to the possible disruptive impact of the ICTs in the cultural and social guidelines of the native communities. A recent analysis of ECLAC states, "one's ethnic group is another factor of the digital divide in Latin America and the Caribbean. The probability of having a computer in one's home is five times greater in the whole of the non-indigenous population than in the homes of indigenous peoples. The probability of having a television is two times higher". The fact that nearly 70% of Latin American homes have televisions offers a false image of democratization and mass access to consumption. However, the process of universalizing formal citizenship has not improved social participation and the political systems maintain a precarious stability.

Rural illiteracy clearly contrasts with urban consumption via the Internet. While infra-human conditions multiply, only a few kilometers from the indigenous communities, wealth, consumption and technological development exceed capacity of united social organization and, often, the governing of our societies. The sensitivity and daily creative capacity of the residents of the large capitals diminishes or disappears before an often inefficient or uncontrolled use of the Internet through domestic connections.

Despite the discouraging data of reality, the scenario of indigenous involvement in the information society also presents opportunities that are stimulated by the indigenous movement as well as by the international community's realization about the role of the native communities for the sustainability of world development. In the last ten years, it has been observed that the indigenous movement has multiplied its course of action and increased its presence in the international forums. It has also increased the consideration of important sectors of the global society regarding its demands and vindications; these processes have given rise to new reflections and conceptualizations on the subject.

From the beginning of inter-ethnic contact, the indigenous peoples developed new survival strategies. Depending on the degree of vitality of the native culture, some strategies tend to the appropriation and assignment of new meaning to those cultural goods produced by the hegemonic society that favor the organizational processes of the communities. There are numerous historical examples, such as the appropriation of the horse or the military tactics of the colonizers, as well as current practices that articulate central aspects of their cosmovision with knowledge from the global society. Such is the case of the complementation of the Andean health system with the proposals of western medicine or the adoption of the new production technologies along with the revaluation of the agro-ecological principles of the American communities. These practices, which associate and interweave different worlds and often opposing conceptions, constitute undeniably intercultural strengths of the indigenous peoples, which facilitate their interaction with the new information paradigm.

The process of ethnic uprising, which has taken place throughout the sub-continent since the 1970s, multiplies the instances of autonomous community organization and stimulates new stages of ethnic awareness that exceed the old, hidden mechanisms of self-destructive resistance. These transformations are mobilizing processes for the revitalization and acceptance of one's identity, which, in many cases, have a positive impact on the transitional internal conflicts and favor a gradual increase in the cohesion of the indigenous groups in order to define and put into effect strategic political projects with a strong cultural base.

Without a doubt, the growing number of indigenous peoples moving to urban environments, one of the most significant changes of recent times, as well as access to formal education, greater participation of women and the practices of political, cultural, communication and information self-management represent opportunities for participation in the ICTs; they are open with respect to the experience accumulated and the lessons learned, which are already showing supportive results for the indigenous stakeholders. Also, the established capacity in human and technical resources, which emerges from the process of indigenous appropriation of the new technologies, serves as a basic platform to increase their participation, help the new users come closer to the ICTs and stimulate the consolidation of the existing social capital.

Among the possibilities in the indigenous social arena, there have also been advances in the basic education of children. Technology has gradually been incorporated in rural zones in order to promote computer literacy. This process, in turn, has awakened interest and motivation of the adults to participate in the proposals for involvement. Also, one hopes that constant technological advancement will contribute to a progressive reduction in costs, which would facilitate becoming connected at prices accessible in a framework of social and economic rationality. The development of new designs also generates expectations about the effective positions of the ICTs as a "bridge" with the spoken word and transmitter of knowledge, contributing in its own way to the reduction of the digital divide.

Finally, it is of great importance to point out that the presence of the indigenous communities in the information systems represents an opportunity for the global society, in terms of the possibility of getting to know the indigenous cultures better and enrich one's life with the contributions of the knowledge of other ancient communities: cosmovision, philosophy, spirituality, scientific and technical knowledge, social relations and relations with nature, etc., which could contribute to forming a more integrated conception of the human condition. At the same time, the diffusion of indigenous cultural values stimulates the destruction of the image currently transmitted in information technology; it generally refers to negative aspects (extreme poverty, illiteracy, malnutrition, etc.) or emphasizes native "picturesque/ folklore" aspects.

Incorporation of Indigenous

After analyzing the social and economic tendencies for Latin America and the Caribbean, it is difficult to imagine, in practice, future scenarios of prosperous and equitable development, with environmental sustainability, and respectful of the identity and culture of the indigenous peoples. As ECLAC expressed, "the utilization of the digitalization process to celebrate linguistic and cultural diversity does not automatically imply a full integration in the global economy. Also, use of the ICTs to foster economic growth does not include the simultaneous strengthening of democratic participation; enjoying the cultural goods, art and entertainment does not automatically improve the health of the members of society and so on".

In a context that stimulates social fragmentation, the proposals supporting a democratic participation in the information society reclaims strategies that encourage advances towards more united forms of relating and redefining a more inclusive "we". Therefore, it is necessary to visualize proposals for innovation and social policies that are reparative to the guidelines of the current economic model. This is possible because, despite the clear global tendencies of cultural homogenization, indigenous efforts to overcome this challenge are continually arising in various Latin American contexts. There are many strategies in this area, which come the communities that have achieved the greatest levels of community cohesion and representation, direct and legitimate, in second- and third-tier organizations. In some cases, the political society and non-indigenous civil society start to support these processes, generally at the local level.

The governments of the Region, the formers of public opinion, the political system and broad sectors of civil society, continue to express their worries and the need to combat the negative consequences of the indigenous exclusion, within the framework of a discourse of respect for ethnic identities and cultural idiosyncrasies. Also, the International Community recognizes that a most efficient course of action is necessary to reverse the information marginalization of the native people. However, in terms of public policies, a consensus has not been reached, which is necessary to act in an integral and coordinated form. Such a consensus would unite governmental forces of the international community and the civil society associations, in order to stimulate the so-called "digital opportunity". A long work experience with indigenous issues shows the good and bad practicesthat indicate the need to join forces and coordinate actions to avoid an overlap of resources, the breakdown of interventions and their counter-productive effects.

In this sense, the current Virtual Workshop on Indigenous Involvement in the ICTS is a relevant space for the constructive discussion and exchange between the participants in order to advance the development of the conceptual bases of a framework for action that facilitates indigenous access to the ICTs as a vehicle of social transformation. The current document is proposed as a preliminary motivational reflection of the debate of the Virtual Workshop as an open space to combine proposals and strategies in the different levels required for an integrated action which, at the same time, has the greatest diversity of criteria, cultural perspectives and experiences.

The sum of contributions, lead by the indigenous organizations or in coordination with them, depending on the various national contexts, could lead to the implementation of a series of proposals articulated in a Regional Strategy for the Reduction of the Information Marginalization of the Indigenous Communities. Following the experiences carried out by ECLAC with numerous indigenous communities of the continent without ceasing to emphasize the following considerations: in the first place, the importance of the active role of the indigenous groups in the process of developing a conceptual-organizational framework that features strategies and opens a path to stimulate the reduction of the digital divide.

Secondly, the strategy is conceived as part of a design of medium- and long-range public policies, intended to facilitate the movement of the native communities towards involvement in the digitalization process; this would minimize the serious risks of remaining marginal to the information society in the modern world. Finally, although far from a universal proposal, the specifications described only attempt to contribute to the social effort to dissolve the prejudice existing in the non-indigenous society and promote actions to improve the quality of life of the native communities. In a first approach, the Regional Strategy is seen as integrating different areas of action and diverse stages or phases of their own duration, which are sometimes simultaneous or complementary, depending on the economic, political and socio-cultural characteristics of each indigenous community and national or sub-regional context:

a. *Revitalization of the ethnic and cultural identity of the indigenous peoples*: the national societies and their public policies can contribute to this process, opening spaces the promote the development of the ethnic organizations as social contributors to of their own economic, social, cultural and information development. The process of ethnic uprising is a key aspect to stimulate the capacity for individuals and communities to appropriate the new technologies.

b. *Definition of a communication policy of significant impact, aimed at the reduction of ethnic discrimination and the digital divide*: the prejudiced behavior and intolerant ideas are expressed daily in the broadest forms of communication, where those who form opinion recreate archaic prototypes of interpretation of the intercultural relations and their routine occurrence. Therefore, this phase opens a long and difficult process of transformation that highlights the social values point of view of the non-indigenous population. This will only be accomplished while there exists, on the part of the political class and civil society together, a commitment to pluralism and the vocation to share, without exception, the benefits of access to the information society.

c. *Revision of the rash defense mechanisms of the values and behavior of the people historically discriminated against*: like all social organizations, the indigenous communities have customs, beliefs, and ways of life that affect their daily actions and which do not necessarily benefit their survival, nor should they be accepted or vindicated solely by virtue of their belonging to those cultures. It will be necessary to encourage multiple and continual instances of self-criticism, lead by the indigenous organizations and communities, in constant dialogue, negotiation or consensus with the non-indigenous civil society, above all, at the local level. The intercultural approach and unprejudiced reflection process about the potentialities of the ICTs to promote local development can contribute to the acceptance and recognition of the advantages of their incorporation in the daily lives of members of the indigenous population.

d. *Self-affirmation of the ethnic identity and distinct cultural of the indigenous peoples, in a scenario of self-management*: this involves the design of new public policies, at local and central levels, which are expressed in the implementation of social, communication and information programs, specifically managed by those interested. These programs are oriented towards generalizing an equitable cultural co-existence, with equality of opportunities for participation in the paradigm of the information society.

The principal guidelines for the implementation of these strategic aspects include the following:

1. Opening multiple spaces of dialogue and debate about the modes transition towards involvement in the information society, between the governmental authorities (central and local) and the legitimate indigenous organizations (in the traditional route or through direct representation). These spaces of settlement will be based on the respect for community organization and the cultural manifestations of the indigenous peoples;
2. Design of consensual policies and actions that correspond to concrete means of reduction of the social phenomenon of information exclusion;
3. Emphasis on two basic principals that guide the spirit of the social programs to conceive and implement: the principle of self-determination so that a community can play an active role in its own development and the principle of self-management as an instrument to learn the concrete tasks that require the gradual incorporation of the population and the indigenous communities into the digitalization process.
4. The development, in collaboration with the interested groups, of a Specific Program for Indigenous Access to the New Information and Communication Technologies, associated with the demands of the communities themselves (civil and human rights, electronic municipal

government, environmental protection, production, bilingual and intercultural autonomous education, integral health, etc.) and coordinated, at local and decentralized levels, with the politics of economic development and basic infrastructure (electricity, telephones, a road network, etc.). This articulation, in the indigenous areas, will promote courses of action that balance the current disadvantageous situation and stimulate the construction of a demand and the creation of local initiatives for involvement in the ICTs.

Incorporation of the minimal conditions of basic infrastructure in the most neglected rural zones and improvement of the existing infrastructure in the entire indigenous settlement area. This should occur in a way that facilitates access to the new users in a number that can become significant for the national figures, above all, in countries such as Guatemala, Ecuador, Bolivia or Peru;

— Reduction of illiteracy and increase in the educational level of the whole of the native population, especially the women;

— Promotion of attitudes favorable for the incorporation of the ICTs, among the leaders as well as the population;

— Emphasis on the transformation in the basic education of girls and boys: incorporation of bilingual education programs (with agents, modes of transmission of knowledge and their own cultural contents) and, in particular, stimulating movement from the traditional pedagogical paradigm towards the proposals of critical pedagogy. This will promote proactive/positive behavior in the children and the development of cognitive frameworks conducive to the use the ICTs;

— Stimulation of the mode of shared access to the ICTs through telecenters in rural and peripheral-urban areas;

— Official recognition, normalization and dissemination of the writing of the indigenous languages, in order to open intercultural information spaces. In such spaces, each indigenous community can express itself in its own linguistic code, which will encourage the production of a non-traditional space for the native languages;

— Identification and training of grassroots, rural and marginal-urban indigenous organizations, which are capable of self-managing community micro-enterprises that involved in the information society;

— Self-identification of local practices that benefit from the use of the ICTs and, in turn, promote their incorporation;

— Stimulus of the self-management of the new technologies and the production of contents; fostering of the process of appropriation and training of the indigenous users;

— The preparation of supervision and control (local and community), which will guarantee the effectiveness of the coordination mechanisms, control the administration of the information resources and supervise their equitable distribution at the community level;

— The opening of sources of work based on the new resources and skills available in the communities;

Development of research on the forms of appropriation, access, modes of use, objectives and projections of the current participation of the indigenous groups and individuals in the information society, focusing in depth on paradigmatic and representative case studies. The design of such participative research, will guide intra-community exploration to decide in which way the ICTs will be incorporated. This will occur on the premise that the indigenous communities can decide to use the ICTs in a different form than other groups of the national societies.

8

Indigenous Peoples of Vietnam

In 1982, the Government of Viet Nam ratified the International Convention on the Elimination of All Forms of Racial Discrimination (CERD). By ratifying the Convention, the Government of Viet Nam committed itself to bring an end to racism and racial discrimination in the country. The examination of the periodic report by Viet Nam offers an opportunity for dialogue with the CERD Committee. Asian Indigenous and Tribal Peoples Network (AITPN) studied the periodic report of Viet Nam with interest. In the periodic report, Viet Nam explicitly denies the existence of racism by stating: "For the Vietnamese people, racial discrimination is unfamiliar and does not exist in the country". As the World Conference Against Racism, Racial Discrimination, Xenophobia and Related Intolerance is little over a month away, the position of the States such as Viet Nam about the denial of the existence of racism and racial discrimination is disturbing.

Indigenous peoples of Viet Nam, presently known as ethnic minorities had collaborated with the Americans during the Viet Nam war. Because of their past association, there are prejudices against indigenous peoples and they face structural and systemic discrimination. The first major democratic uprising of the ethnic minorities in Vietnam took place in Dak Lak and Gia Lai provinces in Central Highlands on 2-6 February 2001. Thousands of indigenous peoples held protest demonstrations unheard of in Viet Nam. This is an indication of the deep discontentment of the indigenous peoples with Hanoi that arose due to denial of autonomy, land appropriation, sponsored settlement of the Kinh, religious intolerance and denial of access to basic facilities like heath care and education. As Hanoi sought to militarily suppress peaceful and democratic dissent, hundreds of indigenous peoples fled into the jungles in Viet Nam in April-May 2001.

Many crossed the international border to Cambodia and were accorded refugee status by the United Nations High Commissioner for Refugees (UNHCR). Many were forcibly repatriated and allegedly faced persecution on their return. Viet Nam has more comprehensive policy on ethnic minorities or indigenous peoples than any other country in the Greater Mekong Sub-region. While AITPN notes the promulgation of laws and regulations covering many aspects of the lives of indigenous peoples as an indication that a policy of promoting the status of indigenous peoples is being pursued by Hanoi, Viet Nam's periodic report contained insufficient data on health, education, welfare and other social and economic conditions of life of the different ethnic minority or indigenous groups. This lack of information makes it difficult to assess properly the implementation of the Convention by the State Party.

Discrimination Against Indigenous Mountain Peoples of Viet Nam seeks to assist the CERD Committee by providing information on discrimination against indigenous peoples in Viet Nam for effective examination of the sixth to the ninth periodic report of the Government of Viet Nam and to enable the CERD Committee to make appropriate recommendations. Earlier, then Ambassador of Viet Nam told the CERD Committee in October 1994 that "the Government of Viet Nam was aware that the elimination of racial discrimination meant guaranteeing ethnic groups an acceptable level of socioeconomic development and giving them preferential treatment".

The same is reiterated in the latest periodic report: "Viet Nam's ethnic policy is aimed at eliminating the gap in economic, cultural and social development between different ethnic groups, and between different ethnic groups, and between them and the whole population, and helping the mountainous areas to catch up with the delta areas so that all groups can advance and attain a prosperous, advanced and happy life, mutually benefiting from comprehensive development, unity and progress". The periodic report further states, "Viet Nam has a consistent policy against all manifestations and forms of racial discrimination whether they are in Viet Na m or elsewhere in the world".

There is no society that can claim to be free from the scourge of racism, racial discrimination, xenophobia and related intolerance. Yet, in the periodic reports to the Committee on the Elimination of Racial Discrimination (the CERD Committee), States from all over the world deny the existence of racism in their country. Consequently, the CERD Committee's Concluding Observations are peppered with bland comments - it expresses concern that there is "no specific legislation prohibiting racial discrimination" or that "racial discrimination as such is not explicitly and adequately penalised in criminal law. " It is essential that CERD Committee unequivocally assert applicability of Article 1 of the CERD recognising Viet Nam's pluralistic, multi-ethnic and multi-cultural society. Indigenous peoples who are known as the ethnic minorities or mountain peoples are part of Viet Nam's pluralistic, multi-ethnic and multi-cultural society.

The Vietnamese Government recognizes the pluralistic and multi-cultural nature of Vietnamese society. In 1995, Government of Viet Nam and United National Development Programme signed a "Framework for External Assistance to Ethnic Minority Development". The Frame Work stated "Ethnic minorities are defined as those people who have Vietnamese nationality, who live in Viet Nam but who do not share Kinh' characteristics such as language, culture and identity. Viet Nam has more than 53 ethnic minority groups with a total population of 9. 9 million, equivalent to over 13 per cent of the population." "The indigenous peoples groups vary in size from less than two hundred to over one million with the ten major groups comprising about 84 per cent of the total ethnic population. The great majority are poor, marginalized, subsistence farmers who practice shifting cultivation often in combination with other farming methods. Although some ethnic groups have settled in the Red River and Mekong Deltas the majority are highland people who live in the northern and western parts of Viet Nam on the borders with Cambodia, the Lao Peoples Republic and the Peoples Republic of China."

The Vietnamese Government further accepted that "The ethnic diversity in Viet Nam is striking and fundamental to an understanding of the socioeconomics situation of the minorities. The diversity manifests itself in a multitude of ways of which language, location of the village, social organizations, agricultural practices, cosmology, religious rites and the status of women in the community are important. Another equally important manifestation is the length, intensity and nature of the exposure to Kinh majority culture that a minority culture has experienced. Northern groups like the Tay, Thai, Nung, H'mong and Dao groups have a history of close interaction which stretches back several centuries. Others like the central highland groups E'de, Muong and Ba-na have only this century come into closer contact with the French and Vietnamese administrations. "

"The ethnic minority languages are divided into three major language groups of which the Austro-Asiatic includes the Khmer, Ba-na, Muong, the Austro-Thai group includes Tay, Thai, H'mong, Dao and Nung languages and the Malayo-Polynesian group which comprises the Cham and Jarai languages. Only eleven of the 53 ethnic groups have a written language of which nine have a Latinized alphabet and two (Cham and Khmer) have Arabic and Pali scripts. In practical terms, however, only very few languages which are linguistically associated are mutually intelligible or understood by native speakers of the respective languages.

Problems in Settlement programme

The problems caused by the settlement programme are exacerbated by the increased pressure exerted by the migrants on the cultivable areas. In many villages of native minorities, land transactions are occurring in the form of sales or rental of land which are recognised only between individuals, possibly by the village chief and in certain cases by the communal authorities. The direct consequence of this market is the occupation of an increasing amount of land by Kinhmigrants, to the detriment of the native populations. This situation, which apparently causes few conflicts, cannot last indefinitely. As soon as the land which is easiest to cultivate profitably is entirely occupied, conflicts may arise, faced with which the minorities are often poorly represented.

On 2-6 February 2001, the conflict burst in Dak Lak and Gia Lai provinces in Central Highlands. Thousands of Ede, Giarai and other indigenous protesters in Daklak and Gia Laiturned out in the streets, unheard of in Viet Nam, to clamour for the return of ancestral lands, among other demands. The demonstrators were fed up with northern migrants-from both the Kinh majority and other ethnic indigenous peoples-encroaching on their land and culture. The protesters reportedly also asked for political autonomy, freedom to practise their Protestant faith and the return of ancestral lands confiscated for coffee plantations. It has also been reported that fears of increased migration spread in late January 2001 with word that 100, 000 people are slated for resettlement in Dak Lak and Gia Lai because of the $3 billion Son La hydropower project.

The government maintains that the protests flared after two minority representatives were briefly detained. According to government's mouthpiece daily, Quan Doi Nhan Dan

(People's Army) on 27 February 2001, a total of 13 regiments and some 20, 000 households were to be settled in a "large economic-defence zone" across the southern part of Dak Lak province and northern part of Bin Phuoc province.

The settlement scheme had sparked protests from the region's minorities, but insisted that an army winning hearts and minds campaign had brought them to an end. "At first, ethnic minority people did not understand the project, " the army daily said. "Some of them, who were incited by evil people, even lodged complaints with the government. Soldiers have arrived to take over the people's land and the people have no land left for living and accommodation, the villagers charged". The local minority people now understood the soldiers' plans to exploit wasteland and barehills, and maintain security at border gates.

As result "many people" from across the districts of Dak Nhau, Dak Rlap, Bom Bo, Loc Ninh and Bu Dang had applied to join the scheme. But the army scheme appeared to run counter to the wishes of the Dak Lak provincial authorities who have called for a halt to immigration to the province. An influx of hundreds of thousands of ethnic Vietnamese settlers over the past two decades fanned the ethnic unrest. Relocation of large numbers of lowland Vietnamese to highland provinces to help clear land to grow coffee and other cash crops is the main reason for the conflict. The problem has been exacerbated by corruption among local officials. Prior to the February 2001 protest, in August 2000, a violent clash erupted in a district in DakLak between minority hill people and Vietnamese settlers in which four officials, including two-piece officers, were slightly injured.

A local official said that in that incident, about 150 members of the Ede minority used sticks and farming tools to attack settlers, burnt some houses and destroyed about two hectares (about five acres) of robust coffee trees. According to Committee for Ethnic Minorities and Mountainous Areas (CEMMA), a governmental body responsible for ethnic minorities, in Lai Chau the Kinh population increased from nine per cent in 1960 to 19 per cent in 1989, while in the Central Highlands, the Kinh population figures in Dak Lak increased from 51 per cent in 1976 to 71 per cent in 1989. Under the 1999 census, indigenous peoples of Gia Lai province were reduced to a minority for the first time. The protests in February 2001 swept virtually all of Gia Lai province's 13 districts. About 400 protesters did manage to gather in the centre of Buon Ma Thuot, capital of Dak Lak province on 3 and 5 February 2001 and blocked parts of the National Road 14 linking Dak Lak and Gia Lai.

The Ministry of Foreign Affairs of the Viet Nam Government acknowledged that 20 protesters were arrested after the February protest. No deaths were reported but state-run media said some police were injured and hospitalized. The fate of the arrested protesters is unknown. Under the Vietnamese Criminal Code rioting and anti-state activity can result in the death penalty. After the protest, the government barred foreign journalists from visiting the area. Phone contact was also severely curtailed. The politburo of Viet Nam Communist Party reportedly instructed provincial leaders to prevent local officials, local journalists and members of local organisations from talking to the foreign press.

Viet Nam's biggest wildlife reserve and the major tourist attraction, Yok Don National Park was temporarily closed down. There are also reports that protests have already been staged in October 2000, but that the Government of Vietnam has apparently succeeded to prevent news from leaking out. After the February 2001 surprising, the Government authorities took foreign correspondents for a guided tour. An indigenous chief, known by the single name Wanh, blamed Protestants for the unrest. The Government of Viet Nam accused "foreign anti-revolutionaries" and "Christian missionaries" to have instigated the uprisings in the Central Highlands. There is undoubtedly paranoia in Viet Nam against "imperialist forces".

However, Viet Nam's concerns against the Christian missionaries from the United States cannot be brushed aside considering the existence of foreign propaganda from some religious fundamentalist groups in the United States to the extent that aggressive proselytizing programs of Christian denominations misuse the right of religious freedom. But, it does not justify Viet Nam's repressive measures against the ethnic minorities. The Government of Viet Nam responded by deployed thousands of soldiers and militiamen after the protest. This was confirmed by government's mouth piece daily Quan Doi Nhan Dan on 27 February 2001. A total of 13 regiments and some 20, 000 households were settled in a "large economic-defence zone" across the southern part of Dak Lak province and northern part of Bin Phuoc province subsequently.

As the Vietnamese authorities begun a military crackdown in earnest, hundreds of indigenous peoples reportedly went into hiding in Viet Nam and Cambodian jungles just across the Vietnamese border. The indigenous peoples primarily from the Jarai, Pnong, and Ede ethnic groups crossed over to Cambodia. A local Cambodian health officialin formed that a large number of infants and small children camped outdoors. Refoulement of the indigenous refugees Most of the fleeing refugees stayed in jungles without food till the officials of the United Nations High Commissioner for Refugees (UNHCR) rescued them. Despite the intervention of the UNHCR, Cambodian authorities forcibly repatriated a large number of Vietnamese refugees.

UNHCR officials had to move more than 150 refugees after reports that Viet Nam authorities had offered a bounty for their return. The group had been in hiding at least two jungle locations in Cambodia until UNHCR staff escorted them to the relative safety of the provincial capital Senmonoron in Mondulkiri province. UNHCR officials monitoring the situation in Mondulkiri province said the decision to move them was made after their continued presence in the jungle became "untenable". Provincial and district-level officials of the Cambodian Government in Mo dulkiri also confirmed that a bounty had been offered by Viet Nam for each minority member returned. O'Reang District, Mondolkiri province - It didn't take much time for Pnong hill tribe member Dien Y Lien to decide to move half a world away to the US from his forest refuge here in Mondolkiri province.

Squatting on hard packed earth in a newly cleared patch of jungle, Dien Y Lien, 38, thought for a few moments, took a long look at his young family crowded under a half-built wooden shelter and came to his conclusion. "We would go to the US, " he said. "We want to live in a peaceful and comfortable country." The Pnong minority have lived in Cambodia for centuries, and one more hill tribe family living among the many villagers here would not make a difference to authorities, he thought But on Tuesday morning six men identified by local sources as Cambodian police and district officials arrived with a truck, loaded Dien Y Lien, his wife Maria Nam Linh, 33, and five children - four girls and a boy - aboard it and disappeared.

They have not been seen since. Both the UN High Commissioner for Refugees and the Office of the High Commissioner for Human Rights in Phnom Penh knew of the family's presence in the province, Montagnard sources reported. About 10 days before they were kidnapped the UNHCR gave the family UN protection documents. They also gave a Mondolkiri deputy governor a copy of the protection document and the general whereabouts of the family in the hope that they would be better protected.

Sources in Mondolkiri province said they believe the seven were driven the 35-km journey to the Dak Dam border crossing with Viet Nam and deposited into the hands of waiting Vietnamese officials. Montagnard sources and provincial officials have confirmed that a bounty is being offered by Vietnamese officials for each Montagnard refugee sent back from Cambodia. Indigenous peoples from Viet Nam have been consistently seeking refuge in Cambodia. They have been consistently repatriated forcibly by the Cambodian authorities in clear violation of the Article 3 of the United Nations Convention Against Torture and 1951 Convention Relating to the Status of Refugees. After refoulement, they have reportedly faced torture, harassment, execution and persecution.

The UN Secretary General's Representative to Cambodia stated: "Ethnic Vietnamese in opposition to the Government in Hanoi have faced problems in Cambodia when they have tried to demonstrate their political opinions. The vice-president of one group, the Free Vietnamese Movement, was arrested in October 1998 together with another member. His whereabouts were unknown at the time of writing, but it was reported that he had been warned before his arrest to stop his activities with the group. Since 1996, over 20 members of this or similar groups have been arrested and deported to Viet Nam where some of them have been imprisoned. Some of those deported had Cambodian identification documents."

Religious Intolerance

Indigenous peoples of Viet Nam are not only ethnically different but they are predominantly Christians especially in the Central Highlands. After the defeat of the Americans in 1975, Vietnamese authorities arrested many religious leaders and held them for years in re-education camps, confiscated properties of the religious groups, closed seminaries and sharply restricted the naming of new religious leaders. The authorities also closed all the Montagnard churches in the highlands, and religious books were forbidden. Vietnam consistently faced credible allegations of extreme religious intolerance. Despite the continuing harassment of Christians in remote areas, the treatment of Viet Nam's religious believers has reportedly improved since the party launched its policy of reforms in the late 1980s.

Nonetheless, religious discrimination remains pervasive. Even today Churches are banned. People practice their religion in houses. The government banned the house churches, especially the Protestant churches. The government states that its opposition to Protestantism was motivated by a desire to preserve the minorities' traditions. But according to indigenous peoples, many elements of the indigenous Bahnars' traditional animist religion, such as feasts, sacrifices and traditional medicine, were themselves outlawed as "extravagant or superstitious."

Religious intolerance remains a part of the State policy. This arises also because of the prejudices against the indigenous peoples who collaborated with the French and later with the Americans. One of the documents-produced by the Bureau of Minority and Religious Affairs in Lao Cai Province in December 1998- charged that Vietnamese Christians have colluded with Viet Nam's enemies since prior to the country's colonization by France in the mid-19th century. "The imperialist enemies and their gangs consider using the exploitation of religion as a very important factor in resisting the revolutionary movement". A document drafted in May 1999 by a Hanoi group called Steering Committee 184 attributes these conversions to short-wave religious radio broadcasts out of the Philippines and hardship in remote areas of Viet Nam. A second document produced by Steering Committee 184 in March 1999 admits that government persecution of Christians often has been counter productive.

Using methods of fighting the contagion of Christianity in minority areas has the opposite effect of making people even more curious. Actually the numbers are growing slowly if we have a relaxed policy and, if we crack down hard, Christianity grows faster. A secret study prepared in January 1999 by the Lao Cai People's Committee calls on officials to inform their citizens that it is "forbidden to listen to the radio station of the enemy," "use illegally smuggled religious materials," "gather many people to study religion" and "collect money or rice to establish an illegal fund." Interestingly, the authors admit that ethnicminority Christians are bold enough to "write petitions to all levels of government, demanding freedom of religion. The majority of Protestant organizations conduct their religious activities without legal recognition, in places of worship or private homes, or even in the forest in the case of ethnic minorities in mountainous areas. These congregations are at the mercy of the goodwill of the authorities, which may either pursue a form of laissez-faire policy or react to activities that are classed as illegal.

The authorities may take any of the following actions in response to illegal activities:

— Suspension of religious services by the security service, financial penalties for religious officials and confiscation of all religious literature;

— Confiscation or even destruction of places of worship;

— Harassment and arrest of pastors;

— The situation appears even more difficult for ethnic minorities in the north of Viet Nam - the Hmong, Hre, Jeh and Jera - because of a sharp rise in conversions to Protestantism;

— Arrest and detention of pastors and faithful, financial penalties, confiscation of religious books, destruction of places of worship and other measures aimed at forcing Protestant believers among these minorities to renounce their faith and desist from all religious activity;

— Protestant religious properties (places of worship, seminaries and educational and health establishments) confiscated after 1975 have not been returned despite requests from Protestant congregations;

— Since 1975, the authorities have authorized only one class of 13 students to receive Protestant religious training. No Protestant theological training establishment is authorized, thus forcing religious congregations to organize private training for pastors. The ordination of pastors, which the authorities want to supervise, is rarely authorized.

9

Genetics of Indigenous Peoples

Indigenous peoples of the world are unique groups who are widely known by our diverse cultures, customs, and languages. Despite our differences, however, we share many similarities. Our early ancestors made significant contributions to astronomy, arts, architecture, agriculture, mathematics, ecology, social science, political science, and genetics. The results of our contributions are evident throughout the world. How far we would have gone in these areas is unknown because our recent ancestors put them aside as they were forced to contend with colonization.

In former times our ancestors fought their battles on land and in courtrooms. Today some of the battles have moved to scientific laboratories and patent offices. Our weapons are awareness, knowledge, and choices, rather than arrows, guns, and treaties. Call it the new wave of colonialism, "the new biotechnology," "the biorevolution, "or "biocolonialism," it is here and will be with us for a long time. In a very broad sense, what we are talking about is "biotechnology".

When we hear the word "biotechnology", many of us turn away our minds, thinking that this field of science seems too hard to understand or that it is "not Indian." Until recently, very few of us had heard about the science of genetics. But we cannot afford to ignore this field of science any longer, because the genomics industry, both public and private, wants and needs the genetic resources that exist within the biodiversity of indigenous peoples' lands and that flows in our veins. The immense resources of technology-rich countries are being pooled in worldwide collaborations in order to carry out genetic research.

Also, numerous researchers are funded by both public and private funds to carry out their own independent research activities. These efforts, combined with increased technological capabilities for genetic sequencing, are fueling a world-wide effort to collect genetic samples, from plants that produce foods or medicines, from animals, and from diverse human populations. The genetic resources that have nurtured the lives of indigenous societies for centuries are at risk of genetic theft. The field of molecular biology is moving ahead extremely fast.

In fact, the field has outpaced the development of new policies and laws that can effectively address the legal, social, and ethical concerns that genetic research raises for society. Scientists and bioethicists regularly have conferences to discuss ethical issues such as genetic discrimination in the workplace or in insurance coverage.

Or they may be concerned about the dilemma parents face when genetic screening of unborn children indicates a predisposition for a disease, but offers no cure for that disease. Others debate the ethics of altering genes in unborn fetuses, human cloning, and animal organ transplants into humans despite the risks of transferring viruses between species. They also often meet to discuss the unique questions raised when they would like to do genetic research on indigenous peoples, but indigenous peoples are rarely at the table to represent our own views. As Indigenous people have taken a more critical look at genetics, many have voiced their concern and have started to speak out against some of the negative aspects of biotechnology. In fact, a widespread movement against genetic theft, or biopiracy, has started to build around the world.

Many of the protestors at the World Trade Organization meeting in late 1999 in Seattle were opposed to the negative impacts biotechnology can have when the interests of corporations are favored over societal needs. Those opposed to the control corporations have over science and genetic resources include a broad range of people, from indigenous peoples to shareholder activists, from students to tenured professors.

Genetics is concerned with studying the genetic composition of life forms at the cellular level, be it viruses, bacteria, plants, animals, or human. The genetic material, or DNA, is found within the cells and contains the hereditary information passed on through reproduction from generation to generation. DNA contains certain biological/chemical instructions that, when combined with environmental influences, result in the biological (physical) development of the organism. Scientists are concerned with understanding the structure and sequences of genes, identifying genes associated with various physical conditions, and they sometimes attempt to change the genetic structure of organisms through genetic manipulations.

Genetics, as a discipline, has little regard for the life forms it manipulates. Their interventions- inserting foreign genetic material into an organism, adding or deleting genes- can permanently alter life forms that have evolved naturally over thousands of years. This contrasts sharply with an indigenous worldview. For us, all life is sacred-it is a gift from the Creator. As indigenous peoples, we carry the responsibility of insuring a healthy future for our children and unborn generations yet to come. This includes a responsibility to respect, protect, and nurture all life. Life is sustained by a healthy environment. In order to carry out our responsibilities to future generations and our environments, we need to understand the nature of the problems we face. Once fully aware, then we are prepared to take action in order to carry out our responsibilities.

The issue of biocolonialism has come knocking at our doors. Like all other unwanted advances of colonization within our lives and territories, genetic prospecting is a reality and is here to stay. Much of life's genetic diversity exists among our peoples and in our territories. Genetic diversity flourishes where lands have not been clear-cut to make way for the expansion of cities, farming, or ranching activities, and where small scale crop diversity is the norm rather than large-scale mono-cropping. Researchers know full well that this is where they will find the genetic diversity, human, animal and plant, needed for their research projects.

Importance of Genetics

Genetics is the study of the structure and function of genes and of the transmission of genes between generations. Knowledge of genetic phenomena has a history that is thousands of years old and probably began when humans first noticed similarities between parents and offspring, or that certain traits or characteristics "run" in families. Ancient civilizations, including the Chinese, Romans, and Egyptians, applied this knowledge to "develop" many different domesticated animals. Throughout the centuries, indigenous peoples in the Western Hemisphere have developed many varieties of plants such as corn, potatoes, beans, squash, and other edibles. Present-day indigenous peoples still maintain different strains of plants, developed over generations of cultivation.

The incredibly fast growth of the "new genetic" is another story altogether. It started when it was found that humans could move portions of DNA (genes) between organisms (human and other life forms), and so the genetic engineering revolution began. And that "revolution", marches on at breakneck speed. Almost daily there are new developments in the "discovery" of "new" genes. Molecular biological techniques have found their way into the courtroom, as documented by the well-publicized trial of O. J. Simpson. In 1997 the world was stunned by the news of "Dolly" the cloned sheep, and two weeks later news coverage featured cloned Rhesus monkeys from a University of Oregon lab. In January of 1998, we learned that longevity might be extended by manipulating certain parts of the chromosome and that a scientist in Chicago was proposing to clone humans. In the year 2000, the UK has proposed to lift its ban on human cloning.

Genetic research in the agricultural world, though less susceptible to sensation in the press, is moving equally fast as scientists are attempting to identify the genes that produce commercially valuable properties by studying plant and animal genetic material. "Traitor Technologies", that engineer seeds to infertile after planting, captured the attention of the press and the public. Further concerns were raised when researchers found that genetically engineered crops were killing the Monarch butterfly.

Genetic Engineering

Genetic engineering is an aspect of genetics that attempts to make changes in the DNA of an organ- ism. Typically, this is done by putting pieces of DNA from an- other source into a life form. When this is done to nonreproductive tissues the changes only remain in effect during the lifetime of the altered individual. However, when this type of manipulation is done during early embryonic stages, the changes can be incorporated into the developing eggs or sperm, and may therefore be passed on to offspring of the manipulated organism.

Genetic alteration of somatic tissues is sometimes called "somatic gene therapy" or "somatic gene engineering", but because of the inexact nature of the science it is more proper just to call it "somatic gene manipulation". Similarly, genetic alterations that can be passed on to future generations should be indentified as "germline manipulation".

In agriculture, a range of genetic engineering techniques has been developed to manipulate the genes or the genetic makeup of living beings to produce a desired commercial result. These technologies are being used in many areas of production, such as pharmaceuticals, industrial raw materials, and food. While proponents of genetic engineering claim that it is precise and safe, there is a great deal of controversy around these claims.

While the term "genetic engineering" sounds like an exact science, in reality it is far from being precise in any predictable manner. Critics of the technology, many of them scientists them- selves, emphasize the unpredictability of genetic manipulation as a primary reason for caution. Critics say that the discipline lacks adequate knowledge of the many dynamic processes that contribute to the development and diversity of different plants and animal species in our world. They observe that the science is being developed and commercialized with too little concern for the risks of not knowing all of the consequences. Among the primary areas of concern, these scientists warn that:

— Transgenic techniques are imprecise. Currently, genetic engineers are not able to fully control where the foreign DNA is inserted into the host organism. This control is important because it is believed that the position of genes can determine what they do. Genetic engineers are not being mindful of the environment of the gene, and the dynamic role that all the other processes and forces in a living being have in shaping the activities of genes.

— Genes can perform more than one function, depending on their environment and the influence of other factors. These multiple functions are not understood, but they are also being ignored. So scientists focusing on the ‚growth genes' to make salmon grow bigger were surprised to find that the young fish also turned pale green. U.S. Department of Agriculture animal genetic engineers using foreign growth hormones to make pigs grow bigger produced pigs with severe arthritis, lethargy, and other disorders. Some of these multiple effects caused by foreign genes may not be so obvious at first, but instead may reveal themselves over time in as yet unimagined ways.

— Projects for the development of genetically engineered plants and animals typically do not try to understand the way that the transgenic organism will interact with other species once released into the world.

Agricultural Genetics

Traditionally, farmers have diversified plant and animal breeds with selective breeding by crossing different varieties from the same species to achieve desired characteristics such as taller plants or sweeter fruits. Nowadays, however, the genetic engineering industry is using approaches that depart radically from traditional agricultural breeding practices. In agriculture, the most common genetic engineering techniques are transgenics and cloning. Transgenics involves the deliberate breaking down of nature's borders, by crossing species that would normally not interbreed. Transgenics works on the assumption that certain genes associated with the performance of certain tasks can be successfully transferred into other life forms, where they will continue to perform the same function.

Genetic engineers identify genes that they believe perform a particular function and then introduce them into the agricultural plant or animal in the hope that these genes will continue to work in the same way in this totally new environment. Examples of transgenic crop and animal experiments that have been attempted include introducing fish genes into tomatoes, petunia flower genes into soybeans, bacteria genes into corn, cow growth hormones into chickens, and human genes into tobacco, kiwifruit, mice, and sheep. Cloning techniques, based on the experiments that produced the cloned sheep Dolly will be used increasingly to mass produce livestock. It is estimated that within 15 years, 85% of livestock in Great Britain will be cloned.

Genetic engineering is being increasingly promoted in agriculture because of the backing of large seed, agrochemical, and livestock companies that are investing bil- lions into the new technologies. Food pro- cessing companies are also encouraging this development, because they see that the new technologies can be used to create raw materials better suited to their manufacturing processes. Largely, genetic engineering is being developed to be able to maintain industrial agricultural practices such as the use of intensive agrochemical and large-scale monocultural (one crop) plantations. So plants and animals are engineered to cope better with the chemical and biological stresses that intensive farming places on them and their environment. According to the companies, the most common aims of genetic engineering techniques are:

— to make plants resistant to agrochemical inputs such as herbicides

— to make plants resistant to pests

— to make plants that can withstand drought conditions

— to make plants and animals "resistant" to diseases and viruses

In addition, genetic engineering in agriculture is being used to push plants and animals beyond their natural limits by £ increasing the productivity of each individual animal

— creating plants that produce raw materials better suited to the processing industry (e.g., trees better suited to the needs of paper and pulp companies)

— creating plants and animals that produce pharmaceuticals or "human" substances In the last decade, genetic engineering in agriculture has boomed.

The fascination of the Western scientific community with the technologies and the promises by the genetic engineering companies of better agriculture have encouraged billions in investment and an extremely cooperative attitude by governments worldwide. Hundreds of thousands of genetically engineered organisms have been released into the environment for field trials. Every living species has suddenly become a reservoir of potentially useful genes, or the possible host for the cultivation of interesting genes or substances that can be later extracted. Meanwhile, commercial cultivation is growing rapidly, due largely to the global reach of the large multinational companies, which have been able to introduce their products almost simultaneously around the world.

In 1999, 100 million acres of genetically engineered crops were cultivated commercially worldwide - a 44% increase from 1998. Over 50% of the US soybean crop and 62% of the Canadian canola harvest in 1999 were genetically engineered.

Implications of Genetic Research

Genetic research in general raises a complex range of legal, ethical, social, spiritual, and political issues which concern indigenous peoples, and society at large. Indigenous peoples, and our territories, are at the forefront of genetic research worldwide. We are immersed in genetic diversity-both in human and environmental (biodiversity) terms. Lands that remain in the control of people indigenous to the area contain the majority of the biodiversity that remains in the world. Our traditional knowledge about our surroundings, as well as many of the members of our own ecosystems, is seen as the "new gold" in a rush to gain commercial benefit from nature. Since indigenous populations represent a significant percentage of the world's human diversity, we are the subjects of scientific curiosity. Indigenous knowledge systems and biological resources are therefore extremely threatened by appropriation.

Indigenous people and nations must prepare themselves to critically evaluate proposals for research involving their people and their territories. Policies which recognize and protect the collective rights of indigenous peoples are lacking.

We must accept the responsibility to put into place policies that protect our interests, and we must come to understand the issues so that we can make fully informed decisions. The following sections will highlight some of the areas of potential concern regarding genetic research and indigenous peoples.

Initially, indigenous peoples were primarily concerned with the Human Genome Diversity Project (HGDP), a worldwide research project initiated in 1992. Today, human genetic diversity research seems to be an aspect of every major genetic research agenda, including the Human Genome Project. Indigenous peoples are the subjects of evolutionary genetic research, genetic research to study differences in how populations react to various pharmaceutical products (pharmacogenetics), and in single nucleotide polymorphism (SNPs) research, to name a few.

Despite these efforts, indigenous peoples are largely unaware of the scale and potential impacts of human genetic research on their communities. The typical human genetic research paradigm treats indigenous peoples as objects of curiosity, rather than partners in research. The research is designed, funded, and implemented without true and meaningful consultation of the studied group. It has become evident that this new area of science and technology poses new challenges with regard to existing ethical practices. Current bioethical protocols fail to address the unique conditions raised by population-based research, in particular with respect to processes for group decision-making and cultural world views.

Genetic variation research is population-based research, but most ethical guidelines do not address group rights. Basic standards in research involving human subjects require that the benefits of the research at least equal the risk. Most population- based genetic research cannot meet this requirement because indigenous peoples are not the intended beneficiaries of the research. As a result, researchers often offer other benefits unrelated to the genetic research such as some short-term medical attention, technology transfer, training opportunities for students, or promises of royalties for any commercial products developed.

Conditions of research designed to protect and benefit the subjects could be formalized in research agreements. But indigenous peoples must be able to monitor and enforce these agreements. But how does one monitor the world-wide exchange of genetic materials and data? What happens when agreements are violated? Who is responsible for the costs associated with enforcement and monitoring agreements? Is money compensation (the only available remedy) the appropriate form of restitution and remediation for broken agreements? These are questions indigenous peoples must take into consideration before entering into research agreements.

Principles and Ethics

Many indigenous peoples regard their bodies, hair, and blood as sacred elements, and consider scientific research on these materials a violation of their cultural and ethical mandates. Immortalization, cloning, or the introduction of genetic materials taken from a human being into another living being is also counter to many indigenous peoples cultural and ethical principles. Indigenous peoples have frequently expressed criticism of Western science for failing to consider the interrelatedness of holistic life systems, and for seeking to manipulate life forms using genetic technologies. Many indigenous people have grave concerns about the short and long-term impacts of introducing genetically-modified life forms into the environment.

By focusing on reactions to changes in genetic materials in organisms (including humans), genetics takes a very mechanistic view of the world. Life forms are viewed as mere machines, in that the research tries to change one part of the "subject" organism in order to get different "output" in terms of, for example, disease resistance or food production. The view is that, with enough experimentation, eventually we will be able to design better "machines". This view is in conflict with a view that recognizes the interrelatedness and interdependence of all living things. Tampering with one aspect of creation necessarily has effects on all other aspects.

Tampering with genetic materials in any life form, which developed over generations in response to years of environmental influence, creates a risk of throwing everything else out of balance as well. That life form had a place where it was specifically adapted to fit in. Tampering with the life form means changing the balance and interrelationships that influenced the development of the organism, which could have broad "ripple" effects.

Genetic Inheritance

Two basic tenets of Euro-American society are that all property should be alienable (for sale) and that all property should be owned by individuals. Current mainstream ethical protocols generally assume that individual consent is all that is necessary for a person to share something of theirs - such as genetic materials or knowledge about something. This is because the protocols, rooted in Euro-American thought, assume that the individual has the right to sell or give away anything that is their own. This thinking is in conflict with indigenous notions of group rights. For example, in many indigenous societies, people may not be free to sell their knowledge because either the knowledge cannot be sold according to the group's ethical principles, or because permission of a larger group is required first.

Also, there may be responsibilities that go hand-in-hand with the holding of traditional knowledge, and that is not usually part of what the Western "purchaser" or researcher is concerned with at all-they just want the knowledge of how something works. Another example is that, if a person's genetic material is sought because they are a member of some indigenous nation, most indigenous people would think that the group ought to have a say in whether the individual's sample may be used as a representative of the nation. After all, it is because the individual is part of the nation that the individual's genetic material is sought at all, and all the members of the nation will be subject to the repercussions of any conclusions drawn from the research.

Therefore, indigenous peoples have a notion of group "ownership" of some things that is in direct conflict with the Euro-American principles, and this means that in areas where we believe we have group rights, these rights are ignored by the mainstream ethical protocols. Much of the current research in genetics is being driven by a strange twist in patent law. Patent laws grant a limited "intellectual property right" to someone who holds a patent. The property right usually lasts from 17 to 20 years. Patents are usually granted for new inventions, as a means of recognizing the inventor's innovation. Currently, the United States Patent Office is granting patents to people who claim to uncover genetic sequences. This means that once a valuable gene is located and isolated, it can be patented, and even mass-produced for commercial purposes.

Under the current law, patents are being granted for portions of all types of genes-human, animal, and plant. But many people are opposed to the idea of patenting genetic sequences, because genetic sequences are part of a life form-which nobody can claim to have invented. Patents were never intended to be granted for the "discovery" of life forms. They were intended to provide some benefit to inventors of things-like mousetraps or toasters. Under the current law, however, even your own genes can be patented, without you even knowing about it.

Often times indigenous peoples are not informed that their DNA can be commercialized through patents and used in the development of new products. The potential commercialization of unique human DNA seems to be a significant motivation behind many research projects. Three cases best exemplify the concern for patenting human genes. The U.S. Secretary of Commerce filed a patent claim on the cell line of 26-year Guaymi woman from Panama in 1993. A wave of international protest and action by the Guaymi General Congress led to the withdrawal of the patent claim in late 1993. The Department of Commerce also filed patent claims on the cell lines of an indigenous person from the Solomon Islands. This patent claim was also later abandoned.

The U.S. Patent and Trademarks Office (PTO) actually approved patents on the cells lines of a Hagahai man from Papua New Guinea. The patents were granted to the U.S. Department of Health and Human Services and the National Institutes of Health (NIH) in March, 1994. Again the patent holders faced public outcry, and in late 1996 the NIH abandoned the patent. However, the Hagahai cell line is now available to the public at the American Type Culture Collection as ATCC Number: CRL-10528 Organism: Homo Sapiens (human) for $216 per sample. At the present time, the US Patents and Trademark Office maintains a policy of granting patents for human genes, and the genetic materials of other life forms. The USPTO is the prevailing model for the protection of intellectual and property rights worldwide, and is currently advocated in international agreements such as the World Trade Organization. Patents on life forms are likely to be a problem for the foreseeable future, unless and until citizens groups and other public advocates are successful in securing legislation that prohibits patents on life.

Immortalized DNA

Genetic samples are frequently "immortalized" for future study utilizing a technique of cell transformation which keeps cells viable for several years. Through immortalization, a single sample is all scientists need to generate unlimited amounts of DNA for future research. The immortalized cell lines can be stored in various gene banks around the world. Control and monitoring of samples is a critical issue, and it is very difficult to prevent abuses such as samples being used beyond the original intent. It is almost impossible to tell who is using them and for what purpose. Additionally, DNA can be extracted from tissues and blood. Once the DNA is extracted, it is frozen and is stored for years. Again, these samples can be transported to several different labs without the consent of the donor and used for studies beyond their original intent.

Collections of biological materials are taken not just from the living, but also from the deceased. For most indigenous peoples this represents a serious violation of the sanctity of our deceased ancestors. In a recent highly-publicized example, the Department of the Interior has approved a plan for taking 10-20 samples from the remains of the Ancient One found at Kennewick, Washington, in order to determine which part of the remains will be the best place to obtain further samples for DNA analysis. These studies are being conducted despite protests from area indigenous peoples.

Expressing a sense of urgency, the Human Genome Diversity Project (HGDP) proposes to collect the DNA samples of indigenous peoples and store the collections in gene banks in order to "avoid the irreversible loss of precious genetic information. lU Referring to indigenous populations as "isolates of historic interest (IHI's)" the HGDP plans to immortalize the DNA of disappearing populations for future study. The initial conceptualization of the HGDP has been widely criticized for its consideration of indigenous peoples as mere research subjects, with little regard for the continued livelihood of the targeted populations. The HGDP has also been sharply criticized for failing to consult with indigenous peoples throughout its planning processes.

Scientists expect to reconstruct the history of the world's populations by studying genetic variation to determine patterns of human migration. In North America, this research is focused on validation of the Bering Strait theory. It is possible these new "scientific findings" concerning our origins can be used to challenge aboriginal rights to territory, resources, and self-determination. Indeed, many governments have sanctioned the use of genomic archetypes to help resolve land conflicts and ancestral ownership claims among Tibetans and Chinese, Azeris and Armenians, and Serbs and Croats, as well as those in Poland, Russia, and the Ukraine who claim German citizenship on the grounds that they are ethnic Germans. The secular law in many nations including the United States has long recognized genetic archetypal matching as a legitimate technique for establishing individual identity.

Genetic Discrimination

The ability to screen a person's genetic material could lead to genetic discrimination. Corporations, for example, may someday demand genetic testing and refuse to hire individuals who carry certain genes. Insurance companies may raise the premiums, or refuse to cover individuals who have been "genetically identified" as having a predisposition for some disease. Already some genetic studies have sought to reinforce social stereotypes and stigmatization in ways such as searching for "the binge drinking gene." Whether the intentions behind the design of such research projects are innocent or not, it remains clear that indigenous peoples must face the real possibility of discrimination and stigmatization in this area as in many other areas of life.

Eugenics and Genocide

Eugenics is an attempt to "improve" the genetic composition of individuals or entire peoples. Genocide is an attempt to eliminate whole peoples from existence. Many people are concerned that genetics may entail forced sterilization or abortion of those found to possess ioundesirablel. genetic sequences. Some geneticists already talk of attempting genetic manipulation on fetuses, in order to "fix" potential genetic problems found in them.

Upon learning about the basics of genetics, some people fear the specter of genetically specific warfare-weapons designed only to impact individuals with certain genetic traits.

Until now, biological warfare has been "sloppy"-along the lines of just introducing a virus in an area where it infects a lot of people. Genetically-based biowarfare would target individuals within a population with specific genetic traits, and not affect other people directly. There are three basic requirements for genetic biowarfare to be possible:

(1) a good understanding of the basic, average human genome;

(2) identification of how different populations differ in their genetic material (the same goal of SNPs (single nucleotide polymorphism) research and human genetic diversity research currently being conducted); and

(3) research discovering how to take advantage of the differences among populations in order to "target" weapons based on genetic differences.

Currently, millions of dollars in the federal budget are being spent to support genetic research. You might question whether this is an appropriate use of federal funds. For example, many public health advocates would like to see federal money currently spent to discover genes associated with diabetes redirected to more practical solutions, like education and other strategies to encourage exercise and dietary changes, as well as providing nourishing foods to people who can't afford to buy food at market prices. Serious questions should be directed at policies whereby vast resources are spent in the search for genetic causes of diseases, and these expenditures are followed by more expenditures, this time for research into how to "fix" people who have "flawed" genetic material.

Public health advocates make a good argument that even to view the problem as a "flaw" in genetic makeup is wrong, and to view the solution as a technological one is wasteful. In many cases, preventative measures would help people deal with their problems in a quicker, more effective, and less costly way. But those interested in conducting genetic research-researchers and bioscience corporations-are not likely to point out that there are more effective uses of public money than finding "techno-fixes." It is up to us to say so if we don't want our tax money spent to support genetic research.

10

Charter of the Indigenous and Tribal Peoples of the Tropical Forests

Statement of the International Alliance of the Indigenous and Tribal Peoples of the Tropical Forests (Established Penang, Malaysia, 15 Feb 1992) (Revised Nairobi, Kenya, 22 Nov 2002)

Article 1

We, the indigenous and tribal peoples of the tropical-forests, present this charter as a response to hundreds of years of continual encroachment and colonisation of our territories and the undermining of our lives, livelihoods and cultures caused by the destruction of the forests that our survival depends on.

Article 2

We declare that we are the original peoples, the rightful owners and the cultures that defend the tropical forests of the world.

Article 3

Our territories and forests are to us more than an economic resource. For us, they are life itself and have an integral and spiritual value for our communities. They are fundamental to our social, cultural, spiritual, economic and political survival as distinct peoples.

Article 4

The unity of people and territory is vital and must be recognised.

Article 5

All policies towards the forests must be based on mutual understanding and respect for cultural diversity and gender perspectives, for a promotion of indigenous ways of life, and an understanding that our peoples have developed ways of life closely attuned to our environment.

Therefore we declare the following principles, goals and demands

Respect for our rights

Article 6

Respect for our human, political, social, economic and cultural rights, respect for our right to self-determination, and to pursue our own ways of life.

Article 7

Respect for our autonomous forms of self-government, as differentiated political systems at the community, regional and other levels. This includes our right to control all economic activities in our territories.

Article 8

Respect for our customary laws and that they be recognized

by national and international law, as equally valid systems of law and decision-making.

Article 9

Where the peoples so demand, nation states must comply with the different treaties, agreements, covenants, awards and other forms of legal recognition that have been signed with us indigenous peoples in the past, both in the colonial period and since independence, regarding our rights.

Article 10

An end to violence, slavery, debt-peonage and land grabbing; the disbanding of all private armies and militias and their replacement by the rule of law and social justice; the means to use the law in our own defence, including the training of our people in the law.

Article 11

The approval and application of the UN Declaration on the Rights of Indigenous Peoples (1993 version), which affirms and guarantees our right to self-determination, and the ratification of ILO Convention 169, which guides States in the application of some of these principles.

Article 12

The setting up of effective international mechanisms and a tribunal to protect us against the violation of our rights and guarantee the application of the principles set out in this charter.

Article 13

There can be no sustainable development of the forests and of our peoples until our fundamental rights as peoples are respected.

Territory

Article 14

Secure control of our territories, by which we mean a whole living system of continuous and vital connection between man and nature; expressed as our right to the unity and continuity of our ancestral domains; including the parts that have been usurped, those being reclaimed and those that we use; the soil, subsoil, air and water required for our self-reliance, cultural development and future generations.

Article 15

The recognition, definition and demarcation of our territories in accordance with our local and customary systems of ownership and use.

Article 16

The form of land tenure will be decided by the people themselves, and the territory should be held communally, unless the people decide otherwise.

Article 17

The right to permanent sovereignty over the use and ownership of the territories which we occupy. Such territories should be inalienable, unleasable, unmortgageable and untransferable.

Article 18

The right to demarcate our territories ourselves and that these areas be officially recognised and documented.

Land rights for our neighbours

Article 19

Legalise the ownership of lands used by non-indigenous peoples who live within and on the forests' margins in the areas that are available once title has been guaranteed to the indigenous peoples.

Article 20

Land reforms and changes in land tenure to secure the livelihoods of those who live outside the forests and indigenous territories, because we recognise that landlessness outside the forests puts heavy pressure on our territories and forests.

Decision-Making

Article 21

Control of our territories and the resources that we depend on: all development in our areas should only go ahead with the free, prior and informed consent of the indigenous people involved or affected. We insist on recognition of our right to veto any developments proposed on our lands without our consent.

Article 22

Recognition of the legal entity of our indigenous institutions and organisations, that defend our rights, and through them the right to collectively negotiate our future.

Article 23

The right to our own forms of social organisation; the right to elect and revoke the authorities and government functionaries who oversee the territorial areas within our jurisdiction.

Development policy

Article 24

Our policy of development is based, first, on guaranteeing our self-sufficiency, material welfare, cosmo-visions and spirituality, as well as that of our neighbours; a full social and cultural development based on the values of equity, justice, solidarity and reciprocity, and a balance with nature. Thereafter, the generation of a surplus for the market must come from a rational and creative use of natural resources developing our own traditional technologies and selecting appropriate new ones.

Article 25

Our right to self-development and to redirect the development process away from large-scale projects towards the promotion of small-scale initiatives controlled by our peoples. The priority for such initiatives is to secure our control over our territories and resources on which our survival depends. Such projects should be the cornerstone of all future development in the forests.

Article 26

The right of our peoples to be broadly informed, consulted and, above all, to participate in the making of decisions on legislation or policies: and in the formulation, implementation or evaluation of any development project, be it at local, national or international levels, whether private or of the state, that may affect our futures directly or indirectly.

Article 27

All major development initiatives should be preceded by social, cultural, health and environmental impact assessments, carried out with the full participation of local communities and indigenous peoples. All such studies and projects should be open to public scrutiny and debate by the indigenous peoples affected.

Article 28

National or international agencies considering funding development projects which may affect us, must set up tripartite commissions - including the funding agency, government representatives and our own communities as represented through our representative organisations - to carry through the planning, implementation, monitoring and evaluation of the projects. In all such negotiations, the right to involve technical advisers and professionals of our choice.

Article 29

The cancellation of all mining concessions in our territories imposed without the consent of our indigenous organisations. Mining policies must prioritise, and be carried out under, our control, to guarantee rational management and a balance with the environment. All mining on our lands should be subject to our free, prior and informed consent and should be carried out subject to freely agreed, openly negotiated, legally binding contracts assented to by our own indigenous institutions, communities and peoples.

Article 30

An end to imposed development schemes and fiscal incentives or subsidies that threaten the integrity of our lives, forests and territories.

Article 31

A halt to all imposed resettlement programmes.

Article 32

The problems caused in our territories by international criminal syndicates trafficking in products from plants like poppy and coca must he confronted by effective policies which involve our peoples in decision-making.

Article 33

Promotion of the health systems of the indigenous peoples, including the revalidation of indigenous medicine and health care, and the promotion of programmes of modern medicine, with measures to ensure our free and equal access to them. Such programmes should allow us to have control over them, providing suitable training to allow us to manage them ourselves.

Article 34

Establishment of systems of bilingual and inter cultural education. These must revalidate our beliefs, religious traditions, customs, and knowledge; allowing our control over these programmes, by the provision of suitable training, in accordance with our cultures; in order to achieve technical and scientific advances for our peoples, in tune with our own cosmo-visions, and as a contribution to the world community.

Article 35

Promotion of alternative financial policies that permit us to develop our community economies and develop mechanisms to establish fair prices for our products.

Forest policy

Article 36

Halt all new logging concessions and suspend existing ones, that affect our territories. The destruction of forests must be considered a crime against humanity and a halt must be made to the various antisocial consequences, such as roads across indigenous cultivations, cemeteries and hunting zones; the destruction of areas used for medicinal plants and crafts; the erosion and compression of soil; the pollution of our environment; the corruption and enclave economy generated by the industry; the increase of invasions and settlement in our territories.

Article 37

Logging concessions on lands adjacent to our territories, or which have an impact on our environment, must comply with operating conditions - ecological, social, of labour, transport, health and others - laid down by the indigenous peoples, who should participate in ensuring that these are complied with. Commercial timber extraction should be prohibited in strategic and seriously degraded forests.

Article 38

The protection of existing natural forests should take priority over reforestation.

Article 39

Reforestation programmes in indigenous peoples' territories must be subject to our free, prior and informed consent and should be prioritised on degraded lands, giving priority to the regeneration of native forests, including the recovery of all the functions of tropical forests, and not being restricted only to timber values.

Article 40

Reforestation programmes on our territories should be developed under the control of our communities. We should select species in accordance with our needs.

Biodiversity and Conservation

Article 41

Programmes related to biodiversity must respect the collective rights of our peoples to cultural and intellectual property, genetic resources, gene banks, biotechnology and knowledge of biological diversity; this should include our participation in the management of any such project in our territories, as well as control of any benefits that derive from them.

Article 42

Conservation programmes must respect our rights to the use and ownership of the territories and resources we depend on. No programmes to conserve biodiversity should be promoted on our territories without our free, prior and informed consent as expressed through our indigenous organisations.

Article 43

The best guarantee of the conservation of biodiversity is that those who promote it should uphold our rights to the use, administration, management and control of our territories. We assert that guardianship of the different ecosystems should be entrusted to us, indigenous peoples, given that we have inhabited them for thousands of years and our very survival depends on them.

Article 44

Environmental policies and legislation should recognise indigenous territories and systems of natural resource management as effective 'protected areas', and give priority to their legal establishment as indigenous territories.

Intellectual Property

Article 45

Since we highly value our technologies and believe that our biotechnologies can make important contributions to humanity, including 'developed' countries, we demand guaranteed rights to our collective intellectual property in both national and international law, and control over the development and manipulation of this knowledge.

Research

Article 46

All investigations in our territories should be carried out with our free, prior and informed consent and under joint control and guidance according to mutual agreement; including the provision for training, publication and support for indigenous institutions necessary to achieve such control.

Institutions

Article 47

The international community, particularly the United Nations, must recognise us indigenous peoples as peoples, as distinct from other organised social movements, non-governmental organisations and independent sectors, and respect for our right toparticipate directly and on the basis of equality, as indigenous peoples, in all fora, mechanisms, processes and funding bodies so as to promote and safeguard the future of the tropical forests.

Education

Article 48

The development of programmes to educate the general public about our rights as indigenous peoples and about the principles, goals and demands in this charter. For this we call on the international community for the necessary recognition and support.

Article 49

We indigenous peoples will use this charter as a basis for promoting our own local strategies for our actions.

11

Futures of Indigenous Peoples

The end of indigenous peoples, globally, and especially for native nations in North America. The great body of Indians will become merged in the indistinguishable mass of population. However, they are not only "still here," but also one of the fastest growing segments of the population of the U. S. Globally, indigenous peoples number some 350 millions, and possibly more depending on how one defines "indigenous". Confrontations and conflicts between states and nonstate peoples are as old as states themselves. Clearly, states have been singularly successful in displacing, absorbing, incorporating, assimilating, or destroying nonstate peoples for the five thousand years that they have existed. Yet, despite myriad dire predictions, and more importantly repeated military and social actions directed against them by states, nonstate or indigenous peoples have not been obliterated.

This would seem to contradict the first point, but actually sustains it, in that "normal accidents" are just those normal or typical events of system functioning. They are not exceptional. Third, following the arguments of Dunaway, while ethnic confict may not have become more comamon since the end of the cold war, it has become more costly to core states and a larger threat to system stability. Hence pressures are intense to minimize ethnic confict. As Dunaway argues, ethnic confict, too, is a normal result of system functioning. Yet the attempts to minimize it may well create more space within which indigenous peoples may survive and resist the inroads of global capitalism and the ideology of consumerism. Fourth, as Wickham argues, 9-11 and the war on terrorism could easily transmute into a new, global, and virulent form of "manifest destiny" in which the United States seeks to export its form of democracy and neoliberalism to the entire planet. Finally, if 9-11 does have impacts on some parts of the system, but not others, this too is important to study and understand.

Colonial expansion into the western hemisphere is tightly connected to the rise of the modern world-system from European states. This usually violent expansion included a land takeover literally on a continental scale, massive labour exploitation systems including genocide or slavery, natural resource extraction that fuelled industrialization, and development of large states. The mythos of an American Revolution misses this central fact which becomes determinative of whether the indigenous peoples become violently incorporated, or not, into and by these states, which are dominated by the United States. Finally, by exploring the puzzle of how people without massive resources, numbers, or weapons can curtail the transformative and often destructive effects of global capitalism.

Indigenous Resistance to Global Capitalism

Indigenous resistance to global capitalism is world wide, diverse, and yet loosely interconnected. Many forms of resistance are covert, echoing Scott's concept of "weapons of the weak"; they often transmute and/or masquerade as something else. For instance, the events in Chiapas have often been cast in the light of a regional, a peasant, or a caudillo driven rebellion. They are less often discussed as an indigenous Mayan rebellion. Movements in the United States, such as American Indian Movement (AIM), are often seen solely in terms of localized ethnic, urban, or racial rebellions.

Indigenous resisters are often far ahead of those who report about them -connected via the United Nations, a large variety of their own organizations, and the internet.

Anna Tsing's, In the Realm of the Diamond Queen, can be read as an account of ways in which local people, in this case Dayaks in Kalimitan, resist state incorporation. Indeed, Tsing's account along with Stoler's account of plantation resistance in Sumatra or Peluso's account of forestry "management" in Java, have as a key component -if not the driving component -the struggle for the survival of indigenous cultures, identities, organization, and economies. This applies to indigenous peoples throughout Southeast Asia and Asia in general. In other cases traditional culture and organization itself is a resource that facilitates resistance and survival. Indigenous resistance struggles are occurring all over the world, even in Europe as, for example, among the Saami. Kurdish activities in West Asia and Miskito resistance in Nicaragua have long been noted as indigenous movements. Gurr's, Minorities at Risk, is a catalog of such movements and Linda Smith's, Decolonizing Methodologies, is itself an act of resistance against the hegemony of European rooted social science concepts.

These movements are so diverse, so fluid in organization, goals, and methods they all but defy summary. Probably the most salient difference between typical class based forms of resistance, as opposed to global capitalism forms of resistance is the emphasis on local community, identity politics, land claims, and rights to a variety of traditional practices, which include alternative family organizations such as matrilineality and/or polygyny, communal ownership of resources such as land, the use of land for sacred ceremonies, and indigenous knowledge, that occasionally includes use of psychoactive substances. Many of these practices contradict, challenge, or threaten deeply held values in state-based systems.

The most fundamental challenge to capitalism, though, comes from communal ownership of resources because it denies the legitimacy of private property rights. Contrary to what many early explorers, missionaries, and colonizers thought, and unfortunately many so-called development experts today may think, it is not that indigenous people do not understand individual ownership. Rather, they have long recognized what many environmental movements are beginning to force capitalists to accept resources are always partially, if not wholly, "public goods" and are thereby sites of contestation. The interactions of environmentalists and indigenous peoples have been something of a mixed bag; although in the first decade of the twenty- first century alliances seem to be becoming more common and antagonism, less so.

Another form of resistance has been the overt, conscious efforts to maintain "traditional culture". Traditional culture, not as static and unchanging, but rather as evolving according to the desires of group members resisting domination, rather than in accord with desires or directions of outsiders. That is, "traditional culture," like all other social forms and structures evolves and changes continuously, if sporadically and unevenly. According to Smelser culture, and hence "traditional culture," are best thought of in relation to domination and dominant groups that change in world-systems according to success or failure of their expansion. Munch and Smelser propose rebuilding paradigms inclusive of these constructs.

Culture building can be another form of resistance. For instance there are 33 tribal colleges in the U. S. These are institutions of higher education, typically equivalents of junior colleges, run by various Native American groups. They differ from the typical U. S. junior college in the number of courses they offer that promote traditional culture, language, crafts, and customs. In some cases, language programmes have been aimed at reviving or reinvigorating a language that has fallen out of use. Indeed, these are often their key missions. That is, tribal colleges are often one institutional means of preserving and enhancing "traditional cultures". Resistance can also take the form of building other localized institutions that conform to traditional cultural values.

The tribal police force, while acting much like any other rural police force in the U. S. , is also culturally sensitive to Navajo traditions and works within them. More direct are the "peace maker courts" which avoid adversarial techniques of Anglo courts by pursuing resolution of disputes, among Navajos, through means that are in accord with Navajo concepts of harmony. Other forms of resistance are less institutionalized, but nonetheless important. Women among the northern Cheyenne have adapted conventional 12 step programmes that address alcohol abuse or spouse abuse to Cheyenne culture, promoting Cheyenne family values. Miller and Chiste discuss the ways in which Native women are producing new feminisms within changing tribal governments.

Another common institution among Native Americans in the U. S. is maintenance of matrilineal family systems, especially through the ownership of property. This often comes at a great price, as missionaries and bureaucratic functionaries have repeatedly attacked matrilineality as "barbaric," unchristian, or chaotic. Native American feminism often organizes in ways that oppose more mainstream feminist movements. Typically Native American feminists focus on issues of identity and cultural preservation as prior to more narrowly focused feminist concerns. Religion can be yet another form of resistance.

Maintenance of religious practices over massive attempts to destroy them, asserts an entirely different way of approaching the supernatural and the sacred. Among the most critical of these practices are lands that are sacred and necessary for religious ceremonies. Today as "new agers" have begun to practice various forms of shamanism, Indian groups have protested such attempts to appropriate Native traditions. The revival of older traditions, such as the Sun Dance, can be another form of religious resistance. These revivals hark back to many revitalization movements. These movements, all of which are somewhat syncretic, preserve many traditional values and have all met with some success in combating the destructiveness of incorporation into the capitalist world-system.

The Longhouse religion has been a source of strength among Iroquois. Russell Th ornton argues persuasively that adoption of the Ghost Dance Religion helped many small groups that had suffered severe demographic loss, due to disease, to recover both demographically and culturally. More recently the Native American Church has been very successful in helping individuals recover from alcoholism. Also NAC has won several court battles that allow members to use peyote. All of these religious traditions are vastly different from the various monotheisms found in the states of the modern world-system. Their survival and growth is an important form of resistance to the ideologies of the modern world-system and to pressures for increasing homogeneity of culture due to various globalization processes.

Moreover, they are tied to "traditional" culture in important ways for continuing resistance to hegemonic domination. Some of the most significant forms of resistance are the various ways that resources are managed collectively, for collective good. Phrased alternatively, there are various ways of pursuing collective rationality. Here one must be careful not to read this as conventional "public goods" administration. This goes much further, in collective ownership of goods -land and livestock most commonly -that are typically individually, privately owned commodities in the capitalist world-system.

One of the more dramatic examples of such resistance is the continuing effort of Lakota peoples to regain control of the Black Hills. Several court decisions, including the U. S. Supreme Court, have determined that the territory of the Black Hills was illegally taken from the Lakota peoples. In accord with U. S. jurisprudence the settlement of this claim has been monetary. The Lakota peoples, however, have steadfastly refused such commodified settlements and have insisted on the return of the land that they consider sacred. The intensity of this commitment is underscored by the relative poverty of Lakota people. Shannon county, South Dakota, where Pine Ridge reservation is located, has been, since 1980, the poorest county in the U. S. Despite the temptation to take the cash settlement, the Lakotas have continued to reject such a settlement and continue to struggle for the return of their land.

Running through all these discussions for Indigenous Peoples in the U. S. has been the issue of sovereignty. Because of initial treaty agreements, indigenous peoples in the U. S. have a special relationship, directly with the U. S. federal government. It is on this legal status that many actions of Native American groups rest. Indeed, sovereignty issues are often the basis of challenges to states around the world and cut to the heart of the interstate system built on the Peace of Westphalia. John Stack argues that various ethnic movements continually challenge the structure and processes of the interstate system and understandings of it. Although Native peoples have met with some success in maintaining sovereignty, they have had to fight on European grounds - within European law.

Recently, one of the more outstanding successes has been to use the doctrine of sovereignty to build various gaming operations. By exploiting the contradictory desires for access to gambling and a desire to forbid it, American Indians have begun to turn considerable profits. But for other groups, such as the Choctaw, this success is fragile and volatile and subject to federal redefinition. The question remains, how much they have had to give up to win these victories. By fighting European civilization on its own turf, they have had to accept some of the premises of that turf.

Thomas Biolsi argues that the law is "a fundamental constituting axis of modern social life -not just a political resource or an institution but a constituent of all social relations of domination". Thus, courts have been a leading institutional means of commodifying everything; especially land. Still, indigenous peoples continue to use legal systems to resist incorporation and global capitalism, when they are available with direct access. Here note an important difference between indigenous struggles in the core or "first" world and those in the "third world" or peripheral areas. The rule of law carries much more force in the first world, or core, and so is a more useful tool there. This difference holds as a "rule of thumb" but finds exceptions in both directions.

Most notable when making this distinction is acknowledging temporal analysis, since North American genocides were common well into the second half of the nineteenth century, even as Canada and U. S. indigenous "sovereigns" were internally recognized. There have been many forms of symbolic resistance. For instance, political pressure has led to several national and/or state parks reserving some areas for traditional Native American ceremonies, such as Bear Butte, Devil's Postpile, Medicine Wheel, etc. Another example has been the movement against the use of Native American images as sports mascots or the national movement to remove the term "squaw" from many place names.

In recent decades there have been movements that have challenged globalizing capitalism. These movements have included those by NGOs such as Cultural Survival, International Work Group on Indigenous Affairs, the Center for World Indigenous Studies, or the United Nations Working Group on Indigenous Populations. There are also several Indigenous organizations. Most of these movements and organizations represent indigenous peoples on both the social group level and collectively, with great variation in their approaches toward issues, the nature of resistance, and the amount of their participation in political spheres. The Zapatista movement centered in Chiapas has been one of the most dramatic.

The Zapatista ideology, and to a large extent Zapatista practices, contradict the logic of capitalism. They reject modernization and development. Mignolo argues that the Zapatista movement constitutes an alternative to greco-roman legacies of state making. The Zapatistas seek to maintain traditional life ways in the face of overwhelming forces to assimilate to capitalist culture and practice in opposition to NAFTA and FTAA. The recent march to Mexico City and the demonstrations in the Zocalo, accompanied by a huge outpouring of civil society in support of the Zapatistas, are some indication of the growing impact of such movements.

The category, "indigenous peoples," itself is a gross simplification of an immense variety of types of social organizations. This diversity is arguably greater than the diversity of types of state organizations found throughout the 500 year history of the "modern world-system," or even the 5000 year history of all states. Either term, "indigenous peoples" or "non-state society," lump this diversity into an overly simple category that emphasizes these differences from states, but little else. Yet, these diferences are key. First, these are not state-based organizations. This, however, does not mean that they did not have identities and political structures. Nor is this to deny that there were indigenous states in North and South America prior to European contact.

Furthermore, some indigenous societies took on, and sometimes lost state-like qualities, including the Cahokia and the Haudenosaunee peoples. The point is, diferences in social organization are crucial, but they are avowedly not assertions about claims to rights, or international status. Second, all these forms of social organization are non-capitalist, a term often glossed as "pre-capitalist." The latter term has two unfortunate connotations. On the one hand, it refers to organizations that preceded the advent of capitalism, taking for the moment that capitalism, as a mode of accumulation is less than 500 years old.

A second, dysfunctional connotation is that such organizations are precursors of capitalism. Thus, at best they are "primitive" forms, and at worst outmoded and outdated. These forms of organization are fundamentally rooted in modes of organization, production, and accumulation that have little to do with capitalist accumulation of capital, and thus resist assimilation into those kinds of systems. That said it is critical to recognize, as Eric Wolf argued so persuasively, that these peoples do, and did, have histories separate and distinct from those of Europeans states, and, indeed, all states. Furthermore, indigenous peoples have been forced to deal with waves of European expansion and the increasing globalization of capitalism over the last 500 years. Many peoples have been incorporated into the capitalist world-system, but far from completely. Many have resisted incorporation heroically, and untold numbers have died doing so.

Indigenous peoples who struggle to preserve much, or some, of their noncapitalist roots -for example, communally held property rights -constitute, by virtue of their continuing existence, a form of anticapitalist resistance to incorporation into the world-system, and a challenge to the assumption of the state as the basic political unit of human social organization. This is yet another way in which the claim to sovereignty by Native American groups is a challenge to the capitalist conception of states. However, the challenge is not only political-economic, but also cultural. Culture and identity politics have become very highly contested issues in recent decades. Within these debates, the names of indigenous peoples are particularly contested.

Such things can become especially insidious when their roots are lost. In order to avoid both reading the past into the present and the present into the past requires distinctions that enable us to describe changes with some precision. On the one hand, some argue that to label chiefdoms "nations" confounds a profoundly modern form of social organization with a much older, and very different form of social organization. On the other hand, others argue that variations among "nations" are sufficiently distinguished by differentiation from the concept of "nation-state"..

The term "indigenous" is inherently troublesome and should be accepted as such. For instance, in mainland Southeast Asia almost everyone is both indigenous and usurped, and typically several times in each role. It is a region where peoples have crossed and recrossed, conquered and reconquered each other for millennia. An ethnic map of Southeast Asia looks like a Jackson Pollock painting. Who is indigenous cannot be settled by conceptual parsing. History is complex and messy. If construct theoretical accounts to deal with it, they must recognize that complexity and messiness. Here use "indigenous" to refer to people who "were in that place" when some others came and usurped some or all of their political control and power and their economic resources.

They should have been there for several generations. However, this, too, is politicized. At times, apologists for usurpation of indigenous territory by the U. S. have argued that this or that "tribe" had just recently conquered their traditional territory from some other "tribe". This argument is conceptually inaccurate, often factually wrong and sometimes downright bogus. For instance, with respect to the founding of the League of the Iroquois see Mann and Fields; or with respect to Lakota claims for the Black Hills see Goodman. All this is compounded by the political/ideological use of such terms. This, of course, is what some of the postmodernist critique is about, the power to make and enforce names. This is compounded by at least two uses of the term "tribe" :

— a generic term that is more-or-less synonymous with "nonstate";

— a technical legal term that refers to treaty-sanctioned and recognized peoples in the U.S.

Rather, they are different forms of social organization. A good deal of confusion is generated by the popular and persistent, yet erroneous, use of "nation," "state," and "nation-state" as synonyms. With respect to "tribe" most of the treaties made by the U. S. , and in most cases by those colonizing forces of expanding world-systems entering into such agreements, were made with "nations" and not tribes. That is, the treaties recognized them as political equivalents, regardless of social organization. Finally, all of these social structures have, themselves, evolved over considerable time. They transform from one thing to another.

An indigenous group that continues to exist today is not a "living fossil". Rather, it too has evolved, often having changed and adapted to a context in which it has been surrounded by one or more, typically hostile, states. Indeed, one of the powerful insights from world-system theory, modern or ancient, is that the fundamental entity evolving is the system itself and that the evolution of any component of a system must be understood within the context of system evolution. Indeed, Rata argues, for the Maori people; their very concept and especially the practice of indigenousness is changing. The salient context today, and into the 21st century is that it is a capitalist world-system that is continuing to evolve and change.

Evolutionary Process

Within these evolutionary processes there are many ways an ethnic or an indigenous group might be destroyed. Genocide, ethnocide, and culturicide share an element of intentional destruction of a group. Genocide is probably the most familiar, and certainly the most brutal, the outright murder of all members of an identifiable descent group, or the attempt to do so. In contrast ethnocide and culturicide involve attempts at to destroy a group's identity, and/or culture, without necessarily killing individual human beings. Ethnocide is an attempt to destroy the identity of a group. In its ideal-typical form it would entail full assimilation of individuals into the dominant group, although some cultural elements might still persist. A key feature here, besides the obvious internal contradiction of destroying an identity but allowing some of its "content" to remain, is that the group, qua a group, disappears.

In contrast, culturicide is an attempt to kill a culture, whether or not its members survive, and whether or not they retain a separate identity. A notorious example is that of Richard Pratt, founder of the Carlisle Indian School, whose explicit goal for the school was "to kill the Indian, but save the man". While Pratt seems seriously retrograde at the beginning of the 21st century,who was a humanitarian reformer in the context of the late 19th century, when many still called for outright genocide. Here the separate identity may survive, but the cultural content is eliminated.

Ethnocide and culturicide are somewhat overlapping processes. Each process, and indeed which process operates, are largely conditioned on the degree to which group distinctions are racialized. Obviously, to the degree that readily visible phenotypically distinctive features mark a group, maintenance of identity in face of destruction of the culture is more possible. Ethnocide, and especially culturicide, are often intimately intertwined with racialization processes. These interconnections warrant further analysis. . As already noted, ethnocide is closely similar to the older concept of assimilation; in which one group adjusts its culture to become progressively more like that of another group. The difference is the clear intent to eliminate the group identity. Culturicide, on the other hand, does not need to destroy the identity as long as the "content" of the identity becomes nearly the same as that of the dominant group, and thus subordinate to the socioeconomic goals, practices, and ideologies of those in power.

For resisting, one way is by remaining small, and therefore relatively nonthreatening, at least to the point that the costs of pursuing ethnocide or culturicide have not been worth while. Another form of resistance has been via relative isolation. This, however, is most often an accident of history - being located within a region of little interest to the state or world-system, owning or controlling resources seen to have no or little value to the larger system. Building upon, or using, a recognized land base to keep the community viable are also resistance forms, but these forms are more of the order of passive resistance. How effective they will be in the long run remains unclear. Clearly, resistance that focuses on symbols runs the risk of allowing culturicide to proceed; in that the identity, via the symbols, is maintained while its content becomes progressively more assimilated to the dominant culture.

However, some of the other forms noted above preserve not only symbols, but also material practices that contradict how capitalism is practiced. They represent alternative ways of organizing human life. What is far from clear, however, is whether these too can ultimately become "merely symbolic". Is an American Indian nation which insists on tribal sovereignty, which administers resources according to principles of collective rationality, yet, which externally participates in a capitalist world-system according to capitalist principles, resisting globalizing capitalism, or slowly evolving into an alternative form of capitalism?. However, such processes are not exclusively modern, occurred since states were frist invented some five millennia ago.

Old and New World System

When a world-system expands, new areas are incorporated, and boundaries are formed and transformed. Incorporated areas and peoples, even when incorporation is relatively limited in degree, often experience profound effects from incorporation and occasionally devastating ones. They also react against and resist these effects to whatever degree possible. Thus, the study of incorporation entails close attention to local conditions, actors, and actions as well as system-wide processes, and especially the complex interactions between the two. Incorporation is a two-way, interactive process. To label this entire range "incorporation" masks important variations and makes it more difficult to understand different processes and outcomes that occur on the frontiers of world-systems.

Some changes induced by incorporation may be reversible, others are not, or only with great difficulty. For instance Dunaway cites comments by a Cherokee chief who lamented in the 1700s that young men had become so dependent on guns that they could no longer use, not to mention produce suitable bows and arrows. Another common result is that indigenous peoples are relocated to "reserve" areas. These go by many names: reservations, reserves, domestic nations, establiciementos de paz, etc. These are often "temporary," where "temporary" can be a century or more. States seek to abolish such reserves for a variety of reasons. Frequently reserves become attractive for further development especially when some formerly unknown or "useless" mineral, such as oil or uranium, becomes valuable due to new technological developments.

States may tire of the administrative and economic overhead of such special status areas and/or peoples. Both have been common in the United States where the special legal status of American Indians generates all sorts of legal and political problems. Eras when a drive for a "national culture" increases can create extensive pressures for assimilation to the dominant culture. One legacy of the obsession with nation-building, common in 20th century third world countries, is for states to become "embarrassed" by the continued existence of "backward" or "primitive" population segments. Their typical response is vigorous, often coercive, drives for assimilation.

The extension of world-systems theory into pre-capitalist settings suggests additional refunements of the analysis of incorporation, which shed some light on commonalities of incorporation in the modern world-system.

— First, incorporation is not one-dimensional, but multidimensional, reflecting four types of world-system boundaries. Thus, incorporation can be economic, political/military, or cultural. The latter assumes that culture, however defined, is a type of information.

— Second, incorporation often creates multiple frontiers, corresponding to each of the boundaries.

— Third, ceteris paribus, incorporation will begin at the furthest boundaries, information and luxury goods, and proceed to narrower, more intense forms along the political/military boundary and finally along the bulk goods dimension.

— Fourth, relations among the dimensions of incorporation are complex theoretically and empirically.

To illustrate, the Lakota were not just loosely connected groups, but quite literally had different sets of sociopolitical connectedness that allowed for greaterfuidity of local and regional decision-making. That is, Lakota peoples may not have been bands, but had an organization more akin to a segmentary lineage system. These systems allowed Lakota to successfully fight U. S. intrusions, and forced the U. S. to use the term "nation" during treaty-making. The same pressures further forced designation of "chiefs" who would head up "tribal councils" that ultimately turn into the form designated in 1934 Indian Reorganization Act reconstructions. Identity and political organization are undiffierentiated for the Lakota until after 1868, when their divisions became a form of cultural domination.

In other parts of the world, the process of attempted incorporation and resistance to it is much older. Indigenous resistance to expanding world-systems, empires, states, and individuals is ubiquitous and has been continual since states were first created. This carries several important implications for analysis of resistance to world-systemic processes.

— First many of the putative evolutionary sequences and/or so-called pristine forms of organization are highly suspect. They are, more often than not, themselves products of long interactions.

— Second, this suggests caution in always attributing the deleterious consequences of incorporation to "capitalism." Rather, there is more continuity in this area between tributary and capitalist world-systems.

— Third, what does seem to be different in the capitalist world-system is the overwhelming power of states relative to indigenous groups, its truly global reach, and the preponderance of capitalist reasons for expansion. The latter include expansion especially for resources, labour, and markets.

— Fourth, the concomitant rise in nation building in the modern world-system, as noted above, has led to much stronger attempts at assimilation of incorporated groups than was common in tributary world-systems.

— Finally, following Eric Wolf, the histories of these encounters are almost exclusively written from the point of view of expanding state systems. Almost universally, these histories take as axiomatic that state-based systems are inherently superior to nonstate systems, and that transforming the latter is "helping" them.

Incorporation into the modern world-system can also have divisive effects. For the White Earth Anishinaabeg, increasing incorporation fractured old clan and band distinctions and created a new division between more and less assimilated Anishinaabeg, or in local parlance, between full-and mixed-bloods. Sandra Faiman-Silva finds much the same processes among the Mississippi Choctaw. Indeed, the full-blood/mixed-blood distinction is an important consequence of incorporation into the European world-system with far-reaching legal consequences. That is, blood quantum becomes covertly connected with development of highly racialized policies that act directly and institutionally indirectly, as agents of domination and subordination.

Even splitting into factions can be the result of the policies, actions, and resistances to incorporation and domination. Partial incorporation can simultaneously transform indigenous peoples and contribute to state building. Kristine L. Jones argues that trade among indigenous peoples and between indigenous peoples and Spanish settlers in the Pampas helped in the process of state-building by fostering increased trade. Gender roles and gender relations are also reshaped by incorporation. Women are often harmed by incorporation even while men may at times benefit, although the entire group usually suffers. There are gender and class differentials in contraception, fertility, labour force participation, and household structure and function. The impacts of incorporation on the social construction of gender and gender relations remain poorly studied.

Survival and Persisting

Even though resistance to incorporation is old, survival of indigenous groups remains problematic. This survival is one of two persisting puzzles:

1) the persistence of ethnic groups and
2) the persistence of indigenous groups.

Both are distinctive in that they are organizations not based on capitalist relations. Let us hasten to say, before someone jumps up to beat us about the head and shoulders with the "primordialist" or "essentialist" bludgeons. Rather, here claim that both types of groups have their fundamental social links around kinship and community, irrespective of how they make their livings. Here confront a basic misunderstanding by Marx, that ties of common work experiences -relations of production -are often not sufficiently powerful to overcome completely ties of kinship and face-to-face community. This is why both nations and movements adopt metaphors of kinship to build solidarity; or to invert Benedict Anderson, that is why the "imagined community," the nation-state, must be imagined. This is not to gainsay that such a transformation might happen, but rather to note that it has not happened completely.

When these ties of kinship and community coincide with ways of making a living, they become extremely powerful in binding people together and in maintaining a sense of solidarity. This is precisely what happens within most indigenous communities. Even where members participate in the wider capitalist economy and its wage-labour processes, they remain tied to their indigenous communities. Thus, it is no accident that the most successful of such groups are ones with a continuously existing land base -even if it is a land base from which they have become widely dispersed. In the homeland, means of making a living, or of surviving, are tied to that land base, tribal identities linked to reservations in the U.S., to traditional lands elsewhere.

Phrased alternatively land still maintains for many indigenous peoples meanings that preceded what Polanyi called the "Great Transformation". This comes out again and again in the resistance statements of indigenous peoples, especially those called "Indians" on the North and Central American continents. Keeping the particular in mind as the ultimate reference point of Indian knowledge. Here power and place are dominance concepts -power being the living energy that inhabits and/or composes the universe, and place being the relationship of things to each other. Deloria is referencing, in Lakota, power as "wakan", and place as "maka", thus establishing connectivity and relationships. Experientially and theoretically, commodification of land and resources is the polar opposite of these philosophies.

Indigenous peoples were not so much unable to understand private property or land boundaries and established monetary value, but were in fact rejecting those concepts as invalid along both spiritual and social value systems. Th at rejection continues, whether found in Crazy Horse's statement: "One does not sell the land which the people walk upon", to the Zapatista's rejection of private ownership of the plantations, and is exemplified, for the White Mountain Apache, in Basso's "wisdom sits in places". Each of these traditions, represents resistance of the highest order to early globalization, .

Indian accumulation of information is directly opposed to the Western scientific method of investigation, because it is primarily observation. Indians look for messages in nature, but they do not force nature to perform functions that it does not naturally do must always keep in mind that traditional knowledge of their people was derived from centuries, perhaps millennia, of experience. Thus stories that seem incredible when compared with scientific findings may indeed represent that unique event that occurs once a century and is not likely to be repeated. Western knowledge, on the other hand, is so well controlled by doctrine that it often denies experiences that could provide important data for consideration.

Knowledge systems are constructed, defended and expressed by both dominant groups and those in resistance. This is profound and demonstrates even deeper issues, though they certainly relate to the land and the cosmos. Fenelon's experience with the Spirit Lake Nation in the Dakotas exemplifies this well. Apparently, "traditionalists" had been telling engineers, especially the Army Corps, "the waters" rose every seventh generation and cleansed the land for renewal. The Corps called that "old Indian talk" until the waters did indeed, rise in the 1990's, and rise all the way to state and federal governments requesting massive intervention. In response, the Corps proposed to build huge pumping stations on the trust reservation lands and dump the excess over the ridge into the Cheyenne River, which flows into the north-running Red River, which goes through Fargo and Grand Forks and then into Canada.

Although the coalition defeated the project and the ridiculous notion of dumping water into one of the nation's worst flooded river basins, experiential knowledge known only through the oral tradition not only predicted this water run, but also observed the beneficial qualities. In this respect, both resistance and cultural survival are important resources, albeit mostly at odds with a system of capitalist accumulation and values based on monetary worth. States, since they were first invented, have necessarily been poly-or multi-ethnic. The ethnically unitary nation-state is a chimera -in the ancient and the modern world. States, or more properly the world-systems within which they are located, always expand. Hence, even if states and world-systems are ethnically homogeneous at their first formation, they quickly incorporate new peoples and become diverse.

In tributary world-systems, constituent states often do not attempt to assimilate those who are ethnically different to the dominant ethnic culture, though some do, they never succeed completely. Rather, they are concerned with the collection of tribute. Clearly, the constituent ethnic groups, within any one state, are hierarchically organized. Egalitarian situations are rare. They are artifacts of peculiarly balanced social forces. Over time, groups do, however, change, transform and transmute into different forms.

In tributary systems, such changes are typically slow, often imperceptible in the short term, so identities are easily confiated with both territory and biology. In recent times these processes have generally sped up, so that situational, reactive, or socially-constructed ethnically is now not only obvious to most observers, but all too typically perceived as "normal," or "natural." There are also abundant examples of the content of identities converging even while the boundaries between then are reinforced. Barth argues, "that a drastic reduction of cultural difference between ethnic groups does not correlate in any simple way with a reduction in the organizational relevance of ethnic identities, or a breakdown in boundary-maintaining processes". But a closer look at most ethnic changes reveals that they typically take generations or centuries to occur, and are often accompanied by much confict.

One consequence of the space-time compression associated with increasing globalization and the various cyclical processes of the modern world-system, especially in recent decades, has been that these pressures for change of identity have become more overt, explicit, and obvious. Hence, not surprisingly, so too have the efforts to resist those pressures become more overt and explicit. The clashes and conficts seem to be most extreme when the incorporated or encapsulated groups are, or recently were, organized according to the logic of a different mode of accumulation.While in some ways obvious, is in other ways obscure. Because such groups are organized according to a different logic, they are more of a threat to the overall system than challengers who are more powerful -economically, politically, or militarily -because they are proof that the logic of the dominant system is not "natural," "normal," "manifest," or "inevitable," but rather has been constructed by human beings, whether consciously or not. In short, by their very continued existence, indigenous peoples are concrete empirical proof that shouts of TINA [There Is No Alternative (to global capitalism)] are patently false. More germane to this discussion is how "manifest destiny" ideologies have informed, if not distorted, much social analysis of indigenous peoples in North America and elsewhere.

Currently, with the end of the cold war and the collapse of any sort of immediately viable socialist alternative to capitalism as an organizing principle for human society, these challenges increase in salience. This, of course, makes the puzzle of their continuing survival all the more puzzling. In part, the answer is that many have. But within capitalist culture's self-conception, whole sale slaughter of human beings for the "crime" of being different has become unacceptable, or at least "gauche."

Discriminatory treatment, ranging from death to social isolation, follows a similar pattern. Thus, other techniques have been tried, most have failed miserably, and often have back fired, strengthening oppositional identities. But also, as in tributary states where the primary concern was that ethnic "others" deliver tribute, not conform, the same is true within the capitalist system where the primary concern is that "others" enter the market and play by capitalist rules. Furthermore, even when such challengers use whatever they gain from "playing the capitalist game" to preserve their non-capitalist organization they have not been perceived as a severe threat to the overall system. There are at least two aspects to this. First, they do not challenge the system in an attempt to replace or overthrow it. Rather, they seek to carve out a niche within it.

Second, most are relatively small -demographically, politically, economically, in resource endowments, etc. Thus, the threats of their existence as alternatives to the dominant mode of organization are outweighed by the self-contradictions that would be made manifest by overt attempts to destroy them. However, people should not lose sight of the very skillful efforts of indigenous leaders to play upon precisely these contradictions to defend their niches within the world-system. Franke Wilmer has observed that one source of indigenous survival in the latter part of the twentieth century, derives from the skills of indigenous leaders to articulate that any justification for eliminating their existence as separate groups, is also a repudiation of the Peace of Westphalia and such "treaties" and therefore the entire interstate system in the modern world. So far, this has been too high of a price to pay.

States and Sovernity

Wallerstein has identified the strong reliance of global capitalism on the nation-state system, and its multitude of connections to military-political networks that prop up and enforce the economic systems and domination. Sklair argues that now the global system is more important than states. While recognizing that world-system analysis has many insights into the global system, he still faults it for relying too much on the state as a unit of analysis. Even as transnational capitalism and the emerging transnational capitalist class seeks to subvert and/or transcend the state in many ways, they also use it extensively. While the processes remain far from clear, the world is in the midst of a considerable shifting of rules and processes that derived from the peace of Westphalia.

The efforts of indigenous groups, as individual groups and as collectivities, are part and parcel of these changes and will play a significant role in them -a role that cannot be ignored. This is because most indigenous peoples represent an alternative to capitalist accumulation that by its very nature poses a perplexing problem, if not a fundamental challenge, to formal state sovereignty. Even as the dialectic outlined above plays out in terms of confiicts between states, indigenous peoples resist from outside the system, often while forced to enact political solutions within individual state structures and regimes.

The United States arguably has the most well-developed and codified relationship with its indigenous peoples, "Indians" who have survived wars and conquest under the treaty system, with Canada following closely over the last two hundred years. Some analysts argue that the Canadians have surpassed the U. S. by recognizing the oral traditions of their "First Nations". While nearly all colonial systems conducted forms of genocide, extending over a five hundred year period well into the nineteenth century, most did not develop treaty based legal systems, but many in Central and South America incorporated American Indian peoples into systems of racial subordination, segregation and partial assimilation as minority groups.

As the state system moved throughout its violent growth and development, it utilized two important concepts in its expansion over the western hemisphere, the Doctrine of

Discovery and the Princes Rights to Conquest. These colonial to Indian relationships were at first with very strong Native Nations, including the early U. S. Some were predicated on treaties and various "non-intercourse" acts, meant to contain and control indigenous peoples with a state actor in the expanding world-system. Within the United States such relationships were known as "tribal sovereignty" for those indigenous peoples surviving the conquest eras, and being able to demonstrate political presence over the next two hundred years.

What then evolved in the United States was a complex set of doubled-up Dual Sovereignty relationships with Federal sovereignty supreme, first with 13 and later up to 50 individual states' sovereignty, along with the contested notions of tribal sovereignty. The newly developing nation-states of the western hemisphere, including the United States, believed they could extinguish tribal claims to sovereignty at a later date. Th at has not proven to be the case. However, indigenous resistance to sovereign and capitalist domination has taken on many forms, which generally relate to hegemonic systems in their classic world-systems typologies.

In reviewing the many examples and cases of indigenous peoples in the western hemisphere, there is a relationship between the legacy of systemic domination type, individual sociopolitical statuses and their contemporary sociopolitical position in the world-system. These relationships may be fairly tightly circumscribed within the Americas, although it is speculative as to how strongly they may be held with various indigenous peoples in other parts of the world, with differing histories and political systems. The effects of hegemonic cycles in core areas are different than those in peripheral areas. They are mediated through cycles of nationalism and nation-building and also are part of the larger tributary to capitalist shift. Survival is also highly problematic, especially in the contemporary world-system.

Until two decades ago when the Canadian courts and political processes gave more credence to both historical treaty rights and contemporary laws concerning separatist sovereignty, the Mohawk of Canada have been relegated to a subsumed and segregated reserve status following the U. S. policy treatment. During their three or four hundred years of cultural domination, they experienced the full range of relationships, including an exchange of gunfire with the military as late as the 1990's. The Mohawk exist under different laws but similar status on both sides of the U. S. Canada border, and thus make a fascinating case of transnational historical ethnicity divided by artificial political borders imposed on them by the dominant groups.

The Lakota represent about two hundred years of confiicts ranging from war, to formal treaty-making with the United States in spectacular negotiations clearly and primarily revolving around claims to sovereignty and control over land. The Lakota were forcefully broken up into six different reservation groups only roughly conforming to tribal relationships and without recognition of the 1868 treaty lands or rights. Recently, anti-hegemonic social movements, from the 1960's have brought these agreements, broken by the United States on multiple occasions, back to the table, and the courts.

The Cherokee were militarily removed under genocidal conditions by the U. S. military; this move was orchestrated by President Jackson in direct opposition to Supreme Court rulings and all legal and moral constraints of the time in respect to the Five Civilized Tribes, forcing what many analysts believe to be the single best example of a constitutional crisis, in that all three sovereigns were in play - federal, tribal, state -and all three divisions of the U. S. government were at odds, with raw power to remove Indian peoples winning out. The primary result was the United States ignoring its manufactured crisis over sovereignty, mainly for the purposes of expanding its realm of control and limiting Indian Country.

The Puyallup make another good example of what starts out as another treaty tribe and though driven out of existence, make a stunning comeback in the late twentieth century to reclaim portions, albeit small, of their earlier claims. The Pequot make an even more compelling story, though eliminated for over three hundred years before the creation of the U. S. A. , receive formal recognition partially by Congressional fiat, and then build a legal anomaly entirely on sovereignty into a stunning economic success through Indian Gaming, Wampanoag people represent the flip side of that story, from once great nations first supporting and then warring with English colonists, and then only getting a limited partial recognition through the court system, with little claims and only nominal sovereignty.

The Yaqui complete the United States examples, straddling the border with Mexico, sometimes warring with both countries, and ultimately getting a forced recognition, although growing substantially in the last two decades in terms of its territorial claim. Mexico, although historically an assimilative nation toward indigenous peoples, treated most of their "Indians" with segregated and discriminatory repression. The Tarahumara peoples, having often difficult relationships within the ejido system of rural land tenure, represent nation-state control over these bounded peoples. Further to the south, and into Guatemala, Mayan descent Indian peoples in Chiapas, Mexico, represent combined armed and sociopolitical resistance to U. S. -led globalization, stating their struggle has been for "500 years" and is against transnational capitalism, hemispheric hegemony, and the repression of the peasant Indian for economic profits.

Primarily with sovereignty and claims to the land as its basis, revolutionary struggle has linked with indigenous resistance and has percolated over hundreds of years under various regimes and economic domination. Legal, socioeconomic, and cultural factors drove mountain indigenous peoples to use arms, illustrating how world-systems shape micro-economic relations, especially when hegemonic decline changes their positions and the activities of dominating elites.

The Miskito in Nicaragua perversely show these contentions in a reverse, namely, that a socialist armed revolutionary government also tries to impose conditions, boundaries, and in a late-stage forced removal, modernized conditions in the world-system, albeit not capitalist. The Sandinistas were, no doubt, responding to hegemonic forces that attempted to employ Miskito people in Honduras to support the Contras. However, the central concerns were against incursions over a limited but existing sovereignty, or in the Miskito case "autonomy" over their lands and sociopolitical life. While the capitalist systems tend to be more invasive of both cultural and political forms of autonomy, socialist systems are also attempting to exercise their sovereignty over societies, and therefore over indigenous peoples, making it incumbent on them to resist the corrosive effects of dominating systems. When hegemonic systems are in decline, these patterns become more apparent.

Reacting to an artificially imposed state political border with real effect, the Yanomami people in Venezuela demonstrate similar issues of an "internal colonialism" spreading out as an arm of a predatory economic system, markedly in Brazil, where it is mostly genocidal. Venezuela, on the other hand, has developed bounded reserve areas, similar to North American patterns, with limited protections but a still invasive market economy with trading posts and timber companies. Gold mines and mineral companies operate freely in Brazilian economic expansion, building peripheries out of Yanomami land where they cannot even be a minority group. Hegemonic decline seems to hasten these activities, and put reserved lands and laws in Venezuela into contention, over sovereignty or limited autonomy. This has been contentious since the IMF accords influenced Amazon development strategies.

The Quechuan people in Ecuador, and in a more complicated set of relationships in Peru, maintain a sizable demographic presence that at times must be taken into consideration. For example, in the recent elections followed by a near military coup, indigenous groups were key to swinging political parties behind one side or another. However, once the immediate objective, always associated with political machinations connected in some manner or form with natural resource extraction, has been achieved, defeated, or no longer matters, the Quechuan peoples are subsumed into the general population again. Separatists' movements, as in Peru, Venezuela and Colombia with different tribal groups, attempt to make short-lived coalitions similar to the above dominant groups operating as nation-states.

Finally, the Native Hawaiians, who have achieved limited sovereignty and in one case territorial autonomy through the practice of legal and political recognition. In this case, states believe the international system of trade forces them to recognize minority separatist groups with documented claims, such as a treaty or formal agreement. Ironically, core countries such as the United States, find themselves no longer able to forcefully eliminate or assimilate indigenous peoples undergoing incorporation processes, instead they enter into negotiations that abide by previous contractual or treaty-like rules, similar to the contracts of international trade and economic development. What remains to be sorted out is how these patterns are shaped and affected by changes in the hegemonic cycle. A key component to this survival is the degree of autonomy or sovereignty.

When systems are in hegemonic decline, there are opportunities to take the relationships described above, primarily of sovereignty/autonomy with a nation-state in a world system governed by international laws and economic agreements upon which capitalism relies, and force new political relationships more advantageous to indigenous peoples. However, states may also contract and respond with greater oppression toward indigenous peoples if they will upset an existing status quo, or simply to nail down those parts of their society under their total control. When indigenous peoples straddle borders these issues become more acute, depending on the particular states involved and the relative strength of the region. Thus hegemonic decline provides both potential opportunities and sometimes grave threats for indigenous groups.

Because a "minority status" is dependent on the dominant policies of the state, levels 5 and 6 hold the most dangerous possibilities for indigenous groups, unless they can engineer movement to the higher levels by gaining some form of autonomy or even limited sovereignty. Historically, being forced into an oppressive minority status was a common feature in the European expansion over the western hemisphere, but currently, less developed or poorer countries are most likely to oppress their indigenous peoples through such definition, or a complete subordination of political, economic and cultural rights.

Bibliography

Barth, Frederick, *Ethnic Groups and Boundaries*. Boston: Little Brown, 1969.

Hall, Thomas D. and James V. Fenelon, "Indigenous Resistance to Globalization: What Does the Future Hold?" Pp. 173-188 in Emerging Issues in the 21st Century World-System: Vol. I: Crises and Resistance in the 21st World-System, edited by Wilma A. Dunaway. Westport, CT: Praeger, 2003.

______________,"The Futures of Indigenous Peoples: 9-11 and the Trajectory of Indigenous Survival and Resistance.", *Journal of World-Systems Research,* 10:1(Winter):153-197, 2004.

Harff, Barbara and Ted Robert Gurr, *Ethnic Conflict in World Politics.* 2nd ed. Boulder, CO: Westview Press, 2004.

Kenner, Charles L., *A History of New Mexican - Plains Indians Relations*. Norman: University of Oklahoma Press, 1969.

Guha, Ramchandra, *The Unquiet Woods: Ecological Change and Peasant Resistance in the Himalaya*. New Delhi: Oxford University Press 1989.

International Work Group for Indigenous Affairs (IWGIA), *The Naga Nation and its struggle against genocide*. Copenhagen: International Work Group for Indigenous Affairs, 1986

Kalpavriksh, G., *The Narmada Valley Project: A Critique*. New Delhi: Kalpavriksh, 1988.

Kumar, Satish, *Human Rights and Economic Development: The Indian Tradition*, Human Rights Quarterly 3(3):47-55, 1981.

Mamoria, C.B., *Tribal Demography in India*, Allahabad: Kitab Mahal, 1958.

Morse, Bradford and Thomas Berger, *Sardar Sarovar: Report of the Independent Review*. Ottawa, Ontario, Canada: Resources Futures International, 1992.

Moser, Rupert R., "The Situation of the Adivasis of Chotanagpur and Santal Parganas, Bihar, India", Copenhagen: International World Group for Indigenous Affairs, 1972.

Parajuli, Pramod, *Grassroots Movements and Popular Education in Jharkhand, India*. Ph.D. dissertation. Stanford University, 1990.

Rubin, Barnett R., *India. In International Handbook of Human Rights*, Jack Donnelly and Rhoda E. Howard, eds. Westport, Connecticut: Greenwood Press, 1987.

Shiva, Vandana, *Staying Alive: Women, Ecology and Development*. London: Zed Books, 1989.

Singh, Jaipal, "Development and Adivasis, Asian Labour" *Indian Labour Forum*, New Delhi. Vol. 1, No. 4. January, 1950.

Singh, K.S., *Tribal Movements in India*, Delhi: Manohar, 1982.

______________, *Economies of the Tribes and Their Transformations*. Delhi: Concept, 1982.

______________, *Tribal Society in India: An Anthropological Approach*. New Delhi: Manohar Publications, 1985.

Index